A Bibliography

of the

Thoreau Society Bulletin Bibliographies

1941–1969

A Bibliography
of the
Thoreau Society Bulletin Bibliographies

1941–1969

A Cumulation and Index

edited by
Walter Harding

cumulated by
Jean Cameron Advena

The Whitston Publishing Company
Incorporated
Troy, New York
1971

INTRODUCTION

Early in the summer of 1941, a small group of Thoreau enthusiasts issued a call for a "Thoreau Birthday Mecca" to Concord, Massachusetts, on July 12th. Much to their pleasant surprise, and despite a stormy day, over a hundred people gathered in answer to the summons. After hearing a few brief talks, lunching together, and visiting some of the shrines of the town, they decided to join together in an informal organization to hold further meetings in summers to come. Thus simply the Thoreau Society came into being, and meetings have been held annually in Concord ever since.

When it was felt that there should be some communication among the members between the meetings, the THOREAU SOCIETY BULLETIN was founded. Bulletin Number One, consisting of one mimeographed sheet, appeared in October, 1941, and with the exception of several occasions during the years of World War II, it has appeared quarterly ever since. It not only reports on the activities of the society and prints (or, occasionally, reprints) articles on Thoreau, but it acts as a general clearing house of Thoreau scholarship.

Beginning with Bulletin Number Two (January, 1942), a checklist of current (or previously overlooked) books, pamphlets, and periodical and newspaper articles became a regular feature of the bulletin. I have had the privilege and pleasure of editing this feature from the beginning and have considered

v

it rather a running detective game to hunt out as many of the constantly appearing pieces of Thoreauviana as I can. But the lists would not be half their size were it not for the constant assistance of faithful members of the Thoreau Society. Hardly a mail goes by without my receiving a letter--or two or three or four--including word or a copy of some elusive new Thoreau item. It would be impossible to acknowledge individually all those who have thus helped (although most of them have been acknowledged in the individual bulletins), but I would be derelict were I not to mention in particular Hilda Adel, Ted Bailey, Margaret Campbell, Richard Epler, and Dorothy Kamen-Kaye, who over the years have sent me a constant stream of such notices.

In the early years of the Thoreau Society, Thoreau was enough out of the mainstream that a typical listing in the quarterly bulletin ran to ten or a dozen items--and often some of these did little more than mention Thoreau's name. But in the intervening thirty years Thoreau has come into his own and a continuing flood of Thoreauviana has poured forth from the presses of the world. We have long since had to abandon attempting to list every mention of Thoreau in print or every reprinting of excerpts from his works. For the past ten years we have limited our checklist to book-length reprintings of Thoreau's works, articles and books entirely devoted to Thoreau, and only such other pieces of Thoreauviana that we feel are of real significance to the Thoreau scholar and/ or enthusiast. Even with these limitations, the quarterly listing has grown to the point where it often includes as many as forty or fifty or sixty items.

These quarterly listings have, I think, served a real purpose over the years in keeping Thoreauvians up-to-date with publications in their field, but with the number of bulletins issued reaching to more than one hundred, searching for a particular item in these listings has begun to parallel searching for the proverbial needle in the haystack. Thus cumulating all these separate listings into a single alphabetization in its turn fulfills a very real need in providing a handy and comprehensive bibliography of Thoreauviana of the past thirty years and incidentally supplementing the Allen, Wade and White bibliographies of earlier periods both in bringing them up to date and listing items that they had overlooked. For this we are all grateful to the compiler for cumulating, editing, correcting, and completing the THOREAU SOCIETY BULLETIN bibliographies and to the Whitston Publishing Company for making the work available.

State University College
Geneseo. New York
March 4, 1971

Walter Harding, Secretary
The Thoreau Society

COMPILER'S NOTES

This is a cumulation of the bibliographies appearing in the THOREAU SOCIETY BULLETIN from its inception in 1941 through #109, 1969. Also incorporated in the cumulation is an index of those first 109 numbers. The listing is alphabetical by author, and title, if anonymous. Thoreau's primary works are entered according to the following order: "editions of, complete and abridged;" "complete in other works;" "translations of, complete and abridged;" "selections from;" "translations of selections of;" "contemporary reviews (i.e. 19th century reviews)."

Translations and reviews of a work are listed after the work. Extended reviews, entered as reviews of the work concerned, are not reproduced, but in each case the THOREAU SOCIETY BULLETIN number is cited.

News announcements and accounts of Thoreau Society annual meetings are entered under "Thoreau Society, transactions of--." Under "Thoreau Society, publications of--" complete entries of all Society Booklets are cited; Bulletins are merely numbered and dated.

Several checklists are entered or interfiled in the appropriate place in their entirety: "Thoreau and the NEW YORK TRIBUNE," by Morrison; "A Preliminary Checklist of Editions of WALDEN," by Harding; "A Preliminary Checklist of the Editions of CAPE COD," by Harber.

A

A., E. "Les Detracteurs de Thoreau," L'UNIQUE [Orleans, France] (September, 1954), pp. 177-178.

A., L. "Mislukte poginingen tot het scheppen ener betere wereld," ALGEMEEN HANDELSBLAD VAN ZATERDAG, February 28, 1948.
> An article on Frederik van Eeden's Dutch Utopia, Walden.

Abbott, M. LIFE OF WILLIAM T. DAVIS. Ithaca: Cornell University Press, 1949.
> Much about the interest of the Staten Island entomologist in Thoreau.

Ackerson, John. "White Birches at Concord," NEW YORK HERALD TRIBUNE, October 10, 1951.
> A poetic tribute to Thoreau.

Adamic, Louis. "What are you doing out there?" NEW YORK TIMES, January 15, 1951. p. 9.
> A quarter-page advertisement sponsored by a group of 17 outstanding citizens calling upon the American people "to protest violations of the right to free opinion" in the spirit of Thoreau's going to jail.

Adams, Agatha Boyd. "In the Abutment of a Rainbow," NATURE WRITERS IN THE UNITED STATES. Chapel Hill: University of North Carolina Press, 1944. pp. 13-14.
> A reading guide to WALDEN and Canby's THOREAU in the STUDY OUTLINES: LIBRARY EXTENSION PUBLICATIONS, X (April, 1944).

Adams, Alexander B. THOREAU'S GUIDE TO CAPE COD. New York: Devin-Adair, 1962.
> A guide to Cape Cod made up of selections from Thoreau's CAPE COD, with an introduction and superb photographs. The selections are re-arranged to fit into an auto tour of the area.

> reviews: AUDUBON MAGAZINE (July, 1963).
> BOSTON HERALD, December 2, 1962.
> BOSTON TRAVELER, October 26, 1962.
> CAPE CODDER, September 12, 1963.
> CHICAGO TRIBUNE, December 9, 1962.
> NARRAGANSETT NATURALIST, VI (1963), 27-28.
> NATIONAL PARKS MAGAZINE (January, 1963).

NATURE CONSERVANCY NEWS (Winter, 1962).
PRESBYTERIAN LIFE (February 1, 1963).
PROVINCETOWN ADVOCATE, December 27, 1962.

Adams, Anthony. "Thoreau in Hall of Fame?" LONG ISLAND SUN-
DAY PRESS, May 22, 1955. p. 21.
Describing Leonard Kleinfeld's collection of Thoreau-
viana.

Adams, Charles H. "Thoreau," YALE LITERARY MAGAZINE, XXXI
(1865).
Yale Literary Prize Essay.

Adams, George. THE MASSACHUSETTS REGISTER...FOR THE YEAR 1852.
Boston: Damrell and Moore, 1852.
Lists Thoreau as a civil engineer (p. 140) and his
father as a lead pencil manufacturer (p. 145).

Adams, George Matthew. "Ballast," CLEVELAND [Ohio] NEWS, October 23, 1941.

--"Influence," BETTER THAN GOLD. New York: Duell, 1949.
pp. 67-68.
"No one can read or study the life and writings
of Henry D. Thoreau without looking anew upon God."

--"Thoreau One of Great U.S. Minds," WORCESTER [Mass.]
GAZETTE, June 10, 1951.
A brief appreciation of Thoreau.

--"Today's Talk," BELOIT [Wis.] DAILY NEWS, June 21, 1944.+

--"Walden Pond," WORCESTER SUNDAY TELEGRAM, August 5, 1951.
p. 2.
"WALDEN is one of the most stimulating books ever
written."

Adams, J. Donald. "Speaking of Books," NEW YORK TIMES BOOK
REVIEW, January 4, 1942. p. 2.
Quotes the last two paragraphs of WALDEN "as a kind-
ling expression of the hope and expectancy in which
life must be lived by those who would keep their
faith in the forging of a better world."

--"Speaking of Books," NEW YORK TIMES BOOK REVIEW, June 6,
1947.
On H. M. Tomlinson's literary debt to Thoreau.

--"Speaking of Books," NEW YORK TIMES BOOK REVIEW, Janaury
11, 1948. p. 2.
More on the origin of "Nothing is so much to be
feared as fear."

--"Speaking of Books," NEW YORK TIMES BOOK REVIEW, March
15, 1953. p. 2.
Emerson and Thoreau contrasted.

2

--"Speaking of Books," NEW YORK TIMES BOOK REVIEW, June
     21, 1953. p. 2.
          On H. M. Tomlinson's interest in Thoreau.

--"Speaking of Books," NEW YORK TIMES BOOK REVIEW, May 6,
     1962.
          A centennial tribute.

Adams, R. P. "Romanticism and the American Renaissance,"
     AMERICAN LITERATURE, XXIII (January, 1952), 419-432.
          Emphasis on Carlyle's influence on Thoreau.

Adams, Raymond W. "The Bibliographical History of Thoreau's
     A WEEK ON THE CONCORD AND MERRIMACK RIVERS," PAPERS OF
     THE BIBLIOGRAPHICAL SOCIETY OF AMERICA, XLIII (1949).
          A scholarly study of the editions of Thoreau's
          first book.

--"Chapel Hill Chaff," CHAPEL HILL [N. C.] WEEKLY, July
     22, 1949.
          On neglect of Walden Pond.

--"Civil Disobedience Gets Printed," TSB #28.
          This was the Presidential Address read at the
          annual meeting in Concord.

--"An Early and Overlooked Defense of Thoreau," TSB #32.

--"Emerson's House at Walden," TSB #24.
          A paper read at the 1948 annual meeting of the
          Thoreau Society in Concord, Massachusetts.

--"Fred Hosmer, the 'Learned Clerk,'" TSB #36.
          The 1951 Presidential Address.

--"Hawthorne and a Glimpse of Walden," ESSEX INSTITUTE
     HISTORICAL COLLECTIONS, XCIV (July, 1958), 191-193.
          Text of a letter from Thoreau to Hawthorne of
          Feburary 20, 1849.

--Letter to the Editor, NEW YORK SUN, April 13, 1945.
          The Cairn controversy.

--"Photograph of the railroad picnic grounds at Walden
     Pond," CONCORD JOURNAL, October 24, 1957.

--"R. J. Hinton on Thoreau," TSB #66.
          Includes a reprint of a prefatory paragraph (by
          Hinton) to an article entitled "Celebration at
          North Elba" in which is printed for the first
          time Thoreau's "The Last Days of John Brown."
          The article appeared in Garrison's THE LIBERATOR
          on Friday, July 27, 1860.

--"A Rap from the Seer of Walden," CHRISTIAN SCIENCE
     MONITOR, October 9, 1954.

Condensation of the 1954 Thoreau Society Presidential Address.

--A review of Carl Bode, editor. COLLECTED POEMS OF HENRY THOREAU. Chicago: Packard and Company, 1943. NEW ENGLAND QUARTERLY, XVII (March, 1944), 114-117.

--A review of Roland Wells Robbins. DISCOVERY AT WALDEN. Concord, Massachusetts: Published by the author, 1947, TSB #19.

--A review of Walter Harding, editor. THOREAU, A CENTURY OF CRITICISM. Dallas: Southern Methodist University Press, 1954, TSB #50.

--"That Claim Again," TSB #67.

--"Thoreau and His Neighbors," TSB #44.
    The article also includes passages by William S. Robinson from WARRINGTON PEN PORTRAITS, 1877, pp. 12-13 passim; by Edward W. Emerson in HENRY THOREAU AS REMEMBERED BY A YOUNG FRIEND, pp. 1-11 passim; by Priscilla Rices Edes who wrote a "caustic appraisal" of Thoreau "on the front flyleaves of a copy of EXCURSIONS;" by Mrs. Daniel Chester French in MEMORIES OF A SCULPTOR'S WIFE; by George F. Hoar in AUTOBIOGRAPHY OF SEVENTY YEARS, I, p. 70. There also appear passages from Ralph Waldo Emerson's "1847 Ode and "The Apology."

    also in: CONCORD JOURNAL, August 13, 1953. p. 1.

--"Thoreau at Harvard," OF THE PEOPLE, edited by Warfel and Manwaring. New York: Oxford University Press, 1942. pp. 407-415.
    A reprint.

--"Thoreau at Walden," LECTURES IN THE HUMANITIES: FIRST SERIES, 1944-1945. Chapel Hill: University of North Carolina Press, 1945. pp. 8-23.

--"Thoreau, Imitators Plus," TSB #14.
    This is a paper delivered at the 1952 annual meeting of the Thoreau society.

--THOREAU NEWSLETTER. Chapel Hill: The Society, January, 1942 (mimeographed).

--THOREAU NEWSLETTER. Chapel Hill: The Society, March, 1942 (mimeographed).
    Reprinted in the CONCORD HERALD, April 16, 1942.

--THOREAU NEWSLETTER. Chapel Hill: The Society, October, 1944 (mimeographed).
    Another of these delightful concoctions of Thoreauana, the first in over two years. Contains a Tho-

reau ghost story.

--Thoreau--Surveyor in the Survey Course," EMERSON SOCIETY
QUARTERLY, XVIII (1960), 2-3.
> An essay in a symposium on teaching Thoreau in
> college classes.

--"Thoreau's Diploma," AMERICAN LITERATURE, XVII (May,
1945), 174-175.
> Correcting the common misunderstanding of Thoreau's
> refusal of his college diploma.

--"Thoreau's Growth at Walden," CHRISTIAN REGISTER, CXXIV
(July, 1945), 268-270.
> An essay on Thoreau's intellectual maturing.

--"Thoreau's Mock-Heroics and the American Natural History
Writers," STUDIES IN PHILOLOGY, LII (January, 1955), 86-
97.
> America's literature has been immeasurably enriched
> by Thoreau's application of the mock-heroic tech-
> nique to natural history.

--"Thoreau's Night in Jail Symbol of Resistance," TRENTON
[N. J.] TIMES, May 6, 1962.
> Centennial tribute syndicated by United Press In-
> ternational.

--"Thoreau's Return to Concord," TSB #96, pp. 1-4.

> also in: CONCORD JOURNAL, July 14, 1966.+

--"Thoreau's Science," SCIENTIFIC MONTHLY, LX (May, 1945),
379-382.
> A discussion of Thoreau as a natural scientist.
> A condensation of this article appeared in the
> CONCORD JOURNAL for June 28, 1945 under the title
> "Thoreau as Scientist."

--"Thoreau's Sources for RESISTANCE TO CIVIL GOVERN-
MENT," STUDIES IN PHILOLOGY, XLII (July, 1945), 640-
653.
> A scholarly study of the origins of Thoreau's
> ideas on civil disobedience.

--"Thoreau's Winged Cat," TSB #68.
> Included is a letter to Mr. Adams from Jimmy W.
> Thomas with an article he found in STARS AND ST-
> RIPES, the Armed Forces Newspaper. The article is
> entitled "West Virginia Youth Finds Cat with 'Wings'."

--"Thoreau's Year after WALDEN," CONCORD JOURNAL, July 14,
1955. pp. 4 passim.
> Reprint of Presidential Address at Thoreau Society
> meeting.

        also in: TSB #52.

  --"WALDEN'S Titles," TSB #46.

  --"Witnessing Walden," TSB #48.
          This is the Presidential Address given to the
          Thoreau Society at Concord, Massachusetts on July
          10, 1954.

Adams, Richard P.   "Architecture and the Romantic Tradition,"
     AMERICAN QUARTERLY, IX (Spring, 1957), 46-92.
          Thoreau's ideas compared to those of Frank Lloyd
          Wright.

Adams, Thomas Boylston.   "Thoreau and Emerson 1957," CONCORD
     JOURNAL, July 25, 1957.
          Sonnet.

  --"The Adams Family Journey Toward Concord," CONCORD JOUR-
     NAL, May 3, 1962.
          Paper read at the opening of the Morgan Library
          Thoreau exhibition on April 25.

  --"Meditation at Walden," BOSTON GLOBE, December 14, 1963.

  --ONE HUNDRED AND TWENTY-TWO YEARS JOURNEY TOWARD CONCORD.
     New York: Pierpont Morgan Library, 1962.
          An address delivered before the Fellows of The
          Pierpont Morgan Library, April 15, 1962.

Adix, Marjorie.   "Phoenix at Walden: D. H. Lawrence Calls
     on Thoreau," WESTERN HUMANITIES REVIEW, VIII (Autumn,
     1954), 287-298.
          An imaginary conversation.

Adler, Mortimer J.   "Civil Disobedience Follows Tradition of
     Henry Thoreau," LONG ISLAND PRESS, August 18, 1963.
          On civil disobedience in the South today.

  --"Thoreau's Act of Passive Resistance Is Remembered,"
     COLUMBUS [Ohio] DISPATCH, May 16, 1965.
          Syndicated column.

"After 100 Years, 'Walden' Rejected," ST. LOUIS POST DISPATCH,
     August 15, 1954.
          A Walden centennial essay mourning the fact that
          Thoreau is not more widely heeded.

Albee, John.   "Channing's Life of Thoreau," SPRINGFIELD REP-
     UBLICAN, February 1, 1903.

Albrecht, Dan.   "Home Town Musings," JOLIET [Ill.] HERALD
     NEWS, March 24, 1954.

Albrecht, Robert C.   "Thoreau and His Audience: 'A Plea
     for Captain John Brown,'" AMERICAN LITERATURE, XXXII

(January, 1961), 393-402.
>An analysis of the revisions Thoreau made in his
>address to make it more effective.

Alcott, Bronson. ESSAYS ON EDUCATION, edited by Walter
>Harding. Gainesville, Florida: Scholars' Facsimiles,
>1960.
>>These essays and reports are valuable on several
>>counts. They reveal Alcott's reverence for and
>>faith in man's nature and life and thus help us
>>to see the "blue-robed man" whom Thoreau celebra-
>>ted in WALDEN. They suggest some, at least, of
>>the "shingles" of thought that two men whittled
>>together: Alcott wrote in one report, "We see no
>>reason why the men of learning and experience who
>>adorn the town should not...contribute greatly to-
>>wards the better education of the children...A Mas-
>>sachusetts Township...is one of the best universi-
>>ties, or may be made so;" and he several times men-
>>tioned his great desire for an atlas of Concord to
>>be done by "the citizen of our time best able to
>>perform the work"--Thoreau. And these reports do
>>much, as Alcott thought they should, toward telling
>>us what life in Concord was like.--J. L. Shanley.
>>TSB #72.

>--THE FORESTER. Berkeley Heights, New Jersey: Oriole Press,
>1962.
>>Reprinted from the April, 1862, ATLANTIC MONTHLY.
>>With a preface by Walter Harding.

>>also in: TSB #78, pp. 2-3.

Alcott, Louisa M. THOREAU'S FLUTE. Berkeley Heights, New
>Jersey: Oriole Press, 1950.
>>Unquestionably the most beautiful edition of Miss
>>Alcott's tribute to Thoreau, printed by Joseph
>>Ishill in an edition "limited to friends and fol-
>>lowers of Thoreau's trends of life."

>>also in: "Poems You Ought to Know," NEW YORK SUN-
>>DAY NEWS, June 21, 1942.

>>translation: "La Flute de Thoreau," translated by
>>E. Armand. L'UNIQUE [Orleans, France] (December 20,
>>1951).

>--A SPRIG OF ANDROMEDA: A LETTER FROM LOUISA MAY ALCOTT
>ON THE DEATH OF HENRY DAVID THOREAU, with an introduction
>by John L. Cooley. New York: Pierpont Morgan Library,
>1962.
>>First printing of Louisa May Alcott's letter of May
>>11, 1862 to Sophia Ford.

Alcott, May. "Concord Scenes," PROVIDENCE JOURNAL, August
>21, 1949. p. 8.

Illustrated review of THOREAU SOCIETY BOOKLET #6.

Alexander, Charlotte A. THOREAU'S WALDEN; ALSO: ON THE DUTY OF CIVIL DISOBEDIENCE. New York: Monarch Press, 1965.
A pony.

Allard, H. A. and E. C. Leonard. "Plants Collected in the Lake Matagamon Region, Piscataquis and Penobscot Counties, Maine," CASTANEA, JOURNAL OF THE SOUTHERN APPALACHIAN BOTANICAL CLUB, X, 1 (1945), 13-30.

Allen, Francis H. A BIBLIOGRAPHY OF HENRY DAVID THOREAU. New York: Johnson Reprint Corporation, 1967.
A facsimile reprint of the original 1908 edition.

--"The French Translation of WALDEN," TSB #38.
A discussion of a French translation of WALDEN by Louis Fabulet, published by La Nouvelle Revue Francaise in 1922 in Paris.

--Letter to the Editor, AUDUBON MAGAZINE, XLVI (September, 1944), 319-320.
A criticism of the "purported" portrait of Thoreau published in the July issue.

--"Thoreau's Arm: A Correction," BULLETIN OF THE MASSACHUSETTS AUDUBON SOCIETY, XXXIII (January, 1950), 385.
It was Emerson, not E. Hoar who said he'd as soon think of taking the arm of an elm as Thoreau's.

--"Thoreau's Collected Poems," AMERICAN LITERATURE, XVII (November, 1945), 260-267.
A critical analysis of Dr. Bode's recent edition, correcting a number of errors and challenging his technique.

--THOREAU'S EDITORS HISTORY AND REMINISCENCE. [Thoreau Society Booklet #7] Chapel Hill: The Society, 1950.

translation: "Historia y Reminiscencia de los Compiladores de Thoreau." CENIT, XI (August, 1961), 3444-3450. Thoreau Society Booklet #7 translated into Spanish.

--"Thoreau's Translations from Pindar," TSB #26.
Printed is an ode which appeared on page 385 of Vol. IV of the DIAL in 1844 but was excluded from Thoreau's "Translations from Pindar" in "EXCURSIONS AND POEMS in the Walden Edition of Thoreau's WORKS and in MISCELLANIES of the Riverside Edition."

"The Francis H. Allen Papers: A Catalog," TSB #34.

"The Francis H. Allen Papers in The Thoreau Society Archives: A Catalog: Supplement," TSB #50.

Allen, Morse S., Earle Osborne, and David P. Edgell. "WAL-
    DEN and How to Teach It," NEWS LETTER OF THE COLLEGE
    ENGLISH ASSOCIATION, IX (December, 1947), 1 passim.
        A report on a panel discussion.

Allen, Walter. THE URGENT WEST: THE AMERICAN DREAM AND
    MODERN MAN. New York: Dutton, 1969.
        A brilliant brief intellectual history of the
        U. S. followed by rather routine discussions of
        individual authors. What he has to say about
        Thoreau--basically that he was Emerson's "American
        Scholar" in the flesh--is well said but not parti-
        cularly original. TSB #108.

Allison, Elliott S. "Me and Thoreau," YANKEE (July, 1967),
    pp. 69 passim.

  --"Thoreau in Vermont," VERMONT LIFE, IX (Autumn, 1954),
    11-13.
        The first thorough treatment of Thoreau's 1856
        visit to Brattleboro.

  --"A Thoreauvian on Red Hill," YANKEE (June, 1950).

Allison, Hildreth M. "Man on a Mountain," APPALACHIA (June,
    1947), 361-363.
        An account of Thoreau's 1860 visit to Monadnock.

Ament, Ernest J. "Socrates and Henry David Thoreau: a
    Study in Civil Disobedience," GRADUATE COMMENT [Wayne
    State University], X (1967), 198-211.

American Academy of Arts and Letters. THE GREAT DECADE IN
    AMERICAN WRITING: 1850-1860: EMERSON: HAWTHORNE: MEL-
    VILLE: THOREAU: WHITMAN: BOOKS AND MANUSCRIPTS: WITH
    PAINTINGS BY FRIENDS AND CONTEMPORARIES OF THE AUTHORS:
    (A CATALOG). New York: American Academy of Arts and
    Letters, 1954.
        A detailed catalog of the fine exhibition held
        for the month of December, 1954.

"Amerikatur og Thoreau's Samlede," BOK MYTT [Norway], Novem-
    ber 2, 1962.
        Ole Kristian Grimnes won a tour of the U. S. from
        Norway for an essay on Thoreau.

Ames, Van Meter. ZEN AND AMERICAN THOUGHT. Honolulu: Uni-
    versity of Hawaii Press, 1962.
        Includes comment on Thoreau and Zen.

Anastas, Peter, Richard Poirier, and Vincent Ferrini.
    "Gloucester's Salute to Thoreau," NORTH SHORE, July 8,
    1967. pp. 2-4.

Anderson, A. D. "Henry David Thoreau," NASSAU LITERARY
    MAGAZINE, XXXIII (1878).

A Princeton undergraduate essay discovered by
Mr. Lownes.

Anderson, Barbara. "Thoreau, New Mexico," TSB #104. pp. 2-3.

Anderson, Charles R. THE MAGIC CIRCLE OF WALDEN. New York:
Holt, 1968.
A detailed belletristic study of WALDEN that yields
many new insights but somehow misses the real
strength and ruggedness of the book. TSB #103.

reviews: BOSTON HERALD, April 7, 1968.
NEW BEDFORD STANDARD TIMES, June 16, 1968.
NEW ENGLAND QUARTERLY (December, 1968).
NEW REPUBLIC (September 14, 1968).
SOUTH ATLANTIC QUARTERLY (Winter, 1969).
WASHINGTON STAR, July 7, 1968.

--"Thoreau Takes a Pot Shot at Carolina Sports," GEORGIA
REVIEW, XXII (Fall, 1968), 289-299.

--"Wit and Metaphor in Thoreau's WALDEN," USA IN FOCUS,
edited by Sigmund Skard. Oslo: Universitetsforlaget,
1966.

Anderson, Esther Howe. "Thoreau and Herbs," THE HERBARIST,
XXVI (1960), 25-30.
On Thoreau's interest in herbs, with quotations
from JOURNALS.

Anderson, George P. "This Year Hall of Fame Electors May
Reach Thoreau," BOSTON GLOBE, July 17, 1955. p. 69.

Anderson, Katherine F. "Thoreau," THE SEER OF CONCORD.
? : Harold Vinal Press, 1928. p. 26.
A sonnet.

Anderson, Oma Carlyle. "Henry David Thoreau," EDUCATIONAL
FORUM, XXX (November, 1965), 78.
A poem.

Andres, Stefan. "Henry David Thoreau: Der Eremit von Wal-
den Pond," PERSPEKTIVEN, III, 10 (1954-1955), 52-71.
A general survey of Thoreau's life and his work;
Andres, whose frame of reference is scholastic
philosophy and Christian mysticism, characterizes
Thoreau as a radical nominalist.

Andrews, George R. "The Return of the Log-Peeler," DART-
MOUTH ALUMNI MAGAZINE (January, 1961), pp. 9-11.
Reminiscences of a two-month experiment in Thoreau-
vian living on Mt. Moosilauke in 1938.

Angelescu, Victor. "Henry Thoreau's 'Night and Moonlight',"
EMERSON SOCIETY QUARTERLY, XXII (1961), 64-67.
An analysis.

Angier, Bradford. "Woodland Retreat," THE BEAVER (June, 1954),
     pp. 38-42.
          Life in the Canadian wilderness inspired by Thoreau.

Angier, Vena and Bradford. AT HOME IN THE WOODS: LIVING THE
     LIFE OF THOREAU TODAY. New York: Sheridan House, 1951.
          Despite Thoreau's injunction in WALDEN not to imi-
          tate him, every year brings a new crop of those who
          retreat to the woods to "live the life of Thoreau
          today." Mr. and Mrs. Angier were Boston writers
          when they decided to live the simple life and built
          themselves a cabin in the far northern wilderness
          of British Columbia. They have truly lived the sim-
          ple life there, and after four years are still en-
          joying it to the hilt. Their book has none of the
          profundity of WALDEN, but it is simple, pleasant
          reading. I think you will enjoy it. --WRH TSB #38.

"Another Forgotten Obituary for Thoreau," TSB #87, p. 3.
          Reprinted from THE NATIONAL ALMANAC FOR 1863.
          Philadelphia: George W. Childs, 1863. p. 640.

"Another Step Has Been Taken to Save Walden's Natural Beau-
     ty," CONCORD JOURNAL, August 4, 1955. p. 2.
          Account of addition to reservation with excellent
          air photo of pond.

"Antiquarian Shows Treasures for WALDEN 1854-1954 Anniver-
     sary," CONCORD JOURNAL, July 8, 1954. pp. 1 passim.
          Account of Concord Antiquarian Society centennial
          exhibition.

Anzai, Shichinosuke. "A Hound, a Bay Horse, and a Turtle-
     dove," in POEMS WITH THEIR TRANSLATIONS, APPRECIATIONS
     AND NOTES. Tokyo: Shinozaki Shoten, 1967. pp. 200-201.
          An explication in Japanese.

Armand, E. "Thoreau, ce qu'il fut et ce qu'on en a dit,"
     L'UNIQUE [Orleans, France] (1959).
          This is the lead article in a special Thoreau sup-
          plement to L'UNIQUE. Also included in the supple-
          ment are: "L'anarchisme 'a la Thoreau'" by John C.
          Scott and Jo Ann Wheeler; "Le 'bachelier de la
          nature' Henry-David Thoreau" by Aime Bailey; "Tho-
          reau et la publicite" by Joseph Wood Krutch; "Re-
          flexions sur Henry-David Thoreau" from ANALYSIS:
          "Thoreau" by Benjamin De Casseres; and "La flute
          de Thoreau" by Louisa Alcott.

Armour, Richard. " Henry David Thoreau," AMERICAN LIT RE-
     LIT. New York: Mc-Graw-Hill, 1964. pp. 54-56.
          A delightful bit of spoofing that comes as a re-
          lief to some of the stuffier histories of American
          literature. If you hold Thoreau too sacred, you
          may be shocked--but that is as it should be. Typ-
          ical is Armour's comment on "I wanted to live deep

and suck out all the marrow of life"--"The picture
of this rugged individualist crouched in a hole he
had dug near his cabin, working away on a bone, is
likely to linger for many a day." TSB #90.

Arnold, Peter. "In Thoreau's Woods," CONNECTICUT CONSER-
VATION ASSOCIATION, I (Spring, 1968), 2-9.
On Thoreau's Easterbrook woods.

Arnstein, Felix. "Henry Thoreau, American," SNOWY EGRET,
XXVI (Autumn, 1962), 12-19.

Ashmun, Margaret. "Thoreau's Walden," NEW ENGLAND MAGAZINE,
XXXVII (February, 1908), 678.
A poem.

Askfelt, Martin. "Brug din tid vel, dit kosteligste eje,"
ROSKILDE [Denmark] TIDENDE, March 11, 1968.
On Thoreau. Text in Danish.

--"Mit liv er kun en strom," INFORMATION [Copenhagen],
September 8, 1966.
On Thoreau in Denmark.

Asklund, Erik. ENSAMMA LYKTOR: STUDIER OCH SKISSER. Stockholm: Kooperativa Forbundets Bokforlag, 1947.
Includes an essay on Thoreau.

Atkinson, Brooks. "Century after Thoreau's Death, America
Knows How 'Great a Son It Has Lost,'" NEW YORK TIMES,
May 8, 1962.
Essay on the centennial meetings.

--"Critic at Large: Value of the Thoreau Society is Dis-
cussed as its 20th Annual Meeting Nears," NEW YORK TIMES,
July 11, 1961.

--"Daughter Recalls Her Mother's Story of Rejecting Thoreau's Proposal," NEW YORK TIMES [Western Edition],
March 12, 1963.

--"Fame Costs $10,774" and "Thoreau Centenary," TUESDAYS
AND FRIDAYS. New York: Random House, 1963, pp. 171-173
passim.
On the Thoreau Centennial.

--"An Introduction to Thoreau's Writings," MODELS FOR COM-
POSITION. Edited by A. A. Glatthorn and Harold Fleming.
New York: Harcourt, Brace, 1967.

--ONCE AROUND THE SUN. New York: Harcourt, Brace, 1951.
Ordinarily we shy away from "daily readings" books,
but here is one we can honestly endorse. It is a
collection of 365 brief essays on assorted subjects
with a great deal of the flavor of Thoreau and frequent mention of him. The entry for Thoreau's birth-

day (pp. 199-201) is an appreciative tribute to
the man. I don't see how you can help but enjoy
this book. TSB #36.

--"Spirit of Frugal Thoreau Resists Efforts to Get His
Bust Installed in Hall of Fame," NEW YORK TIMES, January 19, 1962.

--"Thoreau's Accession to the Hall of Fame Took Long, but
Now Presents Problems," NEW YORK TIMES, October 3, 1961.

--"Thoreau's Message After 150 Years," NEW YORK TIMES,
July 15, 1967.

[Atkinson, J. Brooks]. "River Centennial," NEW YORK TIMES,
August 31, 1939.
An editorial on the centennial of Thoreau's boat
trip.

Atkinson, Oriana. HER LIFE TO LIVE. New York: Popular Library, 1951.
A reissue of the novel BIG EYES with one of its
characters a Thoreau devotee.

Audubon Society. AMERICA MY COUNTRY.   ?   : The Society,
1942.
A pamphlet soliciting gifts, quotes from one of
Thoreau's poems on page 11 and from WALDEN on
page 14.

"August Derleth on Thoreau," TSB #72.
Comments made on January 17, 1960.

Austin, James C. FIELDS OF THE ATLANTIC MONTHLY. San Marino: Huntington Library, 1953.
Includes part of the correspondence between Thoreau and Ticknor and Fields.

Austin, Patricia M. "American Transcendentalism in Thoreau."
Syracuse University, 1936. Unpublished master's thesis.
A mosaic of Thoreau's philosophical writings.

Austin, Thomas D. "Thoreau, the First Hippie," ANKH, I
(Spring, 1968), 12-21.

Ayars, James S. "Civil Disobedience, Yesterday and Today,"
FRIENDS JOURNAL (September 1, 1964), 401-402.
Tracing history of idea from the Old Testament
through Thoreau to modern times.

B., A. "Thought from Thoreau," NEW YORK HERALD TRIBUNE, October 12, 1951.
    A letter to the editor.

B., F. "Thoreau on Winged Cat," WASHINGTON [D.C.] STAR, July 25, 1945.
    A letter to the editor.

Baatz, Wilmer H. "Henry David Thoreau," UNIVERSITY OF ROCH-ESTER LIBRARY BULLETIN, V (Winter, 1950), 35-39.
    On their recent exhibition of Thoreauviana.

Babcock, Franklin L. "Thoreau's House," NEW YORK HERALD TRIBUNE, September 4, 1947.
    A letter to the editor.

Babcock, Frederic. "An Adventure in Living," CHRISTIAN CENTURY, LXII (March 28, 1945), 395-396.
    A brief essay on the Walden experiment.

    --"Among the Authors," CHICAGO SUNDAY TRIBUNE, February 18, 1945.
        On the centennial of Thoreau's going to Walden.

    --"Favorite Classics: WALDEN," CHICAGO TRIBUNE, October 1, 1950. p. 3 passim.
        WALDEN brings serenity to one's life.

    --"In Search of Solitude," in ALL FLORIDA [A Sunday supplement], April 9, 1967.
        On the inspiration of Thoreau.

    --"100th Year of the 'Solitary Rebel's' Immortal WALDEN," CHICAGO TRIBUNE MAGAZINE OF BOOKS, August 8, 1954. p. 3.

Bagg, Edith A. "Fear of Fear," NEW YORK TIMES MAGAZINE, July 26, 1953. p. 4.
    On Thoreau and others as a source for FDR's famous speech.

Bailey, Herbert S., Jr. "Thoreau Changed the World--and the World Changed Him," UNIVERSITY: A PRINCETON QUARTERLY, XXXVIII (Fall, 1968), 15-19.

Bailey, T. L. "Excerpts from Address by T. L. Bailey, Pres. The Thoreau Society," TSB #84. pp. 1-2.

--"A Philatelic Adventure," QUARTERLY JOURNAL BOOK CLUB OF DETROIT, I (Spring, 1968), 12-14.
On background of Thoreau stamp.

Bailly, A. "Les grandes figures: Henry David Thoreau (1817-1862)," L'UNIQUE [Orleans, France], XLIX (June-July, 1950), 134-135.+
An essay quoting extensively from Bazalgette's biography.

Baird, Theodore. "Corn Grows in the Night," MASSACHUSETTS REVIEW, IV (Autumn, 1962), 93-103.

Baker, Carlos. "The Slopes of Kilimanjaro: a Biographical Perspective," NOVEL, I (Fall, 1967), 19-23.
The influence of Thoreau on Hemingway's famous story. Reveals that the protagonist was first named Henry Walden!

also in: AMERICAN HERITAGE, XIX (August, 1968), 40-43 passim. A reprint with revisions.

Baker, Isadore. "On Receiving a Violet from the Grave of Thoreau," A COLLECTION OF POEMS BY AMERICA'S YOUNGER POETS. Philadelphia: Westminister, 1888. p. 87.
A sonnet.

Balch, Francis N. "Ornithologists Alive! IV. Francis H. Allen," BULLETIN OF THE MASSACHUSETTS AUDUBON SOCIETY, XXIX (April, 1945), 89-92.
A tribute to the accomplishments of our foremost editor and bibliographer of Thoreau. TSB #12.

Baldwin, Henry I. "Letter to Gilbert Byron," LIVING WILDERNESS, XXXII (Winter, 1968), 35.
Querying Byron's earlier article on Monadnock.

--"The Vegetation of Mt. Monadnock," FOREST NOTES, XCIX (Fall, 1968), 12-13.
Includes material on Thoreau's botanical notes on the mountain.

Baldwin, Sidney. "Thoreau's Walden Pond," PEORIA JOURNAL STAR, September 7, 1967.

Ball, Max W. "Our Human Resources," THINK (April, 1949), pp. 3-4 passim.
On Thoreau as an economist.

Ballou, Adin. "After Reading Thoreau" sonnets appearing in the NEW YORK HERALD TRIBUNE:
"August Pause," August 28, 1945.
"The Autumn Goes," December 2, 1943.
"Before the Trumpets," November 23, 1944.
"The Bluebird Waits," April 30, 1942.
"Brook Symphony," May 3, 1943.

"Cape Cod Carpet," October 7, 1947.
"Concord in October," October 18, 1958.
"Concord River by Moonlight," 1942.
"Concord River in June," June 25, 1943.
"Concord's Best Skater," December 19, 1946.
"It's Time to Talk of Spring," March 16, 1944.
"January Thaw," January 16, 1943.
"June at Walden Pond," June 30, 1942.
"Leather-Bound November," November 5, 1943.
"The Ledgers of Love," September 28, 1957.
"The Legions Return," 1942?
"Lesson in May," May 16, 1949.
"Let There be Linnets," March 5, 1946.
"Like Flooded Field," March 29, 1946.
"Make Whistles of Your Life," March 29, 1942.
"March Makes a Promise," March 12, 1943.
"Mountainside Dawn," August 17, 1946.
"Mountainside Pasture," July 31, 1938.
"Now in the Woods," February 9, 1943.
"September Equinox," September 25, 1942.
"September's Flower," September 9, 1955.
"Spirit Is Shadow," June 9, 1950.
"The Telegraph Harp," January 31, 1948.
"A Thrush A Day," May 22, 1948.
"Unoccupied Winter," February 3, 1942.
"When the Dark Trumpet Sounds," April (?), 1947.
"Winter Mouse," March 5, 1942.
"Winter Sunset at Walden," February 21, 1944.

--"Essay on Thoreau," NEW YORK HERALD TRIBUNE, July 12, 1943.
 "In recognition of Henry Thoreau's birthday."

--"Flower of the Season," NEW YORK HERALD TRIBUNE, August 13, 1945.
 An editorial on Thoreau's love of water lilies.

--"On Seeing Thoreau's Stove," NEW YORK HERALD TRIBUNE, December 15, 1953.
 A poem.

--"A New England Early Spring," NEW YORK HERALD TRIBUNE, March 14, 1945.
 An editorial on Thoreau's spring notes.

--"The New England Wood Lot," NEW YORK HERALD TRIBUNE, December 21, 1947.
 An editorial.

--"River Program," CHRISTIAN SCIENCE MONITOR, October 10, 1941.
 A poem.

--Sonnets appearing in the CHRISTIAN SCIENCE MONITOR:
 "For a Winter Night," October 15, 1947.
 "High Pilgrimage," June 14, 1944.

"Make Whistles of Your Life," March 18, 1942.
   After reading Thoreau.
"Mountain Cowbells," August 18, 1944.
"November Walk," November 30, 1943.
   After reading Thoreau.
"The Poet's Pine," June 21, 1948.
"Pond Prophet," April 12, 1944.
"Upland Thoughts," August 4, 1945.

--Sonnets appearing in the NEW YORK HERALD TRIBUNE:
   "Blue Warrior," March 14, 1950.
   "The Completed Music," April 30, 1944.
   "Concord New Year," January 1, 1944.
   "The Conquering Corps," February 15, 1950.
   "Fair Haven in February," February 24, 1945.
   "Formula in Fourteen Lines," April 18, 1953.
   "The Melting Stars," January 14, 1954.
   "October at Walden," October 11, 1948.
   "Poet's Purchase," September 26, 1944.
   "Stars over Walden," January 11, 1945.
   "Supper at Sunset," September 13, 1948.
   "The Twilight River," June 26, 1948.
   "The Wilderness Is Near," July 26, 1944.
   "Winter Sunset at Walden," January 3, 1950.

--"Southern Passage," NEW YORK HERALD TRIBUNE, December
   17, 1941.
   A poem.

--"Thoreau's Concord River," NEW YORK HERALD TRIBUNE,
   July 26, 1956.
   A poem.

--"Walden Farmer," BOSTON HERALD, July 27, 1946.
   An After Reading Thoreau sonnet.

[Ballou, Adin]. "Walden Pond's First Citizen," NEW YORK
   HERALD TRIBUNE, June 18, 1945.
   An editorial on the Museum exhibition.

--"The Fluvial Stroll," NEW YORK HERALD TRIBUNE, July
   28, 1957.
   An editorial on Thoreau's river strolls.

Banks, Russell. "The Adjutant Bird," LILLABULERO. [Chapel
   Hill, N. C.], I (Fall, 1967), 7-10.
   On shipping ice from Walden.

Barker, Edna L. S. "Thoreau's Journal, 'Summer'," NEW YORK
   HERALD TRIBUNE, August ?, 1959.
   A poem, reprinted in MONTREAL GAZETTE, September
   3, 1959.

Barlow, Perry. "Oh, you'd like Thoreau!" NEW YORKER (October
   18, 1941).
   A cartoon.

Barnard, William F. "A Day on Old Concord," MARLBORO [Mass.]
ADVERTISER, August 27, 1884.
Comments on Thoreau.

Barnier, John F. "Thoreau's Mirror Imagery." San Diego State
College, 1965. Unpublished master's thesis.

Barton, W. G. "Thoreau, Flagg, and Burroughs," EMERSON SOCIE-
TY QUARTERLY, XV (1959), 51-64.
Reprinted from Historical Coll. of Essex Institute
for 1885.

Barton, William E. "The Great Men of Concord," FUN AND PHI-
LOSOPHY OF SAFED THE SAGE. Boston: Pilgrim Press, 1925.
pp. 83-86.
An amusing account of an interview with a Concord
farmer who knew Thoreau.

Basile, Joseph. "Thoreau's Inevitable, Infernal Railroad,"
THE ATLANTIC 1967/1968 CONTESTS FOR COLLEGE STUDENTS.
Boston: Atlantic Monthly, 1968. pp. 42-52.

Basile, Martha, Dean Soule, Robert Downey, Sondra Olsen, and
David Waite. "Transcript of Students 'Walden' Story
Given at Concord High Graduation," CONCORD ENTERPRISE,
June 24, 1954.
Complete transcription of the commemorative exer-
cises.

Baskin, Leonard. Portrait of Thoreau at 44, MASSACHUSETTS
REVIEW, IV (Autumn, 1962), 42.

"Bas-Relief in Concord Home Links Thoreau to New Bedford,"
NEW BEDFORD STANDARD TIMES, September 8, 1957.
Thoreau and the Ricketsons.

Bass, Althea. "Hawk Flight at Walden," SATURDAY REVIEW OF
LITERATURE, July 25, 1953. p. 31.
A sonnet.

Bates, Caroline. "Walking in Thoreau's Footstep on Cape Cod,"
NEW YORK TIMES, October 11, 1959.
An essay.

Baym, Nina Zippin. "From Metaphysics to Metaphor: the Image
of Water in Emerson and Thoreau," STUDIES IN ROMANTICISM,
V (Summer, 1966), 231-243.

--"The Paradoxical Hero in Thoreau's Writings." Harvard
University, 1963. Unpublished doctoral dissertation.

--"Thoreau's View of Science," JOURNAL OF THE HISTORY OF
IDEAS, XXVI (April-June, 1965), 221-234.

Beardslee, Martin. "Epitaph for Thoreau," THOREAU JOURNAL
QUARTERLY, I (April 15, 1969), 25.
A poem.

--"A Walk to Walden," THOREAU JOURNAL QUARTERLY, I (July 1, 1969), 17-21.

Becker, Klaus. "Der Stil in den Essays von H. D. Thoreau," Marburg, 1952. Unpublished doctoral dissertation.
Rather mystically equates an "inner form" in Thoreau's writing with his world view. Most interesting is Becker's discussion of Thoreau's theoretical statements about writing in relation to his actual practice. Argues that Thoreau's vocabulary is more traditional and less "American" than has generally been supposed. Covers all of Thoreau's writings; emphasizes WALDEN. TSB #105.

Bedau, Hugo Adam. CIVIL DISOBEDIENCE: THEORY AND PRACTICE. New York: Pegasus, 1969.
An anthology of essays (including Thoreau's) on the topic, pro and con. By far the best such volume yet and the analysis of Thoreau's essay by Bedau himself is perhaps the most thoughtful I've yet seen. TSB #107.

Bedichek, Roy. THE SENSE OF SMELL. New York: Doubleday, 1960.
Pp. 198-199, on Thoreau's sense of smell.

Beebe, Howard Percy, Jr. "MacPherson's Ossian in Nineteenth Century American Literature." Cornell University, 1948. Unpublished master's thesis.
Thoreau, pp. 23-35 passim.

Beecher, John. "Homage to a Subversive: For Henry David Thoreau, 1817-1862," FRONTIER (August, 1962).
A poem.

Beers, Henry. "A Pilgrim in Concord," THE YALE REVIEW ANTHOLOGY. New Haven: Yale University Press, 1942. pp. 40-54.

Bemis, Samuel Flagg. "Alum Pond and Walden," NEW ENGLAND GALAXY, X (Summer, 1968), 12-18.
Compares Alum Pond in Sturbridge, Massachusetts, to Walden.

Bengtsson, Frans G. "Henry David Thoreau," introduction to Henry David Thoreau, SKOGSLIV VID WALDEN Stockholm ?, 1924, 1927.
Reprinted in FOLK SOM SJONG [Stockholm ?, 1955], pp. 179-217.

Benson, A. B. "Scandinavian Influences on the Writings of Thoreau," SCANDIVANIAN STUDIES (May, 1941).+

Berkow, Ira. "Will Thoreau's Walden Pond Become 'Walden Puddle?'" MINNEAPOLIS TRIBUNE, October 2, 1966.
On the low water level of the pond.

Bernstein, Daniel J. Letter to the editor. NEW YORK TIMES,
June 23, 1945.
An answer to the Strunsky article of June 4, 1945.

--"Seeks Clippings on Thoreau," CONCORD JOURNAL, January
29, 1942. p. 10.
A letter to the editor.

--"To the Editor," FREE AMERICA (March, 1942), p. 14.
A letter proposing Thoreau as the philosopher of
decentralization, self-sufficiency, and individual
independence--the principles of the magazine.

--"Unpublished Thoreau Letter," SATURDAY REVIEW OF LIT-
ERATURE, (May 30, 1942), p. 15.
A February 15, 1855, letter of Thoreau to Elizabeth
Oakes Smith.

Berry, Edmund. "Thoreau in Canada," DALHOUSIE REVIEW, XXIII
(April, 1943), 68-74.

Berry, Romeyn. "Cabin in the Woods," ITHACA [N. Y.] JOURNAL,
April 9, 1951.
On an annual reading of the spring passages in
WALDEN.

--"State and Tioga," ITHACA [N. Y.] JOURNAL, August 1, 1949.
An essay on Thoreau's writing style.

Berry, Watson. "Thoreau," WATERTOWN [N. Y.] DAILY TIMES,
November 10, 1948.
A letter to the editor about THOREAU SOCIETY BOOK-
LET #5.

Berryman, Charles. "The Artist-Prophet: Emerson and Thoreau,"
EMERSON SOCIETY QUARTERLY, XLIII (1966), 81-86.

Besant, Walter. THE EULOGY OF RICHARD JEFFERIES. London:
Longmans, 1888. 221f.
A comparison of Henry David Thoreau and Jefferies
on p. 221 passim.

Beston, Elizabeth Coatsworth. "Finder, Please Return to Henry
Thoreau," SATURDAY REVIEW OF LITERATURE, XXXVIII (December
17, 1955), 17.
A poem.

Beston, Henry. THE OUTERMOST HOUSE: A YEAR OF LIFE ON THE
GREAT BEACH OF CAPE COD. New York: Rinehart, 1949.
A new edition with new illustrations and forward
of this glorious book on Cape Cod. Innumerable
quotations from and comments on Thoreau.

Bevington, Helen. A CHANGE OF SKY AND OTHER POEMS. Boston:
Houghton Mifflin, 1956.
Including the following on Thoreau:

"The Other Way," p. 99; "The Traveller," p. 79;
"Trip of a Lifetime," p. 107; "Afternoon with a
Savant," p. 130.

--"Do What You Love," ATLANTIC MONTHLY, CLXXVIII (November,
1946), 74.
A poem.

--"Return from Summer," NEW YORKER (September 14, 1946).
A short poem on Thoreau's preoccupation with the
sound of his footsteps.

--"Thoreau and the Farmers of Concord," DR. JOHNSON'S
WATERFALL AND OTHER POEMS. Boston: Houghton, Mifflin,
1946. p. 20.

also in: CHICAGO TRIBUNE, December 8, 1946.
NEW YORKER (January 5, 1946), p. 22.

--"When Found, Make a Note of," 19 MILLION ELEPHANTS AND
OTHER POEMS. Boston: Houghton, Mifflin, 1950. p. 24.
A poem on Thoreau and Whitman.

Bhatia, Kamala. THE MYSTICISM OF THOREAU AND ITS AFFINITY
WITH INDIAN THOUGHT. New Delhi, India: Published by
the author, 1966.
One of the most thoughtful and carefully worked
out discussions of Thoreau and Oriental thought
yet. TSB #98.

"Bibliographia--Henry David Thoreau," BOOKLOVER'S ANSWER, I
(November, 1962), 15-17.
A bibliography.

Bier, Jesse. THE RISE AND FALL OF AMERICAN HUMOR. New York:
Holt, Rinehart and Winston, 1968.
On Thoreau's use of humor, pp. 363-368.

Bigelow, Gordon E. "Summer under Snow: Thoreau's 'A Winter's
Walk,'" EMERSON SOCIETY QUARTERLY, LVI (1969), 13-16.

Bishop, Jonathan. "The Experience of the Sacred in Thoreau's
WEEK," ENGLISH LITERARY HISTORY, XXXIII (March, 1966),
66-91.

Bitter Bachelor. "Thoreau, Fond of Walden Pond, Had Woman-
Free Economy," MINNEAPOLIS TRIBUNE, November 13, 1960.
Humorous essay on WALDEN.

Blackford, Frank. "What Thoreau Started," [Norfolk] VIR-
GINIA PILOT, December 4, 1967.
On CIVIL DISOBEDIENCE.

Blair, John G. and Augustus Trowbridge. "Thoreau on Katahdin," AMERICAN QUARTERLY, XII (Winter, 1960), 508-517.

Blanch, Robert J. "The Synchronized Clocks of Bergson and Thoreau," REV. DES LANGUES VIVANTES [Bruxelles]. XXXIII (September, 1967), 489-492.
Text in French.

Blanchard, Harold H. "Thoreau's Concord," TUFTONIAN, IV (Fall, 1944), 110-118.
An exceptionally good account of a tour of the Thoreau country today, beautifully illustrated with photographs by B. C. Chambers and Mrs. L. A. Sohier, and a new map of Concord by Roberta Blanchard . TSB #11

[Blanchard, Harold]. "Thoreau Collection on Display at Winchester Library," WINCHESTER [Mass.] STAR, May ?, 1945.

Blanding, Thomas. "Walton and WALDEN," TSB #107, p.3.

Blau, Joseph L. "Henry David Thoreau: Anarchist," MEN AND MOVEMENTS IN AMERICAN PHILOSOPHY. New York: Prentice-Hall, 1952. pp. 131-141.

translation: "Henry David Thoreau: Anarquista," FILOSOFOS Y ESCUELAS FILOSOFICAS EN LOS ESTADOS UNIDOS DE AMERICA [Mexico] (July, 1957), pp. 150-163. Translated into Spanish.

Blau, Peter E. "In Memoriam: Henry David Thoreau," BAKER STREET JOURNAL, XIX (September, 1969), 152-153.
On Sherlock Holmes' interest in Thoreau.

Bliven, Bruce. "Mr. Thoreau of Walden Pond," READER'S DIGEST, LXXIX (December, 1961), 225-234.

Block, Louis J. "Thoreau's Letters," DIAL, XVII (October 16, 1894), 228-230.

Blodgett, Harold W. "Prof. Blodgett's Address: Thoreau and Whitman," CONCORD JOURNAL, July 21, 1955. p. 3.
Excerpts from speech at annual meeting.

Blume, Mary. "Thoreau in Paris," NEW YORK HERALD TRIBUNE [Paris Edition], October, 26, 1966.
Interview with Leonard Kleinfeld.

Bode, Carl. THE AMERICAN LYCEUM. New York: Oxford, 1956.
With Prof. Bode's new volume we have the first comprehensive picture of the American Lyceum movement of the pre-Civil War era. Because it gives a broad over-all picture of the movement, there is comparatively little specific detail about Thoreau's part. But the book as a whole will prove important to anyone who wants to understand the background of Thoreau's lecturing career. TSB #55.

--"The Half-Hidden Thoreau," MASSACHUSETTS REVIEW, IV

22

(Autumn, 1962), 68-80.

--"Henry Thoreau as a Poet, with a Critical Edition of
His Poems." Northwestern University, 1941. Unpublished
doctoral dissertation.

--"The Hidden Thoreau," THE HALF-WORLD OF AMERICAN CULTURE:
A MISCELLANY. Carbondale: Southern Illinois University
Press, 1965. pp. 3-15.
  A Freudian study of Thoreau.

--"A New College Manuscript of Thoreau's," AMERICAN LIT-
ERATURE, CCI (November, 1949), 311-320.
  Thoreau's college review of H. N. Coleridge's "In-
  troduction to the Study of the Greek Classic Poets."

--"Rejoinder," AMERICAN LITERATURE, XVII (November, 1945).
  A reply to Mr. Allen. Reveals that the poem "Carpe
  Diem" should be assigned to Thomas Hill rather than
  to Thoreau.

--"The Sound of American Literature a Century Ago," JOURNAL
OF GENERAL EDUCATION, XV (April, 1963).
  On the influence of the lyceum on Thoreau.

  also in: THE HALF-WORLD OF AMERICAN CULTURE: A
  MISCELLANY. Carbondale: Southern Illinois University Press, 1965. pp. 66-84.

--"Thoreau the Actor," AMERICAN QUARTERLY, V (Fall, 1953),
247-252.
  "Thoreau satisfies the idea of Withdrawal and Return more richly and variously for our native culture than does any other American."

  also in: THE HALF-WORLD OF AMERICAN CULTURE: A
  MISCELLANY. Carbondale: Southern Illinois University Press, 1965. pp. 54-62.

--"Thoreau and His Last Publishers," NEW ENGLAND QUARTERLY,
XXVI (September, 1953), 383-387.
  Unpublished letters from Thoreau to Ticknor and
  Fields.

--"Thoreau: The Double Negative," THE YOUNG REBEL IN
AMERICAN LITERATURE. New York: Praeger, 1960. pp. 3-22.
  One of a series of lectures delivered at the American Embassy in London. "Thoreau is never merely negative. He is eager to replace the values he dislikes
  with nobler ones."

--"Thoreau Finds a House," SATURDAY REVIEW OF LITERATURE
(July 20, 1946).
  Annotating a hitherto unpublished letter from Tho-
  reau to Ricketson.

--"Thoreau Society President's Address," CONCORD JOURNAL,
July 20, 1961.
> Excerpts from "The Sound of American Literature a
> Century Ago."

--"Thoreau, with Advice," AMERICAN LITERATURE, XXVIII
(March, 1956), 77-78.
> First publication of Thoreau's letter of January
> 19, 1860 to S. Ripley Bartlett.

--"Thoreau's Last Letter," NEW ENGLAND QUARTERLY, XIX
(June, 1946), 244.
> Another previously unpublished letter, this one
> to his publishers Ticknor and Fields is later
> than any other known letter.

--"Thoreau's Manuscript Poems in Private Hands," EMERSON
SOCIETY QUARTERLY, XIV (1959), 17-18.

> also in: TSB #66 entitled "Thoreau's 'Unpublished'
> Poems."

--"Thoreau's Young Ideas," THE HALF-WORLD OF AMERICAN CUL-
TURE: A MISCELLANY. Carbondale: Southern Illinois University Press, 1965. pp. 95-105.
> Essay on the foreshadowings of Thoreau's more sig-
> nificant ideas in his early poetry.

Bode, Carl, editor. COLLECTED POEMS OF HENRY THOREAU. Chicago: Packard and Company, 1943.
> Thoreau book of the year.

> reviews: TSB #4.
> NEW ENGLAND QUARTERLY, XVII (March, 1944),
> 114-117.
> PHILOLOGICAL QUARTERLY, XXIII (January,
> 1944), 92-94.

--COLLECTED POEMS OF HENRY THOREAU. Baltimore: Johns
Hopkins University Press, 1964. Enlarged edition.

Boewe, Charles. "Thoreau's 1854 Lecture in Philadelphia,"
ENGLISH LANGUAGE NOTES, II (December 1964), 115-122.

Boies, J. J. "Circular Imagery in Thoreau's WEEK," COLLEGE
ENGLISH, XXVI (Feburary, 1965), 350-355.

Boisvert, C. Anne. "Reader Answers Critic of Thoreau,"
SANTA MONICA [Calif.] OUTLOOK, July 21, 1967.

Bolton, Robert. "Henry's Three Chairs," ROTARIAN (September,
1967), pp. 34-35.

Bonner, Willard Hallam. "Captain Thoreau: Gubernator to a
Piece of Wood," NEW ENGLAND QUARTERLY, XXXIX (March, 1965),
26-46.

--"Mariners and Terreners: Some Aspects of Nautical Imagery in Thoreau," AMERICAN LITERATURE, XXXIV (January,
1963), 507-519.

--"Thoreau's Native Port," CANADIAN ASSOCIATION OF AMERICAN
STUDIES BULLETIN [Sir George Williams University, Mont-
real], III (Winter, 1968), 45-72.

--"Thoreau's Other Telegraph Figure," AMERICAN NOTES AND
QUERIES, VII (March, 1969), 99-100.

Bontemps, Ch.-Aug. "L'Anarchisme et le Reel," LES CAHIERS
FRANCS. Paris: ? , 1963.
Comments on Thoreau, p. 91.

Booth, Edward Townsend. "Concord Alluvial," GOD MADE THE
COUNTRY. New York: Knopf, 1946. pp. 186-201.
On Thoreau and his friends as agriculturists.

Booth, Philip. LETTER FROM A DISTANT LAND. New York:
Viking, 1957.
Philip Booth is one of the most gifted and pro-
mising of our younger peots. The title poem of
this, his first volume of poems is a blank verse
letter to Thoreau, telling of the changes that
have come about in Concord and environs in the
past century. (Booth is now a resident of near-
by Lincoln.) It is thought-provoking, penetrating, and beautifully expressed. Quite deserved-
ly it has won the Lamont Poetry Prize. TSB #59.

--"Letter from a Distant Land," POETRY, LXXXVIII (Octo-
ber, 1955), 19-25.
Poem in the form of an open letter to Thoreau.
Title poem of book, LETTER FROM A DISTANT LAND.
New York: Viking, 1957.

--"A Way of Talking About Freedom," CHRISTIAN SCIENCE
MONITOR, June 22, 1961.
Reflections on reading WALDEN.

Born, Helena. "Thoreau's Joy in Nature," WHITMAN'S IDEAL
DEMOCRACY. Boston: Everett Press, 1902. pp. 20-30.
An essay.

Boston Safe Deposit and Trust Company. Advertisement in
BOSTON HERALD, June 15, 1956.
Quotes from WALDEN.

"The Boston Society of Natural History." TSB #17.
Included is the following eulogy of Thoreau:
Jackson, Dr. C. T. "Notice of the death of Mr.
Thoreau," PROCEEDINGS OF THE BOSTON SOCIETY OF
NATURAL HISTORY, IX (May 21, 1862), 70-72.

"Boston's Literary 'Golden Age' As Seen a Century Later:

No. 12--Henry David Thoreau," BOSTON POST, March 29,
1947.
    A brief essay.

Bourinot, Arthur. "Thoreau at Walden Pond," [Montreal]
    GAZETTE, July 31, 1964.
    A poem.

Bowe, Mac. "Meditation Enriches Carmel High Students,"
    SAN JOSE [Calif.] MERCURY, January 18, 1964.
    Experiences of high school teacher who insists
    his students meditate in solitude for four hours
    while reading WALDEN.

Bowling, Lawrence. "Thoreau's Social Criticism as Poetry,"
    YALE REVIEW, LV (Winter, 1966), 255-64.

Boyce, George K. "Modern Literary Manuscripts in the Morgan
    Library," PMLA, LXVII (February, 1952), 3-36.
    A checklist of the library's holdings. Less de-
    tailed than the checklist in THOREAU SOCIETY BUL-
    LETIN #19 so far as Thoreau holdings are concerned.
    TSB #39.

Boyd, Hugh. "Discovery of Henry Thoreau's Work," OTTAWA
    CITIZEN, July 15, 1964.
    Boyd reads WALDEN for the first time.

Boyle, Hal. "He Lives Alone and Likes It," NEW YORK SUN,
    April 30, 1948.
    News account of a South Dakota imitator of Tho-
    reau.

  --"A Southern Thoreau," WORCESTER EVENING GAZETTE, July
    10, 1957.
    On Bert Garner, Tennessee follower of Thoreau.

Boynton, H. W. "Mr. Torrey's Thoreau," NEW YORK TIMES,
    October 20, 1906.

Braden, William. "Yankee Hindoos," THE PRIVATE SEA: LSD
    AND THE SEARCH FOR GOD. Chicago: Quadrangle Books,
    1967. pp. 90-105.
    Discusses the influence of the Transcendental-
    ists in acquainting America with Oriental reli-
    gions. Quotes at length from Thoreau, but con-
    cludes, "Thoreau undoubtedly would have no part
    of LSD were he alive today. In WALDEN he obser-
    ved, 'I prefer the natural sky to an opium-eat-
    er's heaven.' The point is, however, that Thoreau
    could turn himself on, needing only that natural
    sky for a psychedelic, and he was wholly preoccu-
    pied with the modes of inmost being." TSB #100.

Bradford, Robert W. "Thoreau and Therien," AMERICAN LITER-
    ATURE, XXXIV (January, 1963), 499-506.

Bradley, Van Allen. GOLD IN YOUR ATTIC. New York: Fleet, 1958.
>On pp. 72-73 is a description of first edition of WALDEN.

--"WALDEN First Worth $125 Up." PROVIDENCE JOURNAL, August 8, 1958.
>Description of first editions of WALDEN.

Brady, Fred. "He Creates Unseen Beauty," BOSTON HERALD, February 9, 1966.
>Blind artist Merrill Maynard paints a portrait of Thoreau at Walden.

--"History Notes Striped Bass Taken in Large Numbers off Chelsea," BOSTON HERALD, May 29, 1960.
>Includes material on Thoreau's donation of sun-fish to Boston Society of Natural History.

--"Plea to 'Save Walden' Voiced in 1875," BOSTON HERALD, October 4, 1959.
>Reprints excerpts from a HARPER'S MAGAZINE ARTI-CLE. Reprinted in CONCORD JOURNAL, October 15, 1959.

Bratton, F. G. "New England Unitarianism," LEGACY OF THE LIBERAL SPIRIT. New York: Scribner, 1943. pp. 183-200.
>An essay.

Brawner, James Paul. "Thoreau as Wit and Humorist," SOUTH ATLANTIC QUARTERLY, XLIV (April, 1945), 170-176.
>A reply to Lowell's famous assertion that Thoreau had no sense of humor.

Brean, Herbert. HARDLY A MAN IS NOW ALIVE. New York: Morrow, 1950.
>Did Thoreau and Emerson collaborate on a novel that has never been published? That is a central question in a murder mystery centered in present day Concord. We are not murder mystery addicts, but this one kept our interest from beginning to end. Surprisingly Mr. Brean shows a wealth of knowledge about the history of Concord and the great Concord writers. But he could have paid a little more attention to the map of present-day Concord. Once or twice he got his directions somewhat confused. TSB #34.

Breit, Harvey. "Take It On the Lam," NEW YORK TIMES, August 18, 1957.
>A poem.

Brenner, Gerry. "Thoreau's 'Brute Neighbors': Four Levels of Nature," EMERSON SOCIETY QUARTERLY, XXXIX (1965), 37-40.

Bressler, Leo A. "WALDEN, Neglected American Classic,"
ENGLISH JOURNAL, LI (1962), 14-20.

Brickett, Elsie F. "Studies in the Poets and Poetry of
New England Transcendentalism." Yale University, 1934.
Unpublished doctoral dissertation.

Bridgman, Richard. "Holmes, Thoreau, and Ponds," TSB #83.
pp. 1-2.

Briggs, A. E. WALT WHITMAN: THINKER AND ARTIST. New York:
Philosophical Library, 1952.
Pioneer thinking of Thoreau compared with that
of Whitman.

[Briggs, Eugene]. "Manuscript of Thoreau's Journal on
Exhibit at Huntington Library," SAN MARINO [Calif.]
TRIBUNE, July 13, 1944.
An illustrated news article.

Briggs, Olga Hampel. "Walden World," CHRISTIAN SCIENCE
MONITOR, July 8, 1957.
A poem.

Brine, Dexter D. "The Walden Pond Low-Water Mystery,"
BOSTON GLOBE, July 7, 1968.

Broderick, John C. "American Reviews of Thoreau's Posthumous Books, 1863-1866: Check List and Analysis,"
UNIVERSITY OF TEXAS STUDIES IN ENGLISH, XXXIV (1955),
125-139.
Lists and describes many hitherto unnoticed reviews.

--"Bronson Alcott's 'Concord Book'." NEW ENGLAND QUARTER-
LY, XXIX (September, 1956), 365-580.
On Alcott's plans for a never-published book on
Concord which was to have included selections
from Thoreau.

--"Emerson, Thoreau, and Transcendentalism," AMERICAN
LITERARY SCHOLARSHIP: AN ANNUAL/1967, edited by James
Woodress. Durham, North Carolina: Duke University
Press, 1969. pp. 3-16.
Annual bibliography.

--"Imagery in WALDEN," UNIVERSITY OF TEXAS STUDIES IN
ENGLISH, XXXIII (1954), 80-89.
On the "morning" symbol in WALDEN.

--"The Movement of Thoreau's Prose," AMERICAN LITERATURE,
XXXIII (May, 1961), 133-142.

--"Teaching Thoreau," EMERSON SOCIETY QUARTERLY, XVIII
(1960), 3-5.

--"Thoreau, Alcott, and the Poll Tax," STUDIES IN PHILO-
LOGY, LIII (October, 1956), 612-626.
   Demonstrates that Thoreau's refusal to pay his
   tax was a protest against slavery rather than
   against the Mexican War.

--"Thoreau and MY PRISONS," BOSTON PUBLIC LIBRARY QUARTER-
LY, VII (January, 1955), 48-50.
   On Thoreau's interest in Silvio Pellico's book.

--"The Thoreau Family and Concord Fires," TSB #51.
   Thoreau's responsibility for a fire in his woods
   is mentioned in the CONCORD FREEMAN, January 7,
   1842, p. 3.

--"Thoreau's Proposals for Legislation," AMERICAN QUARTER-
LY, VII (1955), 285-290.
   Points out that while most consider Thoreau an
   anarchist, he made many suggestions for govern-
   mental activities.

--"Young Thoreau Asserts Himself," TSB #53.

Bromfield, Louis. "Find the Glorious Hour," THIS WEEK.
   January 13, 1952. p. 1.
   Commentary on a quotation from Thoreau.

Bronson, Wilfred S. "Odd Bedfellows and the Wood Frog's
   Wedding," NATURE MAGAZINE, XXXVIII (April, 1945), 181-
   183 passim.
      A clever bit of satire comparing the frog notes
      of the author, Thoreau and Aristophanes. TSB #12.

BROOK FARM: THE STORY OF THE HISTORICAL SOCIAL EXPERIMENT,
   1841-1847. West Roxbury, Massachusetts: Brook Farm
   Centennial Committee, 1941.

Brooks, Gordon. "We like to think of it as our Walden,"
   YANKEE (June, 1964), 151.
   A cartoon.

Brooks, Van Wyck. THE FLOWERING OF NEW ENGLAND. New York:
   Modern Library, 1941.
      An inexpensive reprint of this important study
      of Thoreau's time.

--SCENES AND PORTRAITS. New York: Dutton, 1954.
      Contains much about Thoreau's friend H. G. O.
      Blake.

Brophy, Liam. "Thoreau: Franciscan Mystic," ECHOES OF
   ASSISSI. Chicago: Franciscan Herald Press, 1958.
   pp. 160-165.

--"Thoreau: an Ideal Holiday Companion," IRISH DIGEST,
   LXXV (September, 1962), 41-43.

Brown, Frances West. "Thoreau and the Modern American House-
wife," FREEMAN, XII (August, 1962), 44-51.
Very clever satire. TSB #82.

Brown, Percy W. "A Metropolite's Notes on Thoreau," RE-AP-
PRAISALS. Cleveland: Privately printed, 1952. pp. 53-
67.
"We may think of Thoreau, first as a transcendental poet in his ever seeking reality over and beyond material phenomena; second, as a nature-mys-
tic in his awareness of some divine presence and
power in nature and man's environment; and third,
--of most importance--as a great artist."

--"Thoreau," LAND AND BORDERLAND. Cleveland: Privately
printed, 1946.
A poem.

Brown, Theodore M. "Thoreau's Prophetic Architectural Program," NEW ENGLAND QUARTERLY, XXXVIII (March, 1965),
3-20.

Bryant, Nelson. "Thoreau's 'Golden Pickerel' Is Missing
as Walden Undergoes Reclamation," NEW YORK TIMES,
September 26, 1968.
Gives details of how Massachusetts Fish and Game
Commission recently killed off all the fish in
Walden Pond in order to stock it with game fish.
Shades of Henry Thoreau! TSB #105.

Buber, Martin. "Man's Duty as Man," MASSACHUSETTS REVIEW,
IV (Autumn, 1962), 55.

Buell, Lawrence. "Transcendentalist Catalogue Rhetoric:
Vision Versus Form," AMERICAN LITERATURE, XL (November,
1968), 325-339.
Includes much on Thoreau.

Buhl, Ingeborg. "Diogenes i Yankeernes Land," POLITIKEN
[Copenhagen], January 31, 1968.
Text in Danish.

Bulkeley, Benjamin R. "Henry David Thoreau, Nature's Lover,"
THE FRIENDLY QUILL (Summer, 1944).
A poem.

Bulkeley, Morgan. "Beatnik with a Difference," BERKSHIRE
EAGLE [Pittsfield, Mass.], July 13, 1967.

--"Thoreau on Greylock," BERKSHIRE EAGLE, June 30, 1960.

--"The Thoreau Society," BERKSHIRE EAGLE, July 20, 1967.

Buranelli, Vincent. "The Case Against Thoreau," ETHICS,
LXVII (July, 1957), 257-268.
One of the most provocative denunciations of

Thoreau yet to appear. Although it repeats the
old charges that he lacks humor and that everyone
couldn't go to live at Walden Pond, it does make
a thoughtful analysis of his philosophy. TSB #62.

--"Rejoinder," ETHICS, LXX (October, 1959), 64-65.

Burd, Van A. "A Louisiana Estimate of an 'American Rousseau:' Sarah Ann Dorsey on Henry David Thoreau," LOUI-
SIANA HISTORY, V (Summer, 1964), 296-309.
A little known Southern novelist writes her praise
of Thoreau's MAINE WOODS in 1871.

Burdett, Bruce E. "The Cult of Thoreau." Brown University,
1955. Unpublished master's thesis.

Burke, William Jeremiah. "Yes, There's Still a Concord,"
MODERN MATURITY (February, 1969), 7-9.
A recent visit to Concord, including the Thoreau
sites.

--, and Charlotte Brooks. "A Walk with Thoreau: Cape
Cod Revisited," LOOK, XXVII (July 2, 1963), 37-41.
Picture essay on Thoreau.

Burling, Francis P. "An Imaginary Conversation," CAPE
CODDER, January 26, 1950. p. 4.
Thoreau returns to see the new Cape Cod super-
highway.

Burnham, Philip E., and Carvel Collins. "Contribution to
a Bibliography of Thoreau, 1938-1945," BULLETIN OF
BIBLIOGRAPHY, XIX (September-December, 1946), 16-18.+
An excellent checklist bringing the Wade and White
bibliography up-to-date. TSB #19.

Burns, E. McN. DAVID STARR JORDAN: PROPHET OF FREEDOM.
Stanford: Stanford University Press, 1953.
Much on the influence of Thoreau on the Califor-
nia educator.

Burns, Henry J. "The Social Philosophy of Henry David Thoreau." Boston University, 1966. Unpublished master's
thesis.

Burns, John R. "Thoreau's Use of the Bible." University
of Notre Dame, 1966. Unpublished doctoral dissertation.
An abstract of the dissertation appears in TSB
#109. p. 8.

Burr, Gray. "The One and Only," MASSACHUSETTS REVIEW, IV
(August, 1962), 92.
A poem.

Burroughs, John. HENRY D. THOREAU. Hartford, Connecticut:
Emerson Society, 1962.

Reprinted from the CENTURY MAGAZINE for July 1882.

Burroughs, Julian. "Burroughs and Thoreau," TSB #21.
Digest of a lecture delivered by Julian Burroughs
in the spring of 1946 at the American Museum of
Natural History in New York City.

Burtscher, William J. THE ROMANCE BEHIND WALKING CANES.
Philadelphia: Dorrance, 1945.
Some notes on Thoreau's walking stick, pp. 153-
154.

Bush, T. N. W. "Thoreau in South Africa," MASSACHUSETTS
REVIEW, IV (Autumn, 1962), 90-91.

Bushee, Ralph. HENRY DAVID THOREAU July 12, 1817-May 6, 1862
AN EXHIBITION HELD IN THE MORRIS LIBRARY. Carbondale,
Illinois: Southern Illinois University Press, Spring,
1965.
A catalog.

Butterworth, H. W. "Concord Writers," YOUTH'S COMPANION
(December 7, 1876).
Much on Thoreau.

Butler, Helen J. "Thoreau's Walden Still Proves Inspiration,"
BAY STATE POST, August 11, 1962.

Butterworth, Hezekiah. "At Walden," CHRISTIAN SCIENCE MONI-
TOR, October 24, 1950.
A brief note on the beauties of Thoreau's Walden
Pond.

Buxton, H. W. "The Solitude of Mr. Thoreau," MANCHESTER
LITERARY CLUB PAPERS, LXVIII (1950-1951), 12-16.

Byron, Gilbert. "Daniel Ricketson Finally Drew Sage of
Concord Here," NEW BEDFORD STANDARD TIMES, June 5, 1966.
Ricketson's friendship with Thoreau.

--"Harvard's Algonquin," LIVING WILDERNESS, XXIX (Summer,
1965), 17-19.
Thoreau and the Indian.

--"Henry Thoreau, Boatman," THOREAU JOURNAL QUARTERLY, I
(July 1, 1969), 9-14.

--"Henry Thoreau: Botanist-Poet," CHRISTIAN SCIENCE MONI-
TOR, December 3, 1962.
An essay.

--Letter to Editor. ATLANTIC MONTHLY, CCXXIV (August,
1969), 26 passim.
On the recent Kazin essay on Thoreau.

--Letter to Henry Baldwin. LIVING WILDERNESS, XXXII

(Winter, 1968), 35.

--"A letter to Henry Thoreau," SATURDAY REVIEW OF LITER-
ATURE (August 30, 1947).
　　　On the difficulties of living the Thoreauvian
　　　life today.

--"Many Area Points on Itinerary for Third Visit Here,"
NEW BEDFORD STANDARD TIMES, June 12, 1966.

--"'An open letter to Thoreau,'" SATURDAY REVIEW OF LITER-
ATURE (June 5, 1948), p. 47.
　　　On Thoreau as an escapist.

--"The Proggers," TSB #89. pp. 1-2.

--"Thoreau and Fellow Mammals." AUDUBON MAGAZINE, LXV
(November, 1963), 374-375.
　　　Thoreau's love of mammals.

--"Thoreau's Mountain: Monadnock," LIVING WILDERNESS,
XXXI (Autumn, 1967), 45-47.

　　　also in:　FOREST NOTES, XCVIII (Summer, 1968),
　　　3-7.

--"To Henry David Thoreau," WHITE COLLAR AND CHAIN.
North Montpelier, Vermont: Driftwind Press, 1945.
p. 26.
　　　A poem. The whole volume is dedicated to Tho-
　　　reau and he is mentioned frequently throughout.

--"What do you know about Henry Thoreau?," TSB #103. p. 6.

--"Your Literary I. Q.: Thoreauvian," SATURDAY REVIEW OF
LITERATURE (September 23, 1967), p. 81.
　　　A quiz.

C., W. J. "Thoreau's Spirit in His Books, Not at Walden Pond or with Relics of Him," BOSTON HERALD, December 2, 1912.

"CEA Member." A letter of antipathy to Thoreau, THE NEWS LETTER OF THE COLLEGE ENGLISH ASSOCIATION, IV, Extra (September, 1942), 4.

"The Cabin Site, Once Again," TSB #17.

Cady, L. V. "Thoreau's Quotations from the Confucian Books in WALDEN," AMERICAN LITERATURE, XXXIII (March, 1961), 20-32.

Cahen, Jacques-Fernand. LA LITERATURE AMERICAINE. Paris: Presses Universitaires de France, 1961.
Thoreau, pp. 27-29.

Cahoon, Herbert. "Some Manuscripts of Concord Authors in the Pierpont Morgan Library," MANUSCRIPTS, XVIII (Fall, 1966), 44-50.
Reprint of 1965 Thoreau Society address.

also in: TSB #92, pp. 2-4.

"The Cairn Controversy," TSB #12.

Caldwell, Jean. "Artist: My Thoreau Real," BOSTON GLOBE, June ?, 1967.
Baskin replies to critics of stamp.

Caldwell, Joshua William. "Thoreau, The Nature-Lover," JOSHUA WILLIAM CALDWELL: A MEMORIAL VOLUME. Nashville, Tennessee: Irving Club, 1909. pp. 205-222.

Caldwell, William A. "Walden and the Tick in the Hall," BERGEN EVENING RECORD [Hackensack, N. J.], November 1, 1961.
A recent visit to Walden Pond.

-- "Who Wouldn't Back Under the Rock?" BERGEN EVENING RECORD [Hackensack, N. J.], December 17, 1958.
On difficulties of living the Thoreauvian life today.

C[alhoun]. H[erbert]. HENRY DAVID THOREAU 1817-1862 AND HIS AMERICA. New York: Morgan Library, 1956.

Prospectus for the exhibition.

Callahan, James L. "Lake Walden's Rooted Trailers," BOSTON
GLOBE, September 15, 1946.
Photographs of the trailer camp at the pond.

Cameron, Kenneth Walter. "Annotations on Thoreau's COR-
RESPONDENCE," EMERSON SOCIETY QUARTERLY, XXIV (1961),
6-105.
Detailed footnotes for the 1958 edition.

--"Anti-Slavery Song Books in Thoreau's Library," EMER-
SON SOCIETY QUARTERLY, XXXVI (1964), 52-121.

--"Books Thoreau Borrowed From Harvard College Library,"
EMERSON THE ESSAYIST. Raleigh, North Carolina: Thistle
Press, 1945.
A check-list. Edition limited to 150 copies.

--"Books Thoreau Desired to Purchase in 1859," EMERSON
SOCIETY QUARTERLY, XXIII (1961), 16.
List based on a MS in Morgan Library.

--"Chronology of Thoreau's Harvard Years," EMERSON SOCIETY
QUARTERLY, XV (1959), 2-108.
Facsimile reproduction of grade books, attendance
records, and other documents pertaining to Thoreau's
Harvard years.

--COMPANION TO THOREAU'S CORRESPONDENCE. Hartford: Transcendental Books, 1964.
Annotations of the 1958 edition with some new
letters added.

--Damning National Publicity for Thoreau in 1849," AMER-
ICAN TRANSCENDENTAL QUARTERLY, II (1969), 18-27.
Hitherto unnoticed editorials on Thoreau.

--"Emerson, Thoreau and the Atlantic Cable," EMERSON SO-
CIETY QUARTERLY, XXVI (1962), 45-86.

--EMERSON, THOREAU AND CONCORD IN EARLY NEWSPAPERS. Hartford: Transcendental Books, 1958.
A collection of facsimile reproductions of newspaper and magazine articles, chiefly from the late
nineteenth century, on Emerson, Thoreau, and other
Concord worthies. There is a wealth of information
imbedded in this volume for the researcher to dig
out. Among the Thoreau items: some of the clippings
from Thoreau's own scrapbook (pp. 5-6); The "Thoreau
Annex" of the Concord FREEMAN (7-15); a poem, "Thoreau," by Muriel Wilton (16); G. W. Curtis's reminiscences of Thoreau (16); an obituary of Thoreau (16);
"Emerson and His Friends," by F. B. Sanborn (44-5);
"The Home of Hawthorne and Thoreau: Thoreau's Succes-
sor," by Munroe (69-71), the most detailed account

I have seen of the man who some years later than
Thoreau built a hut on Walden Pond: "Concord Celeb-
rities" by Brewster (83-85) which suggests Thoreau
once loved an Irish girl; "Old Concord." Anon. (85-
7); "Henry D. Thoreau," Anon. (139-40); "Henry Thoreau's Hermitage" by A. B. H. (145-6); "Thoreau's
Pity" from THE SPECTATOR (146); "Thoreau's Unpublished Works" by E. R. Wiswell (147), mentions a
crayon portrait of Thoreau by his sister Sophia--
what has happened to it?; ["Hawthorne on Thoreau"]
(148); "Thoreau and Literature" from CORNHILL (150);
"Thoreau" from CORNHILL (150); Review of Sanborn's
1882 life of Thoreau (163); "The Relations between
Emerson and Thoreau" Anon. (242-3), an interview
with Elizabeth Peabody; Four Thoreau obituaries
(318-20); Notice of sale of John Thoreau pew (321).
TSB #63.

--"Emerson, Thoreau, and the Poet Henry Sutton," EMERSON
SOCIETY QUARTERLY, I (Fall, 1955), 10-16.
    Discusses Emerson's friendship with a minor English
    poet whom he thought to be an English equivalent of
    Thoreau as a "sayer of No" and reprints Sutton's re-
    miniscences of Emerson's comments on Thoreau.

--"Emerson, Thoreau, and the Society of Natural History,"
AMERICAN LITURATURE, XXIV (March, 1952), 21-30.
    A summary of the relations of Emerson and Thoreau
    with the Boston society and a checklist of the
    books which Thoreau withdrew from the society lib-
    rary. An extremely important source article for
    the student. TSB #40.

--"Emerson, Thoreau, and the Town and Country Club,"
EMERSON SOCIETY QUARTERLY, VIII (1957), 2-17.
    The minutes, constitution, and other records of
    the club which Alcott organized in 1849 and to
    which Thoreau briefly belonged.

--"Emerson, Thoreau, ELEGANT EXTRACTS, and Proverb Lore,"
EMERSON SOCIETY QUARTERLY, VI (1957), 28-39.
    Reproductions with comments of pages from a fa-
    vorite anthology used by Emerson and Thoreau.

--"Emerson, Thoreau, Parson Frost, and 'The Problem',"
EMERSON SOCIETY QUARTERLY, VI (1957), 16.
    A MS note by Thoreau sheds light on the compo-
    sition of Emerson's poem.

--EMERSON'S WORKSHOP. Hartford: Transcendental Books,
1965.
    I, 222 shows a quitclaim deed give to John Thoreau
    Sr., by Julius Mr. Smith of Concord. I, 230-244,
    gives a "List of Persons Qualified to Vote in Con-
    cord, At the Election, 1856," includes names of
    both Henry D. and John Thoreau. Apparently used to

forcast the vote and Thoreau is checked under both
voting for Freemont and doubtful. TSB #91.

--"An Epitaph on the Cover of a Thoreau Journal," EMERSON
SOCIETY QUARTERLY, XIII (1958), 93-95.
  Facsimile reproduction of Thoreau manuscript.

--"Four Uncollected Thoreau Poems, with Notes on the Canon,"
EMERSON SOCIETY QUARTERLY, V (1956), 13-16.
  Texts and facsimiles of manuscripts of four hitherto unknown poems by Thoreau with some corrections
  of Bode's edition of Thoreau's poems.

--"Four Uncollected Thoreau Poems--A Correction," EMERSON
SOCIETY QUARTERLY, VI (1957), 48.
  Calls attention to error in earlier article.

--"Freshman Thoreau Opposes Harvard's Marking System,"
EMERSON SOCIETY QUARTERLY, VIII (1957), 17-18.
  The text of a letter by Thoreau and his classmates
  to the faculty of Harvard opposing the grading system in force in his freshman year.

--"Harvard Rules and Certificates of Thoreau's Day,"
EMERSON SOCIETY QUARTERLY, LII (1968), 86-87.

--"Helen Thoreau Writes to Dr. Shattuck in 1838," EMERSON
SOCIETY QUARTERLY, VI (1957), 48.
  Text of a letter to her physician giving symptoms
  of her illness.

--"Henry Thoreau and the ENTOMOLOGY of Kirby and Spence,"
EMERSON SOCIETY QUARTERLY, XXXVIII (1965), 138-142.

--"Henry Thoreau's Step-Grandmother," EMERSON SOCIETY QUAR-
TERLY, XXII (1961), 54-56.
  Reprints the anonymous "Sketches of the life of
  Mrs. Rebecca Thoreau" from the CHRISTIAN DISCIPLE,
  III (October, 1815), 1-3.

--"Historical Notes on the Concord Academy," EMERSON SO-
CIETY QUARTERLY, XIX, 46-51.
  Reprints various newspaper notices including some
  of Thoreau's teaching there.

--"Jones Very and Thoreau--The 'Greek' Myth," EMERSON SO-
CIETY QUARTERLY, VII (1957), 39-40.
  Points out that legend that Thoreau studied under
  Very at Harvard is false.

--"A Manuscript Fragment of Thoreau's Quebec Journey of
1850," EMERSON SOCIETY QUARTERLY, VIII (1957), 19.
  Facsimile of page of MS.

--"Manuscript Pages from Thoreau's 'Night and Moonlight',"
EMERSON SOCIETY QUARTERLY, XXXV (1964), 82-84.

--OVER THOREAU'S DESK: NEW CORRESPONDENCE 1838-1861.
Hartford: Transcendental Books, 1965.
>Some new Thoreau letters plus material on his
visits to Staten Island and Waterbury, Conn.,
and his aunts' court suit.

--"Ralph Cudworth and Thoreau's Translations of an Orphic
Hymn," EMERSON SOCIETY QUARTERLY, VIII (1957), 31-36.
>Thoreau's use of Cudworth in translating a Greek
poem.

--"Receipt Signed by Thoreau's Father," EMERSON SOCIETY
QUARTERLY, IX (1957), 42.
>Facsimile of bill.

--"The Recent Sale of Thoreau Manuscripts," EMERSON SOCIE-
TY QUARTERLY, XIII (1958), 98-114.
>Facsimile reproduction of catalog of 1958 sale.

>also in: TSB #65 entitled "$32,295 Worth of Tho-
reau Manuscripts!"

--"Reflections on Thoreau at Harvard," EMERSON SOCIETY
QUARTERLY, XLVIII (1967), 87-88.

--"Scattered Thoreau Manuscripts," EMERSON SOCIETY QUAR-
TERLY, XLVIII (1967), 145-149.

--"The Solitary Thoreau of the Alumni Notes," EMERSON SO-
CIETY QUARTERLY, VII (1957), 2-37.
>A thoroughly documented account of Thoreau and his
college class.

--"Some Collections of Emerson Manuscripts," EMERSON SOCI-
ETY QUARTERLY, III (1956), 1-6.
>A bibliography. Includes a number of MSS pertain-
ing to Thoreau.

--"Sophomore Thoreau and Relgious Improvement," EMERSON
SOCIETY QUARTERLY, XLVIII (1967), 82-85.

--"Souvenirs of the Celebration at the Unveiling of Thoreau's Bust in the Hall of Fame," EMERSON SOCIETY QUAR-
TERLY, XXX (1963), 2-5.

--"A Tabular View of Thoreau's Harvard Curriculum," EMER-
SON SOCIETY QUARTERLY, LI (1968), 10-24.

--"Thoreau and Emerson in Channing's Letters to the Wat-
sons," EMERSON SOCIETY QUARTERLY, XIV (1959), 77-85.
>Catalog of a collection recently given to Concord
Free Public Library. Many notations on Thoreau's
last illness. Appendix of material on his friend
Marston Watson.

--"Thoreau and the Folklore of Walden Pond," EMERSON SOCI-

ETY QUARTERLY, III (1956), 10-12.
    Thoreau's sources for some of the folklore in
    WALDEN.

--"Thoreau and Frank Bellew in Concord," EMERSON SOCIETY
QUARTERLY, LI (1968), 141-143.

--THOREAU AND HIS HARVARD CLASSMATES. Hartford: Transcendental Books, 1965.
    Reprints Williams' MEMORIALS OF CLASS OF 1837 plus
    additional material about Thoreau's college days.

    also in: AMERICAN TRANSCENDENTAL QUARTERLY, III
    (1969), 1-32. A reprint of the book.

--"Thoreau and John Evelyn," EMERSON SOCIETY QUARTERLY,
XVIII (1960), 35.
    On the source of a Thoreau quotation from Evelyn.

--"Thoreau and Orestes Brownson," EMERSON SOCIETY QUARTER-
LY, LI (1968), 53-73.

--"Thoreau and Stearns Wheeler: Four Letters and a Reading Record," EMERSON SOCIETY QUARTERLY, XLVIII (1967),
73-81.

--"Thoreau at Harvard: Diligent, Bright and Cheerful,"
EMERSON SOCIETY QUARTERLY, XLII (1966), 1.
    Amos Perry's forgotten reminiscence.

--"Thoreau Bills His Pupils at the Concord Academy,"
EMERSON SOCIETY QUARTERLY, VI (1957), 47-50.
    Facsimiles of bills Thoreau sent his pupils.

--"Thoreau Discovers Emerson," BULLETIN OF THE NEW YORK
PUBLIC LIBRARY, LVII (July, 1953), 319-334.
    Another of Prof. Cameron's extremely important
    source studies, this dealing with Thoreau and the
    "Institute," a Harvard undergraduate club, giving
    records of its meetings and listing the books which
    Thoreau withdrew from its library. TSB #45.

--"Thoreau, Edward Tyrrel Channing and College Themes,"
EMERSON SOCIETY QUARTERLY, XLII (1966), 15-34.

--"Thoreau in the Court of Common Pleas (1854)," EMERSON
SOCIETY QUARTERLY, XIV (1959), 86-89.
    Source material on Thoreau's appearance as a wit-
    ness in a dispute over a water-privilege.

--"Thoreau in the Memoirs of the Concord Social Circle,"
EMERSON SOCIETY QUARTERLY, XIX, 45-46.
    Reprints of reminiscences of Thoreau's neighbors.

--"Thoreau in the Papers of Nathan Brooks and Abel Moore,"
EMERSON SOCIETY QUARTERLY, XIX (1960), 42-45.

Inventory of some MSS in the Concord Free Public Library.

--"Thoreau Manuscripts--Ungathered and Migrant," EMERSON SOCIETY QUARTERLY, XXXV (1964), 84-86.

--"Thoreau, Parker, and Emerson's 'Mousetrap' in the MONITOR (1862)," EMERSON SOCIETY QUARTERLY, VII (1957), 42-45.
    Points out an early version of Emerson's mousetrap proverb applied to Thoreau in 1862.

--"Thoreau, 'Sic Vita'. and HARVARDIANA," TSB #49.
    Probes the possibility of Thoreau's 'Sic Vita' being rejected by the Harvard literary magazine.

--THOREAU'S CANADIAN NOTEBOOK AND RECORD OF SURVEYS. Hartford: Transcendental Books, 1968.
    Reprinted from TRANSCENDENTAL CLIMATE.

--"Thoreau's Diploma Again," EMERSON SOCIETY QUARTERLY, XV (1959), 48-49.
    Evidence that it was fairly usual for Harvard students to reject their M.A. diploma as Thoreau did.

--"Thoreau's Disciple at Walden: Edmond S. Hotham," EMERSON SOCIETY QUARTERLY, XXVI (1962), 34-44.

--"Thoreau's Early Compositions in the Ancient Languages," EMERSON SOCIETY QUARTERLY, VIII (1957), 20-29.
    Facsimiles of two early Greek papers by Thoreau, with comments.

--"Thoreau's Friends and Class Day," EMERSON SOCIETY QUARTERLY, XLIII (1966), 121-139.

--"Thoreau's Gift to the M.H.S. in 1846," EMERSON SOCIETY QUARTERLY, VI (1957), 48.
    Records a gift of an early deed by Thoreau to the Massachusetts Historical Society.

--"Thoreau's Harvard Friends and Temperance," EMERSON SOCIETY QUARTERLY, LI (1968), 137-140.

--"Thoreau's Harvard Friends Discuss Emerson's NATURE," EMERSON SOCIETY QUARTERLY, II (1956), 8.
    Minutes of a Hasty Pudding Club meeting.

--"Thoreau's Harvard Textbooks," EMERSON SOCIETY QUARTERLY, XXIII (1961), 19-111.
    Reprints excerpts from many of Thoreau's college books in facsimile.

--THOREAU'S HARVARD YEARS. Hartford: Transcendental Books, 1966.

Chiefly reprints from EMERSON SOCIETY QUARTERLY.

--"Thoreaus in the Evangelical Missionary Society of Concord," EMERSON SOCIETY QUARTERLY, VII (1957), 52-53.
Records membership of various feminine members of
the Thoreau household in a religious society.

--THOREAU'S LITERARY NOTEBOOK IN THE LIBRARY OF CONGRESS.
Hartford: Transcendental Books, 1964.
A facsimile reproduction.

--"Thoreau's 'Loves Invalides Are Not Those of Common
Wars'--A Correction," EMERSON SOCIETY QUARTERLY, XIII
(1958), 26.
Correction of text of a Thoreau poem.

--"Thoreau's New Poems," EMERSON SOCIETY QUARTERLY, XIV
(1959), 21-32.
Facsimiles of manuscripts in Washington University
Library.

--"Thoreau's Newspaper Clippings in the Morgan College
Notebook," EMERSON SOCIETY QUARTERLY, VII (1957), 51-52.
Facsimiles of several newspaper clippings Thoreau
pasted in an early notebook.

--"Thoreau's Notes from Dubuat's PRINCIPES," EMERSON SOCI-
ETY QUARTERLY, XXII (1961), 68-76.
First publication of some notes Thoreau took and
translated from the French.

--"Thoreau's Notes on the Shipwreck at Fire Island," EM-
ERSON SOCIETY QUARTERLY, LII (1968), 97-99.

--"Thoreau's Three Months out of Harvard and His First
Publication," EMERSON SOCIETY QUARTERLY, V (1956), 2-
12.
Important new light on Thoreau's activities in
1837, including reprinting of his hitherto unknown first appearance in print: an obituary for
Miss Anna Jones in the Concord FREEMAN'S GAZETTE
for November 25, 1837, with an appendix on books
on the American Indian Thoreau might have known
by 1837.

--"Thoreau's Two Books of Pindar," EMERSON SOCIETY QUAR-
TERLY, XXXVIII (1965), 96-112.
Another volume from Thoreau's library found.

--"Thoreau's WALDEN and Alcott's Vegetarianism," AMERICAN
TRANSCENDENTAL QUARTERLY, II (1969), 27-28.

--"Thoreau's Walden Pond," EMERSON SOCIETY QUARTERLY, XXII
(1961), 77-80.
Reproduces a number of newspaper comments on the
Walden Pond case.

--TRANSCENDENTAL CLIMATE. Hartford: Transcendental Books,
    1963. 3 vols.
        A massive collection of documents and resource ma-
        terials relating to Transcendentalism including
        among then "Manuscript Diary of Franklin B. Sanborn"
        (I, 205-243), "An Introduction to Thoreau's Canadian
        Notebook (M.A. 596) and Its Laid-in Papers" (I, 244-
        309), "Thoreau's Reading on Canada" (II, 310-411),
        "Field Notes of Surveys Made by Henry D. Thoreau
        Since November 1849 (II, 413-549), "Early Records of
        the Concord Lyceum" (III, 641-731), "The Lyceum
        Lecturers in Thoreau's Day (III, 732-734), "Thoreau's
        'Paragraphs Mostly Original' (M.A. 608) (III, 901-
        987), "Books Thoreau Read Concerning Concord" (III,
        1012-1021), and "News Reports in Henry Thoreau's
        Fact Book" (III, 1022-1028).

--THE TRANSCENDENTALISTS AND MINERVA. Hartford: Transcen-
    dental Books, 1958. 3 vols.
        These three huge volumes are a veritable gold-mine
        of source material about Thoreau and the Transcen-
        dentalists. Unfortunately we can do little more
        than summarize the Thoreau material made available
        here: facsimile of document appointing Thoreau exec-
        utor of his father's estate, 80; "Thoreau's Reading
        at the Institute," reprinted from BNYPL, 80-89; Read-
        ing of Thoreau's College Friends," reading lists for
        his classmates, 90-129; "Thoreau's Notes on Harvard
        Reading," facsimile reproductions of his college
        reading lists, in 1852, ditto, 818-827; "Thoreau's
        Index at Harvard College," more of his reading notes,
        871-882; "Contents of Thoreau's Lost Notebooks," a
        reconstruction of the index of his early journal,
        883-886; "Emerson, Thoreau and the Town Atheneum,"
        records of Thoreau's help in establishing a local
        reading room, 890-895; "Emerson's Reports as Town
        Committeeman," facsimile reproduction of Concord
        Library reports with details of gifts by the Tho-
        reau family; "Thoreau's 'The Service,'" facsimile
        reproduction of the MS and the Sanborn text. There
        is a tremendous amount of important Thoreau material
        to be mined out of these volumes. It is unfortunate
        that the edition is limited to only 100 copies and
        that it is beyond the financial reach of many Tho-
        reau scholars. Prof. Cameron has notes, and some of
        his college essays, with many annotations, 130-358;
        certificate of baptism of John Thoreau (Thoreau's
        grandfather), 167; Thoreau's autobiographical sketch
        written for his Harvard class book, 223-225; "Un-
        gathered Thoreau Reading Lists," 359-388; "H. D. Tho-
        reau and the Wakeman Sale," facsimile reproduction
        of a portion of the catalog, 400-414; "Discoveries
        in George Moore's Diary," with several references
        to the Thoreau family, 457-473; "Harvard and Thoreau
        Battle Over Books," with facsimile reproductions of
        the correspondence between Thoreau and the Harvard

Library, 474-489; "The Concord Social Library in
1836," facsimile reproduction of catalog of library
Thoreau probably used, 496-506; The Concord Town
Library performed a real service in gathering all
this material together. TSB #63.

--"Two Pages of Thoreau's Notes for CAPE COD," EMERSON SO-
CIETY QUARTERLY, XIX (1960), 38-39.
Notes on a newly discovered manuscript of Thoreau.

--"Two Thoreau Journal Fragments of 1851," EMERSON SOCIETY
QUARTERLY, V (1956), 16-19.
Facsimiles of rough drafts for journals of June 11
and August 8, 1851.

--"An Unidentified French Passage in Thoreau's Notebook,"
EMERSON SOCIETY QUARTERLY, VIII (1957), 36.
Asks the source for an unknown quotation in Tho-
reau's notebook.

--"What Thoreau Taught in 1837," EMERSON SOCIETY QUARTERLY,
LII (1968), 100.

--"The Whereabouts of Thoreau's Natural History Collections,"
EMERSON SOCIETY QUARTERLY, II (1956), 15.
A census.

--"Young Henry Thoreau in the Annals of the Concord Academy (1829-1833)," EMERSON SOCIETY QUARTERLY, IX (1957),
1-42.
Fully documented early records of the Concord Academy which Thoreau attended, including much on Phineas Allen, his teacher.

[Cameron, Kenneth Walter]. "A Brief Glance at the Thoreau
Society," EMERSON SOCIETY QUARTERLY, VII (1957), 54.
A history of our society.

--"Channing's Hymn at Thoreau's Funeral," EMERSON SOCIETY
QUARTERLY, II (1956), 16-17.
Facsimile reproduction of the broadside, with notes.

"Camp Meeting at Walden in 1878," CONCORD JOURNAL, September
12, 1946.
Reprinting an article from BANNER OF LIGHT, a weekly journal of spiritualism, for August 3, 1878
giving an account of an early pilgrimage to the
cairn.

Campbell, Charles L. "An American Tragedy; or, Death in
the Woods," MODERN FICTION STUDIES, XV (Summer, 1969),
251-259.
On Dreiser's interest in Thoreau.

Canby, Henry Seidel. "Back to Nature," THE YALE REVIEW
ANTHOLOGY. New Haven: Yale University Press, 1942.
pp. 116-127.

--"A Book Gandhiji Kept at His Bedside, " FREE PRESS JOUR-
NAL [Bombay], November 12, 1954.

--"From Books to Men," AMERICAN MEMOIR. Boston: Houghton
Mifflin, 1947. pp. 401-408.
On the writing of his biography of Thoreau.

--"Henry David Thoreau," CLASSIC AMERICANS. New York:
Russell and Russell, 1959. pp. 184-225.
CLASSIC AMERICANS, though nearly 30 years old,
is an excellent history of American literature--
or rather a discussion of some masters of American
literature. And by far its best chapter is that on
Thoreau. Although Canby alienated many Thoreauvians
with his 1939 biography, the fact is that as a critic rather than as a biographer, Canby usually has
much of significance to say. And in this essay he
said most succinctly and most clearly what he had
to say. The essay is filled with sentences that
are as pithy as Thoreau's own--sentences that get
right to the heart of Thoreau's philosophy. It
is good to have this volume back in print. TSB #69.

--"Henry David Thoreau," THERE WERE GIANTS IN THE LAND.
New York: Farrar and Rinehart, 1942. pp. 161-168.

--"Henry David Thoreau, Great American," Charlotte [N. C.]
OBSERVER, July 19, 1942.

--Letter to editor, NEWSLETTER OF COLLEGE ENGLISH ASSOCI-
ATION, IV (November, 1942), 2.
On students' attitudes towards Thoreau.

--"A Self-appointed Interpreter to America," CHRISTIAN
SCIENCE MONITOR, December 13, 1945.

--"Setting Your Goal," WORDS TO LIVE BY, edited by William Nichols. New York: Simon and Schuster, 1948.
A brief essay inspired by a quotation from Thoreau.

--THOREAU. Boston: Beacon Press, 1958.
A paperback reprint of the 1939 biography. Since
Canby's is the closest thing there has ever been
to a standard life of Thoreau, it is well to have
it back in print, despite its limitations in both
fact and interpretation and particularly its non-
sense about Thoreau and Mrs. Emerson. It is particularly unfortunate that in reprinting the volume
that no attempt was made to correct the dozens of
errors that have been pointed out by scholars in
the 19 years since it first appeared--errors such
as calling Charles Stearns Wheeler, Charles Stearns
Davis: Benjamin Thatcher, Beebe Thatcher, etc.
TSB #65.

--THOREAU. Gloucester, Mass.: Peter Smith, 1965.

Reprint of 1939 biography.

translation of the 1939 biography: THOREAU, translated into Spanish by Pablo Simon. Buenos Aires: Editorial Poseidon, 1944.

--"Thoreau," GREAT STORIES FROM GREAT LIVES, edited by Herbert V. Procknow. New York: Harpers, 1944. pp. 102-107.
Excerpts from the 1939 biography.

--"Thoreau and Whitman on Democracy," SATURDAY REVIEW OF LITERATURE (July 12, 1941).

--"Thoreau and the Abolitionists," EFFECTIVE READING, edited by Rosenthal, Hummel and Leichty. Boston: Houghton Mifflin, 1944. pp. 65-72.
An extract from the 1939 biography.

--"Thoreau: A New Estimate," SATURDAY REVIEW OF LITERATURE, XXXII (December 3, 1949), 15-16.
Thoreau as seen through his journals. Slightly changed, this was used as the foreword to the new edition of Thoreau's JOURNALS.

--"WALDEN One Hundred Years Later," SATURDAY REVIEW OF LITERATURE (August 7, 1954), 7-8 passim.

Cantine, Holley, et al. "Thoreau and the New Radicals," LIBERATION, VIII (April, 1963), 22-29.
Replies to Staughton Lynd's "Henry Thoreau, the Admirable Radical."

Cantwell, Robert. "Ralph Waldo Emerson and Henry David Thoreau," FAMOUS AMERICAN MEN OF LETTERS. New York: Dodd, Mead, 1956. pp. 75-90.
A brief sketch of Thoreau's life for teen-agers.

Carberg, Warren. "Thoreau Fame Still Expands," BOSTON POST, July 27, 1947.
A long essay on Thoreau's present-day influence.

Cardenas, Eduardo. "Thoreau," BIOGRAFIAS BREVES. Hanover, Pennsylvania: Libros de America, 1963. p. 819.
A brief biography.

Carew, Thomas. THE POEMS OF THOMAS CAREW WITH HIS MASQUE COELUM BRITANNICUM, edited by Rhodes Dunlap. New York: Oxford, 1949.
Contains notes on Carew's influence on Thoreau.

Carl, Ralph F. "The Early Critical Writings of Valery Larbaud," KENTUCKY FOREIGN LANGUAGE QUARTERLY, V (1958), 1-11.
Mentions Larbaud's criticism of Thoreau.

Carleton, Sara King. "The Bean Field," CHRISTIAN SCIENCE
    MONITOR, February 20, 1950.
        A poem.

        also in: NO NEW COUNTRY. New York: Bookman As-
        sociates, 1954. p. 43.

    --"Thoreau," NO NEW COUNTRY. New York: Bookman Asso-
        ciates, 1954. p. 42.
        A poem.

Carlton, James. "Thoreau and the Cockles of Cape Cod,"
    TSB #103, p. 8.

Carman, Bernard R. "Thoreau on Greylock," BERKSHIRE EAGLE
    [Pittsfield, Mass.], July 11, 1956. p. 18.
        Account of Thoreau's visit to the Massachusetts
        mountain.

Carpenter, Frederic I. AMERICAN LITERATURE AND THE DREAM.
    New York: Philosophical Library, 1955.
        Many comments on Thoreau, passim. Concludes that
        Thoreau was the most "clear-eyed" of American
        dreamers because he wished to reform himself and
        not society.

    --"'The American Myth': Paradise (to be) Regained," PMLA,
    LXXIV (December, 1959), 599-606.
        Thoreau's attitude towards primativism and progress.

    --"American Transcendentalism in India," EMERSON SOCIETY
    QUARTERLY, XXXI (1963), 59-62.

Carpenter, Nan Cooke. "Louisa May Alcott on 'Thoreau's
    Flute': Two Letters," HUNTINGTON LIBRARY QUARTERLY,
    XXIV (November, 1960), 71-74.

Carroll, Paul. "The Thoreau Complex among the Solid Schol-
    ars," THE POEM IN ITS SKIN. Chicago: Big Table [Follett],
    1968. pp. 174-187.
        While ostensibly an analysis of a poem by Snodgrass,
        a large portion of this essay is devoted to the ques-
        tion "How was it that a man of such genius for moral
        realities and for creating great American prose [as
        Thoreau] was also such a mean failure in private
        life?" It concludes that Thoreau out of "sour jeal-
        ousy and quiet desperation" refused to put forth the
        effort to win the success he deserved. TSB #108.

Carson, Clarence B. "Henry David Thoreau," THE AMERICAN TRA-
    DITION. Tokyo: Kaibunsha, 1966. pp. 29-30.

Carson, Gerald. "Cape Cod Previsited," NEW YORK TIMES MAGA-
    ZINE, October 9, 1949. pp. 39-41.
        Humorous commemoration of centennial of Thoreau's
        first visit to Cape Cod.

Carson, Herbert L. "An Eccentric Kinship; H.D.T.'s 'A Plea for Captain John Brown'," SOUTHERN SPEECH JOURNAL, XXVII (Winter, 1961), 151-155.

Carstens, Grace. BORN A YANKEE. New York: Macmillan, 1954.
A novel about Cape Cod in which a central character attempts to follow Thoreau's philosophy.

Carter, George F. "Thoreau, the Great Transcendentalist," LITERARY COLLECTOR, VIII (October, 1904), 169-177.
An essay.

also in: HOBBIES, LIV (August, 1949), 139-142.

Casey, Alfredo. "Tiempo y Ambiente de Henry David Thoreau," LA PRENSA [Buenos Aires], January 8, 1950.
Excerpt from a lengthy illustrated article in Spanish.

Cawley, Tom. "As Thoreau Once Expressed It so Well," BINGHAMTON [N. Y.] PRESS, July 21, 1967.

Chamberlain, Allen. "Thoreau on Monadnock," CHRISTIAN SCIENCE MONITOR, April 24, 1947.
An excerpt from the book THE ANNALS OF THE GRAND MONADNOCK.

--"Thoreau's Camps," THE ANNALS OF THE GRAND MONADNOCK. Concord, N. H.: Society for Protection of N. H. Forests, 1968. pp. 70-80.
Paperback reprint.

Chamberlain, John. "Thoreau: A Hippie or Not?" TULSA [Okla.] TRIBUNE, June 17, 1967.

Chandrasekharan, K. R. "Thoreau's Literary Art and His Philosophy," INDIAN ESSAYS IN AMERICAN LITERATURE: PAPERS IN HONOUR OF ROBERT E. SPILLER, edited by Sujit Mukherjee and D. V. K. Raghavacharyulu. Bombay: Popular Prakashan, 1969.

Channing, William Ellery. THOREAU: THE POET-NATURALIST. 1873 edition. A review of, ATLANTIC MONTHLY, XXXIII (February, 1874), 230-231.

--THOREAU THE POET-NATURALIST. 1902 edition.

reviews: ATHENAEUM, January 17, 1903.
BOSTON TRANSCRIPT, November 12, 1902.
INDEPENDENT, LIV (December 11, 1902), 2959-2960.
NATION, LXXV (November 20, 1902), 403.

--THOREAU: THE POET-NATURALIST, edited by F. B. Sanborn. New York: Biblo and Tannen, 1966.
A facsimile reprint of the important, but rare

and hard-to-get 1902 version of Channing's biography of Thoreau.

--"Thoreau Walks Abroad," CHRISTIAN SCIENCE MONITOR, January 28, 1950.
Excerpt from his 1902 biography of Thoreau (p. 12).

Channing, William Ellery the Younger. THE COLLECTED POEMS OF, edited, with an introduction by Walter Harding. Gainesville, Fla.: Scholars' Facsimiles and Reprints, 1967.
Contains all Channing's poems about Thoreau.

C[hapman], C[hanler] A. "Abolitionist 1817-'62," BARRYTOWN EXPLORER, January, 1967.
Sonnet on Thoreau.

Chapman, Ralph. "Birthday of a Book," BRATTLEBORO [Vt.] DAILY REFORMER, August 9, 1954. p. 4.
A guest editorial.

Chapsal, Madeleine. "L'Apotre de L'Ideal Americain," L'EXPRESS [Paris], February 19, 1968, pp. 71-73.
Essay review on recent Thoreau publications in France.

Chari, V. K. "The Question of Form in Thoreau's A WEEK ON THE CONCORD AND MERRIMACK RIVERS," INDIAN ESSAYS IN AMERICAN LITERATURE, edited by Mukherjee and Raghavacharyulu. Bombay: Popular Prakashan, 1969.

Chase, Harry B. "Henry Thoreau, Surveyor," SURVEYING AND MAPPING (June, 1965).

Chase, Mary Ellen. THE LOVELY AMBITION. New York: Norton, 1960.
A delightful novel about an English clergyman who worships Thoreau and eventually comes to America to live. A long passage (pp. 63-66) discusses his love of Thoreau in particular. TSB #73.

--"The Parson and Thoreau." TSB #74, pp. 5-6.
Reprinted from her novel THE LOVELY AMBITION.

Cheney, David M. "Clinton Man Retraces Thoreau's Trail in Wild Maine Woods," WORCESTER [Mass.] TELEGRAM, January 7, 1951. p. 7.
An essay on the Maine Woods today.

Cherry, Robert. "Word Usage in the Writings of Henry David Thoreau." University of Colorado, 1964. Unpublished master's thesis.

Chodorov, Frank. "Henry David Thoreau," ANALYSIS (November, 1945).
An essay on the significance of Thoreau today.

--"Henry David Thoreau," OUT OF STEP. New York: Devin-
Adair, 1962. pp. 197-205.
A salty, vigorous tribute to Thoreau's libertarian
spirit, written in the vein of Thoreau's political
essays.

Christensen, Jack Shields and Robert Boom. THE MATURE AMER-
ICAN. Honolulu: University of Hawaii Press, 1967.
"A profile sketch of Thoreau based on his own
words."

Christie, John Aldrich. THOREAU AS WORLD TRAVELER. New York:
Columbia University Press, 1965.
Thoreau liked to boast that he had traveled much
in Concord, but as Christie proves, he traveled
around the world many times vicariously. He was
an inveterate reader of travel books and from them
received an amazingly wide knowledge of the world
which he in turn wove into his books and essays,
thus achieving a universality. Christie gives an
authoritative survey of Thoreau's reading of travel
literature in a readable and interestingly illustrated book. TSB #94.

reviews: AMERICAN LITERATURE (November, 1966).
BOSTON HERALD, January 12, 1966.
BOSTON TRAVELER, January 12, 1966.
CHICAGO TRIBUNE, January 9, 1966.
DALHOUSIE REVIEW, XLVI (1966), 380-383.
LIVING WILDERNESS (Autumn, 1966).
NEW ENGLAND QUARTERLY (March, 1967).
NEW YORK TIMES, December 26, 1965.

--"Thoreau on Civil Disobedience," EMERSON SOCIETY QUARTER-
LY, LIV (1969), 5-12.

--"Thoreau, Traveler." Duke University, 1956. Unpublished doctoral dissertation.
On Thoreau's interest in travel books.

Christman, Lansing. "Thoreau in New York State," THOREAU
JOURNAL QUARTERLY, I (April 15, 1969), 18-19.

Christy, Arthur. "Thoreau and Oriental Asceticism," ARYAN
PATH, VI (March, 1935).

Chu, Limin. "Self-as-Model: Thoreau," AN INTRODUCTION TO
AMERICAN LITERATURE 1607-1860. Taipei, Taiwan: Book-
mart, 1963.

Clapper, Ronald Earl. "The Development of WALDEN: A GENETIC
TEXT," TSB #107, p. 6.

Clark, Henry Hayden, editor. TRANSITIONS IN AMERICAN LITER-
ARY HISTORY. Durham: Duke University Press, 1954.
Much on Thoreau's position in American literature,

particularly in Alexander Kern's excellent essay, "The Rise of Transcendentalism." TSB #49.

Clarkson, John W., Jr. "A Bibliography of Franklin Benjamin Sanborn," PAPERS OF THE BIBLIOGRAPHICAL SOCIETY OF AMER-ICA, LX (1966), 73-85.
Many articles on Thoreau listed.

--"Wanted in Concord," YANKEE MAGAZINE (April, 1969), 129-132.
On the Sanborn kidnapping and Thoreau's part there-in.

Clendenning, John. "Emerson, Thoreau, and Transcendentalism," AMERICAN LITERARY SCHOLARSHIP: AN ANNUAL: 1964, edited by James Woodress. Durham, N. C.: Duke University Press, 1966. pp. 3-15.
A survey of scholarship.

Clepper, Henry. "The Allagash of Thoreau and 100 Years Later," AMERICAN FORESTS, LXVIII (November, 1962), 12ff.

Clough, Wilson O. "Affirm and Construct--Emerson and Thoreau," THE NECESSARY EARTH: NATURE AND SOLITUDE IN AMERICAN LIT-ERATURE. Austin: University of Texas Press, 1964. pp. 97-115.
A study of "the gradual awareness that the frontier might furnish American writers with a native source of metaphor and analogy in the search for a nation-al expression," this book emphasizes that Thoreau tried to "combine the hardness, the physical vital-ity, of the frontiersman with the reflections of a civilized man," and concludes cogently that "a Tho-reau is a measure of how free a society is or can be. That State which can afford a Thoreau is free."

Clune, Henry W. "Anachronism," ROCHESTER [N. Y.] DEMOCRAT-CHRONICLE, February 2, 1950.
Thoughts on seeing a copy of WALDEN on the news-stand.

--"A Message to Heed," ROCHESTER [N. Y.] DEMOCRAT CHRONICLE, July 15, 1954. p. 19.

--"She Might Have Been Ashamed," ROCHESTER [N. Y.] DEMOCRAT CHRONICLE, May 19, 1957.
Satirical reflections in a night club on Thoreau.

Clynes, Frank. "Dancing Thoreau Shocked a Friend," BOSTON HERALD, January 13, 1963.
Thoreau and Ricketson. Announcement of drive to raise funds to restore Ricketson's house.

Cobb, Robert Paul. "Society vs. Solitude: Studies in Emer-son, Thoreau, Hawthorne and Whitman." University of Michigan, 1955. Unpublished doctoral dissertation.

--"Thoreau and 'the Wild'," EMERSON SOCIETY QUARTERLY, XVIII (1960), 5-7.

Cochell, Shirley. "Thoreau--A Man for Our Times," SCHOLASTIC TEACHER [Junior Edition], LXII (February 15, 1968), 9-10.

Cochnower, Mary E. "Thoreau and Stoicism." University of Iowa, 1939. Unpublished doctoral dissertation.

Coffey, Raymond R. "Thoreau Is Hero of Saigon Students Who Dodge Viet War Draft," BOSTON GLOBE, January 10, 1968.

Cohen, B. Bernard. "The Perspective of an Old Master," EM-ERSON SOCIETY QUARTERLY, LVI (1969), 53-56.
    On "Autumnal Tints."

Cole, Robert C. "Thoreau's Philosophy of Observation." Wake-Forest University, 1961. Unpublished master's thesis.

Coleman, Lucile. "Walden Pond," NEW YORK TIMES, September 22, 1955.
    A poem.

Collard, Edgar Andrew. "Thoreau on the Church," CATHOLIC WORKER, XXVI (October, 1959), 8.
    Excerpts from A YANKEE IN CANADA.

   --"A Yankee Looks at Montreal," THE MONTREAL GAZETTE, September 19, 1959.
    On Thoreau's visit to Canada.

Collette, E. J. "Post Card View of Model of Walden Hut," TSB #32.

Combellack, C. R. B. "Two Critics of Society," PACIFIC SPECTATOR, III (Autumn, 1949), 440-445.
    A comparison and contrast of the lives and phi-
    losophies of Thoreau and Marx.

    translation: "Marx und Thoreau," DIE AMERIKANI-
    SCHE RUNDSCHAU, VI (December, 1949-January, 1950),
    21-26.

"Come Back Mr. Thoreau," WITNESS (December 13, 1956), 7-8.
    An editorial asking for more of Thoreau's inde-
    pendence today.

"Come Spring, Come Wanderlust," READERS DIGEST, LII (April,
1948), 120.
    On Thoreau's love of nature. Reprinted from
    CHRISTAIN SCIENCE MONITOR.

"Commissioners Given Suggestions for New Thoreau Monument,"
    CONCORD JOURNAL, June 13, 1946.
    A suggestion for a marker for the hut.

"The Complete Thoreau," CHICAGO EVENING POST, January 19, 1907.

Conant, Wallace B.   "Franklin Benjamin Sanborn 1831-1917,"
      CONCORD HERALD, March 1, 1945.
            A biography of Thoreau's friend and biographer.

   --"Thoreau's Message," BOSTON DAILY GLOBE, July 13, 1944.
            A letter to the editors on the pertinence of Tho-
            reau. A similar letter by Mr. Conant was printed
            in the BOSTON HERALD for July 9th and in the CON-
            CORD HERALD for July 13th.

   --"Would Thoreau Have Rejoiced?" THE CHRISTIAN CENTURY,
      LIX (March 25), 388.
            A letter to the editor concerning India, saying
            that Thoreau "held the spirit of revolt in check
            through Gandhi."

C[onant], W. B.   "Thoreau As Seen by Concord Authors,"
      CONCORD HERALD, July 9, 1942.

Concord Antiquarian Society.   CLOCK MAKERS OF CONCORD MAS-
      SACHUSETTS.   Concord: The Society, 1966.
            Includes photo of Thoreau's father's clock.

Concord Free Public Library.   BOOKS BY AND ABOUT HENRY DAVID
      THOREAU.   Concord: The Library, 1963.
            An annotated bibliography.

"Concord Sage Talks Frankly about Authors: Frank B. Sanborn
      Gives Twentieth Century Club Snappy Personal Impressions
      of Famous Men," BOSTON HERALD, January 5, 1916.

"The Concord School Recalled.   Mr. Sanborn Speaks at Green-
      acre on Thoreau and William T. Harris," SPRINGFIELD RE-
      PUBLICAN, August 31, 1905.

Condry, William.   "A Hundred Years of WALDEN," DUBLIN MAGAZINE,
      XXXI (January, 1955), 42-46.
            Influence of Thoreau in England.

   --"Nature's Disciple," WISDOM, I (April, 1956), 6-9.
            Reprinted from his THOREAU.

   --"The Sage of Walden Woods," COUNTRY LIFE, CXXXI (May 3,
      1962), 1036-1037.

   --THOREAU.   London: Witherby, 1954, New York: Philosoph-
      ical Library, 1954.
            The first volume in the new English "Great Natural-
            ists" Series, it is written by a Welsh nature warden.
            It is brief, to the point, and well-written, though
            no attempt is made to add any new facts to our know-
            ledge of Thoreau's life. Although the emphasis is
            quite naturally placed on Thoreau's interest in na-
            ture, Mr. Condry has not neglected Thoreau as a phi-

losopher and literary figure, and he has not fallen into some of the misinterpretations of the Canby and other biographies. Altogether it makes a good introduction to Thoreau. TSB #49.

reviews: BRITISH BIRDS, XLVII (October, 1954), 358-359.
COUNTRYMAN, L (Winter, 1956), 374.
MONTGOMERY COUNTY TIMES [England], May 29, 1954.
TIMES LITERARY SUPPLEMENT (September 3, 1954), 559.

--THOREAU. Delhi: Chand and Company, 1962.

translations: MAHAMANA THORO, translated by Sundarji Gokalji Betai. Bombay: Vora, 1962.

THORO, translated by Matilal Das. Calcutta: M. C. Sarker, 1962.

THORO, translated by Yadunath Dattatrey Thatte. Bombay: Majestic Book Stall, 1962.

TORO, translated by K. M. George. Madras: Orient Longmans, 1962. 140pp.

TORO, translated by A. S. Jnanasambandham. Madras: Orient Longmans, 1962.

TORO, translated by G. V. Krsnarau. Madras: Orient Longmans, 1962.

--"Thoreau in Britain," CHRISTIAN SCIENCE MONITOR, October 23, 1954.
An excerpt from his biography.

Conem, Francis B. "Henry-David Thoreau," LA VOIX DE LA PAIX [France], July, 1965.

"Conferencia del Sr. Leopoldo Hurtado," NEUVA ERA [Tandil, Argentina], June 6, 1949.
Account of the Thoreau lecture.

Conn, Howard. THE VALUE OF NON-CONFORMITY. Minneapolis: Plymouth Congregational Church, 1949.
Printing of an excellent sermon on Thoreau's CIVIL DISOBEDIENCE.

Connolly, Myles. "The Greatest Art," THIS WEEK, December 10, 1950.
One of the "Words to Live By" series. Based on a quotation from Thoreau.

Counter, Claude. "Conflits a Concord," JOURNAL D'ESCH [Switzerland], February 3, 1968.

On recent French translations of Thoreau.

Converse, Gordon N. "Thoreau's Cape Cod," AMERICAN FORESTS,
LXV (August, 1959), 24-27.
A series of superb photographs of the cape accom-
panied by quotations from Thoreau. TSB #69.

Conway, Moncure Daniel. A CENTURY AGO WITH THOREAU. Berkeley Heights: Oriole Press, 1962.
Reprinted from Conway's autobiography. Edition
limited to 150 copies.

Cook, Reginald Lansing. "Ancient Rites at Walden," EMERSON
SOCIETY QUARTERLY, XXXIX (1965), 52-56.
Thoreau's use of myth.

--PASSAGE TO WALDEN. Boston: Houghton Mifflin, 1949.

reviews: CHICAGO TRIBUNE, March 20, 1949, by
Frederick Babcock.
CHRISTIAN SCIENCE MONITOR, April 28, 1949.
COMMONWEAL (April 8, 1949).
LIVING WILDERNESS, XV (Spring, 1950), 17-
18, by Harvey Broome.
NEW ENGLAND QUARTERLY, XXII (January,
1950), 542-543, by George Whicher.
NEW YORK HERALD TRIBUNE, April 3, 1949.
NEW YORK TIMES, April 3, 1949.
PROC. ENT. SOC. OF WASHINGTON, LI (October,
1949), 235-236.
SATURDAY REVIEW OF LITERATURE, April 16,
1949.
TSB #27. April, 1949, by Walter Harding.
YANKEE (October, 1949), 89-94.

--PASSAGE TO WALDEN. New York: Russell and Russell, 1966.
New edition with added key to references and cita-
tions.

--"Teaching Thoreau at Middlebury," EMERSON SOCIETY QUAR-
TERLY, XVIII (1960), 7-9.

--"Think of This, Yankees!" MASSACHUSETTS REVIEW, IV (Autumn, 1962), 44-52.

--"This Side of Walden," ENGLISH LEAFLET, LIII (December,
1954), 1-12.
One of the most thoughtful of the centenary essays.

--"Thoreau in Perspective," AMERICAN LITERATURE: A CRITICAL
SURVEY, edited by T. D. Young and R. E. Fine. New York:
American Book Company, 1968. pp. 164-174.

also in: UNIVERSITY OF KANSAS CITY REVIEW, (Winter,
1947), 117-125. Thoreau as evaluated today.

--"Thoreau's Annotations and Corrections in the First
Book of WALDEN," TSB #42.

--"Viola C. White: An Appreciation," TSB #55.

--"West of Walden: on the Wild Side," LIVING WILDERNESS,
XXXII (Summer, 1968), 11-15.
     Text of the 1968 Thoreau Society Presidential
     Address.

Cook, Richard C. "Henry Thoreau's Poetic Imagination: An
Analysis of the Imagery of WALDEN " [Orono] University
of Maine, 1959. Unpublished master's thesis.

--"Thoreau and His Imagery: the Anatomy of an Imagination,"
TSB #70.
     A condensation of Cook's master's thesis.

Cooke, George Willis. "Emerson and Thoreau in the Index
to THE DIAL," EMERSON SOCIETY QUARTERLY, XVIII (1960),
44-49.
     Reprinted from the Rowfant Club edition of THE DIAL.

Cooke, J. W. "Freedom in the Thought of Henry David Thoreau,"
TSB #105. pp. 1-3.

Cooley, John. "Thank You, Henry Thoreau!" CHRISTIAN SCIENCE
MONITOR, August 22, 1967.

[Cooper, Madison]. "Henry Thoreau and Soil Contact," GARDEN-
ING MAGAZINE, VI (February, 1942), 27.

Cordell, Richard A. "Thoreau," ENGLISH AND AMERICAN STUDIES
[Wayo Women's University, Ichikawa, Japan], II (December,
1964), 1-19.

Cordes, Martha R. "Echoes from Walden," BOSTON HERALD, November 5, 1955.
     A poem.

Corita, Sister Mary. "If a man does not keep pace...."
TIME MAGAZINE (October 28, 1966).
     Abstract painting illustrating a line from WALDEN
     as an advertisement for Westinghouse Broadcasting
     Company.

Cosbey, Robert C. "Thoreau at Work: The Writing of 'Ktaadn,"
BULLETIN NEW YORK PUBLIC LIBRARY, LXV (January, 1961),
21-30.

Cosman, Max. "Thoreau and Staten Island," THE STATEN ISLAND
HISTORIAN, VI, 1 (January-March, 1943), 1-2 passim.

--"Thoreau Faced War," PERSONALIST, XXV (Winter, 1944),
73-76.

--"A Yankee in Canada," CANADIAN HISTORICAL REVIEW (March, 1944), 33-37.

Costa, Dick. "1959's Joe Meets 1859's Henry (Thoreau)," UTICA OBSERVER-DISPATCH [N. Y.], January 21, 1959.
      The last of a series of three articles.

"Courage," JOHN O'LONDON'S WEEKLY (June 9, 1950), p. 344.
      The WALDEN reference to "three o'clock in the morning courage" was originally called "two o' clock in the morning courage" by Napoleon.

Cowan, Michael H. CITY OF THE WEST: EMERSON, AMERICA AND URBAN METAPHOR. New Haven: Yale University Press, 1967.
      Frequent reference to Thoreau.

Cowell, Henry and Sidney Cowell. CHARLES IVES AND HIS MUSIC. New York: Oxford, 1955.
      Many details on Ives' interest in Thoreau.

Crawford, Bartholow V. "More Day to Dawn," a review of Harry Lee. MORE DAY TO DAWN. New York: Duell, Sloan and Pearce, 1941.
      AMERICAN LITERATURE, XIV (May, 1942), 183-184.

--, Alexander C. and Morriss H. Needleman. AN OUTLINE-HISTORY OF AMERICAN LITERATURE. New York: Barnes and Noble, 1945.
      Indispensable. If you want to know the biographical facts about Thoreau's friend Jones Very or the bibliography of his companion Ellery Channing, they are here. The pages on Thoreau himself are exceedingly well-done and the Thoreau bibliography in the appendix is the most up-to-date we have seen. TSB #18.

Creevey, Caroline A. Stickney. "The Hermit of Walden," AT RANDOM. New York: Putnam, 1920. pp. 155-161.
      An essay.

Crocket, Douglas. "Walden's Shrunk Since 1850," BOSTON GLOBE, September 30, 1968.
      Report on investigation of Walden by the New England Marine Technology Society.

Cronkhite, G. Ferris. "The Transcendental Railroad," NEW ENGLAND QUARTERLY, XXIV (September, 1951), 306-328.
      Emerson's, Hawthorne's, and Thoreau's reactions to the railroad compared.

Crosbie, Mary. "The Poet by His Pond," JOHN O'LONDON'S WEEKLY, LVI (October 3, 1947), 621.
      A British evaluation of Thoreau.

Crowell, Reid. "Henry Thoreau at Walden Pond," CLASSMATE, LV (August, 1948), 3-4.

A very understanding interpretation for children
of Thoreau's philosophy, in a Methodist Sunday
School paper. TSB #24.

--"Thoreau and Walden Pond," THE OLD INTENSITIES. Dallas:
Published by the author, 1949. p. 37.
A sonnet. Almost all of the poems in this pleasant
volume show the influence of Thoreau. TSB #39.

also in: OREGONIAN, May ? , 1944.

Crowely, Richard C. "Thoreau's Correspondence," COMMONWEAL,
LXX (May 15, 1959), 186.
A violent denunciation of Thoreau.

Crowley, Raymond J. "Thoreau Proposed 'Passive Resistance',"
RICHMOND TIMES DISPATCH, February 27, 1956.
Points out irony that both whites and negroes are
using Thoreau's civil disobedience in the segre-
gation controversy. Reprinted in NEW YORK HERALD
TRIBUNE, March 4, 1956.

Cruickshank, Helen, editor. THOREAU ON BIRDS. New York:
McGraw-Hill, 1964.
Many years ago the late Francis H. Allen gathered
together Thoreau's bird notes from his journals
into an admirable little volume, and when I first
heard of this new volume, I wondered why the job
needed doing over again. But, without disparaging
at all Mr. Allen's fine work, I would like to say
that Mrs. Cruickshank, through her superb editing
and perceptive commentaries, has compiled an in-
dependently worthwhile volume that will attract
both Thoreauvians and bird-lovers. The largest
part of the volume is devoted to selections from
his writings arranged specie by specie, but she
has also gathered together his bird notes at Walden, in the Maine Woods, etc. TSB #90.

reviews: CANADIAN FIELD-NATURALIST (October, 1965).
LIBRARY JOURNAL (November 15, 1964).
MASSACHUSETTS AUDUBON NEWSLETTER (Decem-
ber, 1964).
NEW YORK TIMES, December 6, 1964.

Cummings, Laurence A. "Thoreau Poems in Bixby Washington
University Manuscripts," EMERSON SOCIETY QUARTERLY, XXVI
(1962), 9-27.
Transcriptions and annotations.

Cuneo, Dardol. "Thoreau y la Desobediencia," LA VANGUARDIA
[Buenos Aires], (?).
A brief article on the influence of CIVIL DISOBE-
DIENCE.

Cunningham, Nora B.   "Prose Rambles in Naturalist's Journals,"
        KANSAS CITY TIMES, May 6, 1952.
                Chiefly excerpts from Thoreau's 1852 JOURNALS.

    --"Walden," CHRISTIAN SCIENCE MONITOR, October 16, 1954.
        A sonnet.

    --"WALDEN, Published a Century Ago, Is As Meaningful as
        When It Was Written," KANSAS CITY [Mo.] TIMES, August
        28, 1954. p. 32.

Curtis, Edith Roelker.   A SEASON IN UTOPIA: THE STORY OF
        BROOK FARM.   New York: Nelson, 1961.
                The first, thorough-going, accurate account of
                the Transcendentalist experiment in community
                living. A book that we have long needed. Tho-
                reau is mentioned only very briefly since he
                took no active part in the community, but there
                is a great deal of importance here for a back-
                ground of understanding of his times and of his
                friends.   TSB #77.

Curtis, John L. "The Egghead Corner," DINERS' CLUB MAGAZINE
        (July, 1962), 12.
                Centennial tribute to Thoreau.

"Cynthia Davenport on Thoreau's Ancestry," TSB #107, pp. 7-8.
                A manuscript of a letter from Cynthia M. Davenport
                to F. B. Sanborn is printed.

D

D., P. "Thoreau for Tolstoi," BOSTON GLOBE, August 28, 1950.
If the "Voice of America" broadcasts Tolstoi to
the Russians, perhaps they should broadcast Thoreau to us.

Dabbs, James McBride. "Thoreau--The Adventurer as Economist,"
YALE REVIEW (Summer, 1947), 667-672.
An essay.

Dahlberg, Edward. "Thoreau and Walden," DO THESE BONES LIVE?
New York: Harcourt, 1941. pp. 8-18.

d'Amato, Guy Albert. "Henry David Thoreau (July 12, 1817-
1862): The Devil's Grandchild," MINORITY OF ONE, III
(July, 1961), 9.
A brief essay in praise of Thoreau's spirit of
defiance and revolt.

Damon, Bertah. "Grandma Reads Thoreau," PRESENT TENSE, edited by Sharon Brown. New York: Harcourt, 1946. pp. 297-
302.
A reprint of this delightful essay.

Dana, Mrs. William Starr. HOW TO KNOW THE WILD FLOWERS. New
York: Scribner, 1893.
Filled with quotations from Thoreau.

Daniels, Herb. "Thoreau," THE MODERN ALMANAC. Chicago:
Quadrangle, 1962. pp. 104-105.

Darrow, F. S. "The Transcendentalists and Theosophy," NEW
OUTLOOK, XI (March, 1958), 8-18.
Includes quotations on Thoreau's interest in trans-
migration and pre-existence.

Daugherty, James. HENRY DAVID THOREAU: A MAN FOR OUR TIME.
New York: Viking, 1967.
A beautifully and fully illustrated series of
selections from Thoreau's writings, chiefly WALDEN,
aimed primarily at young people. Daugherty is one
of the foremost children's book illustrators of our
day and this is one of his outstanding books.
TSB #99.

review: NEW YORK TIMES, July 23, 1967.

Davidson, Frank. "Melville, Thoreau, and 'The Apple-Tree

Table'," AMERICAN LITERATURE, XXV (January, 1954), 479-488.
>Shows the relation between the closing pages of WALDEN and a Melville short story.

--"A Reading of WALDEN," EMERSON SOCIETY QUARTERLY, XVIII (1960), 9-11.

--"Thoreau and David Starr Jordan," TSB #109, pp. 5-6.

--"Thoreau's Contributions to Hawthorne's MOSSES," NEW ENGLAND QUARTERLY, XX (December, 1947), 535-542.
>On literary relationship of these two Concord friends.

--"Thoreau's Hound, Bay Horse, and Turtle Dove," NEW ENGLAND QUARTERLY, XXVI (December, 1954), 521-524.
>An analysis of the WALDEN symbol.

Davidson, Jo. "Henry David Thoreau," MASSACHUSETTS REVIEW, IV (Autumn, 1962), 109.
>Photo of bust.

Davies, John. "Centennial of Thoreau's WALDEN," VEGETARIAN NEWS [London, Eng.], XXXIII (Summer, 1954), 60-61.

--"Henry S. Salt: A Personal Recollection," TSB #29.

>translation: CENIT, CXXXVIII (June, 1962), translated into Spanish by V. Munoz.

--"A Letter from England," TSB #21.
>In part a reply to Dr. Herbert Faulkner West's lecture printed in TSB #20.

--"My First Encounter with Thoreau," TSB #106, pp. 5-6.

--"On Reading Thoreau," TSB #45.

--"Thoreau and the Ethics of Food," VEGETARIAN MESSENGER, XLIV (February, 1947), 40-41.
>A British article on Thoreau as a vegetarian.

Davies, William H. THE ADVENTURES OF JOHNNY WALKER TRANG. London: Cape, 1926.
>Includes (p. 180) commentary on Thoreau and his principles.

Davis, Bette. "A New Day Coming," THIS WEEK, July 22, 1956. p. 2.
>The famous actress writes of her interest in Thoreau.

Davis, Grace S. "The Cats of Thoreau," CATS MAGAZINE, XVIII (October, 1961), 7.

--"Thoreau's Cats," CATS MAGAZINE, XVIII (September, 1961), 9-42.

Excerpts on cats from Thoreau's JOURNALS.

Davis, Millard C. "The Influence of Emerson, Thoreau, and
    Whitman on the Early American Naturalists John Muir
    and John Burroughs," LIVING WILDERNESS, XXX (1967), 18-23.

Davis, R. "John Brown First Publicly Championed by Thoreau,"
    LOWELL [Mass.] LEADER, May 15, 1941.

Davis, Rebecca Harding. BITS OF GOSSIP. Boston: Houghton
    Mifflin, 1904.
        Includes an interview with Emerson about Thoreau,
        p. 44.

Davis, T. Y. "A Footnote on CAPE COD." TSB #61.

Daudet, Carlos Ruiz. "Thoreau," EL ECO DE TANDIL [Tandil,
    Argentina], June 3, 1949.
        A brief essay on Thoreau.

Day, Harvey. "Thoreau the Nonconformist," COURIER JOURNAL
    [Louisville, Ky.], May 5, 1952.
        "He could never have kept up with the Joneses and
        would have fled, shrieking, from the gospel of
        Togetherness."

Day, Hem. ARMAND, SA VIE, SA PENSEE, SON ACTION. Paris:
    La Ruche Ouvriere, 1964.
        Thoreau frequently mentioned and quoted.

Day, Rachel C. "To Be Eaten in the Wind," NATURE OUTLOOK
    (November, 1943), 6.
        On Thoreau's wild apples.

Deady, Kathleen. "On Your Own Time," BOSTON POST, May 10,
    1942.

DeArmond, Fred. "Can Dissenters Really Claim Thoreau?"
    HUMAN EVENTS, XXI (May 25, 1968), 10.

"The Death of Hugh Coyle," TSB #33.
        Includes an article reprinted from the CONCORD
    FREEMAN, October 3, 1845. p. 2.

DeCasseres, Benjamin. "The March of Events," NEW YORK DAILY
    MIRROR, September 26, 1945.
        Approving Thoreau for the Hall of Fame.

Decker, Richard. "No, I would not care to hear a chapter
    or two of WALDEN," NEW YORK TIMES, June 9, 1963.
        Cartoon reprinted in TSB #84.

"Dedication of Thoreau House," CONCORD JOURNAL, July 3, 1969.
        Replica of Thoreau's cabin.

Dedmond, Francis B. "A Check List of Manuscripts Relating

61

to Thoreau in The Huntington Library, The Houghton Library of Harvard University, and The Berg Collection of The New York Public Library," TSB #43.

--"Economic Protest in Thoreau's JOURNAL," STUDIA NEOPHIL-OLOGICA, XXVI (1954), 65-76.
> "When Thoreau had his eye on economic conditions and institutions, he could not help but be pessimistic; but when he thought of man with all his possibilities and potentialities, his Transcendental optimism assured him that there still remained some hope of a better world."

--"A Faint Clue on Ellery Channing's Quarrel with Ticknor and Fields," TSB #39.

--"100 Years of WALDEN," CONCORD [Mass.] JOURNAL, June 24, 1954, p. 1 passim.

--"Thoreau and the Ethical Concept of Government," PERSONALIST, XXXVI (Winter, 1955), 36-46.

--"Thoreau as a Critic of Society," TSB #34.
> An abstract of a master's thesis done at Duke University under Dr. Clarence Ghodes in 1950.

--"William Ellery Channing on Thoreau: An Unpublished Satire," MODERN LANGUAGE NOTES, LXVII (January, 1952), 50-52.
> The first printing, with comments, of the Thoreau portions of Channing's Moses Bucolics satire.

Deevey, Edward S., Jr. "A Re-examination of Thoreau's WALDEN," THE QUARTERLY REVIEW OF BIOLOGY, XVII (March, 1942), 1-11.

--, and James S. Bishop. LIMNOLOGY. ? : Connecticut State Board of Fisheries and Game, ? . Bulletin #63.
> Extolls Thoreau as a limnologist.

DeFalco, Joseph M. "'The Landlord': Thoreau's Emblematic Technique," EMERSON SOCIETY QUARTERLY, LVI (1969), 23-32.

--"Thoreau's Ethics and the 'Bloody Revolution," TOPIC [Washington, Pa.], VI (1966), 43-49.

Dempsey, Don P. "Thoreau's Ideas Concerning the Impact of Civilization on the American Primitive Man." San Diego State College, 1964. Unpublished master's thesis.

Derleth, August. AND YOU, THOREAU. Norfolk, Connecticut: New Directions, 1943.
> Nature poems in tribute to Thoreau in the "Poets of the Year" series of pamphlets.

--COLLECTED POEMS 1937-1967. New York: Candlelight Press, 1967.
>Reprints all his many poems about Thoreau.

--CONCORD REBEL: A LIFE OF HENRY DAVID THOREAU. Philadelphia: Chilton, 1962.
>Although there have been numerous attempts, up until now there has not been a satisfactory life of Thoreau written for young people. August Derleth, who is well-known for his "Sac Prairie" novels about life in Wisconsin, has broken through the barrier and written a biography that will not only appeal to young people, but adults as well. It is not sugary. It does not gloss over or play down Thoreau's rebellious nature. For the first time it presents the facts of his life in a clear chronological order. And, most important, it presents Thoreau with a clear understanding of just what his aims were and just what he stood for. An eminently satisfactory book. TSB #81.

>reviews: CENIT (May-June, 1964), 4368.
>NEW YORK TIMES, November 11, 1962.

>translation: UNE CONSCIENCE REVOLTEE: LA VIE d'HENRY D. THOREAU, translated into French by Genevieve Brallion-Zeude. [Paris]: Nouveaux Horizons, 1966.

--CONCORD REBEL: A LIFE OF THOREAU. New York: Avon, 1963 (paper).

--"Homage to Thoreau," RENDEZVOUS IN A LANDSCAPE. New York: Fine Editions, 1952. pp. 3-14.
>Five free verse poems interpreting Thoreau's philosophy.

--"In the End Was His Beginning," HAWK AND WHIPPOORWILL, VI (Spring, 1962).
>A poem on Thoreau's death.

--WALDEN POND: HOMAGE TO THOREAU. With wood engravings by Frank Utpatel. Iowa City: Prairie Press, 1968.
>Excerpts from Derleth's journals about three visits to Walden. As usual, Derleth has stimulating things to say and the volume is a gem of printing. TSB #107.

--WALDEN WEST. New York: Duell, Sloan, and Pearce, 1961.
>A collection of superb short stories and sketches about Sac Prairie, Wisconsin, with one of its announced major themes a series of illustrations of Thoreau's statement that "The mass of men lead lives of quiet desperation." Also includes a number of comments on Derleth's own personal interest in Thoreau. TSB #77.

DesChamps, Grace. "Plaque Once Marked T. Room in Chamberlain Home on Old Road," PROVINCETOWN ADVOCATE, September 27, 1962.

Dewhurst, Dwight. "Henry D. Thoreau," AUTHENTIC [Stoneham, Mass.], October, 1896.

Dias, Earl J. "Daniel Ricketson and Henry Thoreau," NEW ENGLAND QUARTERLY, XXVI (September, 1953), 388-396.
On their friendship.

--"New Bedford Man Was Warm Friend of Thoreau," NEW BED-FORD STANDARD TIMES, May 6, 1962.
On Thoreau's friendship with Daniel Ricketson.

--"Witness to the Transcendental Twist," YANKEE, XXIX (September, 1965), 110-115.
Thoreau and Daniel Ricketson.

Dickens, Robert S. "Henry David Thoreau: A Discussion of his use of the Terms 'Nature' and 'nature'," TSB #71. p. 1.

--"Thoreau and the Abdication of American Philosophy," EMERSON SOCIETY QUARTERLY, XXII (1961), 33-35.

--"Thoreau and the 'Other Great Tradition'," EMERSON SO-CIETY QUARTERLY, XXIX (1962), 26-28.

Dickerson, May Cynthia. WINTER PHOTOGRAPHS FROM THE WOODS AND FIELDS OF MASSACHUSETTS WITH QUOTATIONS SELECTED FROM THOREAU'S JOURNAL ON WINTER IN MASSACHUSETTS. New York: DeVinne Press,   ?   .
A small pamphlet of photographs and quotations.

Dietz, Lew. "A Man to Remember," THE ALLEGASH. New York: Holt, Rinehart and Winston, 1968. pp. 151-163.
A chapter devoted to Thoreau's Maine Woods journeys--and other references to Thoreau occur on almost every page of the last half of the book. It is a gold mine of material for students of Thoreau's MAINE WOODS and a highly readable book besides, filled with anecdotes and folklore as well as history of the area. TSB #106.

also in: DOWN EAST, XIV (June, 1968), 44-45 passim.

"Different Drummer," PROVIDENCE [R. I.] JOURNAL, July 4, 1945.
A centenary editorial.

Dittmer, Bernice. "Thoreau: Emerson's American Scholar." Texas Western College, 1965. Unpublished master's thesis.

Dodd, Edward H., Jr. OF NATURE, TIME, AND TEALE. New York: Dodd, Mead, 1960.
Contains much on Edwin Way Teale's interest in Thoreau.

Dodge, Norman L. "Aunt Maria's Own Copy," MONTH AT GOOD-SPEED'S BOOK SHOP, XXI (November, 1949), 34-36.

Maria Thoreau's copy of A WEEK offered for sale
at $500. Photograph of volume and lengthy com-
mentary.

--"Autograph Pages from Thoreau's JOURNAL," THE MONTH AT
GOODSPEED'S BOOK SHOP, XXIX (January, 1958), 103-105.
Description of MS for sale.

--"First Edition of Thoreau's First," MONTH AT GOODSPEED'S
BOOK SHOP, XXVI (May, 1955), 171-175.
Description and illustrations of a presentation
copy of A WEEK from Thoreau to Savage Landor.

--"Oysters, Clams, and Cape Cod," THE MONTH AT GOODSPEED'S
BOOK SHOP, XXIX (February, 1958), 129 passim.
Description of portion of CAPE COD MS for sale.

--"Travels in Concord," THE MONTH AT GOODSPEED'S BOOK
SHOP, XVIII (January-February, 1947), 113-115.
Photographs and description of a first edition
of WALDEN.

[Dodge, Norman L.]. "Gift to Landor of Thoreau's WEEK,"
EMERSON SOCIETY QUARTERLY, XLVII (1967), 88-89.

--"Walden Pencil-Maker," THE MONTH AT GOODSPEED'S BOOK
SHOP, XXXVII (October, 1965), 2-5.
Describes pack of Thoreau pencils, $100 a dozen!

also in, EMERSON SOCIETY QUARTERLY, XLIII (1966),
97.

Doss, Vernon L. "Thoreau's Minnesota Journal." Mankato
State College, 1961. Unpublished master's thesis.

Doucette, Rita. PARALLEL LIVES. Salem, Mass.: Doucette,
1964 (mimeographed).
A comparison of Thoreau and Truman Nelson.

Douglass, James. "Henry David Thoreau," CATHOLIC WORKER,
XXVIII (May, 1962), 3.
Centennial tribute.

Douthat, Lou. "She Helped Open Cincinnati Medical Colleges
to Women," CINCINNATI POST AND TIMES-STAR, April 12,
1969.
Account of the discovery of an unpublished auto-
biographical MS by a Mrs. Celia Frease which includes a lengthy description of Thoreau, but with
no indication of where she became acquainted with
him.

Downs, Robert B. "Individual versus State," BOOKS THAT
CHANGED THE WORLD. New York: Mentor, 1956. pp. 65-75.
The influence of CIVIL DISOBEDIENCE. Also issued
in hardcovers by the American Library Association.

Drake, Allen. "Thoreau on Society," NARRAGANSETT NATURALIST (Summer, 1963).

Drake, E. " I Hear a Different Drummer." New York: Columbia Records 4-43760, 1967.
A 45 r.p.m. recording, sung by Robert Goulet, about Thoreau.

Drake, William. "Henry Thoreau, Organic Gardener," ORGANIC GARDENING (July, 1956).
Letter to editor quoting Thoreau's comments on organic gardening.

--"The Depth of WALDEN: Thoreau's Symbolism of the Divine in Nature." University of Arizona, 1967. Unpublished doctoral dissertation.
Abstract is reproduced in TSB #107, p. 6.

Dreiser, Theodore. EL PENSAMIENTO VIVO DE THOREAU. Translated into Spanish by Luis Echavarri. Buenos Aires: Editorial Losada, 1944.
Translation of his anthology, LIVING THOUGHTS OF THOREAU.

Drinnon, Richard. "Thoreau's Politics of the Upright Man," ANARCHY [London], III (April, 1963), 117-128.

also in: MASSACHUSETTS REVIEW, IV (Autumn, 1962), 126-138.

translation: "Thoreau y su concepto del hombre probo y justo," RECONSTRUIR [Buenos Aires, Argentina], XXXII (September, 1964), 34-42. Translated into Spanish.

"Drought Perils Walden Pond," CHICAGO TRIBUNE, May 4, 1966.
Syndicated article.

Drucker, D. B. LE JOUR SE LEVE. Avignon, France: Aubanel Editeur, 1955.
Favorable comment on Thoreau's CIVIL DISOBEDIENCE on pp. 140-141.

Dryer, Stan. "Dear Mr. Thoreau," SATURDAY EVENING POST (October 5, 1968).
A delightful little satire on Thoreau's troubles with publishers if he tried to publish WALDEN today. TSB #105.

Dubois, Marjorie B. "Thoreau's WEEK," NEW YORK SUN, February 11, 1949.
A letter to the editor on the centennial of Thoreau's first book.

Ducharme, Jacques. "An American Classic," THINK, XX (November, 1954), 28.

A centennial essay on WALDEN.

also in: P.E.O. RECORD [Mount Pleasant, Iowa], (March, 1960).

Dunham, Mary. "Thoreau Settles by a Pond on Venus," CHRISTIAN SCIENCE MONITOR, May 20, 1955.
Space-fiction parody of WALDEN.

Durfee, Hazard. "Henry David Thoreau on Individuality," FORTUNE (December, 1953), 148.
A full-page colored illustration of Thoreau playing his flute, with a text from WALDEN. One of the Container Corporation of America's series of "Great Ideas of Western Man."

--HENRY DAVID THOREAU ON INDIVIDUALITY. New York: Darien House, 1969.
Huge poster-size reproduction of Container Corp. ad of some years ago.

Duvall, S. P. C. "Robert Frost's 'Directive' Out of WALDEN," AMERICAN LITERATURE, XXXI (January, 1960), 482-488.

Dynnik, M. A., et al. "Thoreau" HISTORY OF PHILOSOPHY. Moscow: Academy of Sciences of the USSR, 1957. II. 549.

"Eagleswood, a Local Social Experiment, Attracted Literary
Giants of the 1800's," PERTH AMBOY [N. J.] EVENING NEWS,
November 12, 1949.
Illustrated account of the community which Thoreau
visited and surveyed. The most detailed account
of this experiment yet to appear. TSB #30.

Earisman, Delbert L. HIPPIES IN OUR MIDST. Philadelphia:
Fortress, 1968.
On Thoreau as a patron saint of the Hippies, pp.
127-131.

[Earle, Peter G.] "Thoreau, teorico de la rebeldia," OVA-
CIONES [Mexico City], August 11, 1963.
With excerpts from Thoreau's writings translated
into Spanish.

Earnest, Ernest. "Thoreau and Little Rock," BEST ARTICLES
AND STORIES (November, 1959).
Thoreau as the spiritual ancestor of Governor
Faubus!

"Easy For Thoreau," BOSTON HERALD, September 20. 1943.
An editorial.

Eaton, Richard J. "Gowing's Swamp," MASSACHUSETTS AUDUBON,
LIII (June, 1969), 31-34.
Thoreau's records of the area and present day
attempts to preserve it.

--"Thoreau as a Botanist: Two Anecdotes," NEW ENGLAND
WILD FLOWER NOTES (Winter, 1968).

Eaton, Walter Prichard. "Thoreau and Nature," TSB #39.
A copy of an address given on July 13, 1946 in
Concord at the annual meeting of the Thoreau So-
ciety.

--"Thoreau Walks Again," BERKSHIRE COUNTY EAGLE, July
19, 1944.
An essay on the Thoreau Society meeting in Concord.

Eby, Cecil D., Jr. "Down East with George Savary Wasson,"
DOWN EAST, XIII (April, 1967), 43-47 passim.
Mentions Thoreau and Wasson.

Eckstorm, Fannie Hardy. "Enter Mr. Thoreau," OLD JOHN NEPTUNE

AND OTHER MAINE INDIAN SHAMANS.   Portland, Maine: South-
worth-Anthoensen, 1945.
> An account of Thoreau's visit with Gov. Neptune.
> Also material on Thoreau's Maine guides.

--"Notes on Thoreau's MAINE WOODS," TSB #51.
> These are notes reproduced by Ralph S. Palmer
> from Mrs. Eckstorm's annotated copy of THE MAINE
> WOODS.

Eddleman, Floyd Eugene.   "Use of Lempriere's Classical
Dictionary in WALDEN," EMERSON SOCIETY QUARTERLY, XLIII
(1966), 62-65.

Edgett, Edwin Francis.   "Thoreau and Emerson on Monadnock,"
BOSTON TRANSCRIPT, September 5, 1931.

"Editions of Thoreau's WALDEN Shown at Fenn," CLEVELAND [Ohio]
PLAIN DEALER, March 28, 1954.
> Account of a centennial exhibition.

[An editorial on the anniversary of Thoreau's death].   NEW
YORKER (May 7, 1949).

Edman, Irwin.   FOUNTAIN-HEADS OF FREEDOM.   New York: Reynal
and Hitchcock, 1942.
> Pages 149-153 devoted to Thoreau's exaltation
> of individuality.

--"To Henry David Thoreau (After Reading a Tribute to
Him in FORTUNE)," NATION, CLIX (September 23, 1944),
346.
> A poem.

"Edwards, Oliver" [Sir William Haley].   "Solitaries," THE
TIMES [London], September 30, 1965.
> "While I found Thoreau a man to admire, he remained
> one I could not like."

"Eenzaamheid Als Experiment" [Solitude as an Experiment],
DE GROENE AMSTERDAMMER, August 31, 1946.+
> Two long articles in Dutch on Thoreau, quoting
> long fragments from WALDEN.

Eglinton, J. Z.   GREEK LOVE.   New York: Oliver Layton, 1964.
> Discusses Thoreau's interest in Edmund Sewall in
> a heavily documented treatise on "Greek love,"
> p. 191 passim.

Eidson, John Olin.   "Charles Stearns Wheeler: Emerson's Good
Grecian," NEW ENGLAND QUARTERLY, XXVII (December, 1954),
472-483.
> Much on friendship of Wheeler and Thoreau.

--CHARLES STEARNS WHEELER: FRIEND OF EMERSON.   Athens:
University of Georgia Press, 1951.

One of the happiest products of research on Transcendentalism in recent years has been the systematic filling in of gaps in the biographies of the members of the movement. Now one more space has been filled--and very adequately filled at that. Wheeler, who died when he was only 26, is one of the minor figures of the movement. But he produced a remarkable amount of work in his short life, and, even more important, acted as a catalyst for both Emerson and Thoreau. Dr. Eidson, in what is obviously a labor of love, has painstakingly run down all the known facts on Wheeler's life--and many previously unknown ones--and put them together in what is unquestionably the definitive biography. Thoreau scholars will find in it much new light on Thoreau's college years including a complete checklist of his college marks and rank (p. 80). There is also as full an account as probably can ever be made of Wheeler's sojourn on Flint's Pond and its influence on the Walden experiment. TSB #38.

reprinted in: EMERSON SOCIETY QUARTERLY, LII (1968), 13-75.

Eifert, Virginia S. "The Botanist, Thoreau," TALL TREES AND FAR HORIZONS: ADVENTURES AND DISCOVERIES OF EARLY BOTANISTS IN AMERICA. New York: Dodd, Mead, 1965. pp. 239-256.
A very readable account of Thoreau's botanical interests as displayed on his 1857 trip to Maine, although oddly enough no use was made of Thoreau's much ampler botanical notes .in his JOURNAL. It does however convey Thoreau's enthusiasm for botany and other chapters in the book give some exciting accounts of the discoveries by other early American botanists. TSB #91.

Eilenberg, Arthur. "Thoreau on Coffee," NEW YORK TIMES MAGAZINE, January 10, 1943. p. 4.

Eiseley, Loren. FRANCIS BACON AND THE MODERN DILEMMA. Lincoln: University of Nebraska Press, 1963.
Contains a lengthy commentary on Thoreau's MAINE WOODS.

Eisenlohr, Herman L. "The Development of Thoreau's Prose " University of Pennsylvania, 1966. Unpublished doctoral dissertation.
Abstract reproduced in TSB #108, pp. 7-8.

Eisinger, Chester E. "Transcendentalism: Its Effect upon American Literature and Democracy," DIE NEURREN SPRACHEN, Beiheft 9. Frankfurt: Mority Diesterweg, 1961. pp. 22-38.

70

Ekirch, Arthur Alphonse, Jr. THE IDEA OF PROGRESS IN AMERICA, 1815-1860. New York: Peter Smith, 1951.
Pp. 162-164 discuss Thoreau's skeptical attitude towards progress.

--"Transcendental Harmony: Thoreau," MAN AND NATURE IN AMERICA. New York: Columbia University Press, 1963. pp. 58-69.

"Ekscentrikas Thoreau," DIENRASTIS DRAUGAS, Liepos 26, 1952, p. 4.
A brief article on Thoreau's eccentricity in a Chicago Lithuanian newspaper.

Eldridge, Oliver. "Un-Concord," CONCORD JOURNAL, December 18, 1959.
Poem on Walden Pond.

Ellis, Charles Mayo (?). AN ESSAY ON TRANSCENDENTALISM, edited by Walter Harding. Gainesville, Florida: Scholar's Facsimiles and Reprints, 1954.
A reprint of a rare annonymous defense of Transcendentalism, originally printed in Boston in 1842. While Thoreau is not mentioned specifically except in the editor's introduction, the essay gives an excellent summary of the beliefs of members of the movement of which Thoreau was a part. TSB #89.

Ellis, J. S. "The Walden Dreamer," CLASSMATE [Cincinnati, Ohio], March 18, 1933.

Ellison, Harlan. "'Repent, Harlequin!' Said the Ticktockman," NEBULA AWARD STORIES, edited by Damon Knight. New York: Pocket Books, 1967. pp. 53-64.
A science fiction story based on Thoreau's CIVIL DISOBEDIENCE and which won the Nebula Award as the best science fiction short story of 1965.

Emans, Elaine V. "Thought for Thoreau," CHRISTIAN SCIENCE MONITOR, October 29, 1960.
A poem.

Emerson, Edward Waldo. HENRY THOREAU AS REMEMBERED BY A YOUNG FRIEND. Concord: Thoreau Lyceum, 1968.
A facsimile reprint of the most delightful short biography of Thoreau. TSB #103.

--"Letter to Miss Nevins," CONCORD SAUNTERER, IV (March, 1969), 6-7.
On Thoreau's French background.

--LETTERS TO EDWIN B. HILL. Ysleta, Texas: Edwin B. Hill, ? .
Two letters from Thoreau's friend and biographer. The second explains the legend of Thoreau's refusal of his college degree.

71

Emerson, Ellen. "Thoreau, One Hundred Years Later: Individualism," CONCORD JOURNAL, June 21, 1962.
Centennial tribute given at Concord High School graduation by Emerson's great-granddaughter.

"Emerson," IJIN WA KUKU OSHIERU (THUS GREAT MEN TEACH US). Tokyo: Dia Nippon Yuben Kai Kodan Sha, 1933. pp. 28-30. On Emerson and Thoreau.

Emerson, Ralph Waldo. An essay on Thoreau in THE SHOCK OF RECOGNITION. New York: Doubleday Doran, 1943.

also in: THE THREE READERS. New York: Readers Club, 1943.

--THE EARLY LECTURES OF, Vol. II, edited by Stephen Whicher, Robert Spiller and Wallace Williams. Cambridge: Harvard University Press, 1964.
This series continues to be a superb piece of editorial work, providing us at last with easily accessible and accurate texts of Emerson's lectures, in this case from 1836 to 1838, so that we may study the development of his thoughts from journal to lecture to essay. Thoreau is not mentioned directly. But since this volume covers the years of their earliest acquaintance, it is essential to an understanding of Emerson's mind when Thoreau first knew him. TSB #90.

--EMERSON: A MODERN ANTHOLOGY, edited by Alfred Kazin and Daniel Asron. Boston: Houghton Mifflin, 1959.
Anthologizes many of Emerson's comments on Thoreau, passim.

--"a forest seer," AMERICAN PHONETIC SPELLING. Concord: Wallace B. Conant, 1946.
Emerson's tribute to Thoreau reproduced.

--THE HEART OF EMERSON'S JOURNALS, edited by Bliss Perry. New York: Dover, 1958.
A paperback reprint of the hardcover edition of thirty years ago. An excellent condensation of Emerson's journals, with many enlightening glimpses of Thoreau and his contemporaries. Dover is to be highly commended for bringing it back into print. TSB #69.

--THE JOURNALS AND MISCELLANEOUS NOTEBOOKS OF, edited by William Gilman et al.
Vol. I. (1819-1822) Cambridge: Harvard University Press, 1960.
The first volume of a projected 16 volume definitive edition of Emerson's journals and notebooks. Not only do they include many important items omitted from the earlier 10 volume edition, but they also correct many misreadings. This first volume

covers the years 1819-1822, so there is little
directly about Thoreau in it. But nonetheless it
is decidedly important for the Thoreau scholar
because it gives us so many new insights into his
closest friend. The editorial work is a marvel to
behold. Never have we seen an edition that so clearly and definitively represents a manuscript with all
its cancellations, interlineations, and so on. It
is a model of editorial practice. It is to be hoped
that scholars and libraries will do their best to
encourage the efforts of the editorial board and the
publishers to complete this project. TSB #73.

Vol. II. (1822-1826) Cambridge: Harvard University
Press, 1961.
The second in the projected 16 volume complete edition of all of Emerson's journals and notebooks.
Like the first volume, it is a magnificent piece of
editing. Although the period covered is still too
early to include any direct mention of Thoreau, the
volume is decidedly important as background material
for understanding Transcendentalism, and thus Thoreau's way of thinking. There is an exceptionally
interesting sketch of President John Adams, and some
of Emerson's early thoughts on "Compensation." Certainly we should all do our utmost to encourage Harvard University Press in the continuance of this magnificent project. TSB #77.

Vol. III. (1826-1832), edited by William H. Gilman and
Alfred R. Ferguson. Cambridge: Harvard University Press,
1963.
Covers the years 1826-1832 including his engagement
and marriage to Ellen Tucker and her death, his
school-teaching, his Divinity School days, his pas-
torate of the Second Church in Boston, and his visit
to Florida. It covers years too early to have di-
ect reference to Thoreau, but it does contain vital
information on the philosophical background of Thoreau's time and the developing interest in Transcendentalism. This volume, as do the earlier ones,
displays the same careful scholarship and editorial
work. It is one of the major projects in American
literary scholarship and every student of American
literature owes it to himself to see that this tre-
mendous undertaking is encouraged in every possible
way. TSB #86.

Vol. IV. (1832-1834), edited by Alfred R. Ferguson.
Cambridge: Harvard University Press, 1964.
This magnificent edition of Emerson's complete
journals and notebooks is gradually approaching the
period of his acquaintance with Thoreau, though it
has not as yet quite reached it. This volume does
however present important background material for a
study of the period, most of important of which is

Emerson's comments on his first trip abroad. This
edition continues to set a model for all such scholarly endeavors. TSB #89.

Vol. V. (1835-1838), edited by Merton Sealts. Cambridge: Harvard University Press, 1965.
This magnificent project, putting Emerson's complete journals and notebooks into print for the
first time, with such meticulous editing that the
handwritten manuscripts are all but recreated, pro-
ceeds on its way. This current volume has more
particular interest to Thoreauvians than the earlier ones because Thoreau himself here first appears
on the pages, the young scholar and neighbor fresh
from Harvard's halls. While no new passages on Thoreau turn up, some of the new passages on Transcendentalism will prove of particular value to the
scholar. TSB #93.

Vol. VI. (1824-1838), edited by Ralph Orth. Cambridge:
Harvard University Press, 1966.
Includes early miscellaneous notebooks with no
mention of Thoreau.

Vol. VII. (1838-1842), edited by A. W. Plumstead and
Harrison Hayford. Cambridge: Harvard University Press,
1969.
The latest installment of this magnificently edited complete edition of Emerson's journals. This
volume includes ten entries on Thoreau, several of
them unpublished in the earlier edition. This edition is absolutely indispensable to any student of
Thoreau. TSB #109.

--"Original Hymn," EMERSON SOCIETY QUARTERLY, I (Fall,
1955), 2.
Reproduces in facsimile broadside of "Concord Hymn"
used on July 4, 1837. Thoreau sang in the choir.

--"Thoreau," PACIFIC SPECTATOR, I (Autumn, 1947), 464-477.
A reprint of the funeral oration.

also in: THE LEAVEN OF DEMOCRACY, edited by C.
Eaton. New York: Braziller, 1964. pp. 365-374.

--THOREAU'S PENCILS: AN UNPUBLISHED LETTER FROM RALPH
WALDO EMERSON TO CAROLINE STURGIS. 19 MAY 1844.
Cambridge, Mass.: Houghton Library, January 6, 1944.
Houghton Library Brochure #4.

Engel, Eduard. GESCHICHTE DER ENGLISCHEN LITTERATUR VON
DEN ANFANGEN BIS ZUR GEGENWART. MIT EINEM ANHANG:
DIE NORDAMERIKANISCHE LITTERATUR, 4th ed. Leipzig:
? , 1897.
P. 529--considers Thoreau a New England version
of Rousseau or Diogenes and a political nihilist,

less important, as a writer, than Margaret Fuller.

Engelhardt, Eleanore. "Thoreau's Rite of Purification."
Marburg: Potodruck von E. Mauersberger, 1963.

Engle, John D., Jr. "To Thoreau (On Reading WALDEN),"
[Portland] SUNDAY OREGONIAN, December 14, 1952, p. 15.
A sonnet.

Engle, Paul. "Henry David Thoreau," NEW ENGLANDERS.   ?   :
Privately printed, (Prairie Press), 1940.
A sonnet.

    also in, WEST OF MIDNIGHT. New York: Random House,
1941. (Quoted from the magazine POETRY by the
GREENSBORO [N. C.] DAILY NEWS, November 23, 1941.)

Engler, Bertha and Ernst Frey, translators. HERBST, AUS
DEM TAGEBUCH VON HENRY DAVID THOREAU. Zurich: Bucher-
gilde Gutenberg, 1947.
A translation of H. G. O. Blake's AUTUMN (1891).

English Literary Society of Japan. CATALOGUE: EXHIBITION
OF NINETEENTH CENTURY AMERICAN LITERATURE. Kyoto
Imperial University, October 25-26, 1941. Kyoto:
The Society, 1941.
Catalog of the collection of Mr. Taro Nagasaki.
Much Thoreau material included.

Ensor, Allison. "Thoreau and the Bible--preliminary Considerations," EMERSON SOCIETY QUARTERLY, XXXIII (1963),
65-70.
Influence of King James version on Thoreau.

Erickson, Richard B. "Sounds of a New England Village,"
NEW ENGLAND GALAXY [Sturbridge, Mass.], IX (Winter,
1968), 3-9.
On Thoreau's notes on sounds.

Erisman, Fred. "T and the Texas Colonel," EMERSON SOCIETY
QUARTERLY, XXXI (1963), 48-49.

Estes, Eleanor. "The Organ Recital," THE MIDDLE MOFFAT.
New York: Harcourt Brace, 1942. pp. 27-59.
Children profit when adults read Thoreau on attics
and give away their stored junk. A story for children.

Estrada, Ezequiel Martinez. "De Los Hombres Libres: Henry
David Thoreau," LA PRENSA [Buenos Aires], June 16, 1957.

Eulau, Heinz. "Wayside Challenger--Some Remarks on the
Politics of Henry David Thoreau," ANTIOCH REVIEW, IX
(Winter, 1949), 509-522.
A provocative discussion of Thoreau's changing
attitude towards government.

EUROPE [Paris, France], XLV (Juillet-Aout, 1967).
Special issue devoted to Thoreau. Includes fol-
lowing (all in French): Roger Asselineau, "Un
Narcisse Puritan," pp. 149-157; Micheline Flak,
"L'Homme de Concord," pp. 158-162; Jean Normand,
"Les Ironies de la Solitude," pp. 162-169; Henry
Miller, "Henry David Thoreau," pp. 169-177; Micheline Flak, "Thoreau et Les Francais," pp. 177-
185; Walter Harding, "L'Influence de 'La Desobeissance Civile," pp. 186-204; H. D. Thoreau, "Plai-
doyer pour John Brown," pp. 204-210; Louis Simon,
"De Desobeir au Crime D'Obeir," pp. 210-219; J. P.
Raudnitz, "Thoreau ou L'Humus Retrouve," pp. 220-
224; H. D. Thoreau, [Various brief extracts], pp.
225-235; Laurence Vernet, "Apercu Bibliographi-
que," 236-238; Laurence Vernet, "Chronologie de la
Vie d'Henry-David Thoreau..." pp. 239-246.

review: "De Charles-Ferdinand Ramuz a Henry
David Thoreau," LE MONDE [Paris], Aout
24, 1967, by Yves Florenne.

Evans, Robert. "Blazing a Trail with Thoreau," BOSTON GLOBE,
September 11, 1960.
A series of articles telling of Evans' retracing
of Thoreau's WEEK journey.

Evans, Robert O. "Thoreau's Poetry and the Prose Works,"
EMERSON SOCIETY QUARTERLY, LVI (1969), 40-52.

"Excerpts from the Autobigraphy of David Loring, Sr,"
TSB #108, p. 7.

F., R. "Gogan Sensei talks on the Zen spirit of Emerson and Thoreau," EIGO SEINEN (THE RISING GENERATION), XLIII (May 15, 1920).

Fabre, Michel. "La Desobeissance Civile," EUROPE [Paris], XLVII (January, 1969), 214-217.

Fadiman, Clifton. "Alimentary," NEW YORKER (May 5, 1956), 37.
        A poem.

--"Reading I've Liked," HOLIDAY, XXXII (December, 1962), 18-19.

--"The Works of Thoreau," AMERICAN PANORAMA, edited by Eric Larrabee. New York University Press, 1957. p. 326.
        The Carnegie Corporation recently decided to distribute sets of 350 books "illustrative not only of good American writing but of the entire range of American thought" to various libraries of the British Commonwealth to aid in a better understanding of the American people. AMERICAN PANORAMA has been issued as a key to this set and each volume of the 350 is evaluated briefly by an outstanding American critic. Canby's edition of THE WORKS OF THOREAU was chosen as one of the 350, and Fadiman was asked to evaluate it. It is his conclusion that, "It is possible that he [Thoreau] will outlast all other American writers of the past 150 years."

Falk, Robert P., editor. AMERICAN LITERATURE IN PARODY. New York: Twane, 1955.
        Contains "The Circulating Library: 1850" (from WALDEN) by Thoreau, and "A Garland of Ibids for Van Wyck Brooks" by Frank Sullivan and "The Retort Transcendental" by E. B. White.

Fallon, Eugene A. "Walden Falling," RALEIGH [N. C.] NEWS AND OBSERVER, August 28, 1955.
        A poem?

Fasel, Ida. "Emily Dickinson's Walden," IOWA ENGLISH YEARBOOK, VII (Fall, 1962), 22-28.
        Thoreau's influence on Emily Dickinson.

Fauchereau, Serge. "Le Philosophe des Bois," LA QUINZAINE
        LITERAIRE [Paris], XLV (February 15, 1968), 11-12.
        On recent French publications on Thoreau.

Faverty, Frederic E. "He Walked Alone--to Immortality,"
        CHICAGO TRIBUNE, October 19, 1958.
        Brief essay on Thoreau.

Federn, Karl. ESSAYS ZUR AMERIKANISCHEN LITTERATUR. Halle:
        an der Saale, 1899.
                This book about American Transcendentalism devotes
                its final chapter to Thoreau. Like Knortz, Federn
                is enthusiastic about Thoreau's attack upon the con-
                ventional wisdom. Though Federn's viewpoint is bas-
                ically the same, his discussion is much more succinct.
                TSB #105.

Feidelson, Charles Jr. "Thoreau," SYMBOLISM AND AMERICAN
        LITERATURE. Chicago: University of Chicago Press, 1953.
        pp. 135-142.
                A weak analysis of Thoreau and his use of the
                organic principle. TSB #44.

    --"Three Views of the Human Person: THE SCARLET LETTER,
        WALDEN, and THE RED BADGE OF COURAGE," REPORTS AND
        SPEECHES OF THE SIXTH YALE CONFERENCE ON THE TEACHING
        OF ENGLISH. Yale University: Master of Arts in Teach-
        ing Program, 1960. pp. 47-52.

Feikema, Feike. BOY ALMIGHTY. St. Paul, Minn.: Itasca,
        1945.
                A novel about a TB sanitarium in which the pro-
                tagonist delights in reading Thoreau.

Fein, Richard J. "WALDEN and the Village of the Mind,"
        BALL STATE UNIVERSITY FORUM, VIII (Winter, 1967), 55-61.

Feinberg, Charles E. WALT WHITMAN: A SELECTION OF THE MANU-
        SCRIPTS, BOOKS AND ASSOCIATION ITEMS. Detroit: Public
        Library, 1955.
                A detailed description of Whitman's copy of Tho-
                reau's WEEK on p. 128.

Fenn, Mary R. "Concord Woods and Fields," TSB #95, pp. 2-3.

    --"Mr. Thoreau and Concord Today," NEW ENGLAND WILD FLOWER
        NOTES (Winter, 1968).

    --"Some New Concord Manuscripts," TSB #101, p. 8.
                Excerpts from letters written by Annie Bartlett
                to her brother Ned Bartlett.

    --TALES OF OLD CONCORD. Concord: Women's Parish Assoc.,
        1965.
                Includes "Centennial Observance of Thoreau's Death,
                May, 1962" and many delightful anecdotes about Tho-

reau and his contemporaries from the First Parish
records.

--"T's Centenary Observed in Concord," CONGRESSIONAL REC-
ORD, November 2, 1962.

--"A Walk with Thoreau," HORTICULTURE (July, 1962), p. 390.
Thoreau and wild flowers.

Fenton, John H. "Walden Pond Stirs New Dispute," NEW YORK
TIMES, July 22, 1967.
On shifting pond to state control.

Ferrando, Guido. H. THOREAU: E IL TRANSCENDENTALISMO AMER-
ICANO. Venice: La Nuova Italia, 1928.
A brief critical study with bibliography.

Ferrer, Jaun. "Enrique David Throeau," LE COMBAT SYNDICAL-
ISTE [Paris], April 4, 1968.
Text in Spanish.

Fertig, Walter L. "John Sullivan Dwight's Pre-publication
Notice of WALDEN," NEQ, XXX (March, 1957), 84-90.
Discovery of a hitherto unnoticed early review of
WALDEN.

Fiedler, Leslie A. THE RETURN OF THE VANISHING AMERICAN.
New York: Stein and Day, 1968.
Includes two long sections on Thoreau's comments
on Indians in A WEEK.

Figueira, Gaston. "Revision de Thoreau," EL DIA (supplemento
1671), [Montevideo, Uruguay], January 31, 1965.
Text in Spanish.

Filippo, Luis Di. "Henry David Thoreau," UNIVERSIDAD [Santa
Fe, Argentina], LIII (1962), 25-39.
Text in Spanish.

--"Thoreau y la Libertad Esencial del Hombre," CLARIN
[Buenos Aires], September 14, 1967.

Fincher, R. H. Letter to the editor, LIFE MAGAZINE (October
13, 1947).
Commentary on the Teale article, "Thoreau's Walden,"
LIFE MAGAZINE (September 22, 1947).

Findley, Francine. FROM WHAT DARK ROOTS. New York: Harper,
1950.
A novel which includes Thoreau as a character.

Fink, Jack E. "A Caveat for Journalists," WORD STUDY, XXXIX
(December, 1963), 7.
On Thoreau's use of the suffix "wise".

Finn, James, editor. PROTEST: PACIFISM AND POLITICS.

New York: Vintage, 1968.
Comments on Thoreau, passim.

Fiorino. AN APPROACH TO H. D. THOREAU. Catania: Tip. dell
'Universita, 1957.
Lecture read at the Fourth Seminar in American
Literature in Rome, on May 2, 1957. (Universita
di Catania. Facolta di Economia e Commercio. Anno
Accademico. Studi Linguistici. 1.).

"The Fire at Fairhaven Bay," TSB #32.
Article reprinted from the CONCORD FREEMAN of
May 3, 1844, p. 2.

Fischer, Ruth. "Thoreau," DARE, III (March, 1965), 8-9.
Brief article in a barbershop magazine on Thoreau's
non-conformity.

Fischer, Walther. "Henry David Thoreau (1817-1862) der
Dichter des 'Walden-Sees' (1854)," ARCHIV FUR DAS STUD-
IUM DER NEUEREN SPRACHEN UND LITTERATUREN BRAUNSCHWEIG,
CLXXXVI (September, 1949), 28-48.
A general introduction to Thoreau's life and
thought.

Fisher, Aileen and Olive Rabe. WE ALCOTTS. New York:
Atheneum, 1968.
"The story of Louisa M. Alcott's family as seen
through the eyes of 'Marmee,' mother of LITTLE
WOMEN." The book is aimed at a young adult audience and tends to be a bit sugary. Thoreau, quite
naturally, appears on a number of pages and is very
well presented. TSB #107.

Fitzhugh, Robert T. "Swapping Cultures," WALL STREET JOURNAL,
March 24, 1960.
On teaching WALDEN in Iran.

Flagg, Wilson. "Thoreau," BOSTON COURIER, October 21, 1883.

Flak, Micheline. "D. H. Thoreau: A Pioneer of Natural Life,"
LA NOUVELLE HYGIENE, LV (November, 1962).
In French.

--HENRY-DAVID THOREAU (1817-1862) OU "L'HOMME REVOLTE."
Paris: La Ruche Ouvriere, 1965.
A pamphlet study of Thoreau's significance. Text
in French. Originally a lecture given at the Foyer
Individualiste d'Etudes Sociales.

--"Henry D. Thoreau: le Desobeissant," PLANETE [Paris],
XL (Mai, 1968), 64-77.

--"Thoreau et les Francais," INFORMATIONS AND DOCUMENTS
[Paris: American Embassy], CCLIV (December 15, 1967),
20-25.

Flanagan, John T. "Henry Salt and His Life of Thoreau,"
    NEW ENGLAND QUARTERLY, XXVIII (June, 1955), 237-246.
    Salt's correspondence with his publisher.

Flatto, Edwin. THE NEW WALDEN. Laredo, Texas: South Pub-
    lishers, 1963.
        A food faddist's manual with quotations from Tho-
        reau.

Flaxman, Seymour. "Thoreau and Van Eeden," in DER FRIEDE:
    IDEE UND VERWIRKLICHUNG, edited by Erich Fromm et al.
    Heidelberg: ? , 1961. pp. 341-352.
        Describes a social experiment in Holland conducted
        by Frederik van Eeden, an admirer of Thoreau.

Fleck, Richard. "Annihilator of Distance," PALMS, PEAKS
    AND PRAIRIES. Francestown, N. H.: Golden Quill Press,
    1967.
        A poem on Thoreau.

--"A Note on Thoreau's Mist Verse," THOREAU JOURNAL QUAR-
    TERLY, I (July 1, 1969), 1-5.

--"Thoreau and Wildness," APPALACHIA (1964), 289-291.

--"Thoreau, Emerson, Whitman in the Western Wilderness,"
    JOURNAL OF AMERICAN NATURE STUDY SOCIETY (Spring, 1969),
    9-11.

--"Thoreau: A National Literature." Colorado State Uni-
    versity, 1961. Unpublished master's thesis.

--"Too Tame for the Chippeway," LIVING WILDERNESS, XXIX
    (Summer, 1965), 20-21.
        Thoreau and "the wild."

Floan, Howard R. "Emerson and Thoreau," THE SOUTH IN NORTH-
    ERN EYES 1831 to 1861. Austin: University of Texas Press,
    1958. pp. 51-70.
        It is Mr. Floan's thesis that most of our mid-19th-
        century Northern authors did not have a true pic-
        ture of the South available when they criticized
        the evils of slavery so harshly. Of Thoreau Floan
        says, "His information about the factual nature of
        Southern slavery was both limited and distorted,
        and his philosophy of extreme individualism was
        inadequate for a problem which called for co-opera-
        tive group action." (p. 63). But unlike the others,
        Thoreau's "attack was not directed at these few,
        however, whom he called 'far-off foes,' but at those
        in the North who were so enslaved by commerce that
        they were not capable of helping the Negro or the
        Mexican." (p. 66). Mr. Floan is unquestionably
        right that Thoreau had a prejudiced and second-
        hand view of the South, but he fails to give ade-
        quate weight to the moral issues involved. TSB #63.

81

Flynn, John J. Jr. "Two Days on the Concord and Merrimac," CONCORD JOURNAL, July 29, 1965.
  Retracing Thoreau's trip.

Foerster, Norman. "Henry David Thoreau: A Critical Sketch," WESTERN FIELD (April, 1906), 194-196.

  --"Thoreau and Old Concord," YALE REVIEW, VII (January, 1918), 430-431.

  --"Thoreau as a Poet," HARVARD MONTHLY (October, 1909), 18-22.

  --"Thoreau's Cabin at Walden Pond," PITTSBURGH DISPATCH, August 28, 1910.

Fogarty, Robert S. "A Utopian Literary Canon," NEW ENGLAND QUARTERLY, XXXVIII (September, 1965), 386-391.
  The Oneida Community comments on WALDEN and WEEK.

Forbes, Esther. O GENTEEL LADY. Boston: Houghton Mifflin, 1926.
  Novel of Boston life in the 1850's, with Thoreau as a minor character (pp. 284-285).

Ford, Arthur L. "A Correction of Thoreau Bibliography."
  A correction of the Thoreau chapter of Lewis Leary's EIGHT AMERICAN AUTHORS: A REVIEW OF RESEARCH AND CRITICISM.

  --"A Critical Study of the Poetry of Henry Thoreau."
  Bowling Green University, 1964. Unpublished doctoral dissertation.
  A reproduction of the abstract appears in TSB #106, p. 7.

Ford, Nick Aaron. "Henry David Thoreau, Abolitionist," NEW ENGLAND QUARTERLY, XIX (September, 1946), 359-371.
  Shows that Thoreau sympathized with the Abolitionists even though he never officially joined their ranks.

Fortas, Abe. CONCERNING DISSENT AND CIVIL DISOBEDIENCE. New York: Signet, 1968.
  Frequent comment on Thoreau's essay.

Fosdick, Raymond B. "Individualism in the Machine Age," NEW YORK TIMES, June 22, 1930.
  Thoreau's philosophy for moderns.

Foster, Charles Howell. A review of COLLECTED POEMS OF HENRY THOREAU, edited by Carl Bode. PHILOLOGICAL QUARTERLY, XXIII (January, 1944), 92-94.

  --, editor. BEYOND CONCORD: SELECTED WRITINGS OF DAVID ATWOOD WASSON. Bloomington: Indiana University Press,

1965.
> Wasson, one of the minor Transcendentalists, rent-
> ed the Texas house from the Thoreaus for several
> years and later mentioned Thoreau fairly frequently
> in his writings--not always favorably. Here is
> the first accurate biography of Wasson, with a num-
> ber of new details on his relationship with Thoreau,
> and a hearty selection from his writings that have
> not been readily available. Foster proposes that
> Wasson's later conservative position is an antidote
> for the extremes of Transcendentalism and that his
> association with Thoreau drove him to that position.
> TSB #93.

"Found Thoreau's Cabin Chimney," NEW YORK SUN, May 4, 1946
(Night edition only).
> Report of a lecture by R. W. Robbins.

Fox, Rod[ney]. "When Thoreau Looked at Iowa," THE IOWAN,
XII (Spring, 1964), 21-24.
> Account of Thoreau's brief visit to the state
> in 1861.

FRAGMENTS. [Thoreau number], III (July, 1965), 1-12.
> Includes Leonard Kleinfeld, "There is More Divin-
> ity in Man Than in God"; Micheline Flak, "Henry
> David Buddha"; Roland Robbins, "House Hunting for
> Thoreau"; H. S. Good, "Henry D's Influence";
> Gladys Hosmer, "Why the Thoreau Society?"; George
> Bringmann, "Thoreau's Civil Disobedience"; Arthur
> Volkman, "Brandywine"; S. A. Mayers, "Yes, Ishtar,
> There Are Individuals"; Jack Schwartzman, "Hermit
> of Disobedience"; Frank Chodorov, "Henry David
> Thoreau"; R. S. Dickens, "Civil Disobedience:
> Philosophy and Tactic"; Edwin Flatto, "Need for
> Sanity"; August Derleth, "Nocturnal Visit"; John
> Peterson, "The Outsiders."

> [Thoreau number], V (April, 1967), 1-12.
> With Articles by W. Harding, G. Ready, O. Johannsen,
> S. Mayers, M. Sherwood, L. Kleinfeld, B. Millard,
> J. Schwartzman, R. Ritchie, A. Borrello, L. Alcott,
> H. Lee.

Fraiberg, Louis. PSYCHOANALYSIS AND AMERICAN LITERARY CRIT-
ICISM. Detroit: Wayne State University Press, 1960.
> Analysis of Ludwig Lewisohn's discussion of Thoreau,
> pp. 149-152.

Francis. "Henry David Thoreau," CHICAGO TRIBUNE, November
11, 1965.
> A poem.

Francis, Robert. "Either Or," MASSACHUSETTS REVIEW, VI
(Spring, 1965), 455.
> Thoreau's opinions on genius.

--"Of Walden and Innisfree," CHRISTIAN SCIENCE MONITOR,
  November 6, 1952.
  A comparison of Thoreau and William Butler Yeats.

--"Thoreau's Mask of Serenity," FORUM, CVI (January, 1947),
  72-77.
  One of the best studies we've yet seen on the problems of the personality of Thoreau. Raises many
  extremely interesting questions. TSB #19.

Franco, Luis. "Hudson y Thoreau," ARGENTINA LIBRE, August
 7, 1941.
  An essay, later reprinted in REPERTORIO AMERICANO
  (Date unknown).

Frank, Waldo. "Henry David Thoreau," Suplemento Quincenal
 de LA PROTESTA [Buenos Aires], (July 30, 1930), 272-273.

--"Thoreau's WALDEN One Hundred Years," NEW YORK TIMES
  BOOK REVIEW, August 8, 1954, p. 7.

Frasconi, Antonio. A VISION OF THOREAU. New York: Spiral
 Press, 1965.
  One of the most beautiful volumes in Thoreau lit-
  erature. CIVIL DISOBEDIENCE illustrated with wood-
  cuts of Thoreau by one of our greatest artists.
  Edition limited to 530 copies. TSB #93.

French, Allen. "Thoreau," HISTORIC CONCORD, A HANDBOOK,
 ETC. Concord: Privately published, 1942. pp. 86-91.

Freniere, Emil A. "Henry David Thoreau, 1837-1847." Pennsylvania State University, 1961. Unpublished doctoral
 dissertation.

--"The Mountain Comes to Concord: Two New Letters from
  Alcott and Thoreau," TSB #75, pp. 2-3.
  The letters are reproduced in the text of the
  article.

Friedell, Egon. CULTURAL HISTORY OF THE MODERN AGE. New
 York: Knopf, 1932.
  On Thoreau's importance in Western culture--Vol.
  III, pp. 213-215.

Friesen, Victor Carl. "Sensuousness in Thoreau's Approach
 to Nature: Conclusion," TSB #103, p. 2.
  A chapter from a master's thesis.

FRIHUG. "Henry David Thoreau, 1862-1962, Til Minne,--Med
 Vyrdnad Og Takksemd," V (Mai, 1962), 1-12.
  The entire issue of this liberal Norwegian mag-
  azine is devoted to a centennial tribute.

Frisbie, Richard P. "Vacation from Quiet Desperation,"
 THE VOICE OF ST. JUDE, XXIV (July, 1958), 20-21.

Brief essay on Thoreau.

"From Walden Pond to Montgomery, Ala," BALTIMORE SUN, February 29, 1956.
        Editorial on use of civil disobedience in the South today.

"Frost and Thoreau: A Query," TSB #88, p. 4.
        Reprints portions of two letters from SELECTED LETTERS OF ROBERT FROST (15 July 1915, and 24 June 1922) in which WALDEN and Thoreau are mentioned.

Frost, Robert and Reginald Cook. "Thoreau's WALDEN," LISTENER [London, Eng.], LII (August 26, 1954), 319-320.
        Transcript of a BBC broadcast.

Frost, Ruth H. "Theo Brown, Friend of Thoreau," NATURE OUTLOOK (May, 1944), pp. 15-19.
        Notes on Thoreau's Worcester friend and possibly the first publication of the third copy of the Worcester portrait of Thoreau.

    --"Thoreau's Worcester Friends: II. Harrison G. O. Blake," NATURE OUTLOOK, III (May, 1945), 116-118.+
        A fine brief study of Thoreau's friend and editor.

    --"Thoreau's Worcester Friends: III. Thomas Wentworth Higginson: His Worcester Years," NATURE OUTLOOK, V (May, 1947), 4-7 passim.
        Another essay in this excellent series.

    --"Thoreau's Worcester Visits," NATURE OUTLOOK [Worcester, Mass.], (February, 1943), 9-15.
        Reprinted from WORCESTER SUNDAY TELEGRAM.

Frothingham, Octavius Brooks. TRANSCENDENTALISM IN NEW ENGLAND: A HISTORY. New York: Harper, 1959.
        Frothingham's book has long been considered the nearest thing we have to a standard history of Transcendentalism. Because Frothingham knew most of the Transcendentalists personally, his history has a peculiar value. But unfortunately it has been out of print for years and brought fabulous sums on the rare book market. Harper has performed a real service in bringing it back into print. It is true the book tends to slight Thoreau as an individual. But as a picture of Transcendentalist movement as a whole, of which Thoreau is a part, Frothingham's book has never been superseded. TSB #69.

Frye, Northrop. "Varieties of Literary Utopias," DAEDALUS, XCIV (Spring, 1965), 323-347.
        Extensive commentary on WALDEN.

Fukuda, Mitsuharu. "Thoreau in Japan," RISING GENERATION

[Tokyo], CXIII (October, 1967), 645-646.
Text in Japanese.

"The Funeral of Thoreau," BOSTON TRANSCRIPT, May 10, 1862.
Reprinted in facsimile in EMERSON SOCIETY QUARTERLY,
II (1956), 16-17.

Fussell, Edwin S. EDWIN ARLINGTON ROBINSON: THE LITERARY
BACKGROUND OF A TRADITIONAL POET. Berkeley: University
of California Press, 1954.
Much on Robinson's interest in Thoreau.

  --"Henry David Thoreau" and "Thoreau's Unwritten Epic,"
FRONTIER: AMERICAN LITERATURE AND THE AMERICAN WEST.
Princeton: Princeton University Press, 1965. pp. 175-
231 and 327-350.
A complex, difficult and often very obscure study
of Thoreau's use of the West, the frontier, and the
Indian as metaphor in his various works. Fussell
has some important things to say but it is a struggle to find out what they are. He approaches Thoreau with no sense of humor and thus, it seems to
me, often misses Thoreau's point. TSB #91.

"G. B. S. on Thoreau," TSB #29.
>Reproduced is a letter written by George Bernard Shaw, on Thoreau, to the secretary of the Thoreau Society.

G., D. "Walden Pond Restyled," CHICAGO TRIBUNE, April ?, 1951.
>A poem.

G., M. "On Reading Thoreau," CHRISTIAN SCIENCE MONITOR, April 24, 1946.
>A brief essay.

Gabriel, Ralph H. "Emerson and Thoreau," THE COURSE OF AMERICAN DEMOCRATIC THOUGHT. New York: The Ronald Press, 1943. pp. 39-51.

Gale, Robert L. BARRON'S SIMPLIFIED APPROACH TO THOREAU'S WALDEN. Woodbury, New York: Barron, 1965.
>Two-thirds of the volume is a summary of WALDEN to help lazy students avoid reading the book, but two chapters on the artistry and the ideas of the book are well done. TSB #94.

--EMERSON AND TRANSCENDENTALISM. Woodbury, New York: Barron, 1966.
>A "guide" to Transcendentalism with many references to Thoreau.

Gandhi, Mahatma. "Duty of Disobeying Laws," COLLECTED WORKS OF MAHATMA GANDHI. Government of India: Ministry of Information and Broadcasting, 1962. VI, 217-218 passim.
>Gandhi's comments on Thoreau.

[Garate, Justo]. "Entornoathoreau," NUEVA ERA [Tandil, Argentina], June 3, 1949.
>A brief essay on Thoreau.

Garber, Grederick. "Unity and Diversity in 'Walking,'" EMERSON SOCIETY QUARTERLY, LVI (1969), 35-40.

Gardner, Elizabeth. "Thoreau Lyceum Opens at Concord House Site," BOSTON GLOBE, December 12, 1966.

Gardner, Isabella. "To Thoreau on Rereading WALDEN," ATLANTIC MONTHLY, CXCI (May, 1953), 52.
>A poem.

also in: YALE REVIEW, XLV (September, 1955), 123.

Garfield, Alva Scott. "A Scott Map of Concord, Massachusetts,"
BOSTON HERALD, April 16, 1950.
A cartoon map with many Thoreau scenes.

Garrison, Joseph M. Jr. "John Burroughs as a Literary Critic:
A Study Emphasizing His Treatment of Emerson, Whitman,
Thoreau, Carlyle, and Arnold." Duke University, 1962.
Unpublished doctoral dissertation.

Gattego, Candido Perez. EL HEROE SOLITARIO EN LA NOVELA
AMERICANA. Madrid: Prensa Espanola, 196?.
Contains a chapter on Thoreau.

Gehr, Harmon M. "A Free Man Speaks to Our Time: On the 100th
Anniversary of the Death of Henry David Thoreau." Pasa-
dena, California: Throop Memorial Universalist Church
[1962], (mimeographed).
Text of a centennial sermon.

"The Gentle Rebel of Walden," NEWS FRONT [New York City], XII
(April, 1968), 36-39.

Gerecht, Asher. "Lives of Quiet Desperation," ESQUIRE (October, 1946), 123 passim.
A weird short story about a printer who suddenly
discovered Thoreau. TSB #108.

Gerstenberger, Donna L. "WALDEN: The House That Henry Built,"
EMERSON SOCIETY QUARTERLY, LVI (1969), 11-13.

Gibson, W. M. and E. H. Cady. "Editions of American Writers,
1963: A Preliminary Survey," PMLA, LXXVIII (September,
1963), 1-8.
On need for a new edition of Thoreau.

Gide, Andre. "An Imaginary Interview," NEW REPUBLIC (February 7, 1944).
Gide tells of his early interest in Thoreau.

Gierasch, Walter. "Bishop Hall and Thoreau," TSB #31.

"A Gift to Wellfleet," BOSTON DAILY GLOBE, June 14, 1958.
Editorial telling of gift of a portion of Thoreau's
CAPE COD MS to the town of Wellfleet, Massachusetts.

"Gifts of Mr. Leonard Kebler," LIBRARY OF CONGRESS QUARTERLY
JOURNAL OF CURRENT ACQUISITIONS, VI (May, 1949), 102-105.
Includes reproduction of one page of MS of a Thoreau college essay on "Whether the Government ought
to educate the children of those parents who refuse
to do it themselves." Also included in Mr. Kebler's
gifts was a first edition of A WEEK.

Gillespie, Paul G. "A Theological Investigation of Civil

Disobedience: With Special Reference to Henry David
Thoreau, M. K. Gandhi, and Martin Luther King, Jr."
New Orleans Baptist Theological Seminary, ? . Un-
published doctoral dissertation.

Gilley, Leonard. "Transcendentalism in WALDEN," PRAIRE
SCHOONER, XLII (1968), 204-207.

Gilman, Hannah. "Henry David Thoreau: The Gentle Rebel,"
MINKUS STAMP JOURNAL, II (1967), 17-18.

Giordan, Alma Roberts. "I, Henry, Too," NEW YORK TIMES,
September 28, 1945.
        A sonnet.

  --"Memo to Thoreau," CHRISTIAN SCIENCE MONITOR, June 27,
1968.
        A poem.

Gittleman, Edwin. JONES VERY: THE EFFECTIVE YEARS 1833-1840.
New York: Columbia University Press, 1967.
On relations of Thoreau and Very.

Glazier, Lyle. "Thoreau's Rebellious Lyric," EMERSON SOCIETY
QUARTERLY, LIV (1969), 27-30.
On "Smoke."

Gleason, Herbert W. "In the Wake of Thoreau's Home Made Boat,"
BOSTON TRANSCRIPT, August 5, 1922.

  --MAP OF CONCORD, MASS. Concord: Thoreau Lyceum, 1968.
        Reprint suitable for framing of map from 1906
        edition of Thoreau's WRITINGS.

  --THOREAU CALENDAR 1969. Concord: Thoreau Lyceum, 1968.
        A superb collection of the Gleason photographs of
        the Thoreau country on a 1969 calendar.

  --"Walden Pond in Thoreau's Day and Ours," BOSTON TRAN-
SCRIPT, December 31, 1924.

"Gleason's Map of Concord," TSB #10.
        The map is printed along with a brief explanation
        and the INDEX TO MAP OF CONCORD.

Gleyton, Marian. Reply to Flagg's essay of October 21, 1883.
BOSTON COURIER, November 4, 1883.

Glick, Wendell P. "CIVIL DISOBEDIENCE: Thoreau's Attacks
upon Relativism," WESTERN HUMANITIES REVIEW, VII (Winter,
1952-1953), 35-42.
        "A more carefully reasoned repudiation of util-
        itarianism does not exist in the entire canon of
        Thoreau's works."

  --"The Native Background of Thoreau's Early Radical Thought,"

REPORT TO THE AMERICAN LITERATURE GROUP. February 10, 1954, p. 8.
    Summary of an M. L. A. speech.

--"Thoreau and Garrisonian Abolitionism." Northwestern University [Chicago], 1950. Unpublished doctoral dissertation.

--"Thoreau and the 'Herald of Freedom'," NEW ENGLAND QUARTERLY, XXII (June, 1949), 193-204.
    Much new information on Thoreau and the abolitionist movement.

--"Three New Early Manuscripts by Thoreau," HUNTINGTON LIBRARY QUARTERLY, XV (November, 1951), 59-71.
    Prints, with enlightening comments, three hitherto unpublished book reviews which Thoreau wrote for his college classes. It includes reviews of (1) THE BOOK OF THE SEASONS; OR THE CALENDAR OF NATURE by William Howitt, (2) THE HISTORY OF THE PROGRESS AND TERMINATION OF THE ROMAN REPUBLIC by Adam Ferguson, and (3) SOME ACCOUNT OF THE LIFE AND WORKS OF SIR W. SCOTT by Allen Cunningham and FAMILIAR ANECDOTES OF SIR W. SCOTT by James Hogg. The manuscripts were found in Thoreau's "Index Rerum" which is in the Huntington Library. TSB #38.

--"Yeats' Early Reading of WALDEN," BOSTON PUBLIC LIBRARY QUARTERLY, V (July, 1953), 164-166.
    On the influence of Thoreau on W. B. Yeats.

--, editor. THE RECOGNITION OF HENRY DAVID THOREAU. Ann Arbor: University of Michigan Press, 1969.
    A selection of 45 critical essays on Thoreau from 1848-1966, ranging from well-known ones such as Emerson's funeral discourse to ones that only the specialist will have been acquainted with. The selection is judicious and representative of both favorable and unfavorable points of view. Brief running comments by Glick are illuminating. A handy survey of Thoreau criticism over the years. TSB #107.

Goldberg, Herbert. "Henry, why are you here?" LOOK MAGAZINE (April 30, 1968).
    A cartoon.

Goldcorn, Isaac. "The Individualist Poet-Philosopher," FORWARD. July 16, 1967. Text in Yiddish.

Golden, Harry. "Thoreau's Message: Ponder on America," PHILADELPHIA BULLETIN, August 8, 1960.
    Essay on Thoreau's message for today.

--"We All Need a Bit of Solitude," CAROLINA ISRAELITE, XVIII (May-June, 1960), 20.

Thoreau teaches us the values of loneliness.

Golightly, John. "Lowell's Attack on Thoreau Delayed His
Fame," PITTSBURGH POST GAZETTE, January 5(?), 1967.

Gonnaud, Maurice. INDIVIDU ET SOCIETE DANS L'OEUVRE DE
RALPH WALDO EMERSON. Paris: Didier, 1964.
Much on Thoreau, passim.

Gordan, John D. FIRST FRUITS: AN EXHIBITION OF FIRST EDI-
TIONS OF FIRST BOOKS BY AMERICAN AUTHORS. New York:
New York Public Library, 1951.
Catalog of a Berg Collection exhibition. Pages
10-12, detailed comments on their seven copies
of A WEEK.

--"A Thoreau Handbill," NEW YORK PUBLIC LIBRARY BULLETIN,
LIX (May, 1955), 253-258.
Facsimile reproduction of the newly discovered
unique handbill advertising Thoreau as a surveyor,
with commentary.

Gottscho, Samuel H. "Thoreau and Wild Flowers," GARDEN
JOURNAL OF THE NEW YORK BOTANICAL GARDEN, VIII (November-
December, 1958), 185-189 passim.

translation: "Thoreau y las flores del campo,"
CENIT (November, 1962), pp. 3891-3894. Translated
into Spanish by V. Munoz.

--"Where the Wildflowers Grow," FLOWER GROWER, XLI (May,
1954), 52-54 passim.
The pleasures of a wild flower lover inspired
by Thoreau. Photographs of Concord wild flowers.

Gould, John. "Washstand to Posterity," CHRISTIAN SCIENCE
MONITOR, July 6, 1966.
On Thoreau's supposedly erecting his cabin in
relation to the vernal equinox.

Gozzi, Raymond D. "An Incoherent Sentence in WALDEN,"
TSB #95, pp. 4-5.

--"The Meaning of the 'Complemental Verses' in WALDEN,"
EMERSON SOCIETY QUARTERLY, XXV (1964), 79-82.

--"Tropes and Figures: A Psychological Study of David
Henry Thoreau." New York University, 1957. Unpublish-
ed doctoral dissertation.
A summary appears in TSB #58.

Graustein, Jeannette E. "Thoreau's Packer on Mt. Washington," APPALACHIA (June, 1957), pp. 414-417.
Identifies the packer who helped Thoreau on his
1858 trip as William H. H. Wentworth.

"The Grave of Henry Thoreau," TSB #37.
>An exact reprint of an article "Henry D. Thoreau"
by Joseph Darling Brown which appeared in SPRAGUE'S
JOURNAL OF MAINE HISTORY, III (January, 1916), 156-
157 and which was originally printed in a May 22,
1890 issue of the DISCATAQUIS OBSERVER.

Gray, Henry David. EMERSON: A STATEMENT OF NEW ENGLAND
TRANSCENDENTALISM AS EXPRESSED IN THE PHILOSOPHY OF ITS
CHIEF EXPONENT. New York: Ungar, 1958.
>The Ungar house has made a real contribution in
bringing back into print after more than 40 years,
this pioneer study of Transcendentalism. Although
the book is centered on Emerson, Thoreau is frequently mentioned, and the book is basic for an
understanding of Thoreau's philosophical background.
It is one of the best organized discussions of Transcendentalist thought, stating explicitly and clearly their views on religion, economics, morals, and
aesthetics. Its one fault is that it fails to take
into consideration the fact that none of the Transcendentalists was ever static in his thought, but
continually changed. TSB #65.

--"Thoreau Stirs Some Thoughts Down Memphremagog Way,"
MONTREAL STAR, July 6, 1968.

Gray, Leonard B. "The Attitudes of Emerson and Thoreau Towards Books." CONCORD JOURNAL, March 31, 1960.

--"Emerson and Thoreau," UNITY (January-February, 1952),
pp. 88-92.
>A provocative contrast of their lives and thoughts
and writings. "The changing conditions of living,
needs, tastes, and man's ability to appreciate will
likely continue to make the reputations of these
two great contemporaries go up and down and change
their relative places. (But) Emerson and Thoreau
belong together and to the ages." TSB #39.

--"The Growth of Thoreau's Reputation." TSB #42.

--"Henry Thoreau and the Transcendental Club," CONCORD
ENTERPRISE, November 20, 1952.
>Thoreau was too independent to be a typical Tran-
scendentalist.

--"Henry Thoreau--Great Individualist," THE CHRISTIAN
LEADER, CXXIV (January 17, 1942), 40-41.
>An appraisal of Thoreau's message by a Congre-
gational minister in Lynn, Massachusetts.

--"Let Thoreau Be Thoreau," CONCORD JOURNAL, May 21, 1942,
p. 7.

--"Thoreau's Famed WALDEN," WORCESTER [Mass.] TELEGRAM,

July 4, 1954.

--"Thoreau's Reading," CONCORD ENTERPRISE, December 31,
1953, p. 8.
>A lengthy discussion of Thoreau's reading, con-
cluding that "his reading and his living and his
writing were closely interrelated and interwoven."

"A Great Discovery at Walden Pond," TSB #15.

Green, David Mason. THE FRAIL DURATION: A KEY TO SYMBOLIC
STRUCTURE IN WALDEN. San Diego: San Diego State College
Humanities Monograph, Vol. I, No. 2, 1966.
>A close examination of the "symbolic structure of
Economy," "Where I Lived," and "Reading" as a clue
to the understanding of WALDEN as a whole. His
conclusions--for example, that "Economy is primarily
a negative "preface" to WALDEN, to which the remain-
der of the book is a positive reply--usually are to
the point. But his "evidence" often does more to
hurt than help his thesis because he persists in
reading "symbolic" intent into Thoreau's every word,
where there is often serious question as to whether
Thoreau had any such intent. (For example, that Thoreau was consciously emphasizing fire, air, earth
and water symbols). Perhaps he himself is conscious
of this weakness of the book, for he protests too
much with such phrases as "It would perhaps be rash
to assume..." or "Perhaps this is a way of saying..."
TSB #97.

Green, George W. "Thoreau," CATHOLIC WORLD (October, 1951), p.67.
>A poem.

Green, Gerald. THE LAST ANGRY MAN. New York: Pocket Books,
1959.
>A novel in which the central character frequently
quotes Thoreau.

Green, Maud Honeyman. "Raritan Bay Union, Eagleswood, New
Jersey," PROC. OF NEW JERSEY HISTORICAL SOCIETY, LXVIII
(January, 1950), 1-20.
>The first authoritative account of the colony which
Thoreau surveyed. Includes a reproduction of Tho-
reau's survey and much about his stay at the com-
munity.

"The Greenacre Lectures," BOSTON TRANSCRIPT, August 14, 1897.
>Sanborn comments on Thoreau.

Greenberg, Abe. "Cliff Robertson and Thoreau," TRIBUNE AD-
VERTISER [N. Hollywood, Calif.], January 25, 1968.
>On Thoreau as a hero of today's teen-agers.

An anonymous review of Greene, D. M. THE FRAIL DURATION,
EMERSON SOCIETY QUARTERLY, XLVIII (1967), 2.

"Greenwich Museum Shows Thoreauiana," NEW YORK SUN, July 20, 1945.
> A brief account of the exhibition.

Grenville, R. H. "Henry Thoreau," NEW YORK TIMES, September 10, 1953.
> A poem.

Gridley, Roy. "WALDEN and Ruskin's 'The White-Thorn Blossom'," EMERSON SOCIETY QUARTERLY, XXVI (1962), 31-34.
> Did Thoreau influence Ruskin?

Griffin, William J. "Thoreau's Reactions to Horatio Greenough," NEW ENGLAND QUARTERLY, XXX (December, 1957), 508-512.
> An explanation of why Thoreau damned Greenough in WALDEN.

Grimnes, Ole Kristian. THOREAU OG VAR EGEN TID. Oslo: De Forente Staters Informasjonstjeneste, [1962].

Griscom, Ludlow. BIRDS OF CONCORD. Cambridge: Harvard University Press, 1949.
> In his last years, Thoreau was much concerned with creating an "Atlas of Concord," including a complete record of all the flora and fauna of the region. Mr. Griscom's volume would certainly fulfill the requirements of the bird section of that atlas. Making use of Thoreau's bird notes, those of William Brewster at the turn of the century, and his own today, Mr. Griscom has compiled an impressive picture of Concord ornithology. It will be indispensable to all those who wish to study the reliability of Thoreau's bird records. Yet it is more than a mere scientific exercise. We found it an exceedingly provocative study. We do wish however to correct two minor factual errors. The famous summerless year (p. 38) was not 1832, but 1812. And the Fitchburg Railroad reached Concord not in 1855 (p. 56), but before Thoreau went out to Walden Pond in 1845. TSB #29.

Griswold, Erwin N. "Dissent--1968 Style," TULANE LAW REVIEW, XLII (June, 1968), 726.
> Includes a strong denunciation of Thoreau's CIVIL DISOBEDIENCE by the current United States Solicitor General.
>
> also in: WASHINGTON [D.C.] STAR, April 21, 1968.

Grobe, Albert and Stanley Newland. GREAT WRITERS: THOREAU. New York: Filmstrip House, [1965].
> Two 10-inch recordings, four filmstrips, and mimeographed script, all boxed, for teaching Thoreau on the high school level. Biographical section very well done. Discussion of his works a little on the

94

weak side. Recordings excellent. Filmstrips, a
series of water-color drawings, well done. TSB #93.

Groff, Richard. THOREAU AND THE PROPHETIC TRADITION. Los
Angeles: Manas Publishing Co., 1961.
An brief but very sympathetic and understanding
discussion of Thoreau's philosophy, placing him
in the tradition of the great prophets of the
past. TSB #91.

G[rondahl], I. C. "Henry David Thoreau," SANDEFIORDS BLAD
[Lordag, Norway], May 5, 1962.
Centennial tribute.

also in: VALDRES [Norway], May 5, 1962.

Groth, J. H. C. "German Backgrounds of American Transcendentalism." University of Washington, 1941. Unpublished
doctoral dissertation.

Gruber, Christian P. "The Education of Henry Thoreau, Harvard, 1833-1837." Princeton University, 1953. Unpublished doctoral dissertation.

Gruenert, Charles F. "Thoreau's Humor in Theory and Practice." University of Chicago, 1957. Unpublished
doctoral dissertation.

Gudzy, N. K. "Leo Tolstoj i Toro," RUSSKO-EVROPEJSKIE
LITERATURNYE SOJAZI: SBORNIK STATEJ K 70-LET IJU SO
DNJA ROZDENIJA AKADEMIKA M. P. ALEKSEEVA. Moscow:
Nauka, 1966. pp. 63-68.

Guidance Associates. CONCORD: A NATION'S CONSCIENCE. New
York: Harcourt, Brace, 1968.
An audio-visual aid aimed at high school literature
classes studying Emerson and Thoreau. The filmstrips are beautifully photographed. The recordings present a good introduction to the philosophy
of the two men, particularly of their social criticism. A worthwhile investment for high school
English courses. TSB #103.

Guilfoil, Kelsey. "The Thoreau Cultists--Are They Insane?"
CHICAGO TRIBUNE, December 1, 1946.
A diatribe against Thoreauvians, reprinted from an
issue of the Chicago Boswell Club publication THE
RAMBLER, where it was issued under the title "Al-
lergy to Thoreau." This article was answered briefly by the following letters in the TRIBUNE: December
8, 1946 by T. Longbaugh, Clara Edmunds Hemingway,
and B. G.; December 15, 1946 by R. L. Hanson; and
on December 29, 1946 by F. A. Tamorgana. For a
lengthier answer, see Harding, Walter. "A Defense
of Thoreau."

Guillet, Edwin C.   "Thoreau's Philosophy,"   TORONTO GLOBE AND MAIL, March ?, 1945.
     A brief letter to the editor commending Thoreau's philosophy.

Gullace, Giovanni.   "WALDEN e l'umorismo di Thoreau," REVISTA DI LETTERATURE MODERNE E COMPARATE [Firenze], XIV (September, 1961), 156-161.

Gundappa, DoVo.   "Thoreau," SWARAJYA [India], 1963 annual number.

Guthrie, Harold N.   "The Humor of Thoreau," Iowa University, 195?.   Unpublished doctoral dissertation.

Guttinger, Fritz.   HENRY DAVID THOREAU (1817-1862).   Zurich, Switzerland: Artemis, 1945.
     A leaflet, in German, issued in conjunction with their edition of WALDEN.

Guy, Don.   "Thoreau Followers Find Hut Expensive," BOSTON GLOBE, June 19, 1969.
     On building replica of Thoreau's cabin.

H., C. C. "Walden Centenary," NEW YORK SUN, September 6,
1947.
        Letter to editor giving a lengthy account of Tho-
        reau's leaving Walden Pond.

H., W. W. "Mt. Greylock Wilder Now than in Thoreau's Time,"
BOSTON HERALD, August 11, 1963.

Hackett, Peter. "Historic Sidelights," BLACKSTONE VALLEY
NEWS TRIBUNE [Whitinsville, Mass.], May 24, 1967.
        An essay on Thoreau on Cape Cod.

--"People Are Reading Thoreau," WORCESTER EVENING GAZETTE,
November ?, 1960.
        Letter to editor on Thoreau's election to Hall of
        Fame.

--"Thoreau Loved Cape Cod's Majestic Beauty, Walked Most
of It," BLACKSTONE VALLEY NEWS TRIBUNE, July 10, 1968.

--"Thoreau's Lasting Influence," WORCESTER TELEGRAM,
April 13, 1960.
        Brief essay.

--"Walk, Walk," WORCESTER SUNDAY TELEGRAM, June 23, 1963.
        On Thoreau as a hiker with particular details of
        his last trip to Cape Cod.

--"When Thoreau Declined a Diploma," WORCESTER EVENING
GAZETTE, May 9, 1961.
        Letter to editor.

Haedens, Kleber. "Pauvres 'Hippies'!" JOURNAL DU DIMANCHE
[Paris], February 11, 1968.
        On new French translations of Thoreau.

Hagenbach, Allen W. CAVE MOOD (THOREAU, ROUSSEAU AND JOHN,
THE BAPTIST REVIVE). Allentown, Pa.: Schlechter's Print-
ers, 1964.
        Amusing comments inspired by Thoreau and others.

--HUT MOOD (THOREAU TAUNTS "MONEY-CHANGER"). Allentown,
Pa.: Published by the author, 1964.
        An unusual little pamphlet commenting on life
        today seen through the eyes of a Thoreauvian.

Hague, William. LIFE NOTES OR FIFTY YEAR'S OUTLOOK. Boston:

Lee and Shepard, 1887.
    A Thoreau anecdote on page 187.

Hale, Christopher. "Self-Made Widow," NEW YORK DAILY NEWS,
    January 6, 1948.
        A serialized novel about a man who simplified his
        life inspired by "that cursed Thoreau."

Hale, Philip. "Lost--a Hound, a Bay Horse and a Turtle Dove,"
    BOSTON HERALD, January 3(?), 1918(?).
        A discussion of the famous passage in WALDEN.

Hall, James Norman. "A Belated Rebuttal." UNDER A THATCHED ROOF.
    Boston: Houghton Mifflin, 1942. pp. 105-116.

Hall, Leonard. "Time to Think," COUNTRY YEAR. New York:
    Harper, 1957. pp. 70-75.
        Brief essay on Thoreau.

Hall of Fame for Great Americans at New York University, The.
    UNVEILING OF THE BUST AND TABLET FOR HENRY DAVID THOREAU,
    edited by Milton Meltzer. New York: New York University,
    1962.
        Program for the ceremonies.

Halle, Louis J., Jr. SPRING IN WASHINGTON. New York: William
    Sloane, 1947.

Halperin, Irving. "Thoreau in Israel," UNIVERSITY COLLEGE
    QUARTERLY, XII (March, 1967), 13-18.
        Expansion of 94 article.

    --"Thoreau on Walking by Day and Night," CANADIAN AUDUBON,
    XXX (January, 1968), 1-4.

Hame, Robert A. "February, Thoreau, and Spring." RENDEZVOUS
    [Pocatello, Idaho], I (Winter, 1966), 23-26.

Hamilton, Franklin Willard. "Henry David Thoreau's Ideas
    For Self-Education of the Individual as Expressed in
    His JOURNAL, 1837-1862." University of Kansas, 1961.
    Unpublished doctoral dissertation.

    --THOREAU ON THE ART OF WRITING. Flint, Mich.: Walden
    Press, 1967.
        A rather good collection of Thoreau's comments
        on writing, style, sentence structure, word choice,
        etc., with a rather platitudinous running commen-
        tary. Final chapter a good summary of Thoreau's
        ideas on writing. TSB #99.

Hammel, Lisa. "The Concord of the Philosophers," NEW YORK
    TIMES, August 23, 1959.
        A tour of Concord including the Thoreau sites.

Hand, Harry E. "Thoreau at One Hundred and Fifty," HARTWICK REVIEW [Oneonta, N. Y.], IV (Spring, 1968), 52-55.

Hanley, Katherine. "WALDEN--Forest Sonata," AMERICAN TRANSCENDENTALIST QUARTERLY, I (1969), 108-110.

Hanley, Wayne. "Geologist Thinks Walden Pond Born Almost as Indians Thought," BOSTON HERALD, January 15, 1956.
On geological formation of Walden Pond.

--"Thoreau Started It," BOSTON HERALD, December 27, 1964.
Thoreau's pioneering in conservation.

Hansen, Arlen and Daniel Smythe. "Unfinished Debates," CHRISTIAN SCIENCE MONITOR, January 22, 1965.
A dialogue on indvidualism and collectivism citing Thoreau.

Hansen, Harry. "Morgan Library Dusts Off Thoreau," CHICAGO TRIBUNE MAGAZINE OF BOOKS, October 14, 1956, p. 8.
Account of exhibition.

Harber, Kenneth. "Birthday Letter," CAPE CODDER, January 27, 1949, p. 1 passim.
Long excerpts from CAPE COD and WALDEN.

--"Preliminary Check-List of the Editions of CAPE COD," TSB #67.

Harding, Walter. "The Apple-Tree Table Tale," BOSTON PUBLIC LIBRARY QUARTERLY, VIII (October, 1956), 213-215.
Traces history of the legend Thoreau quotes in last chapter of WALDEN.

--"A Bibliographical Ghost," TSB #105.
Points out an error in Francis Allen's BIBLIOGRAPHY OF HENRY DAVID THOREAU.

--"A Bibliography of Thoreau in Poetry, Fiction, and Drama," BULLETIN OF BIBLIOGRAPHY, XVIII (May-August, 1943), 15-18.

--"A Bee-Line With Thoreau," NATURE OUTLOOK (February, 1945), 20-21.
A brief essay on Thoreau's favorite method of hiking. In this same issue there is also an essay by Richard C. Potter on "The Concord River" only briefly mentioning Thoreau but telling much of one of his favorite haunts.

--"C. P. Snow and Thoreau," TSB #70.
Snow expresses his opinion of Thoreau in a letter to Harding.

--"C. T. Jackson on Thoreau," TSB #68.
An obituary of Thoreau written by Dr. C. T. Jackson and published in the PROCEEDINGS OF THE BOSTON

SOCIETY OF NATURAL HISTORY, IX (1862-1863), 70-72.

--A CENTENNIAL CHECK-LIST OF THE EDITIONS OF HENRY DAVID
THOREAU'S WALDEN. (Charlottesville: University of Virginia Press for the Bibliographical Society of the University of Virginia, 1954.)
> The modest cover of the Harding check-list is de-
> ceptive. The severely plain cloth binding, in
> color somewhere between Quaker gray and Walden
> blue--a combination Thoreau would have liked,
> covers a book that is as complete as careful schol-
> arship and indefatigable collecting can make it.
> Readers of the Thoreau Society Bulletin need not
> be told that Walter Harding leaves no unconsidered
> trifle out of his consideration nor any overlooked
> bit of Thoreauana anywhere in the world overlooked
> longer than it takes to get an investigatory letter
> there. Here is completeness and accuracy. It is
> a check-list, so the books listed are not collated;
> nor are titles of each item printed, so the slight
> variations in word or punctuation among titles of
> WALDEN are not recorded. It might have been better
> to have omitted separate printings of short select-
> ions from WALDEN. And one might quibble that an-
> thologies of Thoreau writings which include even
> the entire text of WALDEN are not editions of WAL-
> DEN. But no one will quibble about a check-list
> that includes all the WALDENS there have ever been
> and then adds these other things for good measure.
> Particularly, no one will quibble when he can
> praise a book as well compiled and as well printed
> as this one. TSB #46, by Raymond Adams.
>
> also in, BIBLIOGRAPHICAL SOCIETY OF UNIVERSITY
> OF VIRGINIA SECRETARY'S NEWS SHEET #28 (September,
> 1953), Supplement.
>
> reviews: BULLETIN OF BIBLIOGRAPHY, XXI (September,
> 1954), 103.
> ETUDES ANGLAISES, VIII (Avril, 1955).

--"A Century of Thoreau," AUDUBON MAGAZINE, XLVII (March-
April, 1945), 80-84.
> The widening influence of Thoreau.

--"A Century of WALDEN," COLORADO QUARTERLY, III (Autumn,
1954), 186-199.
> An analysis of WALDEN and its influence over the
> last century.

--"A Check-List of Thoreau's Lectures," BULLETIN OF THE
NEW YORK PUBLIC LIBRARY, LII (February, 1948), 78-87.
> A listing of all Thoreau's known lectures giving
> title, date, place, audience reaction, text, etc.
> Two additions to be made since this was published:
> The October 8, 1854 lecture was on "Moonlight", and

October 9, 1859 lecture (on "Life Misspent").

--CIVILIZED DISOBEDIENCE. Geneseo, N. Y.: State University College, 1968.
Thoreau's ideas and campus rebels today.

--"The Correspondence of Henry David Thoreau, 1836-1849." Rutgers University, 1950. Unpublished doctoral dissertation.

--"The Correspondence of Sophia Thoreau and Marianne Dunbar." TSB #33.
Article includes a check-list of letters.

--"The Corruption of WALDEN," TSB #98, pp. 5-6.
Discusses the corruption of WALDEN from the first edition to the first American reprinting during preliminary work for the new edition of Thoreau's works.

--"Daniel Ricketson's Copy of WALDEN," HARVARD LIBRARY BULLETIN, XV (October, 1967), 401-411.
Reproduces a hitherto unpublished cartoon of Thoreau by Ricketson.

--THE DAYS OF HENRY THOREAU. New York: Alfred A. Knopf, 1965.

reviews: AMERICA (January 1, 1966).
AMERICAN LITERATURE (November, 1966).
ATLANTA [Ga.] JOURNAL, November 21, 1965.
AUDUBON MAGAZINE (September, 1966).
BOOK OF THE MONTH CLUB NEWS (July, 1966).
BOSTON GLOBE, February 20, 1966.
BOSTON HERALD, December 26, 1965.
BRIDGEPORT [Conn.] POST, February 13, 1966.
BUFFALO EVENING NEWS, November 13, 1965.
CHICAGO DAILY NEWS, November 27, 1965.
CHICAGO TRIBUNE, November 21, 1965.
CHRISTIAN CENTURY, March 9, 1966.
CHRISTIAN SCIENCE MONITOR, February 10, 1966.
CLEVELAND PLAIN DEALER, November 14 and 16, 1965.
CONCORD JOURNAL, November 11, 1965.
DALHOUSIE REVIEW (Autumn, 1966).
DANBURY [Conn.] NEWS-TIMES, February 26, 1966.
DETROIT BOOK NEWS, December 5, 1965.
EMERSON SOCIETY QUARTERLY, XLV (1966), 98.
ETUDES ANGLAISES, VIII (Avril, 1965).
GENESEO LAMRON, February 18, 1966.
HARTFORD COURANT, September 25, 1966.
HOUSTON CHRONICLE, January 30, 1966.
INDIANAPOLIS STAR, December 26, 1965.
LIBRARY JOURNAL (December 1, 1965).
LIVING WILDERNESS (Autumn, 1966).

LONG BEACH [Cal.] INDEPENDENT, December
29, 1965.
LONG BEACH [Cal.] PRESS TELEGRAM, December
28, 1965.
MADISON CAPITAL TIMES, November 18, 1965.
MIDDLEBURY COLLEGE NEWS LETTER (Spring,
1966).
MONTREAL STAR, January 15, 1966.
NEW ENGLAND QUARTERLY (March, 1967).
NEW HAVEN REGISTER, January 2, 1966.
NEW YORK HERALD TRIBUNE, November 28, 1965.
NEW YORK TIMES, November 16 and December
26, 1965.
NEW YORKER (January 15, 1966).
OMAHA WORLD HERALD, December 5, 1966.
OTTAWA [Ont.] JOURNAL, November 20, 1965.
PLATTSBURGH [N. Y.] PRESS-REPUBLICAN,
March 5, 1966.
PORTLAND [Me.] TELEGRAM, November 28, 1965.
PROVIDENCE JOURNAL, April 17, 1966.
ROCHESTER DEMOCRAT CHRONICAL, January 15,
1966.
ST. LOUIS POST DISPATCH, December 26, 1965.
SAN FRANCISCO EXAMINER, CHRONICLE, June
12, 1966.
SATURDAY REVIEW OF LITERATURE (January 15,
1966).
SCIENCE AND SOCIETY (Summer, 1966).
SOUTH ATLANTIC QUARTERLY (Spring, 1967).
SPRINGFIELD [Mass.] REPUBLICAN, December
19, 1965.
STUDIES IN ENGLISH LITERATURE [Tokyo]
(October, 1966).
SUNDAY OREGONIAN, December 26, 1965.
TIME MAGAZINE (January 14, 1966).
TSB #94, by J. L. Shanley. An extended
review.

--"A Defense of Thoreau," CHICAGO TRIBUNE, December 1, 1946.
    A lengthy reply to Mr. Guilfoil's article.

        also in: YANKEE, XI (March, 1947), 26-27. A
        slightly revised reprinting.

--"'Delugeous' or 'Detergeous'," CEAA NEWSLETTER, I (March,
    1968), 5-6.
        On a word in Thoreau's essay on Carlyle.

        also in: TSB #101, p. 5.

--"Did Thoreau Invent the Term 'Civil Disobedience',"
    TSB #103, p. 8.

--"Do You Recognize Thoreau's Style?," TSB #36.

--"An Early Thoreau Club," TSB #77, pp. 3-4.

--"Emerson, Thoreau, and Transcendentalism," AMERICAN
LITERARY SCHOLARSHIP: AN ANNUAL: 1963, edited by James
Woodress. Durham: Duke University Press, 1965. pp. 3-16.+
A bibliography with comments.

--"Einstein on Gandhi and Thoreau," TSB #45.

--EMERSON'S LIBRARY. Charlottesville: University of Virginia Press, 1967.
Lists many Thoreau books.

--"First Thoreau Edition Volumes to Printer," CHRONICA
[Albany, N. Y.], II (November, 1968), 8-11.

--"Five Ways of Looking At WALDEN," MASSACHUSETTS REVIEW,
IV (Autumn, 1962), 149-162.

translation: "Walden--Piec Interpretacji," TEMATY,
II (Lato, 1963), 129-145. Translated into Polish.

--"Franklin B. Sanborn and Thoreau's Letters," BOSTON
PUBLIC LIBRARY QUARTERLY, III (October, 1951), 288-293.
Sanborn "performed a major service by preserving
in print many Thoreau manuscripts which have since
disappeared and which would otherwise have been
totally lost. But one should approach his work
with caution, realizing that the product is not
pure Thoreau, but rather a Sanbornized Thoreau."
Prints for the first time the original text of
Thoreau's letter to Greeley of May 19, 1848.

--"Frederic Tudor and Walden Pond," TSB #105, p. 8.
Includes an excerpt from the BOSTON TRANSCRIPT
for July 23, 1927.

--"Gandhi and Thoreau," TSB #23.

--"Gene Tunney on Thoreau," TSB #31.
Reprinted from the SATURDAY EVENING POST, May 24,
1941, is an anecdote by Tunney about Thoreau; also
printed is a letter from Tunney to Walter Harding.

--"A Gift from Walden Woods," HOME GARDEN (December, 1967),
29-36.
Unpublished Gleason photographs of the Thoreau
country.

--"The Grave of Thoreau," TSB #69.
A 'photographic reproduction of the drawing' of
Hawthorne's grave in which Thoreau's earlier grave
stone is visible. The drawing originally appeared
in Horatio Bridge's PERSONAL RECOLLECTIONS OF NA-
THANIEL HAWTHORNE. New York: Harper, 1893. p. 180.

--"Harvard Statutes and Laws: Some Footnotes on Thoreau's
College Days," TSB #34.

--"Henry D. Thoreau," NATIONAL WILDLIFE, V (December, 1966), 38-39.

--"Henry D. Thoreau, Instructor," EDUCATIONAL FORUM, XXIX (November, 1964), 89-97.

--"Henry David Thoreau: Philologist," WORD STUDY, XIX, 4 (1944), 7.

--"Henry David Thoreau: WALDEN: OR, LIFE IN THE WOODS," LANDMARKS OF AMERICAN WRITING, edited by Hennig Cohen. New York: Basic Books, 1969. pp. 134-143.

--HENRY DAVID THOREAU'S WALDEN AND CIVIL DISOBEDIENCE: A STUDY GUIDE. Bound Brook, N. J.: Shelley Publishing Co., 1963.
>A guide to Thoreau through questions, biographical sketch, and anthology of criticisms.

>reviews: CONCORD JOURNAL, March 21, 1963.
>WESTERN HUMANITIES REVIEW, XVIII (Summer, 1964), 288-289.

--"Henry Thoreau and Ellen Sewall," SOUTH ATLANTIC QUARTERLY, LXIV (Winter, 1965), 100-109.

>translation: "Henry Thoreau and Ellen Sewall," translated into Japanese by Koh Kasegawa. SHI TO SAMBUN [Tokyo], XIII (April, 1966), 108-115.

--"Henry Thoreau, Ghost Writer," TSB #38.
>Contains an excerpt of an article by Alfred Barron in FOOT NOTES OR WALKING AS A FINE ART which was printed in 1875 by the Wallingford Printing Company in Wallingford, Connecticut.

--"Henry Thoreau: Our American Saint Francis," OUR DUMB ANIMALS, LXXVI (May, 1943), 93.
>On Thoreau's friendship with animals.

--"Hound, Bay Horse, and Turtledove," LITERARY SYMBOLISM, edited by Maurice Beebe. San Francisco: Wadsworth, 1960. pp. 59-62.
>Discussion of the WALDEN image.

--"La Influencia de 'Desobediencia Civil'," translated into Spanish by V. Munoz. RECONSTRUIR [Buenos Aires], XXXIX (December, 1965), 41-50.

--"The Influence of Thoreau's Lecturing upon His Writing," BULLETIN OF NEW YORK PUBLIC LIBRARY, LX (February, 1956), 74-80.
>Comparison of lecture and book versions of A WEEK.

--"Jack London and Thoreau," TSB #57.
>Describes a short story by London in which Thoreau is mentioned.

--"A Late Revision in Thoreau's WALDEN," BIBLIOGRAPHICAL
SOCIETY OF UNIVERSITY OF VIRGINIA SECRETARY'S NEWS SHEET
#25 (November, 1952).
    An indication that Thoreau made additions to the
    text of WALDEN even after it was set in type.

--Letter to the editor, NEW YORK HERALD TRIBUNE, June
8, 1945.
    A reply to M.S.N.'s letter of May 25, 1945.

--Letter to the editor, NEW YORK SUN, April 27, 1945.
    The cairn controversy.

--MR. THOREAU DECLINES AN INVITATION. Richmond, Va.:
Attic Press, 1956.
    Edition limited to 135 copies. Introduction by
    John L. Cooley. Prints, for the first time, Tho-
    reau's letter of December 18, 1853 to the Associa-
    tion for the Advancement of Science, with facsim-
    iles of the letter and the accompanying blank
    filled in by Thoreau.

--"A New Edition of Thoreau," TSB #97, p. 1.

--"A New Sophia Thoreau Letter," TSB #87, p. 4.
    A copy of a letter from Sophia Thoreau to Edmund
    Hosmer is printed.

--"On Teaching WALDEN," EMERSON SOCIETY QUARTERLY, XVIII
(1960), 11-12.

--"A Preliminary Checklist of the Editions of WALDEN," TSB #39.

--"Recent Scholarship on Emerson and Thoreau," THE TEACHER
AND AMERICAN LITERATURE, edited by Lewis Leary. Cham-
paign, Ill.: National Council of Teachers of English,
1965. pp. 81-88.
    Recent scholarship reviewed for high school teach-
    ers.

--A REFERENCE INDEX TO ACCOMPANY THOREAU: MAN OF CONCORD.
New York: Holt, Rinehart and Winston, 1961.

--"The Significance of Thoreau's WALDEN," HUMANIST, V
(Autumn, 1945), 115-121.
    A centennial essay.

--"Some Forgotten Reviews of WALDEN," TSB #46.

--"Some Unfamiliar Glimpses of Thoreau," TSB #69.

--"A Source for a Walden Anecdote," TSB #87.

--"This is a Beautiful World," AMERICAN HERITAGE, XIV

(December, 1962), 106-112.

--"Thoreau," THE WORD [Glasgow, Scotland], VIII (October, 1946), 21.
> An essay on Thoreau as a social philosopher.

> also in: THE BEACON [Melbourne, Austr.] (January, 1947).

--"Thoreau and Bird Songs Celestial," AUDUBON MAGAZINE, XLVI (July, 1944), 234-236.
> Notes on Thoreau's bird lore.

--"Thoreau and the Concord Lyceum," TSB #30.

--"Thoreau and 'Ecology' Correction," SCIENCE , CXLIX (August 13, 1965), 707.
> Thoreau said "geology" not "ecology" in his letter of January 1, 1858.

--"Thoreau and Horace Greeley," TSB #11.
> Reprints articles from the TRIBUNE concerning Thoreau, including: August 2, 1854 (article on slavery in Massachusetts accompanied by editorial by Greeley), August 9, 1854 (ad for WALDEN), July 29, 1854 (digest of WALDEN not printed in TSB #11), and May 10, 1862 (a Thoreau obituary).

--"Thoreau and the Kalmucks: A Newly Discovered Manuscript," NEW ENGLAND QUARTERLY, XXXII (March, 1959), 91-92.
> Text and commentary on a brief unpublished manuscript.

> translation: "Thoreau y Los Calmucos," translated into Spanish by Vladimir Monoz. VOLUNTAD [Montevideo, Uruguay], IV (September, 1959), 4.

--"Thoreau and Kate Brady," AMERICAN LITERATURE, XXXVI (November, 1964), 347-349.

--"Thoreau and Mann on the Minnesota River, June, 1861," MINNESOTA HISTORY, XXXVII (June, 1961), 225-228.

--"Thoreau and the Negro," NEGRO HISTORY BULLETIN (October, 1946).
> On Thoreau's life-long fight for the Negro's freedom.

> translations: "Thoreau y Los Negros," translated into Spanish by V. Munoz. VOLUNTAD [Montevideo, Uraguay], III (March, 1959), 32.

> Translated into Japanese by Koh Kasegawa. SHI TO SAMBUN [Tokyo], XVII (May, 1968), 47-50.

--"Thoreau and the 'Seven Years Itch ,'" AMERICAN SPEECH,

XXIX (October, 1954), 237.
Points out that the citation of this phrase in
WALDEN precedes the earliest DAE entry by forty
years.

--"Thoreau and Timothy Dwight," BOSTON PUBLIC LIBRARY QUAR-
TERLY, X (April, 1958), 109-115.
The influence of Dwight's TRAVELS on Thoreau.

--"Thoreau and the Worcester Ministers," NATURE OUTLOOK,
IX (Spring, 1951), 12-14 passim.
An excursion to the White Mountains by eight Worcester ministers and the little-known letter of
advice which Thoreau wrote to them.

--"Thoreau as Seen by Fredrika Bremer," TSB #54.
A collection of letters published in 1854 titled
THE HOMES OF THE NEW WORLD: IMPRESSIONS OF AMERICA.
New York: Harper, and translated into English from
Scandanavian by Mary Howitt. On pp. 166-167 there
is a paragraph concerning Thoreau.

--"Thoreau at the Boston Music Hall," TSB #105, p. 7.
A review by Daniel Ricketson of a Thoreau lecture given on October 9, 1859 is included.

--"Thoreau at Fire Island," TSB #41.
Contains four excerpts from the NEW YORK TRIBUNE
about Thoreau's visit which appeared on July 25,
1850, July 26, 1850, July 29, 1850, and July 30,
1850.

--"Thoreau at Harvard," HARVARD ALUMNI BULLETIN, LXVI
(March 21, 1964), 468-473.
A chapter from the forthcoming biography.

--"Thoreau at Walden," BULLETIN OF THE ENGLISH LITERATURE
SOCIETY OF HIROSHIMA JOGAKUIN COLLEGE, IX (1965), 1-10.

--"Thoreau Attends Quaker Meeting," FRIENDS INTELLIGENCER,
CI (May 6, 1944), 298-299.

--"Thoreau: The Camper in the Back Yard," HORIZON, VI
(Autumn, 1964), 32-39.
The 1964 Thoreau Society Presidential Address.
Includes a hitherto unpublished drawing of Tho-
reau by Edward Emerson.

--A THOREAU HANDBOOK. New York: New York University Press,
1959. [1961-paper].

    reviews: AMERICAN LITERATURE, XXXII (March, 1960),
             89-90.
             AMERICAN MIDLAND NATURALIST (January, 1960).
             BOOKSELLER (September, 1959).
             CLEVELAND PLAIN DEALER, September 20, 1959.

COLLEGE AND RESEARCH LIBRARIES, XXI
(July, 1960).
CONCORD JOURNAL, August 20, 1959.
GENESEO [N. Y.] LAMRON, October 13, 1959.
GENESEO [N. Y.] LIVINGSTON REPUBLICAN,
October 15, 1959.
HOGAKUZASSI [Journal of Law and Politics,
Osaka City University], VII (1960), 1-42,
by Tokihiko Yamasaki.
LATEST BOOKS (October, 1959).
LIBRARY JOURNAL (August, 1959).
LOUISVILLE COURIER JOURNAL, October 18,
1959.
MASSACHUSETTS AUDUBON (November, 1959).
MODERN LANGUAGE NOTES, LXXV (December,
1960), 711-715.
NATIONAL GUARDIAN, December 28, 1959.
NEW LEADER, November 2, 1959.
PUBLISHERS WEEKLY (September 21, 1959).
ROCHESTER TIMES UNION, October 3, 1959.
SAN FRANCISCO CHRONICLE, November 15, 1959.
SCHOLARLY BOOKS IN AMERICA (August, 1959).
THOREAU SOCIETY BULLETIN #69. by J. L.
Shanley. An extended review.
VIRGINIA QUARTERLY REVIEW (Winter. 1960).
WALT WHITMAN REVIEW (December. 1959).
WESTERN HUMANITIES REVIEW (Autumn, 1959).

--"Thoreau in Japan," TSB #90.
    An account of Harding's lecture series in Japan.

--THOREAU: MAN OF CONCORD. New York: Holt, Rinehart and
  Winston, 1960.
    Although designed primarily as a textbook for col-
    lege students, this volume will interest all Thor-
    eauvians. It is a discriminating "selection...of
    eyewitness reports on Thoreau by his contemporaries".
    It draws on 185 documents and includes reports of
    108 identified writers plus a number of "Anons."
    Not the least of its virtues is the fact that Hard-
    ing has included unfavorable as well as favorable
    opinions; too often the devil's advocate's arguments
    are omitted from reports of "Saint Henry." Much of
    the material will not, of course, be new to mature
    students of Thoreau, but there is excitement in read-
    ing together many vividly concrete accounts of how
    his contemporaries saw and heard him. The "List of
    Documents" and "Biographical Notes on the Authors"
    are helpful.--J. L. Shanley. TSB #74.

    reviews: CONCORD JOURNAL, November 10, 1960.
             COLLEGE ENGLISH, XXII (February, 1961),
             370.
             COMPOSITION AND COMMUNICATION, XII (Decem-
             ber, 1961), 257.

--"Thoreau on the Concord Muster, 1859," THE MONTH AT GOODSPEEDS, XXXIX (April, 1968), 171.

--"Thoreau on the Lecture Platform," NEW ENGLAND QUARTERLY, XXIV (September, 1951), 365-374.
     "He could amuse his audiences and they enjoyed him thoroughly. But he did not have sufficient platform appeal to get across his more abstruse thoughts unless he was roused enough to forget all self-consciousness and deliver a ringing address."

--"Thoreau: Pioneer of Civil Disobedience," FELLOWSHIP, XII (July, 1946), 118-119 passim.
     A centennial essay on the significance of Thoreau's prison experience.

--"Thoreau's CIVIL DISOBEDIENCE," THE COMPASS [West Campton, N. H.] (February, 1943), pp. 13-14 passim.
     Page 12 contains a drawing of Thoreau in jail.

--"Thoreau's Fame Abroad," BOSTON PUBLIC LIBRARY QUARTERLY, IX (April, 1959), 94-101.
     The gradual rise of Thoreau's fame in Europe and Asia.

--"Thoreau's Feminine Foe," PMLA, LXIX (March, 1954), 110-116.
     The first biographical study of the woman who proposed marriage to Thoreau.

--THOREAU'S MINNESOTA JOURNEY, an anonymous review of. MINNESOTA HISTORY (September, 1963).

--"Thoreau's Professor has His Say," TSB #46.
     A criticism by C. C. Felton of Thoreau's translation of THE PROMETHEUS AND AGAMEMNON OF AESCHYLUS.

--"A Thoreauvian in Europe," INTERNATIONAL EDUCATIONAL AND CULTURAL EXCHANGE, IV (Summer, 1968), 1-5.

--"A Thoreauvian in Japan," INTERNATIONAL EDUCATIONAL AND CULTURAL EXCHANGE (Fall, 1965), pp. 20-24.

--"Two F. B. Sanborn Letters," AMERICAN LITERATURE, XXV (May, 1953), 230-234.
     On Thoreau's appointment to an examining committee at Harvard and on the genesis of Channing's COUNTRY WALKING.

--"Uncle Charlie Comes to Concord," NATURE OUTLOOK, VII (Fall, 1948), 7-9.
     An essay on Thoreau's favorite bachelor uncle.

--"Walden: Experiment in Freedom," FREIE ARBEITER STIMME, June 29, 1945.
     A centennial tribute essay on Thoreau's love of

freedom. Translated into the Yiddish by Herman
Frank.

--"Walden's Philosopher as a Tutor of Children," CHRISTIAN
SCIENCE MONITOR, June 30, 1966.

--, editor. THOREAU: A CENTURY OF CRITICISM. Dallas:
Southern Methodist University Press, 1954.

    reviews: AMATEUR BOOK COLLECTOR, V (May, 1955), 14.
                AMERICAN LITERATURE, XXVII (May, 1955),
                291.
                CATHOLIC REVIEW SERVICE (June 6, 1955).
                CHARLOTTESVILLE [Va.] DAILY CAVALIER,
                December 14, 1954.
                CHARLOTTESVILLE [Va.] DAILY PROGRESS,
                December 14, 1954.
                CHICAGO TRIBUNE, January 30, 1955.
                COLLEGE ENGLISH, XVI (April, 1955), 467.
                DALLAS MORNING NEWS, May 1, 1955.
                DALLAS TIMES HERALD, January 2, 1955.
                MISSISSIPPI VALLEY HISTORICAL SOCIETY
                (June, 1955), 166.
                NEW ENGLAND QUARTERLY, XXVIII (June, 1955),
                274-275.
                NEWARK [N. J.] EVENING NEWS, December 30,
                1954.
                OMAHA WORLD HERALD, January 9, 1955.
                RICHMOND TIMES DISPATCH, March 13, 1955.
                SCIENTIFIC MONTHLY (June, 1955), 380.
                SOUTHWEST REVIEW, XL (Summer, 1955), x-xi.
                THOREAU SOCIETY BULLETIN #50, by Raymond
                Adams. An extended review.

--, editor. "Thoreau in the PROCEEDINGS OF THE BOSTON SO-
CIETY OF NATURAL HISTORY," TSB #73, p. 5.

--and Carl Bode. "Henry David Thoreau: A Check List of
His Correspondence," NEW YORK PUBLIC LIBRARY BULLETIN,
LIX (May, 1955), 227-252.
    A list of all known letters written by or to Tho-
    reau, giving location of manuscript, place of pub-
    lication, rating accuracy of printed text, and
    summarizing unpublished letters.

--and Carl Bode, editors. THE CORRESPONDENCE OF HENRY
DAVID THOREAU. New York: New York University Press, 1958.

    reviews: AMERICAN LITERATURE (November, 1959).
                AMERICAN QUARTERLY (Fall, 1959).
                BOOK EXCHANGE (March, 1959).
                BULLETIN OF THE NATIONAL ASSOCIATION OF
                SECONDARY SCHOOL PRINCIPALS (March, 1959).
                CHICAGO TRIBUNE, November 23, 1958.
                CHRISTIAN SCIENCE MONITOR, December 11,
                1958.

COLLEGE ENGLISH (November, 1959).
COMMONWEAL (March 20, 1959).
CONCORD JOURNAL, October 30, 1958.
EMERSON SOCIETY QUARTERLY, XIII.
ENGLISH JOURNAL (February, 1959).
ENGLISH SPEAKING UNION: BOOKS ACROSS THE
SEA (January, 1959).
KEY REPORTER (July, 1959).
NEW ENGLAND QUARTERLY (March, 1959).
NEW LEADER, XLII (June 15, 1959).
NEW YORK HERALD TRIBUNE, March 1, 1959.
NEW YORK TIMES, November 23, 1958.
ROCHESTER TIMES UNION, January 12, 1959.
ST. LOUIS POST-DISPATCH, February 11, 1959.
SAN FRANCISCO CHRONICLE, November 15, 1959.
SANTA BARBARA NEWS-PRESS, March 1, 1959.
TIMES LITERARY SUPPLEMENT [London], August
21, 1959.
THOREAU SOCIETY BULLETIN #65, by J. L.
Shanley. An extended review.
VIRGINIA QUARTERLY REVIEW, XXXV (Winter,
1959).
WALT WHITMAN REVIEW (March, 1959).
WASHINGTON POST, December 21, 1958.
WESTERN HUMANITIES REVIEW (Autumn, 1959).
WORCESTER TELEGRAM, February 7, 1959.

Harmon, Roger J. "Thoreau to His Publishers," AMERICAN LITER-
ATURE, XXV (January, 1954), 496-497.
An unpublished letter by Thoreau.

Harrington, Joe. "All Sorts," BOSTON POST, October 8, 1941.
A brief column on Thoreau's walking.

Harris, Hugh. "Thoreau at Walden: 4th of July 1845," ARYAN
PATH, XVI (July, 1945), 240-245.
A centennial essay from Bombay, India.

Harris, Neil. THE ARTIST IN AMERICAN SOCIETY: THE FORMATIVE
YEARS: 1790-1860. New York: Braziller, 1966.
Thoreau, passim.

Harvard University. "Order of Exercises for Commencement,
XXX August, MDCCCIIIVII," EMERSON SOCIETY QUARTERLY, VII
(1957), 28.
Facsimile of program for Thoreau's graduation
exercises.

--"Order of Performances for Exhibition, Monday, July 13,
1835," EMERSON SOCIETY QUARTERLY, VIII (1957), 28-29.
Facsimile of program for Thoreau's Greek dialogue
on Decius and Cato with M. Clarke.

Harvey, Arthur. THEORY AND PRACTICE OF CIVIL DISOBEDIENCE.
Raymond, N. H.: Mimeographed by the author, 1961.
Much on Thoreau's CIVIL DISOBEDIENCE.

Harvey, Victoria. "Thoreau's Trees," CHRISTIAN SCIENCE MON-
    ITOR, ? .
        A poem.

Hassett, Robert L. "Concord River Flows on as Thoreau Knew
    It," BOSTON HERALD, July 2, 1961.

Hattori, Tanosuke. "Thoreau on Life," KOMYO O OUTE (IN
    PURSUIT OF LIGHT). Tokyo: Ofukaı Shuppan Bu, 1925.   pp.
    75-137.

Hauber, Margaret Francis. "Thoreau, The Humanitarian." Rut-
    gers University, 1939. Unpublished master's thesis.
        An extremely interesting evaluation of Thoreau's
        social interest. TSB #15.

Hauge, Ingvar. "Vismannen fra Walden Pond," DAGBLADET [Oslo,
    Norway], April 16, 1962.
        A centennial tribute on "The Wise Man of Walden
        Pond."

"The Haunting Voice of Thoreau," LOS ANGELES TIMES, July 9,
    1967.
        Excerpts from CIVIL DISOBEDIENCE.

Hausman, Dr. Leon A. "Thoreau on Monadmock," TSB #25.
        This is a condensation of a paper read at the Tho-
        reau Society annual meeting in Concord on July 10,
        1948.

"Hawthorne and Thoreau," T.P.'s WEEKLY [London], VL (Septem-
    ber 22, 1905), 369.
        A notice of Sanborn's "A Concord Note-Book" in the
        September, 1905 CRITIC.

Haymaker, Richard E. FROM PAMPAS TO HEDGEROWS AND DOWNS: A
    STUDY OF W. H. HUDSON. New York: Bookman, 1954.
        Contains much on Hudson's interest in Thoreau.

Hayward, Adrian. "The White Pond Tree," NATURE OUTLOOK, IV
    (November, 1945), 29-36.
        The full history of Thoreau's mysterious submerged
        pine.

Hazard, Lucy Lockwood. "Thoreau, the Intensive Pioneer,"
    THE FRONTIER IN AMERICAN LITERATURE. New York: Barnes
    and Noble, 1941. pp. 164-170.
        A reprint of this provocative analysis of Thoreau's
        intellectual pioneering.

Headley, David. "Three Seasons of Summer's First Monday,"
    WASHINGTON AND JEFFERSON LITERARY JOURNAL, I (1966),
    89-91.
        Poem on Thoreau.

Hedgpeth, Joel W. "A Hundred Years in the Woods," LAND,   IV

(Autumn, 1945), 388-391.
   An excellent summary of the reasons why Thoreau
   seems likely to outlast most nature writers. TSB #15.

--"Reenter the Limerick," SATURDAY REVIEW OF LITERATURE
   (September 2, 1944), p. 16.
   A limerick on Thoreau.

Helfer, Harold. "Honorable Confucius Computer Data," AMERICAN
   LEGION MAGAZINE (August, 1968).
   Humorous poem on Thoreau.

Hellman, George S. "Henry Thoreau as a Versifier," NEW YORK
   TIMES BOOK REVIEW, September 26, 1943, p. 30.
   Review of Bode's edition of Thoreau's poems and
   the 1943 reprint of Canby's life.

--"Unpublished Pages of Henry D. Thoreau," BOSTON HERALD,
   1909?.
   Long quotations from unpublished manuscripts.

Hendrick, George. "Gandhiana at TxU," LIBRARY CHRONICLE OF
   THE UNIVERSITY OF TEXAS, V (Fall, 1954), 43-47.
   Reprints for the first time some of Gandhi's com-
   ments on Thoreau.

--"Influence of Thoreau and Emerson on Gandhi's SATYAGRAHA,"
   GANDHI MARG. (July, 1959), 1-14.
   A survey.

--"The Influence of Thoreau's CIVIL DISOBEDIENCE on Gandhi's
   SATYAGRAHA," AMERICAN LITERATURE: A CRITICAL SURVEY, ed-
   ited by T. D. Young and R. E. Fine. New York: American
   Book Co., 1968.

--"Thoreau and Gandhi's SATYAGRAHA," NEW ENGLAND QUARTERLY,
   XXIX (December, 1956), 462-471.
   At long last an authoritative study of Thoreau's
   influence on Gandhi. TSB #58.

--"Thoreau, F. D. R. and 'Fear'," TSB #62.

--"Thoreau in the Twentieth Century," THE AMERICAN REN-
   AISSANCE: THE HISTORY AND LITERATURE OF AN ERA. Die
   Nevren Sprachen, Beiheft 9. Frankfurt am Main: Moritz
   Diesterweg, 1963. pp. 89-96.

--"Thoreau's CIVIL DISOBEDIENCE in Gandhi's INDIAN OPINION,"
   EMERSON SOCIETY QUARTERLY, XIV (1959), 19-20.
   Reprints excerpts from CIVIL DISOBEDIENCE that Gan-
   dhi had reprinted in his South African newspaper.

--"Thoughts on the Variorum CIVIL DISOBEDIENCE," EMERSON
   SOCIETY QUARTERLY, LVI (1969), 60-62.

--"William Sloane Kennedy Looks to Emerson and Thoreau,"

EMERSON SOCIETY QUARTERLY, XXVI (1962), 28-31.

--, editor. "Pages from Sophia Thoreau's Journal," TSB #61.

"Henry D. Thoreau's AUTUMN," NEW YORK TRIBUNE, October 2, 1892.

"Henry D. Thoreau's WINTER." NEW YORK TRIBUNE, December 26, 1887.

"Henry David Thoreau: 1817-1862," WORCESTER EVENING GAZETTE, May 11, 1962.
 A centennial editorial.

"Henry David Thoreau Exhibit at UVa's Alderman Library," CHARLOTTESVILLE DAILY PROGRESS, June 19, 1954, p. 2.
 Lengthy account of centennial exhibition.

"Henry David Thoreau--Indian Summer at Walden Pond," JOURNEY THROUGH NEW ENGLAND: A GUIDE. Boston: Bowden, 1968. pp. 54-56.

HENRY DAVID THOREAU: THE MAN WHO MOULDED THE MAHATMA'S MIND. New Delhi: Careers Institute, ? .
 Although this 48 page anonymous study which attempts to synthesize the ideas of Thoreau and Gandhi is based on limited sources--the Thoreau biographies by Canby and Krutch and Gandhiji's own AUTOBIOGRAPHY, the parallels of thought and action of "two of the greatest men of modern times" are simply and explicitly stated. It is disappointing, however, that the Indian author did not explore unpublished Gandhi manuscripts to add to our information about the literary influence of Thoreau upon Gandhi.--George Hendrick. TSB #49.

"Henry David Thoreau might have chuckled," NEW YORK TIMES, September 27, 1966.
 Full-page ad for NATIONAL OBSERVER featuring photo of Thoreau.

"Henry F. Thoreau and Bronson Alcott: A Study of Relationships," TEACHERS COLLEGE JOURNAL, XIV (July, 1943), 126-128.

"Henry the Hippie," BOSTON HERALD, July 6, 1967.
 An editorial.

"Henry Thoreau," COOPERATOR, July 9, 1945.
 An editorial.

"Henry Thoreau Applies for a Job in Taunton," CONCORD JOURNAL, July 4, 1963.
 Facsimile of Thoreau's letter of October 6, 1838.

"Henry Thoreau, 'The Service'," NEW YORK TRIBUNE, May 10, 1902.

"Hero: Henry David Thoreau," FORTUNE, XXIX (May, 1944), 152-
153.
    Color plate of Thoreau still life. No. 22 in series
    on heroic Americans.

Hertz, Robert. "England and American Romanticism," PERSONAL-
IST, XLVI (Winter, 1965), 81-92.
    Thoreau discussed as an example.

Heywood, Terence. "Henry David Thoreau," APPALACHIA, XXIX
(June, 1952), 59.
    A sonnet.

Hickok, Benjamin. "The Political and Literary Careers of
    F. B. Sanborn." Michigan State College, 1953. Unpub-
lished doctoral dissertation.
    The first full-length study of Thoreau's friend
    and biographer.

Hicks, John H. THOREAU IN OUR SEASON. Amherst: University
of Massachusetts Press, 1966.
    In 1962 the MASSACHUSETTS REVIEW devoted a large
    part of an issue to Thoreau. It was distributed by
    our society as Booklet 17. It has now been beau-
    tifully reprinted in hard cover form with an ad-
    ditional poem by Robert Francis, and new essays by
    Truman Nelson, C. Roland Wagner, and the editor,
    John Hicks. A truly significant volume, one that
    all Thoreau students will want to own. TSB #95.

    reviews: DALHOUSIE REVIEW (Autumn, 1966).
              LIVING WILDERNESS (Autumn, 1966).
              NEW ENGLAND QUARTERLY (March, 1967).

"Hier Spricht Ein Glucklicher," ARTEMIS BEUCHERPOST [Zurich,
Switzerland] (Spring, 1946).
    A note on the Thoreau Society.

Higashiyama, Masayoshi. "The Environment of Henry David Tho-
    reau," BRITISH AND AMERICAN LITERATURE [Nishinomiya,
    Japan], II (November, 1957).
    Text in Japanese.

  --"A Study of Henry David Thoreau--Man and Nature." Kwansei
    Gakuin University, Nishinomiya, Japan, 195?. Unpublish-
    ed doctoral dissertation.
    Abstract appears in TSB #73, pp. 4-5.

  --A STUDY OF THOREAU. Tokyo(?), 1961(?).
    A new booklength study of Thoreau in Japanese.

  --"Thoreau and the Present Time," RISING GENERATION [Tokyo],
    CXIII (October, 1967), 636-638.
    Text in Japanese.

  --"Thoreau: A Japanese View," ENGLISH AND AMERICAN LITER-

ATURE [Kwansei Gakuin University], VII (October, 1962), 76-83.

--"Tradition and Henry David Thoreau," BRITISH AND AMERICAN LITERATURE, III (June, 1958).
Text in Japanese.

Hildenbrand, Christopher A. A BIBLIOGRAPHY OF SCHOLARSHIP ABOUT HENRY DAVID THOREAU: 1940-1967. Fort Hays, Kansas: Fort Hays Studies: Bibliography Series #3, 1967.
An invaluable checklist of books and articles about Thoreau.

Hill, Edwin B., editor. IN MEMORY OF HENRY D. THOREAU. Ysleta: Hill, 1944.
A brochure reprinting six poems about Thoreau.

[Hill, Edwin B.] "Henry D. Thoreau to George William Curtis," TSB #6.
A reprint of Thoreau's letter of March 11, 1853.
(Ysleta, Texas: Edwin B. Hill, May, 1942).

Hillway, Tyrus. "The Personality of H. D. Thoreau," COLLEGE ENGLISH, VI (March, 1945), 328-330.
A further study into the problem of Thoreau's "coldness."

Himelick, Raymond. "Thoreau and Samuel Daniel," AMERICAN LITERATURE, XXIV (May, 1952), 177-185.
A study of Thoreau's use of quotations from the Elizabethan poet, demonstrating that he used his sources for inspiration rather that interpretation in context.

Hix, Ernest. "Strange as It Seems," BROCKTON [Massachusetts] ENTERPRISE, September 2, 1948.
A syndicated cartoon perpetuating the legend that Thoreau would not pay for his college diploma.

Hoagland, Clayton. "The Diary of Thoreau's 'Gentle Boy'," NEW ENGLAND QUARTERLY, XXVIII (December, 1955), 473-489.
First-hand account of Thoreau's school.

--"Edmund Sewall's Concord Diary," TSB #53.

--"Thoreau as Educator," PLEASURES IN LEARNING [New York University], X (May, 1962), 5-10.

also in: FLORIDA ADULT EDUCATOR, XII (April-June, 1962), 13-16. Reprinted from PLEASURES IN LEARNING (May, 1962).

--"Thoreau's Cove, Walden Pond," THE PLEASURES OF SKETCHING OUTDOORS. New York: Viking, 1947. p. 146.
A drawing.

[Hoagland, Clayton]. "Eighty Years After," NEW YORK SUN,
     May 6, 1942.
                An editorial.

-- "Postscript on Broccoli," NEW YORK SUN, April 4, 1942.
                An editorial, followed by letters to the editor as
                follows: "E. S.," April 8, 1942; F. C. Nicodemus,
                Jr., April 10, 1942; Henry F. Herbermann, April 11,
                1942; Raymond Adams, April 13, 1942.

Hobiltzelle, Harrison. "The War Against War in the Nine-
     teenth Century: A Study of the Western Backgrounds of
     Gandhian Thought." Columbia University, 1959. Unpublish-
     ed doctoral dissertation.

Hoch, David G. "Theory of History in A WEEK: Annals and
     Perennials," EMERSON SOCIETY QUARTERLY, LVI (1969), 32-35.

Hoeltje, Hubert H. "Misconceptions in Current Thoreau Criti-
     cism," PHILOLOGICAL QUARTERLY, XLVII (October, 1968),
     563-570.

-- "Thoreau and the Concord Academy," NEW ENGLAND QUARTERLY,
     XXI (March, 1948), 103-109.
                On Thoreau's school-days and school-teaching.

-- "Thoreau as Lecturer," NEW ENGLAND QUARTERLY, XIX (Decem-
     ber, 1946), 485-494.
                The first detailed study of Thoreau as a lecturer
                with much new information concerning his appearances
                before the Salem Lyceum in particular.

Hoff. "Why can't you lead a life of quiet desperation, like
     everybody else?" NEW YORKER (August 22, 1959).
                A cartoon.

Hoff, Rhoda. "Henry David Thoreau," in WHY THEY WROTE.
     New York: Henry Z. Walck, Inc., 1961. pp. 31-59.
                A well written essay, aimed at teen-agers, on Tho-
                reau as a professional writer. It not only out-
                lines his writing career, but also quotes many of
                his comments on the art of writing, and ends with
                an extensive quotation from CAPE COD as a sample
                of his writing. A good, mature approach to Thoreau
                and one that adults as well as young people should
                find stimulating. TSB #78.

Hoffman, Daniel G. FORM AND FABLE IN AMERICAN FICTION.
     New York: Oxford, 1961.

-- "Thoreau's 'Old Settler' and Frost's Paul Bunyan,"
     JOURNAL OF AMERICAN FOLKLORE, LXXIII (July, 1960), 236-
     238.
                A study in relationships.

Hoffman, George Edward. "Henry David Thoreau," CHRISTIAN

CENTURY, LXVI (April 27, 1949), 527.
A sonnet.

Hoffman, Malvina. "Henry David Thoreau," MASSACHUSETTS REVIEW,
IV (Autumn, 1962), 110.
Photograph of bust.

also in: EMERSON SOCIETY QUARTERLY, XXXI (1963),
79.

Hofmiller, Josef. "Thoreau," VERSUCHE. Munich: ?   , 1909.
pp. 130-165.
Calls attention once again to Thoreau's dissatis-
faction with the complexities of modern civilization.
A competent and unusually colorful essay on Thoreau,
which emphasizes Thoreau's abolitionist sentiments
and activities. Relates Thoreau's civil disobedience
to Separatist theology. Thoreau's personality, he
suggests, is essentially tense like that of the Indian hunters who walked the forests before him--rest-
less, frugal, proud, and silent. TSB #105.

Hofstadter, Samuel H. "The Only Thing We Have to Fear,"
NEW YORK HERALD TRIBUNE, March 21, 1966.
A detailed history of the Thoreau-FDR quotation.

Holden, Raymond P. THE MERRIMACK. New York: Rinehart, 1958.
The latest volume in the Rivers of America series.
Chapter 17, "New Men for a New World," is almost
entirely devoted to a well-written account of Thoreau's voyage on the Concord and Merrimack. But
even more important to the Thoreau student is the
fact that the whole book is filled with data that
help to explain many of Thoreau's allusions in his
first book. Not only that, but the book is decidedly enjoyable reading in itself. A notable addition to a notable series. TSB #66.

Holden, Vincent F. THE YANKEE PAUL: ISAAC THOMAS HECKER.
Milwaukee: Bruce, 1958.
Many comments on Thoreau's friendship with Hecker.

Holder, Alan. "The Writer as Loon: Witty Structure in WALDEN,"
EMERSON SOCIETY QUARTERLY, XLIII (1966), 73-77.

Holley, Sallie. A LIFE FOR LIBERTY: ANTI-SLAVERY AND OTHER
LETTERS, edited by John White Chadwick. New York: Putnam,
1899.
Accounts of an early visit to Walden Pond and to
Thoreau's lecture on "Autumnal Tints" at Worcester.

Hollis C. Carroll. "A New England Outpost: As Revealed in
Some Unpublished Letters of Emerson, Parker, and Alcott
to Ainsworth Spofford," NEW ENGLAND QUARTERLY, XXXVIII
(March, 1965), 65-85.
Contains information on Spofford's early interest

in Thoreau.

--"Thoreau and the State," COMMONWEAL, L (September 9, 1949), 530-533.
"Civil Disobedience" is wrong because it denies the authority of the state.

--"Whitman and William Swinton: A Co-operative Friendship," AMERICAN LITERATURE, XXX (January, 1959), 425-449.
Includes new material on Thoreau's visit to Whitman.

Holmes, John. "Map of My Country," THE KNOWN WORLD. New York: Henry Holt and Company, 1941.
A poem referring to Thoreau.

Holmes, John Haynes. "Thoreau's CIVIL DISOBEDIENCE," CHRISTIAN CENTURY, LXVI (June 29, 1949).
An extended essay originally given as a sermon at Community Church, New York City on May 22nd, commemorating the centennial of the essay.

Holway, Hope. "Thoreau," RADICALS OF YESTERDAY. Norman, Oklahoma: Cooperative Books, 1941.

Homan, John Jr. "Thoreau, the Emblem, and The WEEK," AMERICAN TRANSCENDENTAL QUARTERLY, I (1969), 104-108.

"Homily," PORTLAND OREGONIAN, August 13, 1954.

Hoover, Ira. THE CENTENNIAL OF HENRY DAVID THOREAU. Arden, Delaware: Roberts Studio Press, 1957.
Reprinted from the NEW YORK CALL for July 8, 1917.

--"Figuras Cumbres del Pensamiento Estadounidense: Henry David Thoreau," translated into Spanish by V. Munoz. EL DIA [Montevideo, Uruguay], February 19, 1961.

--"Henry David Thoreau," translated into Spanish by V. Munoz. UMBRAL [Paris], 1967.

--"Un Pensador: Henry David Thoreau," translated into Spanish by V. Munoz. LE COMBAT SYNDICALISTE [Paris], September 30, 1965.

Horri, Ryoho. YAJIN THOREAU [Thoreau, the Unsophisticated] Tokyo: Fujiya Shobo, 1935.
A strange biography of Thoreau, which is fascinating, though it contains a number of factual errors.

Hosmer, Gladys E. H. ALL ABOUT CONCORD. Concord: ? , 1954 (mimeographed).
Checklist of historical resources of the town.

--"An Expansion of the Walden Pond Reservation," TSB #53.
Short article with map drawn by Russel H. Lenz.

--"Phineas Allen, Thoreau's Preceptor," TSB #59.

--"Some Notable Concord Women," CONCORD JOURNAL, November 9, 1961.+
    Brief biographical studies of a number of Thoreau's female contemporaries and neighbors.

--, compiler. THE THOREAU LIBRARY OF ALFRED W. HOSMER GIVEN TO THE CONCORD FREE PUBLIC LIBRARY BY HERBERT BUT-TRICK HOSMER. Concord: Concord Free Public Library, 1949 (mimeographed).

Hosmer, James Kendall. THE LAST LEAF. New York: Putnam, 1912. A description of Thoreau by one of his neighbors, typical of the attitude of Concordians several generations ago, pp. 235-237.

Hough, Henry Beetle. "Thoreau in Today's Sun," TSB #108, pp. 1-4.
    The Presidential Address delivered at the annual meeting.

    also in: CONCORD JOURNAL, July 17 and 24, 1969.

--THOREAU OF WALDEN. New York: Simon and Schuster, 1956. The jacket of this latest biography of Thoreau announces that "detailed critical studies and exhaustive interpretations [of Thoreau]...have made the ordinary reader feel shut out and left behind" and that this new study "offers an earthy, every-day approach to a fascinating and significant American figure." In other words, Mr. Hough intends to offer an introduction to Thoreau for the layman. In many respects he succeeds. His book is highly readable. He does get close to the character of Thoreau. He flavors his book with a large number of direct quotations from Thoreau's writings. And he enlightens it with many anecdotes. To that extent the book certainly serves its purpose. But unfortunately there are negative criticisms that must be made. First, there are many errors. For example, on p. 93, he gives the date of John Thoreau's death as February rather than January, 1842. On p. 100 (and p. 113), he calls J. L. O'Sullivan, O'Donnell. On p. 131, he states the Walden cabin had one window instead of one on each side. On p. 166, he has Thoreau taking the railroad from Cohasset to Bridgewater, when no such railroad exists. On p. 194, he states the second "edition" of WALDEN came out in 1863 instead of 1862. On p. 213, he states Cholmondeley sent Thoreau 24 Indian books rather than 44. On p. 243, he states Thoreau sent word of his Brown lecture to Sanborn rather than the Republican committee. On p. 245, he states Sanborn did not attend the Brown memorial meeting, but Sanborn in his RECOLLECTIONS says he did. On p. 66, he states Tho-

reau commenced his journal at Emerson's suggestion,
but on p. 55, he states Emerson did not meet Thoreau
until after the journal was started. On p. 92, he
states Channing moved to Concord in 1841, but on p.
114, he quotes Thoreau's letter of 1843 to the effect
that Channing had just then moved to Concord. It is
only fair to state that some of these errors have
been made by other biographers and Mr. Hough simply
repeated them. Nonetheless they are errors. Second,
he has not taken advantage of many recent studies.
For example, articles by Adams and McGill would have
given him a more accurate account of Thoreau's life
at Harvard. And, if I may be so immodest, an article of my own solves the mystery of Sophia Foord he
mentions on p. 155. Finally, there are weaknesses
of interpretation. On p. 127, he suggests Thoreau
went to Walden to establish a station on the underground railroad. I know of no evidence that this
is true. Following Canby (although fortunately not
going so far as Canby), he stresses the Lydian Emer-
son--Thoreau relationship and emphasizes a lack of
harmony in the Emerson household to substantiate it.
Again I think he is on weak ground. I have devoted
an unduly large proportion of this review to negative criticism. It is my hope that many of the
book's errors can be corrected in later editions.
For, despite all my criticism, the book has distinct
values. He does present a highly readable biography
and above all he shows his understanding of Thoreau's
personality--which is a great deal more than can be
claimed for some earlier biographers. WH. TSB #55.

reviews: AMERICAN LITERATURE, XXVIII (January,
           1957), 534.
           CHICAGO TRIBUNE, April 22, 1956, by Al-
           fred Ames.
           CLEVELAND PLAIN DEALER, April 22, 1956,
           by Don Keister.
           EMERSON SOCIETY QUARTERLY, VI (1957), 46.
           NEW YORK HERALD TRIBUNE, May 27, 1956.
           NEW YORK TIMES, April 5, 1956, by Charles
           Poore.
           NEW YORK TIMES BOOK REVIEW, April 8, 1956,
           by S. S. Van de Water.
           NEW YORK WORLD TELEGRAM, April 13, 1956.
           NEWSWEEK, April 30, 1956.
           PROVIDENCE SUNDAY JOURNAL, May 13, 1956,
           by R[obert] L. W[heeler].
           REPORTER, May 31, 1956.
           ST. LOUIS POST DISPATCH, January 13, 1957.
           SATURDAY REVIEW OF LITERATURE, XXXIX (April,
           14, 1956), 27, by Louis Halle.

Hourdin, Georges. "Le Premier des non-vilents: Henry David
     Thoreau," LA VIE CATHOLIQUE [Paris], #1209 (October 15,
     1968), 22-23.

Hourihan, Paul. "The Inner Dynamics of the Emerson-Thoreau Relationship." Boston U., 1967. Unpub. doctoral diss.

Houston, Walter Scott. "A Study of Some Aspects of the Criticism of Henry David Thoreau." University of Alabama, 1949. Unpublished master's thesis.
    A survey of the major trends in criticism.

--"Thoreau as Artist." University of Wisconsin, 1935. Unpublished doctoral dissertation.
    Thoreau's attitude toward the problem of literary composition.

Hovaness, Alan Scott. THE STARS. n.p.: n.d..
    Words adapted from WALDEN for soprano, chorus, English horn, celesta, harp, and strings. A copy is on deposit in the Library of Congress.

Hovde, Carl F. "Literary Materials in Thoreau's A WEEK," PMLA, LXXX (March, 1965), 76-83.

--"Nature into Art: Thoreau's Use of His Journals in A WEEK," AMERICAN LITERATURE, XXX (May, 1958), 165-184.
    Important study of the genesis of Thoreau's first book.

--"The Writing of Henry D. Thoreau's A WEEK ON THE CONCORD AND MERRIMACK RIVERS: A Study of Textual Materials and Techniques." Princeton University, 1956. Unpublished doctoral dissertation.
    On the writing of Thoreau's first book.

Hovey, Allen Beecher. THE HIDDEN THOREAU. Beirut [Lebanon]: Catholic Press, 1966.
    An intensive study of Thoreau's earlier writings up through WALDEN, emphasizing in particular their mythological basis and structure. Some of the suggestions (such as that the intersecting lines on Thoreau's map of Walden Pond were intended to symbolize a Christian cross) are fantastic. But they are more than outweighed by some interesting insights into what Thoreau was driving at. TSB #97.

    review: EMERSON SOCIETY QUARTERLY, XLVII (1967), 2.

Hovey, Richard B. "The Christian Gadfly: A Lay Sermon on Thoreau," EDUCATION FORUM, XXIII (January, 1959), 187-191.
    On Thoreau as a Christian.

"How Great a Son," CHICAGO TRIBUNE, May 6, 1962.
    Centenary editorial.

Howard, Leon. LITERATURE AND THE AMERICAN TRADITION. Garden City: Doubleday, 1960.

A brief history of American literature, based on a series of lectures given before university audiences abroad. The section on Thoreau (pp. 155-160) is short and to the point, as is the whole book, but in the few pages he really gets to the heart of Thoreau's meaning, as for example in the following, "Like Emerson, he wanted to reform the world by opening men's eyes to their own potentialities rather than by changing social conditions; but his method was by example rather than by evangelism." TSB #71.

Howarth, William Louis. "Thoreau, The Journalist." University of Virginia, 1967. Unpublished doctoral dissertation. An abstract of Howarth's doctoral dissertation is is reproduced in TSB #107, p. 5.

Howe, M. A. DeWolfe. BARRY FAULKNER"S MEN OF MONADNOCK. Keene, N. H.: Keene National Bank, 1950. The story behind the Faulkner murals; a four page article on "Thoreau's Mountain;" and three full-page color reproductions of the murals.

Howell, Almonte C. "Emerson y el Renacimiento Norte-americano," ENSAYOS SOBRE LITERATURA NORTE-AMERICANA. Guatemala: Universidad de San Carlos, 1948. pp. 28-46. A series of lectures on American literature. Contains much on Thoreau.

Hubbard, Elbert. "Forbes at Harvard," SELECTED WRITINGS OF ELBERT HUBBARD. New York: Wise, 1922. XI, pp. 315 passim. A novel containing letters supposedly written by one of Thoreau's neighbors.

"Hudson and Thoreau," TSB #21. Letter from W. H. Hudson read at the Thoreau Centenary Meeting in Caxton Hall, London, July 12, 1917, and reprinted from THE HUMANITARIAN, August, 1917.

Hudson, Hannah R. HENRY DAVID THOREAU: CONCORD BOOKS. Berkeley Heights: Oriole Press, 1962. "Edition limited to 125 copies for private distribution". Reprinted from HARPER'S MONTHLY for June, 1875.

Hudspeth, Robert N. "A Perennial Springtime: Channing's Friendship with Emerson and Thoreau," EMERSON SOCIETY QUARTERLY, LIV (1969), 30-36.

Huffert, Anton. "Alcott on Thoreau's ATLAS OF CONCORD," TSB #56. Included in the text of the article are excerpts from: Concord [Mass.] School Committee, REPORTS OF THE SCHOOL COMMITTEE AND THE SUPERINTENDENT OF SCHOOLS, 1861, p. 26; and Amos B. Alcott, "Journal

of February 4, 1861," THE JOURNALS OF BRONSON ALCOTT,
p. 334.

--"Thoreau as a Teacher, Lecturer, and Educational Thinker."
New York University, 1951. Unpublished doctoral dissertation.

Hughes, R. "Remembering Eric Gill," AMERICAN, LXXI (September
9, 1944), 556-557.
        A note on the English mystic, and Thoreau.

Hull, Raymona E. "The Cairn at Walden Pond," TSB #102, pp.
5-6.

--"Hawthorne's Efforts to Help Thoreau," EMERSON SOCIETY
QUARTERLY, XXXIII (1963), 24-28.

Humble, Henry Wilbur. "To Thoreau in 1936," LINES ON LITERATI
AND OTHER POEMS. New York: Poetry Publications, 1936.
p. 32.
        A poem.

Hume, Robert A. "February, Thoreau, and Spring," RENDEZVOUS
[Pocatello, Idaho], I (Winter, 1966), 23-26.

Humphrey, Hubert H. "The Thoreau Centenary in Concord,"
CONGRESSIONAL RECORD (November 2, 1962).

--"The Thoreau Society," CONGRESSIONAL RECORD (August 13,
1957), 13184-13188.
        Account of the 1957 annual meeting with text of
        addresses by Zahniser and Mehta.

Hunter, Cliff. "Thoreau on Science," BOSTON HERALD, February
1, 1961.
        Brief letter quoting Thoreau on dangers of science.

"The Huntington Library and Henry Thoreau," SAN MARINO [Calif.]
TRIBUNE, July 13, 1944.
        An editorial.

Hurd, Harry Elmore. "Night Is For Sound," THE AVE MARIA
(October 30, 1943), pp. 551-555.

Hurtado, Leopoldo. "Thoreau en Walden," LA PRENSA [Buenos
Aires], September 16, 1945.
        A lengthy illustrated essay.

Hutchinson, Ken. "dropping a pebble in walden pond," FM AND
FINE ARTS, V (January, 1964), 8-9.
        Wry comment on a modern version of the simple life.

Hutchinson, William R. THE TRANSCENDENTALIST MINISTERS:
CHURCH REFORM IN THE NEW ENGLAND RENAISSANCE. New Haven:
Yale University Press, 1959.
        Although Thoreau is mentioned only briefly in this

book, it is, nonetheless, an exceedingly important volume for those who would understand Thoreau's ways of thinking. Here, in concise, cogent form, is a lucid discussion of the rise of the theory of Transcendentalism and its influence particularly upon the clergy and the religious doctrines of the time. A thoroughly worthwhile book and one that every student of Transcendentalism should own. TSB # 68.

Huth, Hans. NATURE AND THE AMERICAN. Berkeley: University of California Press, 1957.
    A masterly study of the changing attitudes towards nature of the American people over three centuries. Much on Thoreau. "However valuable in theory transcendental doctrines had been in the development of the philosophy of nature as formulated by Emerson, with Thoreau's work in observing nature these ideas would never have received that kind of specific interpretation which made it possible for a widespread public to absorb them" (p. 95). TSB #62.

Hyman, Stanley Edgar. "Henry Thoreau in Our Time," ATLANTIC MONTHLY, CLXXVIII (November, 1946), 137-146.
    An extremely provocative interpretation of Thoreau's writings with much on his supposed use of symbolism. TSB #18.

    also in: THE PROMISED END. Cleveland: World, 1963. pp. 23-25.

-- "Henry Thoreau Once More," MASSACHUSETTS REVIEW, IV (Autumn, 1962), 163-170.

    also in: THE PROMISED END. Cleveland: World, 1963. pp. 39-48.

Iams, Jack. PROPHET BY EXPERIENCE. New York: Morrow, 1943.
A satirical novel with its chief character a
disciple of Thoreau.

review: TSB #12.

--PROPHET BY EXPERIENCE. New York: Armed Services Inc.,
1943.
A special Overseas edition, printed for the armed
forces.

Imaishi, Masayuk. "Thoreau and His Philosophy of Life,"
HIROSHIMA JOGAKUIN UNIVERSITY PUBLICATIONS: COLLECTED
ESSAYS, VI (December, 1966), 97-107.
An essay in Japanese.

"Immortal Yankee." WASHINGTON POST, May 11, 1962.
Editorial on centennial.

"In a Hollow Tree," NEW YORK HERALD TRIBUNE, March 23?, 1958.
Editorial on WALDEN.

"In Sympathy with Fishes," NEW YORK HERALD TRIBUNE, August
12, 1944.
An editorial.

"Indian Envoy Lauds Thoreau at NYU Fete," PROVIDENCE JOURNAL,
May 7, 1962.

Inge, M. Thomas. "Thoreau's Humor in WALDEN," RANDOLPH-MACON
MAGAZINE, XXXVII (March, 1966), 33-44.

Ingraham, Vernon Leland. "Woodland Sage," NEW YORK TIMES,
February 26, 1950.
A poem on Thoreau.

Innerhofer, Helga. "Henry David Thoreau, Seine Stellung zu
seiner Zeit, zu Mensch und Natur." University of Inns-
bruck [Austria], 1951. Unpublished doctoral dissertation.
An enthusiastic and innocent discussion of Thoreau's
personality, without focus. Relies heavily on Canby's
biography in a number of essay-like chapters which
cover almost everything about Thoreau in no great
depth. TSB #105.

"The Insight of Thoreau," THINK, XVII (July, 1951), 28.

"Thoreau was not principally a theorist. He was a
keen observer of the processes of nature.

Ireland, Karen. "Bus Riders' Thoreau," MINNESOTA DAILY [Uni-
versity of Minnesota], May 16, 1960.
Musing on transit ads quoting Thoreau.

Irie, Yukio. "Why the Japanese People Find a Kinship with
Emerson and Thoreau," EMERSON SOCIETY QUARTERLY, XXVII
(1962), 13-14.

Irsiegler, Leopold. "Naturbeobachtung und Naturgefuhl bei
Henry David Thoreau." University of Vienna, 1951. Unpublished doctoral dissertation.

Ishill, Joseph. THOREAU: THE COSMIC YANKEE. Berkeley Heights,
N. Y.: Oriole Press, 1954.
A beautifully printed limited edition of an essay
first published in 1946. TSB #51.

--. et al. THOREAU: THE COSMIC YANKEE: CENTENNIAL APPRECI-
ATIONS. Los Angeles: Rocker Publications Committee, 1946.

review: THOREAU SOCIETY BULLETIN #17.

Ives, Charles. SECOND PIANO SONATA: CONCORD, MASS., 1840-
1860 [Concord Sonata], New York: Arrow Music Press, 1947.

Recordings: New York: Columbia Records, 1948. Recording
is a musical tribute to Emerson, Hawthorne, the
Alcotts, and Thoreau.

New York: Composers Recordings Inc., 1962. (CRI-150).
A new recording, with George Pappastavrou at the
piano, of Ives' major work. The fourth movement is
entitled "Thoreau" and Ives himself has said of it,
"If there shall be a program let it follow his [Tho-
reau's] thought on an autumn day of Indian summer
at Walden." This is the first time the sonata has
been recorded since the advent of long-playing records and the increase of fidelity of reproduction
is notable. TSB #81.

New York: Time Records, 1962. The second recording
of this beautiful sonata in six months, this with
Aloys Kontarsky as the pianist. Very well done. If
anything, superior to the CRI recording. TSB #82.

New York: Columbia Records, 1969. MS-7192, played
by John Kirkpatrick. By far the best recording yet
of the "Concord Sonata" (including of course the
Thoreau movement). It has a brilliance and vibrancy
lacking in all the others. The jacket has a particularly interesting history of the composition of the
sonata and explains why and how this version differs
from the earlier ones. TSB #107.

--"Essays before a Sonata," THREE CLASSICS IN THE AESTHET-
ICS OF MUSIC. New York: Dover, 1962. pp. 103-185.
   Includes the complete text of the 1920 private
   edition, including its provocative essay on Thoreau.

--"Thoreau," ESSAYS BEFORE A SONATA AND OTHER WRITINGS.
New York: Norton, 1962. pp. 51-70.
   The first authentic scholarly text of this provocative essay on Thoreau, hitherto available only
   in a rare private edition.

Jackson, Holbrook. DREAMER OF DREAMS: THE RISE AND FALL OF
19th CENTURY IDEALISM. London: Faber and Faber, 1948;
New York: Farrar and Straus, 1950.
A most provocative study of the philosophies and
interrelationships of Carlyle, Morris, Ruskin,
Emerson, Whitman, and Thoreau. TSB #24.

Jackson, Joseph. THROUGH GLADE AND MEAD, A CONTRIBUTION TO
LOCAL NATURAL HISTORY. Worcester, Mass.: Putnam and
Davis, 1894.
Thoreau frequently quoted and commented on.

Jackson, Robert P. "Thoreau, Chomei and the Working Man,"
AMERICAN BUDDHIST, II (May 15, 1958), 1-2.
Comparison of Thoreau and a 12th century Buddhist.

Jacobs, Briant S. "Henry David Thoreau--Individualist,"
RELIEF SOCIETY MAGAZINE [Salt Lake City], XLIX (August,
1962), 619-624.

--"Thoreau: Man in Nature," RELIEF SOCIETY MAGAZINE, XLIX
(July, 1962), 540-545.

Jacobson, Arthur C. "Tuberculosis and the Creative Mind,"
MEDICAL LIBRARY AND HISTORICAL JOURNAL, V (December,
1907), 225-230.
Includes commentary on influence of tuberculosis
on Thoreau.

Jaffee, Irving. "Thoreau Exhibit," NEW YORK HERALD TRIBUNE,
October 8, 1956.
On Morgan Library exhibit.

Jakeman, Adelbert M. "Walden Echo," THE GOLDEN QUILL AN-
THOLOGY OF THE BOOK CLUB FOR POETRY. Francestown, N. H.:
Golden Quill Press, 1956. p. 78.
A poem.

also in: NEW YORK HERALD TRIBUNE, January 1, 1956.

James, E. H. "Thoreau and The State," THE WORD [Glasgow,
Scotland], XLL (March, 1951), 56.
On Thoreau's political views.

James, Elizabeth Coates. "Reading, by Henry David Thoreau,"
BOSTON GLOBE, January 8, 1942.
A Great Books in Brief article.

"James Russell Lowell and Thoreau's First Book," TSB #35.
Lowell's review of A WEEK.

Japp, Alexander. An anonymous review of THOREAU: HIS LIFE
AND AIMS, by Alexander Japp. ATLANTIC MONTHLY, XLI (May,
1878), 672-673.

Jacques, John. "An Enthusiastic Newspaper Account of Thoreau's
Second Lecture in Portland, Maine, January 15, 1851,"
AMERICAN LITERATURE, XL (November, 1968), 385-391.

Jason, Frank G. "Walden," BOSTON POST MAGAZINE (July 24, 1949).
Brief, well-illustrated rhapsody on Walden Pond.

Jenkins, Lloyd S. "How Bird Pattern Differs from Thoreau's
Day," WORCESTER [Mass.] TELEGRAM, December 24, 1967.

--"Nature Lovers Will Find Much in Thoreau's JOURNAL,"
WORCESTER TELEGRAM, July 6, 1969.

--"Return to Thoreau's Shanty," WORCESTER [Mass.] TELEGRAM,
October 1, 1967.
On Mt. Monadnock.

Joad, C. E. M. "Henry David Thoreau 1817-1862," GREAT NAMES.
New York: Dial, 1926.
A commentary on Thoreau with some selections from
his writings.

"John Dewey on Thoreau...," TSB #30.
Reprinted is a letter from John Dewey to the
Thoreau Society about Thoreau.

John, Godfrey. "Another Look at WALDEN," CHRISTIAN SCIENCE
MONITOR, March 21, 1964.

"John Shepard Keyes on Thoreau," TSB #103, pp. 2-3.
Prints "a letter from John Shepard Keyes to F. H.
Underwood about Thoreau." The letter is dated
November 15th 1886.

Johnson, Thomas H. "Henry David Thoreau," THE LITERARY HIS-
TORY OF THE UNITED STATES, edited by R. E. Spiller, et al.
New York: Macmillan, 1948. III, 742-746.
A bibliography of Thoreau and Thoreauviana to
date.

Johnson, Thomas M. AN INTERVIEW WITH HENRY DAVID THOREAU.
Chicago: Scott, Foresman. 1964.
A 111-frame filmstrip of beautiful color photographs of scenes from Thoreau country with an accompanying narration on a recording both discuss-
ing and quoting Thoreau. It should make an excellent introduction to Thoreau for high school and
early college classes. The text of the recording
is also provided in a pamphlet. TSB #91.

Jones, Arthur Samuel. THOREAU'S INCARCERATION. Berkeley
Heights: Oriole, 1962.
Reprinted from the INLANDER for December, 1898.

Jones, Buford. "'The Hall of Fantasy' and the Early Haw-
thorne-Thoreau Relationship," PMLA, LXXXIII (October,
1968), 1429-1438.

--"A Thoreauvian Wordplay and PARADISE LOST," EMERSON SO-
CIETY QUARTERLY, XLVII (1967), 65-66.

Jones, C. R. MEMENTO MORI: TWO HUNDRED YEARS OF FUNERARY ART
AND CUSTOMS OF CONCORD, MASS ." Concord: Concord Antiquarian Society, 1967.
Includes photographs of numerous Thoreau family
mementoes.

Jones, Evan. THE MINNESOTA: FORGOTTEN RIVER. New York:
Holt, Rinehart and Winston, 1962.
Another superior volume in the "Rivers of America"
series with not only much background material for
Thoreau's trip to Minnesota, but four pages of quo-
tations from Thoreau's comments on the river. TSB
#79.

--"Pick-and-Shovel Historian," COLLIER'S, CXXXVI (August
5, 1955), 28-31.
Illustrated account of Roland Robbins' excavations
at Walden and elsewhere.

Jones, Howard Mumford. THEORY OF AMERICAN LITERATURE.
Ithaca: Cornell University Press, 1949.
Many references to Thoreau.

--"Thoreau and Human Nature," ATLANTIC MONTHLY, CCX (Sep-
tember, 1962), 56-61.
Address delivered at the May centenary in New
York City.

--"Thoreau as Moralist," HISTORY AND THE CONTEMPORARY.
Madison: University of Wisconsin Press, 1964. pp. 127-
144.
Reprinted from ATLANTIC MONTHLY.

Jones, Joseph. INDEX TO WALDEN. Austin, Texas: Hemphill's,
1955.
For any serious student of WALDEN, here is a real
dollar's worth. Not only is there a tremendously
detailed word index that can be used with any edition, but ingenius cross-references of allied
topics, a good map of the pond, and a word-list for
vocabulary study. This is a printed expansion of
his earlier hectographed leaflet. TSB #53.

--"Lugubrious Lucubration," CEA CRITIC, XVIII (March, 1956),
4.

Difficulty of teaching WALDEN to students with poor vocabularies.

--"Thoreau in Hong Kong," TSB #97, pp. 1-3.

--"Transcendental Grocery Bills: Thoreau's WALDEN and Some Aspects of American Vegetarianism," UNIVERSITY OF TEXAS STUDIES IN ENGLISH, XXXVI (1957), 141-154.
Demonstrates that Thoreau's ideas on vegetarianism were fairly common in his day.

--"Villages as Universities: AESTHETIC PAPERS and a Passage in WALDEN," EMERSON SOCIETY QUARTERLY, VII (1957), 40-42.
Points out a possible source in an Elizabeth Peabody essay for an idea in WALDEN.

--"WALDEN and ULTIMA THULE: A Twin-Centennial," LIBRARY CHRONICLE OF THE UNIVERSITY OF TEXAS, V (Fall, 1954), 13-22.
Contrasts the philosophies of Thoreau and his English friend Thomas Cholmondeley.

--WALDEN COUNTRY. Austin, Texas: University of Texas Visual Instruction Bureau, 1958.
24 color-slides, 2x2, with matching quotations from Thoreau's works on 5x8 cards; study guide of 4 pages; fibre packet.

--"Writers Compared," DAILY TELEGRAPH [Napier, New Zealand], September 25, 1953.
Compares lives of Thoreau and Herbert Guthrie Smith.

--, editor. TRIAL INDEX TO THOREAU'S WALDEN. Austin, Texas: University of Texas Press, 1954 (ditto-graphed).

--, et al. "Thoreau, Henry David," AMERICAN LITERARY MANUSCRIPTS. Austin: University of Texas Press, 1961. p. 370.
Lists location of Thoreau manuscripts in American libraries.

Jones, Paul. "Thoreau Anniversary," NEW YORK HERALD TRIBUNE, September 6, 1947.
A letter to the editor on Thoreau's leaving Walden Pond.

Jones, Samuel Arthur. "El Encarcelamiento de Thoreau," translated into Spanish by V. Munoz. CENIT (September, 1962), 3821-3824.

Joost, Nicholas. "A Corollary to Literature," RENASCENCE, XIII (Autumn, 1960), 33-41.
"WALDEN was uniquely American in at least three ways. First, we remark the sharp, indeed painful and exacerbated emphasis on the person against the mass of men. Second, we note the nonchristian yet specifically and

devoutly religious quality of Thoreau's experience
in WALDEN.   Third, we are struck by the pragmatism
here."

"July 4--Centenary of Thoreau's Independence," INTERPRETER,
    July 2, 1945.
        An editorial.

Junkins, Donald.   "Walden in July," NEW YORKER (July 14, 1962),
    75.
        A poem.

        also in: CONCORD JOURNAL, July 19, 1962.

Kahn, Sholom J.   "Thoreau in Israel," TSB #85, pp. 1-2.
　　　　Describes a forthcoming Hebrew translation of Tho-
　　　　reau by World Classics. WALDEN will be translated
　　　　by Reuben Avinoam, and Simon Halkin will contribute
　　　　an introductory essay on CIVIL DISOBEDIENCE.

Kaiser, Leo M.   "Remarks on Thoreau's Translation of Prome-
　　　　theus," CLASSICAL WEEKLY, XLVI (January 5, 1953), 69-70.
　　　　"The work today has significance pretty much as a
　　　　philological curiosity only."

Kalman, David.   "A Study of Thoreau," TSB #22.
　　　　Digest of a longer psychological study done at
　　　　the University of Minnesota.

Kalven, Harry, Jr.   "On Thoreau," CIVIL DISOBEDIENCE, by
　　　　Harrod A. Freeman, et al. Santa Barbara, California:
　　　　Center for Study of Democratic Institutions, 1966. pp.
　　　　25-28.

Kamp, Anton. N. C. WYETH AND THOREAU.   ?   :   ? ,   ? ,
　　　　(mimeographed).
　　　　The text of Mr. Kamp's address before the 1951
　　　　Thoreau Society annual meeting.

Kane, Edward H.   "Thoreau's Words Warn Legislators," BOSTON
　　　　GLOBE, January 4,? 1954.
　　　　Letter to editor citing passage from Thoreau on
　　　　legislators.

Kane, Henry Bugbee.   "Spring at Walden, 1945," BORZOI BATTLE-
　　　　DORE, I (May, 1945), 6-7.
　　　　A comparison with the spring of 1845, in the A.
　　　　A. Knopf house organ.

　--THOREAU'S WALDEN: A PHOTOGRAPHIC REGISTER.   New York:
　　　　Knopf, 1946.
　　　　A study of Walden by camera.

　　　　　reviews: BOSTON POST, December 8, 1946, by O. O.
　　　　　　　　CHICAGO TRIBUNE, August 25, 1946.
　　　　　　　　NEW YORK HERALD TRIBUNE, September 22,
　　　　　　　　1946, by E. W. Teale.
　　　　　　　　NEW YORK SUN, August 23, 1946.
　　　　　　　　SATURDAY REVIEW OF LITERATURE, November
　　　　　　　　23, 1946, by H. S. Canby.
　　　　　　　　THOREAU SOCIETY BULLETIN, #17 (October,
　　　　　　　　1946).

Kane, Russell W. "Freeloaders May Not Be Evil," CLEVELAND
     PLAIN DEALER, February 11, 1968.

--"Thoreau Defender Does Well," CLEVELAND PLAIN DEALER,
     March 2, 1968.
          Harry Wiggins replies to commentary on Thoreau.

Kasegawa, Koh. "The American Dream and Nature," AMERICAN
     LITERATURE: BULLETIN OF TOKYO AMERICAN LITERATURE SOCI-
     ETY, VII (1965), 2-9.

--"Emerson, Thoreau, Melville," THE 36TH GENERAL MEETING
     OF THE ENGLISH LITERARY SOCIETY OF JAPAN, 23-24 May, 1964.
     Meiji University, 1941. pp. 38-42.
          Text in Japanese.

          also in: AOYAMA JOURNAL OF GENERAL EDUCATION
          [Tokyo], V (November, 1964), 15-24. Text in Jap-
          anese but abstract in English.

--"Henry Thoreau and Asa Gray," ENGLISH LITERARY SOCIETY
     OF JAPAN, XXXVII (May 28, 1965), 14-15.

          also in: THOUGHTS CURRENT IN ENGLISH LITERATURE
          [Aoyawa Gakuin University, Tokyo], XXXVIII (1965),
          223-240. Text in Japanese.

--"An Interpretation of Thoreau's 'CIVIL DISOBEDIENCE',"
     AOYAMA JOURNAL OF GENERAL EDUCATION, IV (November, 1963),
     1-19.
          A paragraph by paragraph analysis of the essay.

--"A Limnological Re-examination of Thoreau's WALDEN (A
     Japanese Explication of Mr. E. S. Deevey, Jr.'s study,
     1942)," STUDIES IN ENGLISH AND AMERICAN LITERATURE [Aoyama
     Gakuin University, Tokyo], XII (March, 1966), 1-7.

--"The Natural History Essay in Thoreau," JOURNAL OF COL-
     LEGE OF LITERATURE [Aoyama Gakuin University, Tokyo], X,
     (January, 1967), 31-47.
          Text in Japanese, abstract in English.

--"Nature and Poetic Thought of Thoreau," RISING GENERATION
     [Tokyo], CXIII (October, 1967), 642-644.
          Text in Japanese.

--"Nonviolence in America," AOYAMA JOURNAL OF GENERAL ED-
     UCATION [Tokyo], VIII (November, 1967), 63-70.
          Many references to Thoreau. Text in Japanese.

--"A Note on UNCLE TOM'S CABIN," STUDIES IN ENGLISH AND
     AMERICAN LITERATURE [Aoyama Gakuin University, Tokyo],
     X (March, 1964), 1-10.
          Includes comments on Thoreau's anti-slavery activ-
          ities.

--"Self-Culture in Emerson and Thoreau," STUDIES IN AMER-
ICAN LITERATURE [Tokyo], I (October, 1964), 1-21.

--"Thoreau and the Bhagavad-Gita," THOUGHTS CURRENT IN
ENGLISH LITERATURE [Japan], XXXVI (December, 1963), 43-61.

--"Thoreau and Burroughs," SHI TO SAMBUN [Tokyo], XIX
(March 30, 1969), 42-46.

--"Thoreau and Whitman," THOUGHT CURRENTS IN ENGLISH LITER-
ATURE [Tokyo], XL (December, 1967), 39-54.
     Text in Japanese.

--"Thoreau, CIVIL DISOBEDIENCE ni tsuite," AOYAMA JOURNAL
OF GENERAL EDUCATION, II (November, 1961), 45-61.
     Text in Japanese.

--"Thoreau, THE SUCCESSION OF FOREST TREES," JOURNAL OF
COLLEGE OF LITERATURE [Aoyama Gakuin University, Tokyo],
IX (March, 1966), 53-68.
     In Japanese with abstract in English.

--"Thoreau, A WEEK," AOYAMA JOURNAL OF GENERAL EDUCATION
[Tokyo], VII (November, 1966), 1-8.

--"Thoreau's Humor in CIVIL DISOBEDIENCE," JOURNAL OF
COLLEGE OF LITERATURE [Aoyama Gakuin University, Tokyo],
XI (March, 1968), 41-51.
     Text in Japanese, abstract in English.

--"Thoreau's WALDEN: A Nature-Myth," STUDIES IN ENGLISH
LITERATURE [English Literary Society of Japan], XXXIX
(November, 1963), 213-240.

--"The Transcendentalist View of Man in Emerson and Thoreau," SHI TO SAMBUN, XIX (March 30, 1969), 35-41.

Kashkin, I. "Thoreau," ENCYCLOPAEDIC DICTIONARY OF THE
RUSSIAN BIBLIOGRAPHIC INSTITUTE, 7th Edition, XLI, 645-
648.

Kay, Tom. "The American Way: Henry David Thoreau," ANOKA
[Minn.] HERALD, December 8, 1959.
     A cartoon.

Kazin, Alfred. "Dry Light and Hard Expressions," ATLANTIC
MONTHLY, CC (July, 1957), 74-76.
     Comparison of Emerson and Thoreau.

--"The JOURNAL of Henry David Thoreau," THE INMOST LEAF.
New York: Harcourt, 1955. pp. 103-108.
     Reprinted from NEW YORK HERALD TRIBUNE review of
     Thoreau's JOURNALS.

--"Thoreau and American Power," ATLANTIC MONTHLY, CCXXIII
(May, 1969), 60-68.

Kean, David W. "Thoreauland Revisited: Three Impressions,"
YANKEE, XXX (May, 1966), 62-63 passim.
A native returns to Concord.

Keast, W. R. and R. E. Streeter, editors. "Materials for
Analysis: The Meaning of WALDEN," THE PROVINCE OF PROSE.
New York: Harper, 1956.
Reprints a portion of WALDEN and essays on Thoreau
by Lowell, Canby, White, and Wilder.

Keiper, Elizabeth. "Thoreau's Pen, A Century Ago, Wrote
Truths for Today," ROCHESTER [N. Y.] TIMES UNION, July
16, 1954.
A WALDEN centennial essay.

Keller, Dean H. "Woodbury's Annotated Copy of Thoreau's
Letters," EMERSON SOCIETY QUARTERLY, XLIII (1966), 79-81.

Keller, Karl. "'A Cheerful Elastic Wit': the Metaphysical
Strain in Thoreau," THOREAU JOURNAL QUARTERLY, I (April
15, 1969), 1-17.

Kelley, William Melvin. A DIFFERENT DRUMMER. New York:
Doubleday, 1962.
An exciting new novel about race relations in the
South with its title taken from WALDEN.

Kellner, Leon. GESCHICHTE DER NORDAMERIKANISCHEN LITERATUR.
Berlin: ? , 1913, I.
Places Thoreau in the camp of Melville and Whitman
as a "primitive" writer and argues that he went to
the pond because of mundane concerns rather than
transcendental convictions. Admires Thoreau;s verse,
but attacks the didactic bent in WALDEN, pp. 63-77.

Kennedy, Daniel Edwards. "Thoreau in Old Dunstable," GRANITE
STATE MAGAZINE, IV (December, 1907), 247-250.
Thoreau's visits to southern New Hampshire.

Kent, Corita. "Let the Sun Shine In." Boston: Botolph Group
Center, 1969.
A silk screen print on Thoreau.

Kent, Mrs. Howard W. "A Catalog of the Thoreau Collection in
the Concord Antiquarian Society," TSB #47.

Kent, Phyllida. "A Study of the Structure of Thoreau's A
WEEK ON THE CONCORD AND MERRIMACK RIVERS." Carleton
University, 1967. Unpublished master's thesis.

Kern, Alexander C. "American Studies and American Literature:
Approaches to the Study of Thoreau," COLLEGE ENGLISH,
XXVII (March, 1966), 480-486.

--"Introducing Thoreau as Artist and Man," EMERSON SOCIETY
QUARTERLY, XVIII (1960), 12-14.

--"Thoreau's 'Sir Walter Raleigh'," CEAA NEWSLETTER, I
(March, 1968), 4-5.

Kessler, Milton. "The Good Death: For Henry D. Thoreau a
Century Later," EMERSON SOCIETY QUARTERLY, LVI (1969),
3.
A poem.

Kesterton, David B. "Hawthorne and Nature: Thoreauvian Influence?" ENGLISH LANGUAGE NOTES, IV (March, 1967), 200-
206.

Ketcham, Ralph L. "Reply to Buranelli's Case Against Thoreau," ETHICS, LXIX (April, 1959), 206-209.

Keyes, Langley Carleton. "He Journeyed Far," CHRISTIAN
SCIENCE MONITOR, May 31, 1945.
A sonnet on Thoreau.

--THOREAU: VOICE IN THE EDGELAND. Chapel Hill: University
of North Carolina Press, 1955.
A sequence of 209 sonnets weaving an intellectual
biography of Thoreau. The octaves are fashioned
from Thoreau's own words; the sestets are Mr. Keyes'
commentaries. It is interesting to see that Thoreau's prose can so easily be converted into poetry.
But the sestets are the more rewarding for they display Mr. Keyes' keen insight into the mind of Thoreau. WH TSB #55.

reviews: CHARLOTTE [N. C.] OBSERVER, January 1, 1956
RICHMOND [Va.] NEWS LEADER, December 29,
1955.

--"What Did Thoreau Really Think of Cape Cod's Great Beach?"
FALMOUTH [Mass.] ENTERPRISE, May 19, 1967.

Kieran, John. "Extracts from a Book with a Service Record,"
NEW YORK SUN, January 13, 1943.

--"Letters Received and Contents Noted," NEW YORK SUN,
June 16.
A comparison of Thoreau and Gilbert White.

--"Philosophy in the Making," WORDS TO LIVE BY, edited by
William Nichols. New York: Simon and Schuster, 1948.

King, Bruce. "Thoreau's WALDEN," ETUDES ANGLAISES, XVII
(July, 1964), 262-268.

King, Martin Luther Jr. "A Legacy of Creative Protest,"
MASSACHUSETTS REVIEW, IV (Autumn, 1962), 43.

--STRIDE TOWARD FREEDOM. New York: Ballentine Books, 1958.
King cites Thoreau as inspiration for his non-
violent revolt against segregation, pp. 41 passim.

Kingsbury, Kermit. "A Walk Around Walden on a January Day,"
    WORCESTER EVENING GAZETTE, January 6, 1960.
        Photographic essay.

Kinnaird, Clark. "The Happy Man," NEW YORK JOURNAL AMERICAN,
    July 12, 1965.
        Syndicated column on Thoreau.

Kirchner, Wm. Harry Jr. "Henry David Thoreau as a Social
    Critic." University of Minnesota, 1938. Unpublished
    doctoral dissertation.

Kiser, Martha Gwinn. GAY MELODY. New York: Longmans Green,
    1949.
        For those of you who want to introduce Thoreau to
        the younger generation, here is a new book, a novel
        of life in Concord written for teen-age girls. It
        is a veritable encyclopedia of customs of mid-19th
        century American life, perhaps too much so, for the
        plot is awkward and stilted. Thoreau wanders in
        and out of the pages, but the chapter entitled "A
        Day at Walden Wood" is entirely devoted to a visit
        to the cabin and contains as good an exposition of
        Thoreau's philosophy for young people as I've seen.
        I once heard a novelist say that Thoreau stole the
        show every time she tried to include him in one of
        her books. That must have happened here, for his
        chapter is by far the liveliest of the book,--WH,
        TSB #27.

Klein, Richard P. "Limerick on Thoreau's bluebird," CLEVE-
    LAND PLAIN DEALER, May 7, 1961.

Kleine, Don W. "CIVIL DISOBEDIENCE: The Way to WALDEN,"
    MODERN LANGUAGE NOTES, LXXV (April, 1960), 297-304.
        The essay and the book are consistent in philosophy.

Kleinfeld, Leonard F. "[Albert Jay] Nock Lauds Thoreau,"
    FRAGMENTS, IV (April, 1966), 9.

    --"Henry David Thoreau; the Apostle of Individual Hap-
    piness," translated into Japanese by Koh Kasegawa. SHI
    TO SAMBUN [Tokyo], XVIII (September, 1968), 22-29.

    --HENRY DAVID THOREAU CHRONOLOGY. Forest Hills, New York:
    Printed for the author, 1950.
        This is the first detailed chronology of Thoreau's
        life and it fills a long-felt need. Particularly
        helpful are the parallel chronologies of literature,
        American, and world history. It should be an in-
        dispensable tool to any research student and a help
        to the general reader. TSB #32.

    --Letter to the editor, NEW YORK SUN, April 13, 1945.
        Cairn controversy.

--"Stones for the Cairn," HEAR YE [Acton, Mass.], February, 1969.
>A play originally performed at a Thoreau Society annual meeting.

--"Thoreau's Pursuit of Happiness," FRAGMENTS, I (April, 1963), 3.

--"Tres Enfoques de Thoreau," CENIT (May-June, 1964), 4365-4368.
>Translated into Spanish by V. Munoz from FRAGMENTS.

Klomp, Henry DeWitt. THE GAME. New York: Pageant, 1967.
>A satirical novel on college English departments. One of characters has much to say on Thoreau since he is writing a book on him.

Kloss, Gerald. "The Philosopher at Walden," MILWAUKEE JOURNAL, September 3, 1954.

Klossner, Erich S. "Thoreau's Walden Pond," WINGS, XIII (Autumn, 1957), 17.
>A poem.

Knortz, Karl. EIN AMERIKANISCHER DIOGENES, HENRY D. THOREAU. Hamburg: ? , 1899.
>A brief monograph in two sections; the first section celebrates Thoreau's attack on the shams of society and Christianity; the second relates his life and ideas to those of Goethe, Zimmermann, Christ, Nietzsche, Faust, et al. A wild and often irrelevant exercise in critical broken-field running. TSB #105.

--GESCHICHTE DER NORDAMERIKANISCHEN LITERATUR. Berlin: ? , 1891, I. pp. 283-293.
>Characterizes Thoreau as a vehement abolitionist. Though dubious about what he takes to be Thoreau's escapism, Knortz admires Thoreau's practical ideas, such as his views on education. Calls attention to Thoreau as a critic of society and concludes that his writings will be considered among the classics of American literature. TSB #105.

Knox, John B. "Thoreau's WALDEN Still Important in World Affairs," WINONA [Minn.] DAILY NEWS, September 20, 1954.
>Reprinted under varying titles in DALLAS [Tex.] MORNING NEWS, August 8, 1954 and TRENTON [N. J.] TIMES-ADVERTISER, August 29, 1954.

Koehler, Martha P. "Thoreau's Walden," RALPH WALDO EMERSON AND OTHER POEMS. Philadelphia: Dorrance, 1967. p. 18.
>A poem.

Koopman, Louise O. "The Thoreau Romance," MASSACHUSETTS REVIEW, IV (Autumn, 1962), 61-67.

Kopp, Charles C. "The Mysticism of Henry David Thoreau." Pennsylvania State University, 1963. Unpublished doctoral dissertation.

Korell, Jason H. "Thoreau Reborn at New Lyceum," LOWELL [Mass.] SUN, July 8, 1966.
Account of new Thoreau Lyceum.

Korell, Priscilla A. "Walden Pond Now National Historical Landmark," LOWELL SUN, July 12, 1965.

Kotera, Yukimasa. "Explanation on Thoreau's WALDEN," KONGO-YOTEKI [Osaka, Japan], CCIII (May 25, 1965), 1-28.

--"On the Anniversary of the 150 Years of Thoreau's Birthday," KONG-YOTEKI, CCXX (1967), 1-30.
Text in Japanese.

Kramer, Aaron. THE PROPHETIC TRADITION IN AMERICAN POETRY, 1835-1900. Rutherford, N. J.: Fairleigh Dickinson University Press, 1968.
A fantastically comprehensive survey of the reactions of 19th century American poets to such social issues as the War with Mexico, slavery, immigrants, and Indians. In Thoreau's case, his prose on these subjects is given as close scrutiny as his poems and he emerges as one of the few on the liberal side on each of these issues. Kramer describes him as one of "the greatest souls of the century." TSB #108.

Kramer, Sid and Sonia Kramer. "Thoreau Job Done on Walden Creator," THE EVENING NEWS [Washington Square College, N. Y. U.], December 9, 1948, pp. 1-3.
A detailed account of a meeting devoted to Thoreau.

Krastin, Alexandra. "He Took to the Woods 100 Years Ago," SATURDAY EVENING POST (June 30, 1945).
A long essay on Thoreau's Walden experiment and its influence today, illustrated with some superb kodachrome photographs of Concord scenes. TSB #12.

Kreymborg, Alfred. MAN AND SHADOW: AN ALLEGORY. New York: Dutton, 1946.
A long poem with frequent mention of Thoreau.

Krogh, Lee V. "Thoreau: An Inquiry into the Question of His Status as a Poet." Mankato [Minn.] State College, 1961. Unpublished master's thesis.

Krokel, Fritz. "Der gerade Weg des H. D. Thoreau," DER SPEICHER (1948), pp. 93-117.
Stresses Thoreau's protest against the tyranny of the majority and the eclecticism of his religious views.

141

Krutch, Joseph Wood. "GBS Enters Heaven (?)," SATURDAY REVIEW
OF LITERATURE, May 24, 1952.

        also in: SATURDAY REVIEW READER NO. 2. New York:
        Bantam, 1953. pp. 205-211. A delightful imaginary
        interview between GBS and Thoreau in the after-world.

--HENRY DAVID THOREAU. New York: William Sloane Associates, 1948.

        reviews: ATLANTIC MONTHLY, CLXXXII (December, 1948),
        113-114.
        BULLETIN OF THE MASSACHUSETTS AUDUBON SO-
        CIETY, XXXIII (November, 1949), 298-300,
        by F. H. Allen.
        CHICAGO DAILY NEWS, February 9, 1949, by
        Sidney J. Harris.
        CHRISTIAN SCIENCE MONITOR, October 21,
        1948.
        CHRISTIAN UNITARIAN REGISTER, CXXVII
        (March, 1949).
        COMMONWEAL, XLIX (October 15, 1948), 17,
        by Mason Wade.
        FREEDOM [London, England], X (April 2,
        1949), 2.
        JOHN O'LONDON'S WEEKLY [London, England],
        LVIII (April 15, 1949), 235.
        LIBRARY JOURNAL, LXXIII (September 1,
        1949), 1189.
        LIVING WILDERNESS, XIV (Summer, 1949),
        19-20, by Paul H. Oehser.
        NATION, CLXVII (October 16, 1948), 433-
        435, by Carl Bode.
        NATURE MAGAZINE, XLI (December, 1948),
        506-507, by Howard Zahniser.
        NEW ENGLAND QUARTERLY, XXII (January,
        1950), 540-542, by Sterling Lanier.
        NEW REPUBLIC, November 8, 1948.
        NEW YORK EVENING SUN, October 4, 1948,
        by John Cournos.
        NEW YORK HERALD TRIBUNE, October 3 & 6,
        1948.
        NEW YORK TIMES, October 3 & 4, 1948.
        NEW YORKER (October 16, 1948), 133-134.
        PROCEEDINGS OF THE ENTOMOLOGICAL SOCIETY
        OF WASHINGTON, LI (June, 1949), 132-133.
        PROGRESSIVE (March, 1949).
        SATURDAY REVIEW OF LITERATURE, XXI (Novem-
        ber 13, 1948), by Milton Crane.
        THOREAU SOCIETY BULLETIN #25, October,
        1948.
        TRENTON [N. J.] TIMES, November 7, 1948,
        p. 10.

--"Henry David Thoreau and Society Today," BULLETIN OF
THE AMERICAN ACADEMY OF ARTS AND SCIENCES, XXI (October,

1967), 3-12.

--"If You Don't Mind My Saying So,: AMERICAN SCHOLAR, XXXVII (Winter, 1967), 15-18.
On CIVIL DISOBEDIENCE.

--"A Kind of Pantheism," SATURDAY REVIEW OF LITERATURE, XXIII (June 10, 1950), 7ff.
Nature writers, particularly Thoreau, evaluated.

--THE LAST BOSWELL PAPER. Woodstock, Vermont: Elm Tree Press, 1951.
660 copies printed for Philip and Fanny Duschnes. A beautiful reprinting of the article in the SATURDAY REVIEW OF LITERATURE (July 21, 1951), 13-15 passim. A conversation between Thoreau and Dr. Johnson in the Elysian Fields. Quite the most delightful essay of the year. But don't believe it when they tell you Wyeth's painting of Hubbard's Bridge is Walden Pond. TSB #37.

--"A Little Fishy Friend," NATION, CLXIX (October 8, 1949), 350-351.
Commemorating centennial of A WEEK. Thoreau began new epoch in nature writing because he was willing to regard objects of nature as his fellow-creatures without qualification or condescension. R.A. TSB #30.

--MORE LIVES THAN ONE. New York: Sloane, 1962.
Much on his interest in Thoreau.

--"Quiet of Walden Pond Still Sounds thru the World," CHICAGO TRIBUNE, November 29, 1959.
Brief essay.

--"Thoreau and Sir Thomas Browne," TSB #29.

--"Thoreau on Madison Ave.," SATURDAY REVIEW OF LITERATURE, XXVIII (January 29, 1955), 9-10 passim.
A delightful "interview" with Thoreau on modern advertising.

translation: "Thoreau et la publicite," translated by A. Prudhommeaux. L'UNIQUE (1955).

--"Thoreau's Literary Reputation," CHRISTIAN SCIENCE MONITOR, May, 1949.
An excerpt from his book on Thoreau.

--THE TWELVE SEASONS: A PERPETUAL CALENDAR FOR THE COUNTRY. New York: Sloane, 1949.
A series of twelve delightful monthly essays on nature, with frequent reference to Thoreau. TSB #28.

--"Who Was Henry Thoreau?," SATURDAY REVIEW OF LITERATURE (August 19, 1967), pp. 18-19 passim.

--"Wilderness as a Tonic," SATURDAY REVIEW OF LITERATURE
(June 8, 1963), pp. 15-17.
    On Thoreau's theory of "the wild."

--"The Wilderness at Our Doorstep," NEW YORK TIMES BOOK
REVIEW, June 21, 1953, p. 1 passim.
    On the influence of American nature writers on
    English. "Thoreau is still the greatest of them
    all."

--, E. W. Teale and L. Bryson. "Henry Thoreau: WALDEN,"
INVITATION TO LEARNING, II (Summer, 1952), 115-122.
    Transcription of radio broadcast.

"Krutch on Thoreau," WESTERN HUMANITIES REVIEW, IX (Summer,
1955), 279-280.
    On Thoreau's "blasphemy" against the machine.

Kurtz, Kenneth. "Thoreau and Individualism Today," EMERSON
SOCIETY QUARTERLY, LVIII (1960), 14-15.
    Part of symposium.

Kuyk, D. A. Jr. "A Thoreau Exhibition," RICHMOND TIMES DIS-
PATCH, June 20, 1954.
    A lengthy account of the University of Virginia
    Library centennial exhibition.

Kwiat, Joseph J. "Thoreau and George Minott," AMERICAN SPEECH,
XX (February, 1945), 78.

--"Thoreau's Philosophical Apprenticeship," NEW ENGLAND
QUARTERLY (March, 1945).
    A scholarly study of the influence of Thoreau's
    college reading in philosophy upon his thought.
    A reply to Raymond Adams' "Thoreau's Literary
    Apprenticeship" of some years ago.

Kyria, Pierre. "Henry David Thoreau et L'Esprit de Liberte,"
COMBAT [Paris], February 8, 1968.
    On recent French translation of Thoreau.

Lacey, James F. "Thoreau in German Criticism: an Annotated Bibliography," TSB #105, pp. 4-6.

LaForte, R. S. "The Political Thought of Henry D. Thoreau: A Study in Paradox," EDUCATIONAL LEADER, XXIII (July, 1959), 41-51.

Lake, Ivan Clyde. "Concord Villager: Henry David Thoreau," NEW YORK HERALD TRIBUNE, September 10, 1950.
    A poem.

    also in: KALEIDOGRAPH, XXII (August, 1950), 3.

Lalli, Biancamaria Tedeschini. HENRY DAVID THOREAU. Roma: Edizioni di Storia e Letteratura, 1954.
    The first book-length study of Thoreau in Italian.

Landis, Benson Y. "The Decentralist at Walden Pond," CHRISTIAN CENTURY, LXII (July 11, 1945), 810-811.
    Thoreau's economic theories.

  --"The Squatter at Walden," ADVANCE, CXXXVII (July, 1945), 16-17.
    A centennial essay.

  --"The Squatter's Hut at Walden," AMERICAN JOURNAL OF ECONOMICS AND SOCIOLOGY, IV (April, 1945), 327-332.
    A still further expansion of Thoreau's economic theories, the most thorough of the series.

  --"Where History is Everything, or, Concord Revisited," TOWN AND COUNTRY CHURCH, LXIX (March, 1951), 9-10.
    Thoughts on Thoreau while on a pilgrimage to Concord.

Lane, Lauriat, Jr. "On the Organic Structure of WALDEN," AMERICAN LITERATURE: A CRITICAL SURVEY, edited by T. D. Young and R. E. Fine. New York: American Book Co., 1968. pp. 187-198.

    also in: COLLEGE ENGLISH, XXI (January, 1960), 195-202.

  --"Prose as Architecture: Thoreau and Theodore Winthrop on the Maine Woods," CANADIAN ASSOCIATION FOR AMERICAN STUDIES BULLETIN, II (Spring, 1966), 17-24.

  --"Thoreau at Work: Four Versions of 'A Walk to Wachusett',"

BULLETIN OF NEW YORK PUBLIC LIBRARY, LXIX (January, 1965), 3-16.

--"Thoreau's Response to the Maine Woods," EMERSON SOCIETY QUARTERLY, XLVII (1967), 37-41.

--"Thoreau's Two Walks: Structure and Meaning," TSB #109, pp. 1-3.

--"WALDEN, the Second Year," STUDIES IN ROMANTICISM, VIII (1969), 183-192.

--, editor. APPROACHES TO WALDEN. San Francisco: Wadsworth, 1961.
> Lane has "tried to give the reader a set of materials helpful for the understanding and appreciation of WALDEN." It includes a brief analysis by Lane of ways to read WALDEN (quite the best part of the book), excerpts from Thoreau's journals and correspondence showing ideas similar to those in WALDEN, typical 19th and 20th century criticisms of WALDEN by Lowell, Stevenson, Hyman, Morris, etc., a collection of E. B. White's comments on Thoreau, a series of comments, questions and topics for writing on WALDEN, and an extensive bibliography. It should help both the student and the teacher to attain a more thorough understanding of WALDEN. TSB #76.

Lang, Berel. "Thoreau and the Body Impolitic," COLORADO QUARTERLY, XVIII (Summer, 1969), 51-57.

Langland, Joseph. "How It, So Help Me, Was," MASSACHUSETTS REVIEW, IV (Autumn, 1962), 53-54.
> A poem.

Langton, Jane. THE TRANSCENDENTAL MURDER. New York: Harper and Row, 1964.
> An amusing murder mystery, set in contemporary Concord, which involves such skullduggery as unearthing a love-affair between Emily Dickinson and Thoreau, and murdering someone by dropping a bust of Louisa May Alcott on her head. The secretary of the Thoreau Society is one of the central characters! TSB #87.

> review: CONCORD JOURNAL, February 20, 1964.

Lapin, Adam. "On the 135th Anniversary of Henry Thoreau," THE WORKER [New York], July 27, 1952, p. 7.
> A Communist tribute to Thoreau!!! "His meaning for today is to be found in his realization that he, the most non-political of human beings, had to engage in political struggle if he were not to betray himself and his love of life and nature."

Larter, Nancy. "Thoreau's Thought Was That You Learn More
About Nature by Practicing Humanity," BOSTON HERALD,
October 24, 1961.

Lask, Thomas. "College Seminar Honors Thoreau," NEW YORK
TIMES, May 15, 1967.
On Nassau Community College Thoreau Festival.

LasVergnas, Raymond. "Le Triomphe de Thoreau," LES NOUVEL-
LES LITTERAIRES [Paris]. February 29. 1968.
On recent French translation of Thoreau.

Lathrop, George Parsons. "On Thoreau," BROOKLYN STANDARD
UNION, December 19, 1894.
Detailed report of a lecture on Thoreau.

Lauter, Paul. "Thoreau's Prophetic Testimony," MASSACHUSETTS
REVIEW, IV (Autumn, 1962), 111-123.

Lavan, Spencer. "A Concept of God in the Writings of Emerson and Thoreau," LIBERAL'S CHALLENGE, XI (Spring, 1958).

Lawrence, Wes. "Beautiful Concord River," CLEVELAND PLAIN
DEALER. December 29, 1964.
Its association with Thoreau.

--"Breakfast Commentator: Bainbury's Summer Diary,"
CLEVELAND PLAIN DEALER, June 27, 1962.
Account of a visit to Walden.

--"How Thoreau and Clevelander Won 1960 Election," CLEVE-
LAND PLAIN DEALER, February 26, 1961.
Ted Bailey's part in election of Thoreau to Hall
of Fame.

--"Observes Henry Thoreau Day," PLAIN DEALER [Cleveland, O.],
July 15, 1967.

"A Lead Pencil Diploma," TSB #74, pp. 7-8.
The diploma is reproduced on page 8.

Leary, Lewis. ARTICLES ON AMERICAN LITERATURE APPEARING IN
CURRENT PERIODICALS: 1920-1945. Durham: Duke University
Press, 1947.
An excellent bibliography of all recent magazine
articles on American literature. There are five
pages of items listed on Thoreau (pp. 110-115).
It is indispensable to anyone studying American
literature. TSB #21.

--"A Century of WALDEN," NATION, CLXXIX (August 7, 1954),
114-115.

--"A Man of Few Affairs," SATURDAY REVIEW, XLV (May 5,
1962), 12-13.
A centennial tribute.

--"Thoreau," EIGHT AMERICAN AUTHORS, edited by Floyd Stovall. New York: Modern Language Association, 1956. pp.
153-206.
> So rapidly have the studies of Thoreau proliferated
> in recent years that your secretary, for example,
> finds that he has more than 3000 books, pamphlets,
> and periodical articles in his Thoreau files. It
> is obvious therefore that the average person cannot
> hope to read thru all this material and weed out the
> worth-while from the repetitious or mere trash. For-
> tunately now Prof. Leary has come to our rescue with
> his fifty-three page annotated bibliography of ma-
> terials by and about Thoreau. Prof. Leary has ap-
> parently read everything of value on the subject
> and has chosen from that mountainous pile all that
> is really significant to the Thoreau student and
> then provided ample and clear directions as to just
> how it may be found. He has not tried to bring any
> new material to light, but he has shed a great deal
> of light on what is available. While his bibliogra-
> phy by no means replaces the more exhaustive check-
> lists of Allen, Wade, and White, it will no doubt
> prove more valuable to the student, because his is
> a critical bibliography. Incidentally, the other
> seven authors included in this group bibliography
> are Poe, Emerson, Hawthorne, Melville, Whitman,
> Twain, and James. TSB #58.

--"The Thoreau Society Presidential Address," TSB #80, pp.
1-3.

--"Walden Goes Wandering: The Transit of Good Intentions,"
NEW ENGLAND QUARTERLY, XXXII (March, 1959), 3-30.
> Detailed account of the Dutch F. van Eeden's Walden
> experiment.

--"Wilderness Is Where You Find It," CONGRESSIONAL RECORD
(November 2, 1962).

[Leary, Lewis]. A CENTENARY COMMEMORATION. New York: Thoreau Society, 1962.
> Program of the centennial meetings.

Leavitt, H. Walter. KATAHDIN SKYLINES. Orono, Maine: University of Maine Press, 1942 (Revised 1946), Maine Technology Experiment Station Paper No. 40.
> A detailed discussion of Maine's highest mountain
> with much new naterial on Thoreau's excursions there.

Lee, Harry. MORE DAY TO DAWN. New York: Duell, Sloan and
Pearce, 1941.
> The major Thoreau book of the year. Thoreau bio-
> graphy in verse.
>
> review: Thoreau Society Bulletin #1.

-- "Wartime Economies," LIBERTY MAGAZINE (March 26, 1943).
   A poem.

Lee, Leon H. THE LITERARY ANTECENDENTS OF HENRY DAVID THO-
   REAU'S CIVIL DISOBEDIENCE. Lexington, Ky.: University
   of Kentucky Press, 1964.
      Kentucky Microcards, Series A., No. 189.

Lehigh University Library. THE DEMOCRATIC IMAGINATION.
   Bethlehem: Lehigh University Library, 1968.
      Catalog of an exhibition including a section of
      Thoreau materials.

Lehrman, N. L. "Why I Like Thoreau," TSB #54.

Leidecker, Kurt F. "That Sad Pagan Thoreau," VISVABHARATI
   QUARTERLY (November, 1951-January, 1952), 218-259.
      One of the lengthiest and most thorough studies
      of Thoreau's orientalism to date.

Leigh, Betty. "Concord Meadows (Remembering Thoreau),"
   BOSTON POST, August 6, 1942.
      A poem.

Leighton, Caroline C. A SWISS THOREAU. Boston: ?   , 1890.
      A pamphlet comparing Thoreau with Amiel.

Leisy, Ernest E. "Francis Quarles and Henry D. Thoreau,"
   MODERN LANGUAGE NOTES (May, 1945).
      A brief note on Thoreau's interest in Quarles.

   -- "Sources of Thoreau's Borrowings in A WEEK," AMERICAN
   LITERATURE (March, 1946).
      An extremely important scholarly study of the
      sources used for Thoreau's first book. Because
      of its significance, I shall include here a few
      corrections of its text made by F. H. Allen:
      "'Were it the will of heaven,' etc., as it ap-
      pears in MISCELLANIES is attributed by Thoreau to
      Plutarch as a quotation from Pindar. It appears
      in PLUTARCH'S MORALS: TRANSLATED FROM THE GREEK BY
      SEVERAL HANDS, London, 1718, vol. III, p. 123,
      where Plutarch is quoting Pindar. So both Emerson's
      Commonplace Book and Thoreau are right...Another of
      Leisy's notes seems to need a little revision--that
      for p. 414. Here 'day' in the singular is correct,
      but the earlier editions of the WEEK have the in-
      correct 'days'. They also give the third line in-
      correctly as 'Sweet dews,' etc., instead of 'The
      dew,' etc." TSB #16.

   -- "Thoreau and Ossian," NEW ENGLAND QUARTERLY (March, 1945).
      Another brief note, on Thoreau's interest in Ossian.

   -- "Thoreau's Borrowings in WALDEN," NOTES AND QUERIES
   (January 16, 1943), 46.

A request for identification of passages.

Lemaitre, Renee. "Les Transcendentalists," INFORMATIONS AND
DOCUMENTS [Paris], CCIV (September 15, 1964), 32-37.
Background essay with much on Thoreau.

[Lemaitre, Renee]. "Actual ite du Philosophe H. D. Thoreau,"
HUMANISME [Centre de Documentation du Grand Orient de
France], LXXIII (Mars, 1969), 5-16.

Lennon, Florence Becker. "The Voice of the Turtle," TSB #15.
The article was written "after a series of inter-
views with Wm. Sherburne Osgood of Colorado Springs,
the son of Ellen Sewall Osgood."

--"WALDEN Centennial Celebration at City Library With Exhibit," BOULDER [Col.] DAILY CAMERA, February 19, 1945.
With an essay on Thoreau's life and significance.

"Leslie Stephen on Thoreau," TSB #105, p. 8.
Includes an excerpt from HOURS IN A LIBRARY. New
York: Putnam, 1907. IV, 132-133.

Lessing, O. E. BRUECKEN UBER DEN ATLANTIK: BEITRAGE ZUM
AMERIKANISCHEN UND DEUTSCHEN GEISTESLEBEN. Berlin:
?   , 1927. pp. 69-75.
Portrays Thoreau as a GEMÜTLICH, good-humoured,
and industrious burgher and attacks the clichés
which characterize Thoreau as a Yankee-Stoic or a
latter-day St. Francis of Assisi. Suggests Thor-
reau's Walden sojourn was a sentimental and un-
necessary prank.

Leviero, Harry P. "Walden Pond Preserves Site Thoreau Used
as a Sanctuary," NEW YORK HERALD TRIBUNE, August 31, 1947.
A brief article for the tourist trade. Filled with
inaccuracies. TSB #21.

Lewis, R. W. B. THE AMERICAN ADAM. Chicago: University of
Chicago Press, 1955.
One of the most thoughtful and provocative analyses
of 19th century American literature in recent years.
A study of the "Adamic myth," the popular belief
of the time that in America man had found a new
opportunity to break away from the past and begin
all over again as an "innocent in paradise." Quite
appropriately Thoreau is one of the first authors
he discusses (pp. 20-27, et passim) and his analysis of the "re-birth" symbol in WALDEN is one of
the most enlightening and convincing I have seen.
He demonstrates effectively how much Thoreau's protest was a part of the intellectual milieu of the
time. TSB #55.

Lewis, Sinclair. "One-Man Revolution," THE MAN FROM MAIN
STREET. New York: Random House, 1953. pp. 240-242.

Reprinting his vital analysis of Thoreau's opposition to totalitarianism.

Ley, Ruth. "Hard Luck Led to Good," BOSTON GLOBE, July 12,
1946.
An account of Mr. Robbins' find.

"Library Receives Gift from Plymouth of Literary Interest,"
CONCORD JOURNAL, December 4, 1958.
Free Public Library receives 100 MS letters by
Thoreau's friend Ellery Channing.

Liddell, Bettie Cassie. "Gardener at Walden," CHRISTIAN
SCIENCE MONITOR, May ?, 1954.
A poem on Thoreau.

Lidman, David. "Thoreau Design by Leonard Baskin," NEW YORK
TIMES, April 9, 1967.
Probably the most detailed of articles on the new
Thoreau stamp. Other articles: WESTERN STAMP COL-
LECTOR, April 15, 1967; CONCORD FREE PRESS, April
13, 1967; CHRISTIAN SCIENCE MONITOR, April 13, 1967.

"Life in the Woods," NEW YORK TRIBUNE,   ?   , 1849?.
A hitherto unnoticed brief contemporary account
of Thoreau's experiment at Walden.

also in: YOUTH'S COMPANION (July 19, 1849).
YOUTH'S COMPANION. Boston: Houghton Mifflin, 1954.
p. 903.

Lin, Yutan. ON THE WISDOM OF AMERICA. New York: Day, 1950.
Numerous references to Thoreau.

Linscott, Robert Newton. "$3 a Week as a Start," NEW YORK
TIMES BOOK REVIEW, February 6, 1966.

Little, Jan. "Rain Forest Walden," CHRISTIAN SCIENCE MON-
ITOR, November 6, 1968.
On reading WALDEN in the tropics.

Lloyd, J. William. "Thoreau, the Husband of Nature," FREE
SPIRIT (September, 1919), pp. 47-58.
An essay.

Locke, Walter. "Trends of the Times," ATLANTA JOURNAL, August 31, 1944.
An editorial wondering how Thoreau would fare in
certain foreign countries were he alive today.

Lombardo, Agostino. "L'arte di Henry David Thoreau," BEL-
FAGOR, XIV (November 30, 1959), 674-685.

--LA RICERCA DEL VERO: SAGGI SULLA TRADIZIONE LITTERARIA
AMERICANA. Roma: Ed. di storia e letteratura, 1961.
Includes a chapter on Thoreau.

Longstreth, T. Morris. "Allen French: An Appreciation,"
    CONCORD JOURNAL, October 10, 1946.
        A beautiful tribute to a great Thoreauvian.

--"An Atmosphere of Choice," CHRISTIAN SCIENCE MONITOR,
    May 28, 1951.
        An interpretation of Thoreau's ideas of friendship.

--"Doctor Johnson's Block-head," CHRISTIAN SCIENCE MONITOR,
    March 3, 1953.
        Johnson and Thoreau contrasted on rules for good
        writing.

--HENRY THOREAU: AMERICAN REBEL. New York: Dodd, Mead,
    1963.
        A brief fictionalized biography of Thoreau for teen-
        agers. Mr. Longstreth (acting secretary of the Tho-
        reau Society during World War II) catches the flavor
        of Thoreau's life, but often concocts imaginary con-
        versations and incidents and occasionally transposes
        events quite out of their sequence--as for example,
        having Thoreau talking to Emerson years before Emer-
        son moved to Concord. TSB #86.

        reviews: BOOKWEEK (April 12, 1964).
                  NEW YORK TIMES, November 10, 1963.

--HIDEOUT. New York: Macmillan, 1947.

--"An Idyl Out of Season," CHRISTIAN SCIENCE MONITOR,
    March 4, 1944.
        An essay on Thoreau and huckleberry picking.

--"The Man Who Sought Peace with Himself," NEW YORK TIMES
    MAGAZINE, July 1, 1945.
        A centennial essay.

--"On Thoreau's Coldness," CHRISTIAN SCIENCE MONITOR, Au-
    gust 25, 1944.
        The theory presented that Thoreau was even more
        capable of warm friendly relations with his fellow-
        men that he ever suspected.

--"Our Most Famous Hill," CHRISTIAN SCIENCE MONITOR, Novem-
    ber 5, 1943.
        Thoreau and Fair Haven Hill.

--"Thoreau and the Thrushes," CHRISTIAN SCIENCE MONITOR,
    June 8, 1944.
        An essay.

--"Thoreau as Writing Instructor," CHRISTIAN SCIENCE MON-
    ITOR, July 12, 1945.

--"The Three Thousand Mile Shelf," CHRISTIAN SCIENCE MON-
    ITOR, November 26, 1946.

A suggestion that the United States Congress re-
publish some of the great classics of American literature in order to get them back into print and that
Thoreau's JOURNALS in particular be one of the first
of these.

--TWO RIVERS MEET IN CONCORD. Philadelphia: Westminster,
1946.

      reviews: CHRISTIAN SCIENCE MONITOR, April 13, 1946.
                SATURDAY REVIEW OF LITERATURE, April 27,
                1946.
                THOREAU SOCIETY BULLETIN #15.

Loomis, C. Grant. "Henry David Thoreau as Folklorist,"
WESTERN FOLKLORE, XVI (April, 1957), 90-106.
Points out in detail that Thoreau's works are a
gold mine of folklore, proverbs, folktales, super-
stition, etc.

--A WALK IN CONCORD: IN MEMORIAM HENRY DAVID THOREAU 1817-
1862. Fort Bragg, Calif.: Gull Press, 1961.
A moving poetical tribute to Thoreau.

Lorch, Fred. Wm. "Thoreau and the Organic Principle in
Poetry." University of Iowa, 1936. Unpublished doctoral dissertation.

"'Lost'Thoreau Volume in Exhibit," NEW YORK HERALD TRIBUNE,
October 3, 1956.

"Louisa May Alcott Recalls Her Friend," TSB #18.
Reprinted is an article from Louisa May Alcott's
monthly column, "Merry's Monthly Chat with His
Friends," which appeared in MERRY'S MUSEUM for
March, 1869.

"Loves and Lovers," BOSTON POST, March 12, 1949.
Summarizes Canby's chapters on Thoreau in love.

Low, Alvah H. "The Concord Lyceum," OLD-TIME NEW ENGLAND,
L (Fall, 1959), 29-42.

"Lowell and Thoreau," NOTES AND QUERIES (January 16, 1943), pp.
40-41.
A reprinting by the editors of NOTES AND QUERIES
of Thoreau's June 22, 1858, letter to Lowell in
protest of dropping the pine tree sentence from
"Chesuncook".

Lowell, Anna C. SEED-GRAIN FOR THOUGHT AND DISCUSSION: A
COMPILATION. Boston: Ticknor and Fields, 1856. 2 vols.
An anthology which includes many quotations from
Thoreau. One of the very earliest such anthol-
ogizations of Thoreau.

Lownes, Albert E. "Arthur Fifield and Thoreau's CIVIL DIS-
OBEDIENCE," TSB #86, p. 4.
Lownes contends that the pamphlet, The Simple Life
Series No. 4, ON THE DUTY OF CIVIL DISOBEDIENCE
published by Fifield in 1903 interested many people
in Thoreau.

--"Some Statistics about Thoreau's WEEK," TSB #66.

Lucas, Alec. "Thoreau, Field Naturalist," UNIVERSITY OF
TORONTO QUARTERLY, XXIII (April, 1954), 227-232.
"Thoreau is both philosopher and scientist--a
field naturalist, one of the forerunners of an in-
creasing number of people who today visit the woods
and fields simply for the personal pleasure of quiet
hours spent in learning something about the plants
and animals they find there."

Ludlow, Robert P. "Thoreau and the State," COMMONWEAL, L
(September 23, 1949), 581-582.

Ludlum, Robert P. "Thoreau and Blackburn," A TRAIN OF THOUGHT,
XIII (December, 1960), 1-4.
Influence of Thoreau on Blackburn college curriculum.

Ludwig, Jack. "Confusions: Thoreau in California," NOBLE
SAVAGE, I (1960), 208-248.
An hilarious short story about a beatnik worship-
er of Thoreau.

Ludwig, Richard M. LITERARY HISTORY OF THE UNITED STATES:
BIBLIOGRAPHY SUPPLEMENT. New York: Macmillan, 1959.
Ten years ago in these pages we reviewed the first
edition of the LHUS and described it as "a major
event in our literary history." The most valuable
part, we thought, was the bibliography volume and
the intervening years have confirmed us in that
opinion. Now Mr. Ludwig has brought the bibliography section up-to-date, adding, for example 68
items to the Thoreau section. And since Thoreau
scholarship has been at its best for the past decade, that list includes many important works. In-
evitably there are omissions--some understandable,
others curious--why for example has the one PMLA
article on Thoreau in the past 10 years been omitted? And why have the two W. E. Channings been
lumped together in one confusion? But despite these
faults, this supplement is an invaluable tool that
all scholars of American literature will want on
their desks. TSB #69.

Lundquist, James. "An Apology for Henry," NATIONAL REVIEW
(August 13, 1968), p. 806 passim.

Lunt, Dudley C. Letter to editor, NEW ENGLAND QUARTERLY,
XXVIII (June, 1955), 259-262.

Reply to Carl Bode's earlier review of Lunt's edition of Thoreau's WEEK with Bode's reply to Lunt.

--"Moosehead Lake," WILMINGTON [Del.] MORNING NEWS, February 16, 1961.
On Thoreau in the Maine Woods.

Lynd, Staughton. "Henry Thoreau: the Admirable Radical," LIBERATION (February, 1963), pp. 21-36.

--INTELLECTUAL ORIGINS OF AMERICAN RADICALISM. New York: Pantheon, 1968.
Thoreau, passim. An especially interesting comparison of the literary styles of Thoreau and Karl Marx, pp. 93-95.

Lyon, Melvin E. "Walden Pond as Symbol," PMLA, LXXXII (May, 1967), 289-300.

Lyon, Peter. "Where Thoreau Lived," HOLIDAY, XXXI (May, 1962), 170-177 passim.
Centennial tribute.

Lyons, L. M. "Concord to Honor Man It Jailed for Not Paying Taxes," BOSTON GLOBE, July 5, 1942.
A preview of the Society's 1942 meeting.

Lyons, Nathan. "The Figure of William Ellery Channing," MICHIGAN QUARTERLY REVIEW, VII (April, 1968), 120-126.
Includes comments on Thoreau.

Lyons, W. A. "A Walden Reflective," BOSTON HERALD, May 16, 1953.
A poem.

M., C. E. "Hop in, Henry," SATURDAY REVIEW (July 22, 1961).
Cartoon on Thoreau hitchhiking to Walden.

M., W. G. "Migrants," CHRISTIAN SCIENCE MONITOR, October 26,
1953.
A poem on Thoreau.

Maass, Edgar. "Thoreau," DAS INNERE REICH, VI (June, 1939),
310-334.
Argues that Thoreau, in his attack upon the almighty dollar and technological encroachments
upon the individual, developed revolutionary anti-
capitalistic ideas. Emphasizes Thoreau's HEIMAT-
GEFUHL and his admiration for the defeated yet
proud Indian race.

McAleer, John J. "Thoreau's Epic CAPE COD," THOUGHT, XLIII
(Summer, 1968), 227-246.
The first extended scholarly evaluation of CAPE
COD.

--"Transcendentalism and the Improper Bostonian," EMER-
SON SOCIETY QUARTERLY, XXXIX (1965), 73-78.
On teaching WALDEN in a Catholic college.

McCabe, Charles R. "I Like My Sub-Standard of Living!"
NEW YORK HERALD TRIBUNE, March 29, 1958.
Essay on pleasures of Thoreau's plan of simple
living.

McCarthy, Mary E. "H. D. Thoreau and the Echoes," NEW
HAMPSHIRE NEWS [Manchester], July 23, 1967.
A poem.

McClintock, Marshall. THE STORY OF NEW ENGLAND. New York:
Harpers, 1941.
A history for juveniles with a full page litho-
graph in color of Thoreau at Walden by C. H. De-
Witt, p. 18.

McCord, David T. TROUT IN THE MILK. [Cambridge, Mass.], 1957.
A cleverly written appeal for the Harvard [Univer-
sity] Fund, parodying the style of Thoreau.

also in, IN SIGHT OF SEVER. Cambridge: Harvard
University Press, 1963. pp. 268-271.

McCormick, Edgar L. "T. and Higginson," EMERSON SOCIETY QUAR-
TERLY, XXXI (1963), 75-78.

McCormick, Rory. "When Laws Should Be Broken," AVE MARIA
(November 30, 1963), 11-15.
On Thoreau's CIVIL DISOBEDIENCE.

McCoy, Fitz. "Thoreau's Walden Revisited," HATTIESBURG [Miss.]
AMERICAN, May 8, 1965.

McCutcheon, John T., Jr. "Was Thoreau a Hippy?" CHICAGO
TRIBUNE, July 27, 1967.

McDermott, William F. "McDermott on Old Books," CLEVELAND
PLAIN DEALER, October 8, 1958.
The first of a series of articles describes Tho-
reau as selfish.

--"McDermott on Thoreau," CLEVELAND PLAIN DEALER, October
18, 1958.
Rebuttal of above article.

--"McDermott's Mailbag," CLEVELAND PLAIN DEALER, October
31, 1958.
Another rebuttal by a reader.

MacDonald, George. LILITH: A ROMANCE. London: Allen and
Unwin, 1895.
This once-popular novel opens with a two-page
quotation from Thoreau's "Walking".

McDonald, Lawrence. "Henry Thoreau--Liberal, Unconventional,
Nudist," SUNSHINE AND HEALTH (January, 1943).
Thoreau as a pioneer nudist.

--"Thoreau on Discipline," WALDEN ROUND ROBIN #27 (November, 1945).
Thoreau's philosophy of temperance. The ROUND ROBIN
itself will be of interest to a great many. It is
"a digest of friendly letters among seekers of over-
flowing life," and is dedicated to the principles
of Thoreavian friendship.

McDonnell, Thomas P. "The Books I Can't Forget," CRITIC
(October, 1959), 71-73.
Discussion of Thoreau's MEN OF CONCORD.

--"HDT's Journal Reveals Early Irish Friendships," PILOT
[Boston, Mass.], February 19, 1967, pp. 7-8.

--"Walden Revisited," MASSACHUSETTS REVIEW, IV (Autumn,
1962), 148.
A poem.

MacDougall, Sally. "Thoreau Fan Studies at Walden Pond,"
NEW YORK WORLD TELEGRAM, September 20, 1948, p. 23.

About Rella Ritchell and Thoreau. Similar anonymous
article, "Poetess, Here 21 Yrs., Became World Famous."
BROOKLYN EAGLE SUN, September 12, 1948, p. 10.

Macdougall, Walter M. "The Lower Lakes," DOWN EAST, XIII
(April, 1967), 22-27 passim.
Much on Thoreau's Maine Woods routes.

McDowell, Tremaine, editor. AMERICA IN LITERATURE. New York:
Crofts, 1944.
Contains "The Walden Experiment" by Thoreau (226-
232) and White's "Retort Transcendental", 232-234.

McFeely, Otto. "Gandhi's New England Ideas," TIME MAGAZINE
(July 21, 1947).
A letter to the editor on Thoreau's influence on
Gandhi.

McGehee, Judson D. "The Nature Essay as a Literary Genre:
An Intrinsic Study of the Works of Six English and Amer-
ican Nature Writers." University of Michigan, 1958.
Unpublished doctoral dissertation.
Includes Thoreau.

McGill, Frederick T., Jr. CHANNING OF CONCORD: A LIFE OF
WILLIAM ELLERY CHANNING II. New Brunswick: Rutgers
University Press, 1967.
The first book-length biography of Thoreau's closest
friend. Filled with all sorts of new information.
Essential reading for anyone who wishes to understand Thoreau's background. Advances the interesting thesis that Channing's eccentricities helped to
temper Thoreau's own. TSB #102.

--"Thoreau and College Discipline," NEW ENGLAND QUARTERLY,
XV (June, 1942), 349-353.

McGill, Ralph. "Concord's Past Buried in Cemetery," SCOTTS-
DALE [Ariz.] PROGRESS, June 26, 1961.
Thoughts on Thoreau's grave.

McGrail, Thomas H. "A Thought on Thoreau," Unidentified
English-language Haifa, Israeli newspaper, December 4,
1953.
Announcing that a Hebrew translation of WALDEN
is in the process.

McIntosh, James H. "Thoreau's Shifting Stance Towards Nature:
A Study in Romanticism." Yale University, 1967. Un-
published doctoral dissertation.
A reproduction of the abstract appears in TSB #109.

MacKaye, Benton. "Thoreau on Ktaadn," LIVING WILDERNESS, IX
(September, 1944), 3-6.
Thoreau's philosophical views on the mountain
reviewed.

McKee, Christopher. "Thoreau: A Week on Mt. Washington and in Tuckerman Ravine," APPALACHIA, XXX (December, 1954), 169-183.
>A detailed study of Thoreau's 1858 mountain trip, correcting many errors of previous accounts.

--"Thoreau's First Visit to the White Mountains," APPALACHIA, XXXI (December, 1956), 199-209.
>Many new facts discovered about the mountain journey Thoreau took with his brother in the midst of their WEEK trip.

--"Thoreau's Sister in the White Mountains," APPALACHIA, XXIII (December, 1957), 551-556.
>Diary of Sophia Thoreau's 1870 visit to the White Mountains.

McKenna, Richard. "Quest for Education," PLEASURES IN LEARNING [N. Y. U.], XIII (May, 1965), 5-11.
>A novelist's interest in Thoreau.

--"The Quest for Learning," NATIONAL OBSERVER, March 11, 1963.
>A novelist tells how reading WALDEN changed his life.

McKinsey, Folger. "I and Henry Thoreau," BALTIMORE SUN, January 28, 1946.
>A poem.

MacLachlan, C. H. "The Spiritual Life of Henry D. Thoreau," VEDANTA AND THE WEST, CXCI (May, 1968), 46-59.+
>Reprinted from PRABUDDHA BHARATA for June, 1965.

--"Vivekananda and Thoreau," VEDANTA AND THE WEST, CLXXXIII (November, 1967), 18-36.
>Reprinted from PRABUDDHA BHARATA for May, 1967.

McLaughlin, Elizabeth. "Thoreau and Gandhi: The Date," EMERSON SOCIETY QUARTERLY, XLIII (1966), 65-66.

McLean, Albert F., Jr. "Addenda to the Thoreau Correspondence," BULLETIN OF NEW YORK PUBLIC LIBRARY, LXXI (April, 1967), 265-267.

--"Thoreau's True Meridian: Natural Fact and Metaphor," AMERICAN QUARTERLY, XX (Fall, 1968), 567-579.
>The most important study yet of Thoreau as a surveyor. TSB #106.

Maclean, Hugh N. "The Pattern of WALDEN," THE ELENSIS OF CHI OMEGA, LXII (May, 1960), 235-239.

McMillan, Pat. "Thoreau," CONCORD FREE PRESS, July 13, 1967.
>A poem.

McNamara, Simpson. "Thoreau and Walden," NEW YORK HERALD

TRIBUNE, July 12, 1955.
A poem.

McNear, Everett. A Drawing of Thoreau on the March, 1949 and
1951 page of the Kemberly-Clark Corporation calendar.

Macone, John C., Jr. Letter to the editor, LIFE MAGAZINE
(October 13, 1947).
Another commentary on the Teale article.

MacShane, Frank. "WALDEN and Yoga," NEW ENGLAND QUARTERLY,
XXXVII (September, 1964), 322-342.

Madden, Edward H. CIVIL DISOBEDIENCE AND MORAL LAW IN NINE-
TEENTH CENTURY AMERICAN PHILOSOPHY. Seattle: University
of Washington Press, 1968.
The first authoritative study of the idea of civil
disobedience among Thoreau's contemporaries. A
well written and most important study for those who
wish to know the background of Thoreau's essays.
Well points out that Thoreau was by no means unique
in his ideas in his time. TSB #103.

Madison, Chas. A. "Henry David Thoreau: Transcendental Individualist," ETHICS, LIV (January, 1944), 110-123.

also in: CRITICS AND CRUSADERS: A CENTURY OF AMER-
ICAN PROTEST. New York: Henry Holt, 1947. pp. 174-
193. Study of Thoreau as an anarchist.

Madson, John. "The Abashed Savage." STORIES FROM UNDER THE
SKY. Ames: Iowa State University Press, 1961.
Calls Thoreau "the Spartan Scoutmaster of Walden
Pond."

Magorian, James. "Transcendentalist," ALMOST NOON. Chicago:
Ibis, 1969. p. 31.
Poem on Thoreau.

Mahabharata. THE BHAGVAT-GEETA, translated with notes by
Charles Wilkins, introduction by George Hendrick. Gainesville, Fla.: Scholars' Facsimiles and Reprints, 1959.
As Canby has said, the Bhagvat-Geeta was one of
the two most influential books on Thoreau. Yet the
Wilkins translation that Thoreau used has been generally unavailable for more than a century. Even
Emerson could not find a copy to purchase in the
1860's. So George Hendrick and SF&R have performed
a notable service to the students of Thoreau's
thought in publishing this facsimile of the edition
Thoreau and Emerson were most familiar with. Hendrick's introduction is brief but Thoreau's interest
in the book is adequately covered (pp. xi-xiii).
TSB #69.

Mahanay, Vera F. "An Analysis of Joy in the Writing of Henry

160

DAVID THOREAU." San Diego State College, 1964. Unpublished master's thesis.

"Mahatma Gandhi and Thoreau," INDIA NEWS, October 1, 1962, p. 8.

Majumdar, R. "Virginia Woolf and Thoreau," TSB #109, pp. 4-5.

"Malloony, J. P." "Letter from Concord, Mass," CHRISTIAN SCIENCE MONITOR, November 11, 1941.
A brief but interesting article referring to Thoreau.

Maloney, Russell. "Baruch of the U. S. A.," CORONET (October, 1945).
Proclaims Bernard Baruch to be a great devotee of Thoreau's writings!

Mangione, Jerre. "Oliver Arb," TSB #96, p. 6.

Mann, Helen B. "The Man Who Went to Live All Alone," JACK AND JILL, LX (March, 1947), 9-12.
A sketch of Thoreau in a children's magazine.

Manning, Clarence A. "Thoreau and Tolstoy," NEW ENGLAND QUARTERLY, XVI (June, 1943), 234-243.

"Man's Ingratitude to Nature," NEW YORK SUN, August 11, 1949.
Editorial on neglect of Walden Pond.

"Manuscripts in the Clifton Waller Barrett Library of American Literature in the University of Virginia Library," TSB #90, pp. 1-2.

Marcus, Mordecai. "Eugene O'Neill's Debt to Thoreau in A TOUCH OF THE POET," JOURNAL OF ENGLISH AND GERMAN PHILOLOGY, LXII (April, 1963), 270-279.

--"WALDEN as a Possible Source for Stephen Spender's "The Express," TSB #75, p. 1.

Marcus, Morton J. "Events at Walden Pond," ST. LOUIS POST DISPATCH, September 1, 1957.
A poem.

Markle, Carl, Jr. "The Shores of Walden--and Beyond: A Study of Henry David Thoreau's CIVIL DISOBEDIENCE and Its Influence." Oakland [Mich.] University, 1967. Unpublished master's thesis.

Marks, Mabel H. "When Thoreau Died," TSB #11.
A poem.

Marshall, James Morse. "The Heroic Adventure in "A Winter Walk'," EMERSON SOCIETY QUARTERLY, LVI (1969), 16-23.

Martin, James J. MEN AGAINST THE STATE. DeKalb, Ill.: Adrian Allen, 1953.

Contains references to Thoreau's influence on American anarchism.

Marx, Leo. THE MACHINE IN THE GARDEN. New York: Oxford, 1964.
A thoughtful and enlightening discussion of the con-
flict between technology and the pastoral idea in
America. Pp. 242-265 discusses Thoreau's WALDEN,
shedding a good deal of light on Thoreau's attitude
towards such examples of mechanization as the railroad and concluding that Thoreau solved the dilemma
by realizing that the "golden age" can be achieved
only through private or literary experience rather
than through a mechanized society. TSB #90.

--"Thoreau's Excursions," YALE REVIEW, LI (Spring, 1962),
363-369.
"All of his successful works are accounts of excursions....Thoreau uses the story of an excursion as
a vehicle for a spiritual quest." Reprinted from
the new Corinth paperback edition of EXCURSIONS.

--"The Vision of Henry Thoreau, A Study in the Social and
Political Ideas of American Romanticism." Harvard University, 1941. Unpublished honors thesis.

--"Walden as Transcendental Pastoral," EMERSON SOCIETY
QUARTERLY, XVIII (1960), 16-17.
Part of symposium.

Mason, Herbert. "Thoreau on 'Walking'," CATHOLIC WORKER,
XXIX (October, 1962), 3.

Massachusetts, Commonwealth of. Supreme Judicial Court.
JOHN E. NICKOLS ET AL. V. WILLIAM G. ANDREW ET AL.
Suffolk County, March, 1960.
Save Walden Court case.

Mathews, J. Chesley. "The Interest in Dante Shown by 19th
Century American Men of Letters," DANTE ALIGHIERI: THREE
LECTURES. Washington: Library of Congress, 1965.
Includes notes on Thoreau's interest.

Mathieson, Theodore. ISLAND IN THE SAND. Indianapolis:
Bobbs-Merrill, 1964.
A novel for teen-agers wherein a 17-year-old boy
retires to the Oregon dune country with a copy of
WALDEN as a guide.

Mattfield, Mary S. "THE WEEK: The 'Way In' to WALDEN," CEA
CRITIC, XXX (October, 1967), 12-13.
On using A WEEK as an introduction to WALDEN in
the classroom.

Matthews, Alice C. "I've business with this drop of dew,"
CHRISTIAN SCIENCE MONITOR, January 31, 1966.
A poem.

Matthews, J. C. "Thoreau's Reading in Dante," ITALICA (June, 1950).
> One of the most thorough studies of Thoreau's reading yet.

Mattiessen, Francis O. AMERICAN RENAISSANCE. New York: Oxford University Press, 1941. [paper, 1967].
> Contains a great deal on Thoreau and his friends.

--"WALDEN: Craftsmanship vs. Technique," GIVING FORM TO IDEAS, edited by Egbert S. Oliver. New York: Odyssey Press, 1946. pp. 466-73.
> Reprinting a portion of AMERICAN RENAISSANCE. Also reprinted are "On the Fitchburg Railroad" (pp. 454-463) from WALDEN, and comments on Thoreau by Hawthorne and Prudence Ward (pp. 463-466).

Mavi, E. "Franklin D. Thoreau," NEW YORK HERALD TRIBUNE, May 6, 1958.
> Letter to editor on FDR's indebtedness to Thoreau for the "fear" quotation.

Max, Patrick. Letter of comment on Kazin article, entitled "Thoreau and American Power [ATLANTIC MONTHLY (May. 1969)]." ATLANTIC MONTHLY, CXXIV (July, 1969), 30.

Maxfield-Miller, Elizabeth. "Elizabeth Hoar of Concord and Thoreau," TSB #106, pp. 1-3.

Mayer, Frederick. "Invitation to Understanding," WISDOM (November, 1956).
> An appreciation of Thoreau.

--"Thoreau," THE GREAT TEACHERS. New York: Citadel, 1967. pp. 259-272.

--"Thoreau and Utopia," A HISTORY OF AMERICAN THOUGHT. Dubuque, Iowa: Brown, 1951. pp. 158-169.

Maynard, Theodore. ORESTES BROWNSON: YANKEE, RADICAL, CATHOLIC. New York: Macmillan, 1943.
> A biography of Thoreau's teacher with much about their friendship.

Mayrand, Robert T. "Thoreau on Clothing," SOL-64 [Sherman Oaks, Calif.], I (1964), 46-53.
> A nudist magazine looks at Thoreau's thoughts.

Mehta, G. L. "Thoreau and Gandhi," CONCORD JOURNAL, August 15, 1957.
> Text of his address at the annual meeting.
>
> also in: NEW OUTLOOK (October, 1957).

Meigs, Peveril. "The Cove Names of Walden," TSB #104, pp. 5-7.
> Map on page 6.

Meltzer, Milton and Walter Harding. A THOREAU PROFILE. New
York: Crowell, 1962.
This is a novel and certainly useful introduction
to Thoreau. The text does in fact present a profile
by means of material in which original sources pre-
dominate; the reader is invited to round out the
figure for himself. The material is generally well
chosen and simply organized, chronologically for
the most part but, in part, topically; the major
periods and interests of Thoreau's life are thus
emphasized. The many illustrations of people, build-
ings, scenes, and newspaper items are very interesting and help greatly in enabling the reader to re-
create Thoreau's world. There is, perhaps, a little
too much space given to pictures of 'reliques.' The
book will whet the reader's appetite for Mr. Harding's future biography of Thoreau.--J. Lyndon Shanley. TSB #82.

reviews: AUDUBON MAGAZINE (July, 1963).
CHICAGO TRIBUNE, December 9, 1962.
CHRISTIAN SCIENCE MONITOR, November 21,
1962 and November 29, 1962.
CONCORD JOURNAL, November 22, 1962 and
July 24, 1969.
HARTFORD TIMES, December 10, 1962.
MADISON [Wis.] CAPITAL TIMES, December 20,
1962.
NEW YORK STANDARD, January 27, 1963.
ROCHESTER TIMES-UNION, January 12, 1963.
VINEYARD GAZETTE, December 28, 1962.

--A THOREAU PROFILE. Concord, Mass.: Thoreau Lyceum, 1969
(paper).

Melville, Herman. PIAZZA TALES, edited by Egbert S. Oliver.
New York: Hendricks, Farrar, Straus, 1948.
A new edition with notes on the relationship of
Thoreau and Melville.

review: NEW YORKER (February 12, 1949), by Alfred
Kazin.

Menger, W. H. "Thoreau's WALDEN MS," TRACE, XLIV (Autumn,
1961), 209-215.

Merchant, Jane. "Exception to Thoreau," CHRISTIAN SCIENCE
MONITOR, May 20, 1955.
A sonnet.

Merrifield, Richard. "100 Years After," YANKEE MAGAZINE
(July, 1954), 68-69.

Merritt, Diana Lejeune. "Writer of Journals," MANCHESTER
[Eng.] GUARDIAN WEEKLY (January 11, 1951), p. 10.
A brief essay on Thoreau at Walden.

Merton, Thomas. "The Wild Places," CATHOLIC WORKER (June, 1968).

Meserve, Harry C. "What is Loyalty?"   ?   , 1951.
    A mimeographed sermon on Thoreau's CIVIL DISOBEDIENCE
    distributed in 1951 by the Unitarian Church of the
    Larger Fellowship.

Metzger, Charles Reid. THOREAU AND WHITMAN: A STUDY OF THEIR
    ESTHETICS. Seattle: University of Washington Press, 1961.
    A sequel to Prof. Metzger's EMERSON AND GREENOUGH,
    this little volume continues his study of the Tran-
    scendentalists' theories of aesthetics. Since Tho-
    reau never formulated his ideas into an essay on
    the subject, Prof. Metzger has been forced to cull
    his ideas from the whole body of his work. As we
    might expect, Thoreau was more interested in the
    practical application than the theory of esthetics,
    and it is perhaps in the field of architecture that
    he had the most pertinent comments to make. Thor-
    eau was consistent in following the organic theory
    in every field of art. Prof. Metzger's book is a
    useful summary and evaluation of Thoreau's thoughts
    on the subject. TSB #78.

    review: NEW ENGLAND QUARTERLY (September, 1962).

--"Thoreau on Science," ANNALS OF SCIENCE, XII (September,
    1956), 206-211.
    Thoreau's philosophical approach to nature was close
    to the modern science of ecology.

--"The Transcendental Esthetics in America: Essays on Emer-
    son, Greenough, Thoreau, and Whitman." University of
    Washington, 1954. Unpublished doctoral dessertation.

Middlebrook, Samuel. "Henry David Thoreau," GREAT AMERICAN
    LIBERALS, edited by G. R. Mason. Boston: Starr King
    Press, 1956. pp. 69-79.

Mielziner, Janice. "Henry David Thoreau, Music Lover,"
    THOREAU JOURNAL QUARTERLY, I (July 1, 1969), 15-16.

Milch, Robert J. WALDEN OR LIFE IN THE WOODS AND ON THE DUTY
    OF CIVIL DISOBEDIENCE: NOTES. Lincoln, Neb.: Cliff's
    Notes, 1965.
    A crib.

Miller, F. DeWolfe. CHRISTOPHER PEARSE CRANCH AND HIS CAR-
    ICATURES OF NEW ENGLAND TRANSCENDENTALISM. Cambridge:
    Harvard University Press, 1951.
    Despite its long and formidable title, this is
    the most delightful book of its type that I have
    seen. Cranch was one of the minor Transcenden-
    talists, a friend of both Emerson and Thoreau.
    For his own amusement he made a series of cari-

catures of his friends and of their most famous
writings. Only two had ever been published. Now
Mr. Miller has gathered 18 of them together with a
brief biography of Cranch and an essay explaining
the cartoons. At times he tends to reach too much
significance into the drawings and is a little pon-
tifical in style. But it is one of the rare excursions into the humorous side of the movement and
will add much to your understanding and enjoyment.
I know I will find them useful tools in teaching
from now on. TSB #36.

Miller, Henry. "Henry David Thoreau," STAND STILL LIKE A
    HUMMINGBIRD. New York: New Directions, 1962. pp. 111-
    118.
        Now Miller has collected the brilliant essay he
        wrote on Thoreau for a privately printed edition
        of three of Thoreau's political essays some six-
        teen years ago. It is still one of the most potent
        discussions of the present-day efficacy of Thoreau's
        political ideas and it is good to see that it will
        now have a larger audience. Thoreauvians will also
        want to read many of the other essays collected in
        this stimulating volume. Thoreau is quoted directly
        frequently and there is hardly a page that does not
        display the close similarity in philosophy of Miller
        and Thoreau. TSB #81.

    --"Thoreau's Hard Road," PEACE NEWS [London], December 28,
    1962.

Miller, Perry. CONSCIOUSNESS IN CONCORD: THE TEXT OF THOREAU'S
    HITHERTO "LOST JOURNAL" (1840-1841) TOGETHER WITH NOTES
    AND A COMMENTARY. Boston: Houghton Mifflin, 1958.
        One of the most intriguing gaps in the standard
        edition of Thoreau's JOURNAL has been that from
        July 30, 1840 to January 22, 1841. Scholars had
        known of the existence of the MS for years, but
        other than letting Canby glance at it for a few
        minutes, its owner had not permitted its release.
        It was finally acquired by Morgan Library in 1956.
        And now at last it has been published.
            Readers expecting to find a new Thoreau master-
        piece or sensational new material on the Ellen
        Sewall romance are going to be disappointed. There
        is less there than Canby "found" in his cursory
        glance. And Miller wisely has not tried to make
        much out of little. But they will find early
        drafts of many of Thoreau's early lectures and es-
        says, with enlightening comments by Miller on their
        revisions. And from about December 1, 1840 on,
        some superior fragments of natural history essays.
            Although it is good to have this "missing" jour-
        nal in print, actually Miller's long introduction,
        it seems to me, is more important than the text
        itself. He wisely does not attempt to answer ques-

tions on the meagre evidence of the MS, But he does
ask some questions that should provoke Thoreau scholars into some much-needed thinking: Just how much
was Thoreau in love with Ellen? What was his attitude towards Edmund Sewall? How did Thoreau and Emerson differ in style, technique, and outlook? Did
Torrey and Allen adopt the wisest technique in editing the JOURNAL? These are all questions that Miller asks. And Thoreau students are going to have
to do some real thinking on the subjects if they are
going to be honest with themselves. TSB #63.

reviews: AMERICAN LITERATURE, XXXI (May, 1959), 198-
201.
BALTIMORE SUN, June 25, 1958.
BERKSHIRE EAGLE, June 21, 1958.
BOSTON GLOBE, June 22, 1958.
BOSTON HERALD, July 28, 1958.
BRIDGEPORT [Conn.] POST, June 29, 1958.
CAMBRIDGE [Mass.] CHRONICLE SUN, August
21, 1958.
CAPITOL PRESS [Salem, Ore.], July 4, 1958.
CHICAGO TRIBUNE, June 22, 1958.
CHRISTIAN SCIENCE MONITOR, June 26, 1958.
COLUMBUS DISPATCH, July 13, 1958.
CONCORD JOURNAL, June 19, 1958.
EMERSON SOCIETY QUARTERLY, XIII (1958).
FORT WAYNE NEWS SENTINEL, June 29, 1958.
HARTFORD COURANT, July 6, 1958.
HARTFORD TIMES, July 19, 1958.
HOUSTON POST, July 8, 1958.
LEWISTON-AUBURN INDEPENDENT, August 16,
1958.
LIBRARY JOURNAL (June 15, 1958).
LOS ANGELES MIRROR AND NEWS, July 7, 1958.
LOS ANGELES TIMES, July 8, 1958.
MIAMI NEWS, June 22, 1958.
MILWAUKEE JOURNAL, June 29, 1958.
MINNEAPOLIS TRIBUNE, June 29, 1958.
NASHVILLE TENNESSEAN, July 13, 1958.
NATION, CLXXXVII (December 6, 1958), 428-
431.
NEW LEADER, XLII (June 15, 1959), 16.
NEW YORK HERALD TRIBUNE, June 22, 1958.
NEW YORK POST, June 22, 1958.
NEW YORK TIMES, June 22, 1958.
NEW YORK WORLD TELEGRAM, June 23, 1958.
NEWSWEEK (June 23, 1958).
OMAHA WORLD HERALD, August 17, 1958.
PROVIDENCE JOURNAL, June 22, 1958.
ROCHESTER TIMES-UNION, November 17, 1958.
ST. LOUIS GLOBE DEMOCRAT, July 6, 1958.
SAN FRANCISCO CHRONICLE, June 26, 1958.
SATURDAY REVIEW OF LITERATURE (July 5, 1958).
SOUTH ATLANTIC QUARTERLY (Spring, 1959).
SPRINGFIELD REPUBLICAN, June 29, 1958.

TIME (July, 1958).
TULSA WORLD, July 27, 1958.
WASHINGTON POST AND TIMES, June 22, 1958.
WILMINGTON MORNING NEWS, July 15, 1958.
WILMINGTON NEWS, July 10, 1958.
WORCESTER TELEGRAM, July 20, 1958.

--"The Responsibility of Mind," AMERICAN SCHOLAR, XXXI
(Winter, 1961-1962), 51-69.
An "eloquent symptom of the dislocation between the
sensitive mind and the confessedly insensitive environment in which the machines have corralled us
is a steady enlargement of the popular regard for
Henry Thoreau."

--"Thoreau in the Context of International Romanticism,"
TSB #73, pp. 1-4.
Delivered at the Thoreau Society 1960 Annual Meeting.

also in: NEW ENGLAND QUARTERLY, XXXIV (June, 1961),
147-159. and NATURE'S NATION. Cambridge: Harvard
University Press, 1967. pp. 175-183.

--THE TRANSCENDENTALISTS. Cambridge: Harvard University
Press, 1950.

--, editor. THE AMERICAN TRANSCENDENTALISTS. New York:
Doubleday Anchor Books, 1957.
This book is not to be confused with Miller's
earlier THE TRANSCENDENTALISTS, although like that,
this is an anthology of the writings of the group.
But whereas that was aimed at the specialist, this
is aimed at the general reader--and a superb intro-
duction for the general reader it makes too. Of
Thoreau's works it includes selections from the
JOURNAL (pp. 69-85), "Walking" (143-148), 16 poems
(230-247), and "Life without Principle" (308-329).
One error should be pointed out, Cranch's poem on
p. 262 should be titled "Enosis" not "Gnosis."
TSB #62.

Mills, Edgar M. "Expansion of Recreational Areas Looms,"
CHRISTIAN SCIENCE MONITOR, June 28, 1955, p. 7.
On expansion of Walden Reservation.

--"Greater Walden Pond Area Slated," CHRISTIAN SCIENCE
MONITOR, August 4, 1956, p. 1.
Announces further enlargement of the state reser-
vation. Map on page 2.

Milne, Gordon. GEORGE WILLIAM CURTIS AND THE GENTEEL TRA-
DITION. Bloomington: Indiana University Press, 1956.
Comments of Thoreau's friendship and editorial
dealings with Curtis, passim.

Milne, Louis J. and Margery J. "Henry David Thoreau: Dreamer,"

FAMOUS NATURALISTS. New York: Dodd Mead, 1952. pp. 99-
106.
>A children's biographical sketch.

Mirachi, J. "And that goes for Henry David Thoreau, Too!"
NEW YORKER (July 18, 1964).
>A cartoon.

"'Missing' Thoreau JOURNAL," NEW YORK TIMES, October 3, 1956,
p. 35.
>Shown at Exhibition in Morgan Library.

"Mr. Sanborn's Thoreau," CRITIC (July 29, 1882), 197-198.

Mitchell, Edwin Valentine. IT'S AN OLD CAPE COD CUSTOM.
New York: Vanguard, 1949.
>The opening word of this pleasant volume is "Thoreau"
>and references to him continue throughout. It is
>a fascinating compilation of fact and legend of the
>cape. Our only quarrel is that there is no index.
>TSB #28.

Moecket, Fred. "On Thoreau's Grave," CONCORD JOURNAL, January 4, 1962.
>A poem.

Moiles, Bill. "Henry D. Thoreau Pens Columnist a Missive,"
WORCESTER DAILY TELEGRAM, March 10, 1959.
>On Walden Pond's being stocked with trout.

--"Our Man Thoreau Views Some Cats," WORCESTER TELEGRAM,
June 27, 1952.
>Excerpts from Thoreau's JOURNALS on his cat Min,
>with comments.

--"A Poisoned Opinion of Mountain Laurel," WORCESTER TELE-
GRAM, June 1, 1965.
>On Thoreau's 1851 visit to Worcester.

"Thoreau Put No Faith in Groundhog Day," WORCESTER TELE-
GRAM, February 2, 1960.
>On Thoreau and woodchucks.

--"Thoreau Saw Some Use in August Floods," WORCESTER TELE-
GRAM, August 30, 1955.
>Thoreau's comments on floods.

--"Thoreau Seems Better Companion Than Most," WORCESTER
TELEGRAM, February 17, 1961.

--"Thoreau Would Frown on 'No Parking' Signs," WORCESTER
TELEGRAM, May 1, 1957.
>Account of a visit to Walden Pond.

--"Thoreau Would Vote for Cape Cod Park," WORCESTER TELE-
GRAM, May 16, 1958.

--"Thoreau Would Want Trout in Walden Pond," WORCESTER TELE-
GRAM, March 5, 1959.

--"Thoreau's Groundhog Perhaps Most Famous," WORCESTER TELE-
GRAM, February 2, 1963.

--"Thoreau's Voice Still Stirs His Countrymen," WORCESTER
TELEGRAM,   ? .
        On current popularity of Thoreau.

--"We Love Humanity Even When It Teems," WORCESTER TELEGRAM,
July 4, 1963.
        On a visit to Walden Pond.

Moldenhauer, Joseph J.   "The Extra-vagant Maneuver: Paradox
in WALDEN," GRADUATE JOURNAL, VI (Winter, 1964), 132-
146.

--"Images of Circularity in Thoreau's Prose," TEXAS STUDIES
IN LITERATURE AND LANGUAGE, I (Summer, 1959), 245-263.

--"A New Manuscript Fragment by Thoreau," EMERSON SOCIETY
QUARTERLY, XXXIII (1963), 17-21.
        Part of an early draft of "Autumnal Tints."

--"A Recently-Discovered Addition to the Thoreau Correspondence," TSB #84, p. 4.
        An annotated copy of the letter is included.

--"The Rhetoric of WALDEN." Columbia University, 1964.   Unpublished doctoral dissertation.
        An abstract of the dissertation appears in TSB #91,
        pp. 3-4.

--"The Rhetorical Function of Proverbs in WALDEN," JOURNAL
OF AMERICAN FOLK-LORE, LXXX (April, 1967), 151-159.

--"Thoreau to Blake: Four Letters Re-Edited," TEXAS STUDIES
IN LITERATURE AND LANGUAGE, VIII (Spring, 1966), 43-62.

Moloney, Michael F.   "Henry David Thoreau: Christian Malgre
Lui," AMERICAN CLASSICS RECONSIDERED, edited by Harold
C. Gardiner.   New York: Scribner, 1958.   pp. 193-209.

--"WALDEN: A Centenary," AMERICA, XC (March 27, 1954),
635-638.
        A centennial essay.

Monaghan, James.   "Thoreau in Nantucket," PROCEEDINGS OF THE
NANTUCKET HISTORICAL ASSOCIATION: 48th ANNUAL MEETING,
(1942?), 24-30.

Mondale, R. Lester.   "Henry David Thoreau and the Naturalizing
of Religion," UNITY, CXXXVII (March-April, 1951), 14-17.
        On Thoreau's religion of nature.

Moneyhun, George. "Civil Disobedience: Shape of Debate and Historical Setting," CHRISTIAN SCIENCE MONITOR, July 20, 1968.

Monteiro, George. "Birches in Winter: Notes on Thoreau and Frost," CLA JOURNAL, XII (December, 1968), 129-133.

--"'Delugeous' or 'Detergeous'?--a Contextual Argument," CEAA NEWSLETTER, II (July, 1969), 4-5.
On a puzzling word in Thoreau's essay on Carlyle.

--"First Printing of a Hawthorne Letter," AMERICAN LITERATURE, XXXVI (November, 1964), 346.
Hawthorne's letter to Epes Sargent about Thoreau was published in HARPER'S WEEKLY for November 1, 1879.

--"Redemption through Nature: A Recurring Theme in Thoreau, Frost and Richard Wilbur," AMERICAN QUARTERLY, XX (Winter, 1968), 795-809.

Moraes, Frank. "Gandhi Ten Years After," FOREIGN AFFAIRS. January, 1958.
Brief mention of Thoreau's influence.

also in: CONGRESSIONAL RECORD: APPENDIX (January 30, 1858), pp. A889-A892.

Mordell, Albert. "Roosevelt and Thoreau," SATURDAY REVIEW OF LITERATURE, September 13, 1947.
A letter to the editor on the source of F.D.'s "nothing to fear but fear."

"More Doctoral Dissertations on Thoreau," TSB #107, pp. 5-6.+

"More on the Cairn," TSB #12.

More, Paul Elmer. "A Hermit's Notes on Thoreau" and "Thoreau's Journal," SHELBURNE ESSAYS ON AMERICAN LITERATURE. New York: Harcourt Brace, 1963. pp. 199-229 passim.
Two important essays of half a century ago in Thoreau, now readily available in an inexpensive paperback.

"More WALDENS," TSB #6.
1942 editions.

Moreau, Louis. PORTRAIT OF THOREAU. Berkeley Heights, N. J.: Oriole Press, 1962.
Special printing of a woodcut portrait of Thoreau.

Morgan, Arthur E. THE PHOLOSOPHY OF EDWARD BELLAMY. New York: Kings Crown Press, ? .
The second chapter deals, in part, with Thoreau's debt to India.

Morgan, Charles. "Walden and Beyond," THE LONDON TIMES, November 9, 1947, p. 3.
    The British novelist comments at length on Thoreau.

Morgan, James. "Dollar-a-Day Thoreau," BOSTON GLOBE, December 4, 1962.

Morison, Samuel E. "Gee, Wotta Style," BOSTON GLOBE, June 3, 1962.
    Acceptance speech upon receipt of the Gold Medal of the National Institute of Arts and letters. Devoted to Thoreau's style.

Morley, Christopher. "Thoreau," OFF THE DEEP END. Garden City: Doubleday, 1928. pp. 332-335.
    Brief but caustic evaluation of Thoreau.

Morley, Felix. Editorial on Thoreau, NATION'S BUSINESS (April, 1953), 17-18.

Morrell, Richard. "Monadnock Is a Mountain Strong," YANKEE, (October, 1968), p. 96ff.
    Includes section on Thoreau's visits to the mountain.

Morris, Charles R. AN ESSENTIAL VOCABULARY FOR THE READING OF WALDEN, BY HENRY D. THOREAU. Milton, Mass.: Charles R. Morris, 1946.
    A study of Thoreau's word usage for students.

Morris, John. "Thoreau: Gentle Anarchist," RELIGIOUS HUMANISM [Yellow Springs, Ohio], III (Spring, 1969), 62-65.

Morris, Wright. "To the Woods: Henry Thoreau," THE TERRITORY AHEAD. New York: Harcourt Brace, 1958. pp. 39-50.
    THE TERRITORY AHEAD is a volcanic discussion of American literature that is bound to arouse controversy. Morris feels (1) that Thoreau at Walden was facing, not fleeing from life, (2) that Thoreau "turned to Nature as D. H. Lawrence turned to Sex, and both transformed what they saw, what they found, to suit the needs of their genius"; and (3) "We forget that Thoreau...after two years in the woods called off the experiment...We prefer to think that he is permanently anchored at Walden Pond." TSB #65.

Morrison, Helen Barber. "Thoreau and the New York Tribune: A Checklist," TSB #77.+
    See Thoreau and the New York Tribune.

--An anonymous review of THOREAU TODAY, by Helen Morrison. EMERSON SOCIETY QUARTERLY, XIV (1959), 42.

Morsberger, Robert E. "'I Prefer Not To': Melville and the Theme of Withdrawal," UNIVERSITY COLLEGE QUARTERLY, X (January, 1965), 2.

Morton, Kent. "Thoreau, One Hundred Years Later: Civil Dis-
    obedience," CONCORD JOURNAL, June 21, 1962.
        Another Concord High School graduation speech.

Moser, Edwin I. "Henry David Thoreau: the College Essays."
    New York University, 1961. Unpublished master's thesis.
        Includes the text of most of Thoreau's known college
        essays.

   --"The Order of Fragments of Thoreau's Essay on 'L'Allegro'
    and 'Il Penseroso'," TSB #101, pp. 1-2.

   --"Thoreau's Theme Grades," TSB #91, pp. 1-2.

Moses, George L. "Thoreau Had Salty View of Cape Cod," NEW
    BEDFORD STANDARD TIMES, May 6, 1962.
        Essay on Thoreau's visits to Cape Cod.

Moss, Sidney P. "'Cock-a-Doodle-Doo!' and Some Legends in
    Melville Scholarship," AMERICAN LITERATURE, XL (May,
    1968), 192-210.
        Denies Melville based his short story on Thoreau.

"Mrs. Alcott Writes Mrs. Thoreau a Letter," TSB #69.
        The manuscript of the letter is printed.

Mulder, Arnold. "Benjamin Franklin: Teacher of Composition,"
    COLLEGE ENGLISH, III (February, 1942), 485-486.
        On the pages mentioned is a paragraph devoted to
        Thoreau's composition in relation to his experience.

Mulvaney, Tom. "The Genesis of a Lyric: Yeats' 'The Lake
    Isle of Innisfree'," TEXAS QUARTERLY, VIII (Winter, 1965),
    160-164.

Munoz, Vladimir. "A los Cien Anos de la Muerte de Thoreau
    (1862-1962)," VOLUNTAD [Montevideo, Uruguay] (June, 1962).
        Centennial essay.

   --"Ante el Centenario de la Meurte de Thoreau," EL PLATA
    [Montevideo, Uruguay], June 9, 1962.
        Centennial essay.

   --CORRESPONDENCIA SELECTA DE JOSEPH ISHILL. Mexico City:
    Ediciones Tierra y Libertad, 1967.
        Frequent comments on Thoreau.

   --"Una Cronologia de Henry David Thoreau," LE COMBAT
    [Paris], March 30, 1967.+

        also in: RECONSTRUIR [Buenos Aires], XLVIII (May,
        1967), 44-48. Text in Spanish.

   --"Desobediencis Civil," TIERRA Y LIBERTAD [Mexico], Feb-
    ruary, 1969.
        Commentary on recent foreign editions of Thoreau's
        essay.

--"En Torno al Naturalismo. Barrell y Thoreau," CENIT (April, 1955), 1528-1530.

--"Enrique David Thoreau o El Hombre Rebelde," TIERRA Y LIBERTAD [Mexico] (August, 1966).

--"En Filosofo de Walden," CENIT, X (April, 1960), 2989-2994.
    An extended discussion of Thoreau's thought.

--"Henry David Thoreau," L'ADUNATA DEI REFRATTARI [New York City], XLVI (September 2, 1967), 5-6.
    Text in Italian.

--"Henry David Thoreau," RUTA [Caracas], V (May, 1967), 1-2 passim.
    Text in Spanish.

--"Henry David Thoreau: EL Hombre de WALDEN," TIERRA Y LIBERTAD [Mexico] (February, 1964).
    Text in Spanish.

--THOREAU: EL QUIJOTE DE WALDEN. Montevideo, Uruguay: Ediciones Voluntad, 1958.
    A tribute to Thoreau in Spanish.

--"Thoreau y Hudson," VOLUNTAD [Montevideo, Uruguay], IV (May, 1960).

    also in: CENIT, X (December, 1960), 3237-3238.
    Text in Spanish.

--"Viaje con Thoreau," UMBRAL [Paris], LXXII (January, 1968).+
    Text in Spanish.

--"Vidas Ejemplares: Henry David Thoreau," VOLUNTAD, II (January, 1958), 4-5.+
    Extended essay in Spanish in Uruguayan anarchist monthly.

Munson, Gorham. "First Penobscot Vacationist," PENOBSCOT: DOWN EAST PARADISE. Philadelphia: Lippincott, 1959. pp. 15-41.
    An account of Thoreau's visits to Maine, including many new details concerning his voyages from Boston to Bangor and a thoughtful critical account of his tours of the Maine Woods. This book is an important source book for background material on Thoreau's Maine visits. There is also extensive information about Fannie Hardy Eckstorm, the foremost authority on Thoreau's MAINE WOODS. TSB #68.

--"Maine's First Vacationist," DOWN EAST, V (January, 1959), 26-35.
    On Thoreau's visit to the Maine Woods. Superb color

photographs of the region.

Murphy, Kathy. "A Different Drummer," PRACTICAL ENGLISH
(March 6, 1964), 18.
A teen-ager looks at Thoreau.

Murphy, Mischa. "Thoreau...The Thinking Man's Nudist,"
MR. SUN [Hollywood, Calif.], I (December, 1966), 18-20.

Murphy, Richard J. "Remarks at Thoreau Stamp Ceremony,"
CONCORD FREE PRESS, July 13, 1967.

Murphy, Russ. "Do You Believe in Dreams," NEWARK [N. J.] STAR-
LEDGER, April 4, 1949, p. 22.
Syndicated column analyzing Thoreau's dream of his
controversy with his brother over Ellen Sewall!

Murray, Donald. "The Sage of Walden," SPIRAL [New Utrecht
High School, Brooklyn, N. Y.] (January, 1956), pp. 34-35.
Impressionistic account of visit to Walden.

Murray, James G. HENRY DAVID THOREAU. New York: Washington
Square Press, 1968.
A volume in the "Great American Thinkers" series.
Billed as a biography of Thoreau's mind, it does
analyze his thought, but fails to trace its development. Because he feels WALDEN and "Civil Disobedience" are "too familiar," he instead concentrates
on such fugitive pieces as "Sir Walter Raleigh."
Generally it is a sensitive appraisal, though it
tends to over-formalize Thoreau's thought. And as
is the case with virtually all critics of Thoreau,
his words seem prosaic when set against the vibrant
phraseology of Thoreau. TSB #105.

Myers, Helen. "John Burroughs Sought Secluded Nook to Write,
Built 'Slabsides'," [Poughkeepsie], NEW YORKER (May 2,
1948).
With much on Burroughs' interest in Thoreau.

Myers, John M. "A Check-list of Items Published by the Private Press of Edwin B. Hill," AMERICAN BOOK COLLECTOR,
XVIII (October, 1967), 22-27.
Many of Hill's Thoreau editions described. In same
issue: Adrian Goldstone, "The Search for Edwin B.
Hill," p. 19; G. H. Muir, "Edwin Bliss Hill, pp.
20-21.

N., M. S. "Blaming Henry D. Thoreau," NEW YORK SUN, March 9, 1946.
> A letter to the editor blaming the current strikes on "the reading of the essay on 'Civil Disobedience' stimulated by the centenary of the hut at Walden Pond."

--Letter to the editor, NEW YORK HERALD TRIBUNE, May 25, 1945.
> Questions Thoreau's eligibility for election to Hall of Fame on grounds that he seceded from Union on writing his essay on "Civil Disobedience."

--"Reminiscences of an Unofficial Guide," CONCORD JOURNAL, October 10, 1946.
> Recollections of serving as a guide to the Thoreau sites in Concord sixty years ago.

--"Thoreau on Mining," NEW YORK SUN, January 31, 1949.
> Suggests issuing a Thoreau postage stamp.

Nadeau, Raymond. "Walden Raped," NEW ENGLAND REVIEW [P.O. Box 542, Waterbury, Conn.], I (July, 1969), 14-15.

Nagy, Michael F. "Thoreau's Concord a Century Later," BOSTON GLOBE, May 11, 1969.

Nair, Pyarelal. THOREAU, TOLSTOY AND GANDHIJI. Calcutta: A. K. Banerji, 1958.

Narayanan, K. P. "Thoreau's Walden," HINDU (December, 1961).
> Tells of a Hindu's visit to Walden.

Nash, Roderick. "Henry David Thoreau: Philosopher," WILDERNESS AND THE AMERICAN MIND. New Haven: Yale University Press, 1967. pp. 84-95.

Nassau [N. Y.] Community College. ARTIST OF THE WORD: A THOREAU FESTIVAL. Garden City: Nassau Community College, 1967.
> Program of the festival.

--"Festival of American Poets: Henry David Thoreau," VIGNETTE [Garden City], May 9, 1967.

--Student paper devoted to Thoreau festival.

--"Homage to Henry David Thoreau," LIBRARY NEWSLETTER, II
(May, 1967), 1-4.

Nehru, B. K. "Henry David Thoreau--A Tribute," INDIA NEWS, I
(May 11, 1962), 8.
The Hall of Fame address.

    also in: NEW OUTLOOK, XV (1962), 48-54.

Nehru, Jawaharlal. Letter on Thoreau, MASSACHUSETTS REVIEW,
IV (Autumn, 1962), 89.

Nelson, Truman. "The Battle of Walden Pond," NATIONAL PARKS
MAGAZINE, XXXIV (December, 1960), 4-6.+
Detailed account of the Save Walden Committee's
work.

--THE PASSION BY THE BROOK. New York: Doubleday, 1953.
Thoreau appears several times in this fine novel
on Brook Farm. TSB #43.

--THE SIN OF THE PROPHET. Boston: Little, Brown, 1952.
A fine new historical novel based on Theodore Parker and the Anthony Burns incident. Thoreau enters
as a background character, delivering his "Slavery
in Massachusetts" address in Framingham. The theme
of the novel is based on a quotation from Thoreau's
CIVIL DISOBEDIENCE. TSB #39.

--THE SURVEYOR. Garden City: Doubleday, 1960.
A novel about John Brown in Kansas with frequent
references to Thoreau.

--"Thoreau and the Paralysis of Individualism," RAMPARTS
(March, 1966), pp. 16-26.
On Thoreau and John Brown.

--"Walden on Trial," NATION (July 19, 1958).
An account of the Save Walden Committee hearings.

    also in, WESTERN HUMANITIES REVIEW, XII (Autumn,
    1958), 307-311.

Nelson, William Stuart. "Thoreau and American Non-violent
Resistance," MASSACHUSETTS REVIEW, IV (Autumn, 1962),
56-60.

--"Thoreau and the Current Non-violent Struggle for Inte-
gration," TSB #88, pp. 1-4.
Delivered at the annual meeting of the Thoreau
Society, July 11, 1964, and reprinted from the
CONCORD JOURNAL.

Nesmith, Mike. "Different Drum," Capitol Records, BMI-2:35
2004, 1968.
A 45-rpm recording by the Stone Poneys.

Neufeldt, Leonard Nick. "The Wild Apple Tree: Possibilities of the Self in Thoreau." University of Illinois [Urbana], 1966. Unpublished doctoral dissertation.

Nevinson, Henry W. FIRE OF LIFE. New York: Harcourt Brace, 1935.
> Includes account of visit to Walden Pond, pp. 378-380.

--LAST CHANGES LAST CHANCES. London: Nisbet, 1928.
> An extended tribute to Thoreau and quotation from WALDEN, pp. 226-227.

"New England Rebel," MD, VI (October, 1962), 131-134.
> Picture essay on Thoreau.

"The New England Spirit," THE TIMES LITERARY SUPPLEMENT [London] (November 22, 1947), p. 602.
> An essay on the New England writers in general with some on Thoreau.

"A New England Town," AMERICAN TRANSCENDENTAL QUARTERLY, II (1969), 41.
> An account of an 1856 visit to Concord with commentary on Thoreau. Reprinted from HOME JOURNAL FOR THE CULTIVATION OF THE MEMORABLE, THE PROGRESSIVE, AND THE BEAUTIFUL.

"New Foundation to Establish Thoreau Center for Concord," CONCORD FREE PRESS, June 16, 1966.
> On the new Thoreau Lyceum.

"A New Roof for Henry Thoreau's Walden House Reborn," HEAR YE! [Acton, Mass], June, 1969.

"New Thoreau Item," TSB #2.
> Printed is a letter from the manuscript room of the New York Public Library: to Wm. H. Sweetser, Esqu., Charlestown, Mass., from Henry D. Thoreau.

"A New Thoreau Letter," TSB #15.
> A previously unpublished letter written by Thoreau to the Boston Society of Natural History.

"New Thoreau Memorial," CONCORD ENTERPRISE, April 22, 1948.
> A photograph of the new memorial at the Walden Pond cabin site.

Newcomb, Charles King, THE JOURNALS OF, edited by Judith Kennedy Johnson. Providence, R. I.: Brown University Press, 1946.

> review: THOREAU SOCIETY BULLETIN #16.

Newman, Elmer S. "Thoreau's Dilemma," SCIENCE, CLIX (January 26, 1968), 379.

On Thoreau and the AAAS.

Newsom, William. "Thoreau, One Hundred Years Later: Simplicity," CONCORD JOURNAL, June 21, 1962.
Another Concord High School graduation address.

Ney, Lew. Letter to the editor, CONCORD JOURNAL, June 7, 1945.
Suggesting that a replica of Thoreau's hut be built at Walden Pond.

--Letter to the editor, NEW YORK SUN, June 15, 1945.
Another letter on Thoreau's hut.

Nicholas, William H. "Literary Landmarks of Massachusetts," NATIONAL GEOGRAPHIC, XCVII (March, 1950), 279-310.
Photographic essay with several Thoreau scenes.

Nichols, Charles E., Jr. "Thoreau on the Citizen and His Government," PHYLON, XIII (1952), 19-24.

Nichols, William W. "Science and the Development of Thoreau's Art." University of Missouri [Columbia], 1966.
Unpublished doctoral dissertation.
The abstract is reproduced in TSB #106, p. 6.

Nickols, John E. "Thoreau and the Pig," TSB #77, p. 1.

"Night Warbler Song Mystified Thoreau," NEW BEDFORD STANDARD-TIMES, July 30, 1967.

Nishikawa, Kojiro. THOREAU GENKO ROKU [MEMOIRS OF THOREAU].
Tokyo: Naigai Suppan Kyokai, 1912.

Nitkin, Nathaniel. "Wild, the Mountain of Thoreau," NEW ENGLAND QUARTERLY, IX (Fall, 1967), 35-43.
On Mt. Katahdin.

Noble, W. Carey. "Undetected Plagiarism," NEW YORK SUN, July 20, 1948, p. 14.
A letter to the editor on the source of FDR's "nothing to be feared."

Noé, Heinrich. "Henry David Thoreau," BEILAGE ZUR ALLGEMEINEN ZEITUNG, CXVI (May 18, 1892), 1-5.
The earliest German essay on Thoreau characterizes WALDEN as a book of ideas related in spirit to the novels of Jean Paul Richter.

Nordell, Roderick. "Notes on Winter Words at Walden," CHRISTIAN SCIENCE MONITOR, January 19, 1963.

Norman, Charles. TO A DIFFERENT DRUM: THE STORY OF HENRY DAVID THOREAU. New York: Harper, 1954.
Fourteen years ago Hildegarde Hawthorne wrote a young people's biography of Thoreau, CONCORD'S

179

HAPPY REBEL. It was a readable volume, but many
of us felt it reflected too strongly against Thoreau's basic ideas. Now Charles Norman has at-
tempted a young people's biography. We wish we
could be enthusiastic, for there is a need for
such a book, but so far as we are concerned, Mr.
Norman has failed. He has obviously done a great
deal of background reading in Thoreau's works, the
standard biographies, and the memoirs of Thoreau's
friends. But he has failed to assimilate the material, quoting great hunks verbatim that are far
beyond the vocabulary and interest of a school boy.
And, what is worse, he has ignored recent research
on Thoreau's life and so has perpetuated many legends about Thoreau that have long since been proved
false. I am afraid this book would drive young
people away from Thoreau instead of toward him.
It's too bad. TSB #49.

reviews: APPALACHIA, XXX (December, 1954), 312-313.
CHICAGO TRIBUNE, November 14, 1954.
CONCORD JOURNAL, October 21, 1954.
NEW YORK TIMES, March 6, 1955, by E.L.B.

translation: UN HOMBRE SOLO, translated into Spanish
by M. H. Calichio. Buenos Aires: Editorial Agora,
1959.

North, Sterling. "Being Out of Step Became Symbol of Thoreau's Life," BOSTON HERALD, October 25, 1959.
A brief essay.

--"The Man Who Got Away From it All," NEW YORK WORLD TELE-
GRAM, October 31, 1959.
Essay on Thoreau.

--"Of Walden Revisited," NEW YORK WORLD TELEGRAM, August
11, 1953, p. 18.
An evaluation of WALDEN.

--"Thoreau of Walden Pond," GARY [Ind.] POST TRIBUNE,
January 3, 1960.
A brief essay.

--THOREAU OF WALDEN POND, illustrated by Harve Stein.
Boston: Houghton Mifflin, 1959.
Any attempt to write a children's biography of
Thoreau is a real challenge. Several capable
authors have tried it and failed. There is always
the danger of over-sentimentalizing, of emphasizing
Thoreau the nature man at the expense of Thoreau
the rebel. Sterling North has taken up the challenge and, it seems to me, has met it more success-
fully than any other author to date. He has written a biography that has enough of Thoreau's love

of nature to appeal to the young person, and yet
he has not hesitated to discuss Thoreau's ideas of
civil disobedience, economy, and government--being
careful to use a vocabulary that would not overwhelm
the child. Granted he is a little condescending at
times--condescending towards Thoreau, that is--but
on the whole he has succeeded in writing a biography
of Thoreau that should appeal to the child and at
the same time give the child a fairly accurate picture of Thoreau's life and mind.
    Although the book is handsomely printed and
sumptuously illustrated, we find it hard to conceive
of Thoreau's ever having looked quite as hay-seedy
as Mr. Stein portrays him. TSB #69.

Notice of Sale of Thoreau's MS Journal to Stephen H. Wakeman,
    BOSTON TRANSCRIPT, July 10, 1907.

Notice of the Walden Edition of Thoreau, T. P.'s WEEKLY [Lon-
    don], XI (June 19, 1908), 776.

Numata, Makoto. METHODOLOGY OF ECOLOGY. Tokyo: Kokon-Shoin,
    1967.
        Frequent reference to Thoreau as ecologist. Text
    in Japanese.

Nutt, Howard. "Thoreau", POETRY, LX (May, 1942), 66-68.
        A poem.

Nyren, Dorothy. "The Concord Academic Debating Society,"
    MASSACHUSETTS REVIEW, IV (Autumn, 1962), 81-84.

Nyren, Karl. A DIFFERENT DRUMMER. Lexington, Mass.: Sander-
    line Films, 1965.
        A ten-minute, 16mm. sound film.

"Obituary of Sophia Thoreau," SPRINGFIELD REPUBLICAN, October 10, 1876.

"October," MASSILLON [Ohio] INDEPENDENT, September 30, 1955.
Editorial on Thoreau's attitude toward autumn.

O'Donnell, Charles Robert. "The Mind of the Artist: Cooper, Thoreau, Hawthorne, Melville." Syracuse University, 1957. Unpublished doctoral dissertation.

Oehser, Paul. "Pioneers in Conservation," NATURE MAGAZINE, XXXVIII (April, 1945), 188-190.
A large portion of this essay is devoted to Thoreau's interest in conservation.

--"Thoreau: Exponent of Silence," TSB #72.
This paper was read at the annual meeting of the Thoreau Society at Concord, Mass., July 9, 1960.

also in: CONCORD JOURNAL, July 14, 1960 and NEW OUTLOOK, XIV (June, 1961), 29-35.

--"The Word 'Ecology'," SCIENCE, CXXIX (April 17, 1959), 992.
Points out that Thoreau uses the word ten years before it was supposedly invented!

[Oehser, Paul]. "Flower of New England," WASHINGTON [D.C.] POST, July 5, 1945.
A centennial editorial.

"Off-Beat Americans: Henry David Thoreau," NEW YORK SUNDAY NEWS, March 20, 1960.
An editorial: "Maybe we Americans can afford to have a few of such lazybones in every generation, to keep us aware of the fact that if all or most of us were to turn into Henry David Thoreaus, our national power, glory and well-being would depart in a matter of days or weeks."

Ogata, Toshihiko. "The Influence of the Oriental Scriptures on WALDEN," REVIEW OF ENGLISH LITERATURE [Kyoto University] XX (March 20, 1967), 125-171.
Text in Japanese.

O'H., J. "Any Thoreauvians in Holland?" DE KOERIER, May 10, 1946.

A note on the Thoreau Society in a Dutch paper.

Okumura, Osama. "Miller et le Moi Authentique," SYNTHESES [Brussels], XXII (February, 1967), 89-95.
Much on Thoreau and Henry Miller.

Oliver, Egbert S. "Cock-A-Doodle-Doo! and Transcendental Hocus-Pocus," NEW ENGLAND QUARTERLY, XXI (June, 1948), 204-216.
Melville's use of A WEEK as a source for his short story.

--"Melville's Picture of Emerson and Thoreau in 'The Confidence-Man'," COLLEGE ENGLISH, VIII (November, 1946), 61-72.
An identification of Egbert in Herman Melville's novel as Thoreau.

--"The Rise of American Understanding of Asia," UNITED ASIA, IX (June, 1957), 149-156.
Brief mention of Thoreau.

--"A Second Look at Bartleby," COLLEGE ENGLISH, VI (May, 1945), 431-439.
An identification of the central figure of this short story by Herman Melville as Thoreau.

--"Thoreau and the Puritan Tradition," EMERSON SOCIETY QUARTERLY, XLIV (1966), 79-85.

--"Thoreau Finds the Dawn in Asia," STUDIES IN AMERICAN LITERATURE. Ram Nagar, New Delhi, India: Eurasia Publishing Company, 1965. pp. 33-39.
"The Orient became part of Thoreau's life, thought, and expression."

also in: KOREAN SURVEY, II (November, 1953), 6 passim and NEW OUTLOOK, VI (December, 1953), 8-13 passim.

Olsen, M. E. "Thoreau: Poet-Naturalist of Walden," SNOWY EGRET, XVII (Spring, 1951), 3-15.
A eulogistic tribute.

O'Malley, Charles J. "Wreck at Cohasset Recalled," BOSTON POST, October 8, 1946.
The story of the wreck of the brig ST. JOHN which Thoreau described in CAPE COD, telling of the location of the graves of the victims.

"On Quoting Thoreau," TULSA [Okla.] TRIBUNE, October 27, 1967.
An editorial.

"100th Anniversary of Naturalist's Death," PROVIDENCE JOURNAL, May 6, 1962.

Onuska, J. T. "Teach the Soul," NEW YORK TIMES BOOK REVIEW, February 6, 1966, p. 47.
> Identifies an unfamiliar quotation in CIVIL DIS-OBEDIENCE.

Ord, Samuel. "Against Thoreau," NATION (November 13, 1954).
> Replies to Lewis Leary's recent article on Thoreau, denouncing it. Leary replies here with another letter.

Orth, Ralph H. "A Volume from Thoreau's Library," TSB #87, p. 1.

Ortmayer, Roger. "Prescription for Today: The Story of Thoreau," MENNONITE YOUTH, LXVI (November 13, 1951), 719-720.
> An interpretive criticism, reprinted from ONWARD.

Osann. "Tizzy," DURHAM SUN, June 6, 1961.
> Cartoon on teen-ager's essay on Thoreau.

Ostrander, G. M. "Emerson and Thoreau and John Brown," MISSISSIPPI VALLEY HIST. REVIEW, XXXIX (March, 1953), 713-726.

Owens, Olga. "Bookstall Gossip," BOSTON POST, August 15, 1954.
> A WALDEN centennial essay.

"Ownership of Thoreau House Changes," WORCESTER EVENING GAZETTE, February 2, 1960.
> Photograph of Worcester house where Thoreau often visited Theo Brown.

Ozana, Anna. "Varianten des 'einfachen Lebens' von Henry D. Thoreau bis Ernst Wiechert," WELT UND WORT, VIII (1953), 145-149.
> Distinguishes and criticizes the primitivism of writers like Thoreau, D. H. Lawrence, Hemingway, and Ernst Wiechert, a German contemporary of Hemingway. Wiechert, the critic feels, represents a decadent and meaningless protest against civilization as opposed to Thoreau's sound principles.

P., A. K. "Henry Thoreau Would Starve at Walden Now," PROV-
IDENCE EVENING BULLETIN, June 26, 1964.
Denounces Thoreau's comments on newspapers.

P., M. "Thoreau-Alcott House May Be Opened to the Public,"
WORCESTER [Mass.] GAZETTE TELEGRAM, July (?), 1948.
Account of Thoreau Society fund drive.

Pacey, Desmond. FREDERICK PHILIP GROVE. Toronto: Ryerson,
1945.
Many comments on Thoreau's influence on Grove.

Packard, William. "Infinite Expectation and Thoreau," WALL
STREET JOURNAL, July 12, 1967.

"A Page from Thoreau," DENVER POST, November 23, 1956.
Editorial on Thoreau's influence on Gandhi.

Paine, Barbara B. "Harvard's Botanical Treasures," THE
HERBARIST, XXVI (1960), 19-23.
On Thoreau's herbarium.

--"Thoreau's Wildflowers: a 100-Year Record," AUDUBON
MAGAZINE, LXIII (July, 1961), 194-197.
How Mrs. Edmund Fenn of Concord and Mr. Richard
Eaton of Lincoln are confirming Thoreau's wild-
flower records of a century ago.

Paine, Tom. "Another Thoreau, So Badly Needed," CONCORD JOUR-
NAL, July 6, 1967.

Palches, Lois Grant. "Enjoying Life Thoreau-ly," NEW HAMP-
SHIRE TROUBADOUR, XXI (May, 1951), 4-10.
On living life today on the Thoreauvian plan.

Paludan, Jacob. OM THOREAU. Copenhagen, Denmark: Kunst Og
Kultur, 1949.
A reprint of the foreword to the new Danish edition
of WALDEN.

Paquette, Gerald. "Words of Thoreau Cited," MINNEAPOLIS
TRIBUNE, March 30, 1968.
On CIVIL DISOBEDIENCE.

Paris, Leonard. "Rugged Individualist: Henry David Thoreau,"
SENIOR SCHOLASTIC, LXXI (December 13, 1957), 14.

Brief biography for high school students.

Parke, Fran. "Today's Protestors Carry on Old Battle of Conscience vs. Law," LANCASTER [Pa.] NEW ERA, March 6, 1969.
    Many comments on Thoreau.

Parkhurst, Winthrop. Letter to the editor, NEW YORK SUN, April 13, 1945.
    A tribute to Thoreau.

Parr, W. Holton. "Communication," CONCORD JOURNAL, September 5, 1946.
    A letter to the editor complaining about the lack of markers for the Walden hut site.

Parsons, Thornton H. "Thoreau, Frost, and the American Humanist Tradition," EMERSON SOCIETY QUARTERLY, XXXIII (1963), 33-43.

Parsons, Vesta M. "Thoreau's THE MAINE WOODS: An Essay in Appreciation," HUSSON REVIEW [Bangor, Maine], I (Fall, 1967), 17-27.

Pascal, Joseph. FLORILEGE DE LA PENSEE FRANCAISE. Paris: Debresse Editeur, 1956.
    Contains many quotations from Thoreau.

"Path to Thoreau's Door Grows Wider," CHICAGO TRIBUNE, August 11, 1946.
    An interview with Edwin W. Teale on the present popularity of Thoreau.

Paul, Sherman. "Resolution at Walden," ACCENT, XIII (Spring, 1953), 101-113.
    On symbolism in WALDEN.

    also in: INTERPRETATIONS OF AMERICAN LITERATURE, edited by Fridelson and Brodkorb. New York: Oxford, 1959. pp. 161-175.

    CRITICAL APPROACHES TO AMERICAN LITERATURE, edited by Browne and Light. New York: Crowell, 1965. I. pp. 164-177.

    AMERICAN LITERATURE: A CRITICAL SURVEY, edited by Young and Fine. New York: American Book Company, 1968. pp. 199-212.

--THE SHORES OF AMERICA: THOREAU'S INWARD EXPLORATION. University of Illinois Press, 1958.
    In this book Thoreau criticism has at long last reached maturity--W. H. TSB #66.

    reviews: AMERICAN LITERATURE (November, 1959).

AMERICAN QUARTERLY (Fall, 1959).
CHICAGO TRIBUNE, January 4, 1959.
COLLEGE ENGLISH (January, 1960).
JEGP, LVIII (July, 1959), 551-555.
NATION, CLXXXVIII (April 18, 1959), 345-346.
NEW LEADER, XLII (June 15, 1959), 16.
THOREAU SOCIETY BULLETIN #66, by Walter Harding.
WASHINGTON POST, December 21, 1958.
WESTERN HUMANITIES REVIEW (Autumn, 1959).

--"Thoreau's 'The Landlord': 'Sublimely Trivial for the Good of Men'," JOURNAL OF ENGLISH AND GERMANIC PHILOLGY, LIV (October, 1955), 587-591.
Important analysis of one of the few essays Thoreau wrote for the commercial market. TSB #54.

--"The Wise Silence: Sound as the Agency of Correspondence in Thoreau," NEW ENGLAND QUARTERLY, XXII (January, 1950), 511-527.
Lengthy discussion on Thoreau's sense of sound.

--, editor. THOREAU: A COLLECTION OF CRITICAL ESSAYS. Englewood Cliffs, N. J.: Prentice-Hall, 1962.
A collection of fourteen 20th-century essays and two poems on Thoreau by William Butler Yeats, Lewis Mumford, Max Lerner, Stanley Edgar Hyman, Leo Stoller, F. O. Matthiessen, Heinz Eulau, Laurence Stapleton, and others. The volume is probably most important for getting William Drake's analyses of WALDEN and A WEEK into print and Edwin S. Fussell's brilliant analysis of the book about the American Indians that Thoreau never got around to writing. The remaining essays make a fairly good survey of criticism of Thoreau except that there is no negative criticism and that too many of them repeat each other particularly on the symbolism of rebirth in WALDEN--an important idea, granted, but one that hardly needs being said in one volume by four different authors. It is unfortunate too that the book suffers from careless proof-reading. TSB #81.

PAUNCH. [Thoreau number], XXIV (October, 1965), 1-50.
Wade Thompson, "The Uniqueness of Henry David Thoreau" R. D. Callahan, "WALDEN: Portrait of the Critics' Saint as a Young Daydreamer": Kingsley Widmer, "The Prophet's Passional Ethos: Henry David Thoreau." A series of studies of Thoreau by followers of Wilhelm Reich and Paul Goodman. Typical comment: "Thoreau seems the most castrato of the great secular moralists." TSB #93.

Payne, Roger. WHY WORK?: THE COMING AGE OF LEISURE AND PLENTY. Boston: Meador, ? .

A reissue of this classic of the practical application of Thoreau's philosophy today.

Peabody Institute Library. MR. EMERSON LECTURES AT THE PEA-
BODY INSTITUTE. Baltimore: Peabody Institute Library,
1949.
Emerson and Burroughs discuss Thoreau. A beautifully printed pamphlet.

Pearce, Roy Harvey. THE SAVAGES OF AMERICA. Baltimore:
Johns Hopkins University Press, 1953.
Commentary on Thoreau and Indians, pp. 146-150.

Pearson, George P. "Thoreau's Cairn," OLD CAMBRIDGE AND
OTHER POEMS. ? : ? , 1928.

Pebworth, Ted-Larry. "Evelyn's Lay Fields, Digby's Vital
Spirits, and Thoreau's Beans," TSB #101, pp. 6-7.

Pederson, Lee A. "Americanisms in Thoreau's JOURNAL," AMER-
ICAN LITERATURE, XXXVII (May, 1965), 167-184.

translation: ENGLISH LANGUAGE LABORATORY OF OITA
KOGYO DAIGAKU, I (November, 1968), 1-33. Translated into Japanese by Tsuotomu Shigematsu.

--"Thoreau's Source of the Motto in CIVIL DISOBEDIENCE,"
TSB #67.
Pederson contends that the motto "That government
is best which governs least,' is an "alteration of
the motto of THE UNITED STATES MAGAZINE, and DEM-
OCRATIC REVIEW.

translation: "La Fuente del Lema de Thoreau en
DESOBEDIENCIA CIVIL," translated into Spanish by
V. Munoz. VOLUNTAD, IV (May, 1960).

--"Thoreau's Rhetoric and Carew's Lines," TSB #82, p. 1.

Pellet, Kent. "Henry David Thoreau--a Reflection," GARDEN-
ING MAGAZINE, VI (February, 1942), 28.

Perkins, Frederick. "Nature in Thoreau and Burroughs,"
COLLEGIAN (February, 1889), pp. 119-126.

Perkins Institute for the Blind. A letter from Thoreau, THE
LANTERN [Perkins Institute for the Blind], XXIX (March
15, 1960), 2.
Quotes hitherto unrecorded letter by Thoreau apply-
ing for a position at the Institute.

"Personal Items," HERALD OF PROGRESS, III (May 24, 1862).
A hitherto unnoticed news item on Thoreau's death,
in a Spiritualist newspaper.

Peterson, George L. "Century after T, Walden Is Still Tran-
quil," MINNEAPOLIS STAR, September 20, 1962.

--"When H. D. Thoreau Visited Minnesota," MINNEAPOLIS STAR,
August 20, 1962.

[Peterson, George L.]. "Walden Centenary," MINNEAPOLIS STAR-
JOURNAL, July 3, 1945.
A centennial editorial.

Petteys, D. F. "A Complaint to R. W. E.," NEW YORK TIMES,
December 9, 1968.
A poem about Thoreau.

Pettigrew, Richard C. "Thoreau," NEW YORK HERALD TRIBUNE,
June 26, 1949.
A poem.

also in: POETRY CHAPBOOK, VII (Summer, 1949), 89.

Philbin, Philip J. "Thoreau," CONGRESSIONAL RECORD (May 23,
1962), pp. A3870-A3871.
Centennial tribute.

Photograph of the new memorial, LOWELL SUN, April 28, 1948,
p. 17.

Pickard, John B. "The Religion of 'Higher Laws'," EMERSON
SOCIETY QUARTERLY, XXXIX (1965), 68-72.
Analysis of WALDEN chapter.

Pierra. "Lines about Thinkers," CHRISTIAN SCIENCE MONITOR,
March 7, 1941.

Pileser, Tiglath. "By the Way," STATUS AND DIPLOMAT, XVIII
(April, 1968), 12-15.
On Thoreau's influence today.

Piper, Walter E. "Here's Evidence World Could Be a Lot Easier,"
FOOD MARKETING IN NEW ENGLAND, XVI (September, 1955), 15.
Reprints newly discovered document signed by Tho-
reau's grandfather.

--"Ice at Walden Pond," Boston, Mass.: Station WEEI, February 11, 1954.
Mimeographed copy of a broadcast.

--"A Salute to Henry David Thoreau," Boston, Mass.: Station
WEEI, July 10, 1952.
Mimeographed copy of a broadcast.

--"Thoreau's Map of Walden Pond," Boston, Mass.: Station
WEEI, January 21, 1954.
Mimeographed copy of a broadcast.

--THOREAUVIANA 1817-1955. Boston: Massachusetts Department
of Agriculture, 1955 (mimeographed).
A birthday tribute.

also in: CONCORD JOURNAL, July 21, 1955, p. 1 passim.

--"The University in the Sugar Bush," Boston: Massachusetts
Department of Agriculture, March 24, 1955.
Mimeographed text of a broadcast, on Thoreau's
experiments with maple sugar.

Pisanti, Tommasa. "Ottocento e Novecento: Henry D. Thoreau,
Francis S. Fitzgerald," NUOVA ANTOLOGIA, 1967 (November,
1964), 413-416.

Plagemann, Gentz. THE STEEL COCOON. New York: Viking, 1958.
A novel about life in the Navy in World War II.
The central character, Tyler Williams, carries a
copy of WALDEN with him constantly. We wrote the
author, asking why, and he replied, "As to why
Tyler Williams carried his WALDEN with him, I'm
afraid I can't really tell you. It was an intui-
tive, more than a conscious act of selection, I
think. Wasn't it Socrates who said that a man
should live so that when the city was beseiged, he
could leave with all of his belongings on his back?
Naturally, when Tyler Williams' city was beseiged,
he would leave with his Bible and His WALDEN, which
might be said to be the sum total of his possessions, in faith and personal philosophy." A strange-
ly compelling novel. TSB #66.

Pochmann, Henry A. "Henry David Thoreau," GERMAN CULTURE IN
AMERICA: PHILOSOPHICAL AND LITERARY INFLUENCES: 1600-
1900. Madison: University of Wisconsin Press, 1957.
pp. 423-436.
Most extensive study yet of the influence of German authors on Thoreau, concluding, "Thoreau was
not much influenced." TSB #67.

--NEW ENGLAND TRANSCENDENTALISM AND ST. LOUIS HEGELIANISM:
PHASES IN THE HISTORY OF AMERICAN IDEALISM. Philadelphia:
Carl Schurz Memorial Foundation, 1948.
A very important study of the relationship between
the Concord Transcendentalists and the St. Louis
group. It is a scholarly piece of work, but thoroughly readable. An essential book for any student
of American Transcendentalism. TSB #28.

Poger, Sidney. "Thoreau: Two Modes of Discourse." Columbia
University, 1966. Unpublished doctoral dissertation.
A reproduction of the abstract is found in TSB #106,
p. 7.

Poirier, Richard. A WORLD ELSEWHERE: THE PLACE OF STYLE IN

AMERICAN LITERATURE. New York: Oxford, 1966.
        Thoreau, passim; pp. 84-89, analysis of puns in
        WALDEN.

Polak, Henry S. L. "Gandhi and Thoreau," TSB #45.
        This article was reprinted from the NEW YORK EVENING
        POST. The author explains how he printed Thoreau's
        ON THE DUTY OF CIVIL DISOBEDIENCE in the INDIAN
        OPINION (which he edited) in 1907. The essay was
        also printed and distributed as a pamphlet.

Poole, Lynn. "Henry Thoreau Wanted to Live," TOLEDO BLADE,
        July 3, 1960.
        On Thoreau at Walden.

Pops, Martin L. "An Analysis of Thoreau's CAPE COD," BULLETIN
        OF NEW YORK PUBLIC LIBRARY, LXVII (September, 1963), 419-
        428.

Porte, Joel Miles. EMERSON AND THOREAU: TRANSCENDENTALISTS
        IN CONFLICT. Middletown, Conn.: Wesleyan University
        Press, 1966.
        The first detailed study of the philosophical dif-
        ferences between Thoreau and Emerson. He finds
        Thoreau to be more a Lockean sensualist than Tran-
        scendentalist. (Actually he was both; the terms
        are not necessarily contradictory). He places the
        blame for the cooling of the friendship of the two
        men on Emerson's jealousy of Thoreau's intellectual
        integrity and Thoreau's belief that Emerson was
        hypocritical. Porte makes some strong charges and
        undoubtedly overstates his case, but his book is a
        provocative and stimulating one. TSB #95.

        review: CHRISTIAN SCIENCE MONITOR, March 29, 1966.

    --"Emerson, Thoreau and the Double Consciousness," NEW
        ENGLAND QUARTERLY, XLI (March, 1968), 40-50.

    --"Love and Thoreau: a Lexicon of Hate," UNIVERSITY REVIEW,
        XXXI (Spring, 1965), 191-194.

    --"Thoreau on Love," UNIVERSITY REVIEW, XXXI (December,
        1964), 111-116.

Porter, Betty H. "Emerson and Thoreau: Implications for
        School Programs," THE TEACHER AND AMERICAN LITERATURE,
        edited by Lewis Leary. Champaign: NCTE, 1965. pp. 89-
        94.
        Teaching Thoreau in high school.

Porter, Eliot. "In Praise of Wildness," AMERICAN HERITAGE,
        XIV (December, 1962), 112-120.

    -- IN WILDNESS IS THE PRESERVATION OF THE WORLD.

191

San Francisco, Sierra Club, 1962.
>Unquestionably the most beautiful Thoreau book ever
published. Quotations from Thoreau illustrated with
photographs.

>reviews: ATLANTIC MONTHLY (February, 1963).
EXPLORER, November, 1962.

--The Same. New York: Ballentine, 1967. (paper).

Porter, Harriette Wilburr. "Birds of the Walden Seasons,"
FRONTIERS, XXII (December, 1957), 42-45.
>Brief essay on bird notes in Thoreau's writings.

Porter, Lawrence C. "Transcendentalism: A Self-Portrait,"
NEW ENGLAND QUARTERLY, XXXV (March, 1962), 27-47.
>Much on Thoreau's Transcendentalism.

Potter, David. "Sonnet" (Lake Walden, Thoreau's silent haunt
of old,") NATURE OUTLOOK, 1: 2 (February, 1943), 15.

P[otter], G[eorge] W. "He Marched Alone," PROVIDENCE [R. I.]
JOURNAL, September 11, 1954.

>also in: PROVIDENCE BULLETIN, September 11, 1954.

--"Henry Thoreau," PROVIDENCE [R. I.] EVENING BULLETIN,
December 7, 1951.
>"Thoreau's Walden Pond hut belongs immortally to
the heritage of this country."

--"Walden," PROVIDENCE [R. I.] EVENING BULLETIN, December
21, 1951.
>WALDEN is primarily not a nature essay but "a study
in values."

Poulet, Georges. STUDIES IN HUMAN TIME, translated from
French by Elliott Coleman. Baltimore: Johns Hopkins
University Press, 1955.
>Thoreau's attitude towards time on pp. 334-337.

--STUDIES IN HUMAN TIME, translated from French by Elliott
Coleman. New York: Harper Torchbooks, 1959. (paper).

Preston, Howard. "Thoreau's Lessons Ignored," CLEVELAND NEWS,
December 24, 1959.
>Brief, humorous essay on Thoreau's simple life.

Price, Fanny. "R. L. S. and Thoreau," NOTES AND QUERIES
(January 2, 1943) p. 18.
>A note on influence of Thoreau's lines in A WEEK
("Monday"): "The ship becalmed, at length stands
still, The steed must rest beneath the hill." on
Stevenson's famous lines "Home is the sailor, home
from the sea, And the hunter home from the hill."

Price, Lucien. "Concord's Non-Conformist," BOSTON [Mass.] GLOBE, August 8, 1954, p. 20.

--"Dialogue in Limbo," CLEVELAND SYMPHONY PROGRAM, April ?, 1955, pp. 771-776.
    A play with Thoreau as a minor character.

A. Prinzinger, d[er] J[unger]. HENRY D. THOREAU, EIN AMER-IKANISCHER NATURSCHILDERER. Salzburg: ? , 1895.
    A brief monograph which impressionistically charac-terizes Thoreau's relation to nature. Relates Thor-reau to the back-to-nature cult and calls attention to "Walking," "A Winter's Walk," and Thoreau's ex-periences in Maine.

Pritchard, John Paul. "Cato in Concord," CLASSICAL WEEKLY, XXXVI (October 5, 1942), 3-5.

--"Henry David Thoreau," RETURN TO THE FOUNTAINS. Durham, N. C.: Duke University Press, 1942. pp. 60-67.

Proctor, Edwin W. "From Thoreau's Seat," HARTFORD COURANT, September 23, 1945.
    A poem.

Profile of Walden Pond, CONCORD JOURNAL, October 17, 1968.
    Diagram of the pond made by the New England Marine Technology Society.

Proper, D. R. "Thoreau liked the Keene Area," KEENE [N. H.] EVENING SENTINEL, June 30, 1964.

"Prophets in Solitude," THE TIME LITERARY SUPPLEMENT [London] (February 14, 1948), 93.
    Review of the English edition of Canby's edition of Thoreau's WORKS, with comments on Thoreau's influence on Gandhi.

Pulos, C. E. "WALDEN and Emerson's 'The Sphinx," AMERICAN TRANSCENDENTAL QUARTERLY, I (1969), 7-11.

Pulsifer, Harold Townsend. COLLECTED POEMS. Waterville, Me.: Colby College Press, 1954.
    A sonnet, "Thoreau," p. 35.

Pyarelal. THOREAU, TOLSTOY AND GANDHIJI. Calcutta: Benson, 1958.
    A good account of Gandhi's interest in Thoreau writ-ten by his personal secretary. TSB #102.

    also in: STATESMAN [New Delhi], January 30, 1957.+ and NEW OUTLOOK, X (May, 1957), 3-11.

Quaal, Ward. "Favorite Author," CHICAGO AMERICAN, March 22, 1959.
>A radio station manager chooses Thoreau as his favorite author.

Quack, H. P. G. DE SOCIALISTEN. Amsterdam, Holland: van Kampen and Zoon, 1901.
>Pp. 238-242, on Thoreau.

Quinn, Arthur Hobson, editor. THE LITERATURE OF THE AMERICAN PEOPLE. New York: Appleton, 1951.
>Mr. Quinn's comments on Thoreau (pp. 270-273) sound like something out of the mid-nineteenth century. He dismisses Thoreau as a poor stylist, bewails the fact that his Journals have been printed, and ends up evaluating the notorious Lowell essay as one of the soundest appraisals of Thoreau. TSB #43.

Quinn, John Robert. "Walden Pond in Winter," NEW YORK TIMES, July 16, 1958.
>A poem.

Radetsky, Peter. "Thoreau and Taoism." University of Colorado, 1966. Unpublished master's thesis.
    Abstract in TSB #98, p. 6.

Rady, George Russell. "Thoreau," THE BLUE BELL [Montreal, Que.], XLI (April, 1962), 26-28.
    A centennial tribute.

--THOREAU AND THE TELEGRAPH, illustrated by Thoreau Mac-Donald. Montreal: Privately printed, 196?.

"Ranger Spreads His Poncho, Takes Off," CAPE CODDER (February 17, 1966).
    Confirms Thoreau's observations on Cape Cod winds.

Rao, E. Nageswara. "Thoreau and Gandhi: A Comparison," ARYAN PATH, XXXVII (August, 1966), 361-364.

"A Rare Thoreau Broadside," TSB #54.
    A reproduction of a broadside announcing a memorial service for John Brown.

Reaver, J. Russell. "Thoreau's Way with Proverbs," AMERICAN TRANSCENDENTAL QUARTERLY, I (1969), 2-7.

"Recent Thoreauana," TSB #1.
    A review of MORE DAY TO DAWN by Harry Lee.

"The Reception of Thoreau's First Book," TSB #27.
    Reprinted is a review of A WEEK ON THE CONCORD AND MERRIMACK RIVERS which originally appeared in the NEW YORK TRIBUNE on June 13, 1849 and was written by George Ripley.

Reel, Lois. "He Didn't Give a Hoot," CLEVELAND [Ohio] PLAIN DEALER, August 4, 1954.
    A poem parodying Whittier.

Reeves, Jean. "2 WNY Men Harken to Words of Thoreau--ALL 110,000," BUFFALO EVENING NEWS, September 24, 1960.
    Account of the editing of Sherwin and Reynolds, INDEX TO WALDEN.

Reglis, Eugen. "Hojas de mi Calendario," TIERRA Y LIBERTAD [Mexico] (April, 1965).

Reid, John T., editor. THOREAU AND INDIA. New Delhi [India]:
    United States Information Service, 1962.
        A booklet issued to commemorate the centennial of
        Thoreau's death. Includes: John Reid, "Prefatory
        Note," p. 4; Braj Kumar Nehru, "Thoreau: the Non-
        conformist," pp. 5-11; Mervin R. Lowe, " Henry
        David Thoreau: a Rebel for Our Times," pp. 13-20;
        Manning Hawthorne, "Thoreau: A Universal Spirit,"
        pp. 21-27; John T. Reid, "After Re-reading Walden,"
        pp. 28-34; "Thoreau on the Holy Books of India,"
        pp. 35-39; "For Further Reading on Thoreau," pp.40-41.

Reid, Mark. "Fish in the Sky," THE SHAMELESS NUDE, edited by
    Charles Cropsey and Jill Browner. Los Angeles: Elysium,
    1963. pp. 112-119.
        A spoof with Thoreau in a mental hospital being
        interviewed by psychiatrists.

Reinfeld, Fred. THE GREAT DISSENTERS. New York: Crowell,
    1959.
        Includes a chapter on Thoreau. Written for teen-
        agers.

Reinhardt, Charles A. "Principle's Price," FELLOWSHIP EX-
    CHANGE [Unitarian Fellowship, Boston, Mass.], XX (Novem-
    ber, 1963), 1-14.
        "An orchestration" of selections from Thoreau and
        others.

Relgis, Eugen. ALBORES DE LIBERTAD. Buenos Aires: Ed. Re-
    construir, 1959.
        Describes on page 68 a translation of WALDEN into
        Roumanian by Panait Musiou that was published some-
        time between 1900 and 1916.

"Reminiscences of Thoreau, I," TSB #38.
        Reprinted from RALPH WALDO EMERSON by William
        Hague. New York: Putnam, 1884. p. 12.

"Reminiscences of Thoreau, II," TSB #38.
        Reprinted from "Here in Boston", TIME AND THE HOUR,
        I (1896), 3-4.

Renzi, Emilia. "La 'Contestazione' di Henry-David Thoreau,"
    VOLONTA [Rome] (February, 1969).

"Rep. Eaton Steering Walden Bill to Final Enactment," CONCORD
    JOURNAL, July 14, 1955, p. 1 passim.
        On addition to reservation.

"Report of an Address by F. B. Sanborn at Greenacre on the
    Religion of Thoreau," BOSTON TRANSCRIPT, August 22, 1908.

Reynolds, Horace. "Thoreau, Emerson, and Taxes," CHRISTIAN
    SCIENCE MONITOR, September 30, 1963.

On Thoreau's payment of his 1840 poll tax.

Reynolds, R. C. and J. S. Sherwin. "Variant Punctuations in Two Editions of WALDEN," TSB #74, pp. 1-5.

Ribbins, Dennis. A NOBLE EXERCISE. Waupan, Wisc.: ? , 1967 (mimeographed).
    A lengthy study of Thoreau's attitudes towards reading.

Rice, Edwin B. "Wants Another Thoreau to Make the Scene," BUFFALO EVENING NEWS, February 18, 1969.
    Letter to editor.

Rich, Adrienne Cecile. "Concord River," NEW YORKER (September 12, 1953).
    A poem.

    also in: THE DIAMOND CUTTERS AND OTHER POEMS. New York: Harper, 1955. pp. 55-57.

--"Walden 1950," A CHANGE OF WORD. Cambridge: Harvard University Press, 1951.
    A sonnet.

Rich, Everett. "No Solitude at Walden Pond Where Thoreau Found Peace," WATERTOWN [N. Y.] DAILY TIMES, July 2, 1953.
    Account of a visit to Concord reprinted from KANSAS CITY STAR.

Rich, Stephen G. "Thoreau." NEW YORK TIMES BOOK REVIEW, September 12, 1954.
    A letter to the editor on the pronunciation of Thoreau's name.

Richardson, Laurence Eaton. CONCORD RIVER. Barre, Mass.: Barre Publishers, 1964.
    A thorough and detailed account of the history of Thoreau's favorite rivers (despite its title it includes the Assabet and Sudbury as well as the Concord) illustrated with a number of beautiful photographs. An excellent reference book for those wishing a fuller knowledge of the Thoreau country. TSB #90.

Richmond, Bruce L. THE PATTERN OF FREEDOM. Stockholm, Sweden: Ljus English Library, 1943.
    Quotes from CIVIL DISOBEDIENCE.

Riegel, Kurt. "Zum Thoreau-Echo im Spatwerk O'Neills," GERMANISH-ROMANISCHE MONATSSCHRIFT, XVIII (April, 1968), 191-199.
    Influence of Thoreau on Eugene O'Neill.

Rihani, Ameen. "From Concord to Syria," THE PATH OF VISION.

New York: White, 1921.

Ring, Elizabeth. "Fannie Hardy Eckstorm: Maine Woods His-
    torian," NEW ENGLAND QUARTERLY, XXVI (March, 1953), 45-
    64.
        On Thoreau's Maine Woods' biographer.

Rinhart, Floyd and Marion Rinhart. AMERICAN DAGUERREIAN ART.
    New York: Clarkson Potter, 1967.
        On page 30 is reproduced a supposed daguerreotype
        of Thoreau that is very obviously not that.

Rinzler, Elsie E. "Thoreau: The Medium and His Message,"
    ENGLISH JOURNAL, LVII (November, 1968), 1138ff.

Ritchell, Rella. "Thoreau--July 12, 1943," CONCORD JOURNAL,
    July 15, 1943.
        A poem.

        also in: SCARS AND OTHERS.   ?   : Walden Press,
        1953.

    --"Thoreau: Poet and Philosopher," TSB #41.

Robbins, Roland Wells. "A Communication re: Thoreau Under-
    ground," CONCORD JOURNAL, November 8, 1945.
        A suggestion that Concordians become better ac-
        quainted with their most famous native son.

    --"Discovery at Walden,"   ?,   ?.
        A brochure announcing lectures by the discoverer
        of the hut site.

    --DISCOVERY AT WALDEN. Concord, Mass.: Published by the
    author, 1947.
        Illustrated and with an introduction by Walter
        Harding.

        reviews: AMERICAN LITERATURE, XIX (November, 1947),
                  276, by Raymond Adams.
                  BOSTON GLOBE, March 26, 1947.
                  BOSTON POST, August 17, 1947, by H. B. Kane.
                  CHICAGO TRIBUNE, February 23, 1947, by
                  Frederick Babcock.
                  CONCORD ENTERPRISE, February 13, 1947.
                  CONCORD JOURNAL, February 13, 1947.
                  NEW ENGLAND QUARTERLY (Summer, 1947), by
                  Townsend Scudder.
                  NEW YORK HERALD TRIBUNE, March 16, 1947.
                  YANKEE, XII (February, 1948), 41, by
                  A[llison] E[lliott].

    --"House Hunting for Henry D. Thoreau," TSB #92, pp. 1-2.
    1965 Thoreau Society Presidential Address.

-- and Evan Jones. HIDDEN AMERICA. New York: Knopf, 1959. Roland Robbins is well-known to every member of the Thoreau Society as the discoverer of the exact site of Thoreau's Walden cabin. In Chapter 2, entitled "Go Thou My Incense Upward from This Hearth" (pp. 16-35), Robbins tells again the story of his work at Walden Pond. HIDDEN AMERICA is a fascinating account of the work of the "pick and shovel historian" and will be of particular interest to all Thoreauvians. TSB #69.

Robert, Derek. BELLBIRD ELEVEN. London: Hamish Hamilton, 1965.
    Account of a British sailor's attempt to establish his own Walden in the Australian bush. Thoreau frequently quoted and many of the chapters paralleling WALDEN in both title and content.

Roberts, Kenneth. "Be Yourself," THIS WEEK MAGAZINE (June 27, 1948), 2.
    Quotations from and comments on WALDEN.

--"On Somplicity," WORDS TO LIVE BY, edited by William Nichols. New York: Simon and Schuster, 1948.

Robinson, E. Arthur. "Thoreau's Buried Short Story," STUDIES IN SHORT FICTION. [Newberry College], I (Fall, 1963), 16-20.
    The "Baker Farm" chapter in WALDEN.

Robinson, James R. "Civil Disobedience," CONSCIENTIOUS OBJECTOR [N. Y.], IV (February, 1942), 8.
    Applies Thoreau's essay ON THE DUTY OF CIVIL DISOBEDIENCE to contemporary pacifism.

Robinson, Jeff. "Who's for Psychology," MINUS ONE [London, England]. July, 1966.
    An attack on Bode's "Half-Hidden Thoreau."

Rocker, Rudolf. "Henry David Thoreau," SOLIDARIDAD [Montevideo, Uruguay], May 1, 1959, pp. 50-52.

--"El Pensamiento de Thoreau," RECONSTRUIT, [Buenos Aires], XXIV-XXV (April-May, 1964).

--PIONEERS OF AMERICAN FREEDOM, translated from the German by Arthur E. Briggs. Los Angeles: Rocker Publications Committee, 1949.
    Mr. Rocker devotes more than half a chapter to Thoreau in his study of American liberalism and radicalism, and he declares that "Of all the spiritual representatives of American liberalism, Thoreau was perhaps the most profound and consistent. The book as a whole is an authoritative study of the liberal tradition in America. The bibliography

is particularly helpful for further reading. TSB #29.

translation: "Emerson y Thoreau," translated into Spanish by D. A. de Santillan in EL PENSAMIENTO LIBERAL EN LOS ESTADOS UNIDOS. Buenos Aires: Editorial Americalee, 1944. pp. 44-60.

Rodabaugh, Delmer. "Thoreau's SMOKE," EXPLICATOR, XVII (April, 1959), 47.
　　Explication of the poem.

Rohman, David G. "An Annotated Edition of Henry David Thoreau's WALDEN." Syracuse University, 1960. Unpublished doctoral dissertation.

　--"The Executive Deity, A Rhetorical Analysis of 'Economy' in WALDEN." Syracuse University, 1955. Unpublished master's thesis.

　--"Second Growth in WALDEN," PAPERS OF THE MICHIGAN ACADEMY OF SCIENCE, ARTS, AND LETTERS, XLVII (1962), 565-570.

　--"Thoreau's Transcendental Stewardship," EMERSON SOCIETY QUARTERLY, XLIV (1966), 72-77.

　--"WALDEN I and WALDEN II," PAPERS OF THE MICHIGAN ACADEMY OF SCIENCES, ARTS, AND LETTERS, XLVIII (1963), 639-648.
　　Thoreau's and B. F. Skinner's WALDENS compared.

Roland, Albert. "Do It Yourself: A Walden for the Millions," THE AMERICAN CULTURE, edited by Hennig Cohen. Boston: Houghton Mifflin, 1968.

Rolfe, Henry W. "Cummings Davis's 'Stars to Walden'," TSB #30.

Rolland, Romain. THE LIFE OF VIVEKANANDA. India: Advaita Ashrama Himalayas, 1953.
　　Much on the influence of Thoreau.

Rose, E. J. "The Wit and Wisdom of Thoreau's 'Higher Laws'," QUEEN'S QUARTERLY, LXIX (Winter, 1963), 555-567.
　　Analysis of WALDEN chapter.

Roseliep, Raymond. "Song Sparrow," POETRY, CXI (February, 1968).
　　Poem on Thoreau.

Rosenthal, Bernard. "Thoreau's Book of Leaves," EMERSON SOCIETY QUARTERLY, LVI (1969), 7-11.
　　On "Autumnal Tints."

Ross, Donald, Jr. "Hawthorne and Thoreau on 'Cottage Architecture!" AMERICAN TRANSCENDENTAL QUARTERLY, I (1969), 100.

--"The Style of Thoreau's WALDEN." University of Michigan, 1967. Unpublished doctoral dissertation.
A reproduction of the abstract appears in TSB #108.

Ross, Francis D. "Rhetorical Procedure in Thoreau's 'Battle of the Ants'," COLLEGE COMPOSITION AND COMMUNICATION, XVI (February, 1965), 14-18.

Ross, Ivan T. OLD STUDENTS NEVER DIE. Garden City: Doubleday, 1962.
Murder mystery in which one of the characters frequently quotes from Thoreau.

Rothovius, Andrew. "Great Dissenter was Friend of Monadnock," PETERBOROUGH [N. H.] TRANSCRIPT, July 27, 1967.

Rowlands, John J. SPINDRIFT. New York: Norton, 1960.
Includes comments on Tudor's cutting of the ice on Walden Pond in 1845 (pp. 70-72) and on Thoreau's visit to Cape Cod (pp. 202-204).

--"When Massachusetts Shipped Ice from Lake Walden to India," BOSTON TRANSCRIPT, July 23, 1927.

"The Rowse Crayon of Thoreau," TSB #30.
Reprinted is a portion of a letter to Alfred W. Hosmer from Eben J. Loomis.

Roy, Claude. "Defense des Americains," NOUVEL OBSERVATEUR [Paris], February 14, 1968, pp. 32-33.
On recent French translation of Thoreau.

Royce, Elizabeth S. "The Interview," NEW YORK STATE EDUCATION, LII (April, 1965), 12-13.
Satire on Thoreau in a modern school.

Ruland, Richard. THE REDISCOVERY OF AMERICAN LITERATURE. Cambridge: Harvard University Press, 1967.
Includes extended commentary on the criticisms of Thoreau by Matthiessen and P. E. More.

--TWENTIETH CENTURY INTERPRETATIONS OF WALDEN. Englewood Cliffs: Prentice-Hall, ? , also paper?
A reprinting of nine recent essays on WALDEN with excerpts from twelve others. The stress is on myth and symbolism.

Runge, Paul F. "Discover Your Own Walden," AUDUBON MAGAZINE (May-June, 1949).
Largely on Thoreau.

Russell, Francis. "The Concord and the Merrimack: A Voyage

after Thoreau," APPALACHIA (June, 1956).
Illustrated account of a retracing of Thoreau's
WEEK."

--"Thoreau's River Journey," CHRISTIAN SCIENCE MONITOR,
July 1, 1953.
An essay on A WEEK.

Russell, Frank Alden (Ted Malone, pseud.). "Henry David Thoreau," AMERICAN PILGRIMAGE. New York: Dodd Mead, 1942.
pp. 199-215.

Russo, Louis. "Summer at 'Blue-Eyed' Walden," BOSTON GLOBE,
August 18, 1946.
Photographs of the swimming beach at Walden.

"Rutgers Professor [F. T. McGill] Contends Thoreau Was Not
a Hippie," NEW YORK TIMES, January 5, 1968.

Ruzicka, Rudolf. NEW YEAR'S KEEPSAKE. Boston: Merrymount
Press, 1927.
A wood-engraving of Walden Pond.

Sadoya, Shigenobu. "Henry Thoreau in Japan," STUDY OF CURRENT
ENGLISH [Tokyo] (December, 1967), pp. 52-53.
Says Thoreau was first introduced into Japan by
Hosuke Koyama in TEIKOKU BUNGAKU, XI, 7 (1905).

Sagendorph, Robb. "Two Roads to Adventure," THIS WEEK (March
24, 1957), 2.
Brief tribute to Thoreau.

St. Armand, Barton L. "Thoreau Comes to Brown," BOOKS AT
BROWN, XXII (1968), 121-141.
Detailed account of the Albert Lownes collection
of Thoreauviana recently given to Brown University.

Saito, George. "Concord and Thoreau," RISING GENERATION
[Tokyo], CXIII (October, 1967), 644-645.
Text in Japanese.

--"Walden Pond," JIYU [Freedom] (August, 1963), 154-159.
Account of a visit to Walden Pond. Text in Japanese.

--"Walden Pond: Essay and Photographs," ENGLISH TEACHER'S
MAGAZINE [Japan], XVI (1967), 44-48.

Saito, Hikaru. "Thoreau Singing Lively Like a Cock," RISING
GENERATION, CXIII (October, 1967), 638-639.
Text in Japanese.

--"The Transcendentalists, Emerson, Thoreau and Others,"
A HANDBOOK OF BRITISH AND AMERICAN LITERATURE; 18TH-19TH
CENTURIES, edited by Natsuo Shumuda. Tokyo: Nan'un-do,
1966. pp. 558-577.

Sakamoto, Masayuki. "Retreat to the Original Point: A Portrait
of Thoreau," RISING GENERATION, CXIII (October, 1967),
640-642.
Text in Japanese.

--"Thoreau the Frontier Saunterer," ESSAYS, XV (1963), 15-
29.+

Salak, Joseph. "The Nudist Philosopher," AMERICAN SUNBATHER
[Spokane, Wash.], XVIII (March, 1966), 32-34.
Detailed discussion of Thoreau as an advocate of
nudism.

Sale of Thoreau MSS. by the Anderson Auction Co., N. Y.,
BOSTON TRANSCRIPT, May 19, 1905.

Salomon, Louis B. "The Practical Thoreau," COLLEGE ENGLISH,
XVII (January, 1956), 229-232.
Excellent article refuting most popular misconceptions of Thoreau's ideas with quotations from
his works. A god-send for any teacher of WALDEN
and CIVIL DISOBEDIENCE.

--"The Straight-Cut Ditch: Thoreau on Education," AMERICAN
QUARTERLY, XIV (Spring, 1962), 19-36.

Salt, Henry S. "A Group of Unpublished Letters by Henry S.
Salt to Joseph Ishill," Berkeley Heights, N. J.: Oriole
Press, 1942.
Letters by one of the greatest authorities on Tho-
reau. Edition limited to 50 copies only.

--LIFE OF HENRY DAVID THOREAU. New York: Haskell House,
1968.
A facsimile reprint of the 1896 short version of
Salt's great life of Thoreau. In many respects
this is still the best of all biographies of Thoreau. TSB #107.

--LIFE OF HENRY DAVID THOREAU. Hamden, Conn.: Archon Books
[Shoestring Press], 1968.

--"One World at a Time," CUM GRANO. Berkeley Heights, N. J.:
Oriole Press, 1931. p. 100.
A poem.

Salyer, Sandford. MARMEE, THE MOTHER OF LITTLE WOMEN. Norman:
University of Oklahoma Press, 1949.
A well-written but somewhat sentimental addition to
the ever-growing list of biographies of Thoreau's
friends. Thoreau receives little direct mention,
but it gives a good background picture of his times.
It is an understanding biography of a long-suffering
woman and will particularly delight all those who
have loved LITTLE WOMEN. The book is an exceptionally beautiful piece of printing. But why, did they
omit an index? TSB #27.

Sanavio, Piero. "Nota su Henry David Thoreau," LETTERATURE
MODERNE, VIII (April, 1958), 218-225.

Sanborn, Franklin Benjamin. "At the Breakfast Table," BOSTON
ADVERTISER, March 18, 1892.
On Thoreau's reading.

--HENRY D. THOREAU. New York: Houghton Mifflin, 1882.

reviews: ACADEMY, XXII (October 14, 1882), 271-272.
AMERICAN, IV (July 15, 1882), 218.

DIAL, III (August, 1882), 70-71.
HARPER'S MONTHLY, LXV (Sept, 1882), 631-
632.
LITERARY WORLD, XIII (July 15, 1882), 227-
228.
NATION, XXXV (July 13, 1882), 34-35.

--"John Brown's Burial Service," MIDDLESEX PATRIOT [Concord],
December 22, 1899.
Thoreau's part therein.

--LIFE OF HENRY DAVID THOREAU. Boston, New York: Houghton
Mifflin, 1917.

review: BOSTON TRANSCRIPT, March 7, 1917.
BOSTON TRANSCRIPT, May 29, 1917, by E. E. F.

--THE LIFE OF HENRY DAVID THOREAU. Detroit: Gale Research,
1968.
Facsimile reprint of the rare final biography of
Thoreau by Sanborn.

--"More Views of Concord Men," BOSTON TRANSCRIPT, August
10, 1906.

--"Our American Hermit," CHRISTIAN SCIENCE MONITOR, January 25, 1947.
A reprinting from the 1889 biography of Thoreau.

--THE PERSONALITY OF THOREAU. Boston: C. E. Goodspeed,
1901.

reviews: CRITIC, XLVI (January, 1905), 93.
NATION, LXXIV (February 6, 1902), 114.
NEW YORK TIMES, January 11, 1902.

--"Relation of Emerson and Thoreau," BOSTON HERALD, May
26, 1896.

--"The Religion of Thoreau," BOSTON TRANSCRIPT, August 22,
1908.

--"Rowse's Portraits of Emerson and Thoreau," BOSTON TRAN-
SCRIPT, June 5, 1901.

--"Thoreau and Emerson," FORUM, XXIII (April, 1897), 218-
227.

--"Thoreau and the Walden Woods," BOSTON HERALD, May 26,
1896.

Sanborn, Kate. "Bachelor Authors as Types," MY FAVORITE LEC-
TURES OF LONG AGO. Boston: Privately printed, 1898.
Thoreau described as a typical bachelor author,
pp. 75-77.

Sanborn, S. "Sanborn's Arrest," CONCORD JOURNAL, December
24, 1959.
> Account by his sister of F. B. Sanborn's arrest in
> the John Brown case, with particulars of Thoreau's
> part.

Sanborn, Victor Channing. "Franklin Benjamin Sanborn, A. B.,"
KANSAS HIST. COL., XIV, 58-63.
> On Thoreau's friend and biographer.

Sanchez, L. A. "Henry David Thoreau," REVISTA IBEROAMERICANA,
VI (February, 1943), 95-102.

Sanders, Frederick K. "Mr. Thoreau's Timebomb," NATIONAL
REVIEW, XX (June 4, 1968), 541-547.
> A conservative looks at CIVIL DISOBEDIENCE.

Sanford, Charles L. "Classics of Reform Literature," AMER-
ICAN QUARTERLY, X (Fall, 1958), 295-311.
> Includes much comment on Thoreau.

--"Emerson, Thoreau, and the Hereditary Duality," EMERSON
SOCIETY QUARTERLY, LIV (1969), 36-43.

Sargent, George H. "Thoreau's Personality," BOSTON TRANSCRIPT,
December 14, 1901.

Sarma, Sreekrishna. "A Short Study of Oriental Influence upon
H. D. Thoreau with Special Reference to WALDEN," JAHRBUCH
FUR AMERIKASTUDIEN, I (1956), 76-92.
> Argues that from an Indian point of view Thoreau
> may be considered a Jnanayogi, i.e., a Yogi whose
> path is intellectual rather than emotional. In
> addition Sarma discerns in Thoreau traces of Karma-
> yoga, the path of action.

Scanlon, Lawrence. "Thoreau's Parable of Baker Farm," EMERSON
SOCIETY QUARTERLY, XLVII (1967), 19-21.

Schechter, Betty. THE PEACEABLE REVOLUTION. Boston: Houghton
Mifflin, 1963.
> The story of non-violent resistance, tracing it
> from Thoreau, through Gandhi to Martin Luther King.
> Although written for young people, it is a thorough-
> going and well-written account of the spread of Tho-
> reau's doctrine of civil disobedience that will ap-
> peal equally well to adults. Particularly of in-
> terest in the light of civil disobedience in the
> South today. TSB #84.

Schejbal, Jaroslav. "Henry David Thoreau," LITERARNI NOVINY,
XXXVIII (September 22, 1967).
> Text in Czech.

Scherman, David and Rosemarie Redlich. LITERARY AMERICA.

New York: Dodd, Mead, 1952.
>An album of photographs of the scenes that inspired American authors. The Thoreau pages (40-43) are especially effective. TSB #39.

Schiffman, Joseph. HENRY DAVID THOREAU, ACTIVIST. New York: McGraw-Hill, 1969, McGraw-Hill Sound Seminars #75626.
>A clear, straight-forward and well-expresses tape-recorded summary of Thoreau's life and exposition of his ideas, aimed particularly at today's students. An excellent classroom introduction to Thoreau for today. TSB #108.

--"WALDEN and CIVIL DISOBEDIENCE: Critical Analyses," EMERSON SOCIETY QUARTERLY, LVI (1969), 57-60.

Schiller, Andrew. "Thoreau and Whitman: The Record of a Pilgrimage," NEW ENGLAND QUARTERLY, XXVIII (June, 1955), 186-197.
>Detailed account of the friendship of the two.

--"Thoreau in the Undergraduate Survey Course," EMERSON SOCIETY QUARTERLY, XVIII (1960), 17-19.

Schlesinger, Arthur M., Jr. THE AGE OF JACKSON. Boston: Little, Brown, 1945.
>According to reviews this has several pages of interpretation of Thoreau's philosophy in the light of Jacksonian democracy.

--"Jackson and Literature," NEW REPUBLIC, CXIV (May 27, 1946), 765-768.
>Condensed from the book THE AGE OF JACKSON.

Schlick, Ernst. "Ein Held der Vereinigten Staaten," ZEIT-SCHRIFT FUR GEOPOLITIK, XXX, 5 (1959), 7-9.
>Emphatically calls attention to the value of civil disobedience in the modern world; suggests Thoreau's influence on Gandhi.

Schmidtchen, Paul V. "Rugged Individualist," HOBBIES (August, 1968).

Schnittkind, H. T. and D. A. Schnittkind. "Thoreau's Adventure into the Simple Life," LIVING ADVENTURES IN PHILOSOPHY. New York: Hanover House, 1954. pp. 230-239.

Schoenberger, H. W. "Henry David Thoreau," SOME WRITERS OF OLDER NEW ENGLAND, edited by Percival Hunt et al. Pittsburg: University of Pittsburg Press, 1928. pp. 41-47.

Scholz, Franz. "Pollution Costs $40 Million," LOWELL [Mass.] SUN, September 7, 1969.
>This and following articles recount a retracing this

summer of Thoreau's week on the Concord and Merrimack Rivers, emphasizing in vivid and sickening
terms the destruction of those rivers by pollution.

--"Pollution Menaces Riverside Residents," LOWELL SUN,
September 3, 1969.

--"A Week on the Concord and Merrimack Rivers with Apologies
to Henry David Thoreau," LOWELL SUN, August 31, 1969.

Schott, Webster. "Materialism Casts Its Spell on Pond Where
Thoreau Sought the Ideal Life," KANSAS CITY [Mo.] STAR,
August 28, 1954.

Shreffler, Philip A. "Holmes and Thoreau," BAKER STREET JOUR-
NAL, XIX (September, 1969), 149-151.
More on Sherlock Holmes and Thoreau.

Schroeder, Fred. E. H. "Andrew Wyeth and the Transcendental
Tradition," AMERICAN QUARTERLY, XVII (1965), 559-567.
Influence of Thoreau on his art.

Schuchat, Theodor. "WALDEN, 100 Years Old, Still Has a Word
for the Wise," WASHINGTON [D.C.] POST, August 9, 1954,
p. 9.

Schultz, Howard. "A Fragment of Jacobean Song in Thoreau's
WALDEN," MODERN LANGUAGE NOTES, LXIII (April, 1948),
271-272.
A source for a bit in WALDEN.

Schwaber, Paul. "Thoreau's Development in WALDEN," CRITICISM,
V (Winter, 1963), 64-77.

Schwartzman, Jack. "Henry David Thoreau: The Hermit of Disobedience," REBELS OF INDIVIDUALISM. New York: Expo-
sition Press, 1949. pp. 54-62.
A unique account of Thoreau's Judgment Day trial
with Thoreau quoting his books in self-defense, and
being sentenced to reincarnation as a tree. TSB #27.

--"Yes, Ladies, There Is an Innisfree! (Thoreau's Influence
on Yeats)," NASSAU REVIEW [Garden City, N. Y.], I (Spring,
1968), 14-25.

Scott, Louise. "And a Small Cabin Built There," EDUCATIONAL
FORUM, XXVI (January, 1962), 232.
Sonnet on Thoreau.

--"Walden," CONCORD JOURNAL, August 10, 1961.
A sonnet.

Scott, Winfield Townley. "Walden Pond in the Nuclear Age,"
NEW YORK TIMES MAGAZINE, May 6, 1962, pp. 34 passim.
A centennial tribute.

Scudder, Townsend. CONCORD: AMERICAN TOWN. Boston: Little, Brown and Co., 1947.

--"Henry David Thoreau," THE LITERARY HISTORY OF THE UNITED STATES, edited by Spiller, Thorp, Johnson and Canby. New York: Macmillan, 1948. I, 388-415.

--"Henry David Thoreau," THE LITERARY HISTORY OF THE UNITED STATES. New York: Macmillan, 1953.
   A new edition.

--"Thoreau's Hut Fitted like a Coat," CHRISTIAN SCIENCE MONITOR, May 20, 1947.
   An excerpt from CONCORD: AMERICAN TOWN.

Scutch, Alexander F. "Backward--or Forward--to Nature?" NATURE MAGAZINE (November, 1946), 457-460 passim.
   A contrast between Thoreau's Walden experiment and one by the author in a remote section of Costa Rica.

Seaburg, Alan. "An Introduction to Thoreau," TSB #107, p. 3.

--"Min Thoreau," TSB #101, pp. 7-8.

--"That Man Thoreau," CONCORD JOURNAL, June 15 and 22, 1967.

--"A Thoreau Document," TSB #109, p. 5.
   A Thoreau obituary in THE CHRISTIAN REGISTER for May 17th.

--"Thoreau's Favorite Farmer," TSB #102, pp. 1-4.

--"Thoreau's Neighbor: George Melvin," SNOWY EGRET, XXXI (Autumn, 1967), 25-30.

Seal, Gabriel. "Henry Thoreau," COUNTRYMAN [Burford, Oxfordshire, England], LIII (Summer, 1956), 325-330.
   A general essay.

Sebenthall, R. E. "Thoreau," COLORADO QUARTERLY, X (Autumn, 1961), 133.
   A poem.

Seefurth, Nathaniel H. THOREAU: A VIEW FROM EMERITUS. Chicago: Seefurth Foundation, 1968.
   A delightfully written evaluation of the significance of Thoreau today.

      also in: EMERSON SOCIETY QUARTERLY, LIV (1969), Supplement.

Semmens, Frank. "Thoreau's Changing Attitudes: a Study of Metaphor and Meaning in WALDEN." State University of New York at Oswego, 1968. Unpublished master's thesis.

Semple, Dugald. JOY IN LIVING: AN AUTOBIOGRAPHY. Glasgow:
Maclellan, 1957.
Autobiography of a Scottish nature writer and
advocate of the simple life, with frequent mention
of the influence of Thoreau.

Sergeant, Elizabeth Shepley. ROBERT FROST: THE TRIAL BY
EXISTENCE. New York: Holt, 1960.
Many comments on Frost's interest in Thoreau.

Seven Gables Bookshop. HAWTHORNE AND THOREAU. New York:
Seven Gables Bookshop, 1949.
A catalog of books pertaining to Hawthorne and
to Thoreau.

Seybold, Ethel. "Thoreau for Everyone," EMERSON SOCIETY QUAR-
TERLY, XVIII (1960), 19-21.

--THOREAU: THE QUEST AND THE CLASSICS. New Haven: Yale
University Press, 1951.

> reviews: AMERICAN LITERATURE, XXIII (November, 1951),
> 385-386, by John Paul Pritchard.
> AMERICAN QUARTERLY, IV (Winter, 1952), 363-
> 366.
> NEW ENGLAND QUARTERLY, XXIV (September,
> 1951), 399-402, by Sherman Paul.
> THOREAU SOCIETY BULLETIN #35.
> TIMES LITERARY SUPPLEMENT [London], August
> 24, 1951, p. 527.

--THOREAU: THE QUEST AND THE CLASSICS. Hamden, Conn.:
Archon Books, 1969.
A reprint.

Shafer, Burr. "Through History with J. Wesley Smith," SATUR-
DAY REVIEW OF LITERATURE, April 13, 1946.
A cartoon of Thoreau at Walden Pond.

Shanley, J. Lyndon. THE MAKING OF WALDEN. University of
Chicago Press, 1957.
Undoubtedly the most important book on Thoreau of
the year--in fact, in some years. Prof. Shanley
has untangled the mess of WALDEN manuscripts in
Huntington Library and discovered therein large
portions of seven different drafts of the book, including almost all of the first draft. On the basis
of his discovery he is able to show us clearly just
how Thoreau developed, polished, and refined his
masterpiece. Most important of all, he gives us
the nearly complete text of the first draft--which
in itself is an amazingly polished work of art. A
particularly valuable portion of the book is Mr.
Shanley's emphasis on the structure of WALDEN--a
discussion which belies the popular claim that the

book is formless. And we agree heartily with his
thesis that Thoreau was <u>not</u> unhappy and frustrated,
as many would claim. This is a must book for any
Thoreauvian and one of the outstanding books in the
history of American literary scholarship. TSB #61.

reviews: CHICAGO TRIBUNE, November 3, 1957.
EMERSON SOCIETY QUARTERLY, XIV (1959), 37.
REPORTER, January 23, 1958.
TIMES LITERARY SUPPLEMENT, March 7, 1958,
p. 129.

--MAPS OF CONCORD. Evanston, Ill.: Published by the author,
1950.
An excellent relief map of the Thoreau country.
TSB #33.

--"The Pleasures of Walden," CONCORD JOURNAL, July 16, 1959.
A condensed version of the Presidential Address at
the annual meeting.

translation: "Placeres de Walden," translated into
Spanish by Vladimir Munoz. CENIT, XII (January,
1962), 3575-3579.

--"Thoreau's Geese and Yeat's Swans," AMERICAN LITERATURE,
XXX (November, 1958), 361-364.
Demonstrates that Yeats was influenced by WALDEN
when he wrote "The Wild Swans at Coole."

--A review of THE CORRESPONDENCE OF HENRY DAVID THOREAU,
edited by Walter Harding and Carl Bode. TSB #65.

--A review of THE DAYS OF HENRY THOREAU, by Walter Harding.
TSB #94.

--A review of A THOREAU HANDBOOK, by Walter Harding. TSB
#69.

Shapiro, Leo. "A Beauty of Nature in Love with Thoreau,"
BOSTON GLOBE, October 31, 1968.
A PLAYBOY girl of the month confesses her love
for Thoreau.

Shear, Walter, Lewis. "Thoreau's Imagery and Symbolism."
Madison: University of Wisconsin, 1961. Unpublished
doctoral dissertation.

Sheean, Vincent. MAHATMA GANDHI. New York: Knopf, 1955.
Pp. 77-78, contains a rather garbled account of
Gandhi's interest in Thoreau.

Sheehan, Arthur and Elizabeth Odell. ROSE HAWTHORNE: THE
PILGRIMAGE OF NATHANIEL'S DAUGHTER. New York: Farrar,
Straus and Cudahy, 1959.

A biography of Hawthorne's younger daughter, written
especially for Roman Catholic children. There are
several discriptions (pp. 22-23 passim) of the visits
from Thoreau which are notable chiefly for their
misrepresentation of Thoreau as an awkward cross-
patch. The book as a whole, however, gives an interesting picture of Rose Hawthorne's charitable
work. TSB #69.

Shepard, Odell. "Approaching Thoreau Through Modern Scholarship," EMERSON SOCIETY QUARTERLY, XVIII (1960), 23-26.

--"Unconsciousness in Concord," EMERSON SOCIETY QUARTERLY,
LII (1968), 3-8.
A reprint.

S[hepard], O[dell]. "A River and Three Lovers," CHRISTIAN
SCIENCE MONITOR, January 22, 1925.

Sherlock, Chesla C. "Walden, the Rendezvous of Thoreau,"
HOMES OF FAMOUS AMERICANS. Des Moines: Meredith, 1926.
I, 205-216.

Sherwin, J. Stephen and Richard C. Reynolds. A WORD INDEX TO
WALDEN WITH TEXTUAL NOTES. Charlottesville: University
of Virginia Press, 1960.
Thoreau scholars have long felt the need for a concordance of WALDEN and at last the need is filled.
Here is an index of every single word in the book,
giving the exact location as to page and line of
each occurence except for the 122 words that occur
more frequently than 100 times each--and for these
there is a word count. But the book has other uses
as well as those of a concordance. New insight is
given into Thoreau's vocabulary and its patterns of
usage. And so carefully have the authors studied
word variants that they have provided a number of
new insights into Thoreau's exact meaning. We hope
in a future issue of our bulletin to persuade them
to present some of their new findings. Meanwhile
all students of WALDEN will find this volume a tremendously handy reference work. TSB =73.

reviews: BUFFALO EVENING NEWS, September 24, 1960.
ROCHESTER TIMES-UNION, November 7, 1960.
also in: EMERSON SOCIETY QUARTERLY, LVII (1969).
Supplement. A reprint with corrections of the
original edition.

Sherwin, Stephen. "A Thoreau Ground-Swell?" ST. LOUIS POST-
DISPATCH, December 7, 1958.
"The chances for a substantial increase in Thoreau's
popularity are exceedingly slim until there is a
large adult reading public."

Sherwood, Mary p. "The Library Elm." CONCORD JOURNAL. February 23, 1961.
> Events which have occurred through the years near a recently cut down elm.

--"The Biography of Colonial Inn." CONCORD TOWN (September, 1964), p. 1 passim.
> [CONCORD TOWN is a new monthly magazine for Concord visitors.]

--"Did Thoreau Foreshadow a Third Culture Synthesis?" THOREAU JOURNAL QUARTERLY, I (July 1, 1969), 22-29.

--"Fanny Eckstorm's Bias." MASSACHUSETTS REVIEW, IV (Autumn, 1962), 139-147.

--"The Hut Discoverer," CONCORD TOWN (July, 1964), pp. 13-15 passim.
> On Roland Robbins.

--"Julian, Abbie, and the River Lilies," CONCORD TOWN (April, 1964), p. 2 passim.
> Thoreau sends some children after water lilies.

--"May, 1862," CONCORD TOWN (May, 1964), p. 6 passim.
> On Thoreau's death.

--"Our Three Little Rivers," CONCORD TOWN (June, 1964), p. 1 passim.
> On Thoreau's boating.

--"Red Bridge." CONCORD TOWN (May, 1964), p. 1 passim.
> Thoreau carves Ellen Sewall's initials.

--"Thoreau Island," THOREAU JOURNAL QUARTERLY, I (January 15, 1969), 20-22.
> On the recent renaming of an island is the Penobscot for Thoreau.

--"Thoreau's Penobscot Indians," THOREAU JOURNAL QUARTERLY, I (January 15, 1969), 1-13.

--"Where Can I See Thoreau's Hut?" CONCORD TOWN (July, 1964), pp. 9-12.

Shigematsu, Tsutomu. "On Thoreau's Doctrine of Simplicity," BULLETIN OF STUDIES OITA WOMEN'S JUNIOR COLLEGE, I (April, 1969), 75-86.

--"A Study on the Sun in WALDEN," BULLETIN OF OITA KOGYO DAIGAKU, I (December, 1968).

Shively, Daniel. AGAINST FEAR. Indiana, Pa.: Published by the author, 1968.
> Philosophical speculations permeated with references

to and quotations from Thoreau.

Shuman, R. Baird. "Thoreau's Passage on the 'Frozen-Thawed'
Apple," EMERSON SOCIETY QUARTERLY, XVIII (1960), 34-35.
A hitherto unknown 1-page draft of a portion of
"Wild Apples" reveals some minor word variations.

Shute, Ernest X. "Concord, Massachusetts," STUDIO NEWS MAGA-
ZINE [Friend, Neb.] (January, 1960), p. 24.
A sonnet on Thoreau.

   --"Thoreau and Emerson: Twin Stars in History's Literary
Firmament," STUDIO NEWS MAGAZINE (September-October, 1959),
p. 24.
An essay.

   --THOUGHT TRAILS. Boston: Bruce Humphries, 1956.
A collection of poems "dedicated to Thoreau,"
and with brief reference to Thoreau in one poem.

Sibley, Celestine. "Thoreau Spoiled Work Plans at Cabin,"
BUFFALO COURIER EXPRESS, July ?, 1960.
Thoreau is used to justify loafing on a vacation.

Sillen, Samuel. "Thoreau in our Time," LOOKING FORWARD.
New York: International, 1955. pp. 153-163.
Marxist approach to Thoreau.

"Simon Brown's Journal," TSB #76, p. 3.
"Excerpts from the unpublished journal of Simon
Brown."

Simon, Myron and Thornton H. Parsons. TRANSCENDENTALISM AND
ITS LEGACY. Ann Arbor: University of Michigan Press,
1966.
Many good articles on the movement. Albert Gilman
and Roger Brown, "Personality and Style in Concord,"
pp. 87-122, is the most authoritative study yet of
the stylistic differences between Thoreau and Emerson. TSB #98.

Simpson, Lewis P. "The Short Desperate Life of Henry Thoreau,"
EMERSON SOCIETY QUARTERLY, XLII (1966), 45-56.

Sinks, Don. A drawing of Thoreau at his Walden cabin. CHICAGO
TRIBUNE MAGAZINE OF BOOKS, August 8, 1954, p. 1.
A full-page colored illustration.

Sisson, Jonathan. "Notes on Walden Pond," IVORY TOWER [Univer-
sity of Minnesota], XIV (May, 1967), 26-29.

"Site of Thoreau Hut Established," CONCORD JOURNAL, January
10, 1946.
Mr. Robbins' discovery, with a photograph of the
excavation.

Skard, Sigmund. "Grunnfjellet i oss: Henry Thoreau," DAD
    OG DIKT. Oslo: Det Norske Samlaget, 1963. pp. 248-261.
    Text in Norse.

Skinner, B. F. WALDEN TWO. New York: Macmillan, 1948.
    Add this to the ever-increasing bibliography of
    Thoreau in fiction. Mr. Skinner's novel is an
    account of a modern utopian community in the
    Middle West, inspired in part by the philosophy of
    Thoreau's WALDEN. As LIFE has recently pointed out,
    however, the philosophy of the managers and plan-
    ners of Walden Two is a gross perversion of the
    original WALDEN. While it is true that the phi-
    losophy of the simple life and the doing away with
    all needless luxuries in a search for the very mar-
    row of life motivates these leaders, the atmosphere
    of the community is completely sterile of the free-
    dom of thought and the independence that are the
    fundamental characteristics of Thoreau's mind. The
    novel is thought-provoking, to say the least. But
    no one can honestly call it an expression of the
    Thoreauvian philosophy. TSB #24.

    also in: DESIGNS OF FAMOUS UTOPIAS, edited by
    Donald and Allan Orrick. New York: Rinehart, 1959.
    pp. 55-62. A condensed version.

Skwire, David. "A Check List of Wordplay in WALDEN," AMER-
    ICAN LITERATURE, XXXI (November, 1959), 281-289.

Slater, Joseph. "Caroline Dall in Concord," TSB #62.

--, editor. THE CORRESPONDENCE OF EMERSON AND CARLYLE.
    New York: Columbia University Press, 1964.
    Of all Emerson's correspondences, unquestionably
    the most important was that with Carlyle, yet the
    only edition has been the Norton one of 1883 edited
    by 19th rather than 20th century standards. Now
    Slater has brought out a completely up-to-date
    edition edited with impecable scholarship. Thoreau
    is, of course, frequently mentioned particularly in
    the early years when Emerson was hailing him as his
    "man of Concord." TSB #90.

Smith, Bess Foster. "The Vision of Thoreau," FELLOWSHIP IN
    PRAYER, XIV (August, 1963), 8-9.

Smith, Bradford. "Thoreau: Civil Disobedience," MEN OF PEACE.
    Philadelphia: Lippincott, 1964. pp. 144-156.
    In a collection of studies of fifteen men from
    ancient times to the present who dedicated them-
    selves to the abolition of war, Smith presents a
    good brief summary of Thoreau's attitude toward
    reform as it changed from "Civil Disobedience"
    through "Slavery in Massachusetts" to the John

Brown essays. Thoreauvians will also be particularly interested in the chapter on Gandhi since it presents a very clear picture of the application of
Thoreau's theories today. TSB #90.

Smith Corporation, A. O. Advertisement in WALL STREET JOURNAL,
December 28, 1956.
Quotes Thoreau's poem "Inspiration."

Smith, Edmund Ware. "Along Thoreau's Canoe Trail," FORD TIMES,
LI (March, 1959), 2-9.

Smith, Edwin F. "Thoreau's Note Books," SCHOOL MODERATOR,
September 4, 1884.
A review of "Spring" and "Summer" in a Grand Rapids
Michigan paper.

Smith, Edwin S. "A Thoreau for Today," MAINSTREAM, XIII
(April, 1960), 1-24.+
Ostensibly a review of recent books on Thoreau,
actually a penetrating discussion of Thoreau's
ideas. TSB #71.

Smith, John Sylvester. "The philosophical naturism of Henry
David Thoreau with special reference to its epistemo-
logical presuppositions and theological implications."
Drew University, 1948. Unpublished doctoral dissertation.

Smith, Kenneth J. "Henry David Thoreau: America's Hippie,"
EXISTENTIALISM AND ETHICAL HUMANISM. Kanona, N. Y.:
J. & C. Transcripts, 1969. pp. 43-55.

Smith, Marion Whitney. ALGONQUIAN AND ABENAKI INDIAN MYTHS
AND LEGENDS. Lewiston, Maine: Central Maine Press, 1962.
Much on Thoreau and the Neptune family.

--STRANGE TALES OF ABENAKE SHAMANISM. Lewiston, Maine:
Central Maine Press, 1963.
Frequent references to Thoreau's Maine trips.

Smith, Marjorie W. "Kipling and Thoreau's Mother Figured in
History of the Crystal [Restaurant]," KEENE [N. H.]
SENTINEL, January 3, 1968.

Smith, May Riley. "The Scarecrow," POEMS. New York: Poet's
Guild, 1929.

Smith, S. S. Steel engraving of Rowse crayon of Thoreau.
Concord: Thoreau Lyceum, 1966.

Smythe, Daniel. "Henry D. Thoreau--1969," THOREAU JOURNAL
QUARTERLY, I (April 15, 1969), 24-25.
A poem.

--"Thoreau and People," THOREAU JOURNAL QUARTERLY, I
(April 15, 1969), 21-22.

--"Thoreauvian Journey," CHRISTIAN SCIENCE MONITOR, May 6, 1969.

Snow, Edward Rowe. A PILGRIM RETURNS TO CAPE COD. Boston: Yankee Publishing Company, 1946.
> While this book is often awkward in literary structure, it is probably the most complete and authoritative volume on Cape Cod today. Mr. Snow hikes over much the same territory that Thoreau covered and much more too. He gives an excellent picture of the Cape today and frequently throws new light on many of Thoreau's experiences. There is a particularly good account of the present state of the Wellfleet Oysterman's house. It should be required reading for all who want a fuller understanding of Thoreau's CAPE COD. TSB #19.

--"Salvage Silver Coins from Old Pirate Hulk WHIDAH in Waters off Cape Cod," BOSTON POST, October 5, 1947, p. 12.
> With quotations from Thoreau on the same wreck.

--"Thoreau in Provincetown," CHRISTIAN SCIENCE MONITOR, January 7, 1947.
> A reprinting of a brief section from A PILGRIM RETURNS TO CAPE COD.

Snyder, Helena A. "Thoreau's Philosophy of Life with Special Consideration of the Influence of Hindoo Philosophy." Heidelberg University, 1902. Unpublished doctoral dissertation.
> Written in English, this dissertation appears to be the first extensive treatment of Thoreau's relation to Oriental thought. Though of historical interest on this account, it is superficial and unhistorical in regard to its "special consideration." Most interesting and original is Snyder's discussion of Thoreau's idealism, which convincingly ties together his civil disobedience, his curious notions about love and friendship, his negative attitude toward reform movements, and even his comments on music. TSB #105.

"Sobre Henry D. Thoreau Diserto Leopoldo Hurtado en e Ateneo," ELXECO DE TANDIL [Tandil, Argentina], June 7, 1949.
> Account of a lecture on Thoreau by Mr. Hurtado.

"Sophia Foord Again". TSB #47.

"Sophia Thoreau," EMERSON SOCIETY QUARTERLY, XVIII (1960), 42.
> Reprinting of SPRINGFIELD REPUBLICAN obituary of 1876.

"A Southern Matron Looks at Thoreau," TSB #104, p. 7.
> An entry from the diary of Mary Boykin Chesnut, November 28, 1861.

Sowerby, Henry. "Withdrawal and Return," CHRISTIAN SCIENCE
MONITOR, May 20, 1964.
On Thoreau at Walden.

Spatz, Claire. "Why Thoreau Spent One Night in Milwaukee,"
HISTORICAL MESSENGER OF MILWAUKEE COUNTY HISTORICAL SOCI-
ETY, XVIII (December, 1962), 3-9.

--, editor. WALDEN: CHAPTER NOTES AND CRITICISM. New
York: American R. D. M. Corp., 1962.
A "pony" to help students to avoid reading WALDEN!

Spector, Robert. WALDEN AND CIVIL DISOBEDIENCE. Boston:
Student Outlines Co., 1964.
A "trot" in the "Hymarx" series.

Spencer, Benjamin T. THE QUEST FOR NATIONALITY: AN AMERICAN
LITERARY CAMPAIGN. Syracuse: Syracuse University Press,
1957. pp. 86-87.
On nationalism in Thoreau's writings.

Spiller, Robert E. THE CYCLE OF AMERICAN LITERATURE: AN
ESSAY IN HISTORICAL CRITICISM. New York: Macmillan,
1955.
Much on Thoreau, passim.

Spofford, Walter R. "How Harvard Acquired its Thoreau Common-
place Book," TSB #54.

"Spring-Rests of Thoreau Coach Come to Light," MOOSEHEAD
GAZETTE [Dexter, Maine], February, 1966, p. 1.

Staerk, Melanie. "On the Side Lines," SWISS REVIEW OF WORLD
AFFAIRS, XI (September, 1961), 18.
On Thoreau's preference for the "mixed life," his
affection and his happiness.

Stanton, Will. "The Friends of Sammy," McCALL'S (January,
1964), 73.
A short story with a Thoreau devotee as one of
the characters.

Stark, L. M. and R. W. Hill. "Guggenheim Gift," BULLETIN OF
THE NEW YORK PUBLIC LIBRARY, LVII (January, 1953), 43-
46.
Description of some important Thoreau manuscripts
and books recently given to the New York Public
Library.

Starr, John T. "Moosehead: Thoreau's North Woods Lake,"
AMERICAN FORESTS, LXX (June, 1964), 19-23.

Steel, Kurt. "Prophet of the Independent Man," PROGRESSIVE,
IX (September 24, 1945), 9.
An excellent brief essay on Thoreau. TSB #13.

Stein, Roger. JOHN RUSKIN AND AESTHETIC THOUGHT IN AMERICA: 1840-1900. Cambridge: Harvard University Press, 1967. Comment on Thoreau and Ruskin, pp. 90-93.

Stein, William Bysshe. "An Approach to Thoreau," EMERSON SOCIETY QUARTERLY, LVI (1969), 4-6.

--"A Bibliography of Hindu and Buddhist Literature Available to Thoreau thru 1854," EMERSON SOCIETY QUARTERLY, XLVII (1967), 52-56.

--"Melville Roasts Thoreau's Cock," MODERN LANGUAGE NOTES, LXXIV (March, 1959), 218-219.
    Melville's "Cock-a-Doodle-Do" considered as a reply to Thoreau's "Walking."

--"Thoreau's First Book: A Spoor of Yoga," EMERSON SOCIETY QUARTERLY, XLI (1965), 4-15.

--"Thoreau's Hound, Bay Horse, and Turtledove," TSB #67.

--"Thoreau's WALDEN and the Bhagavad Gita," TOPIC [Washington and Jefferson College], IV (Fall, 1963), 38-55.

--"Thoreau's A WEEK: The Path of AUM," WASHINGTON AND JEFFERSON LITERARY JOURNAL [Washington, Pa.], I (1966), 9-16.
    [The entire issue is dedicated to Thoreau.]

--TWO BRAHMAN SOURCES OF EMERSON AND THOREAU. Gainesville, Florida: Scholars' Facsimiles and Reprints, 1967.
    Reprints Rajay Rammohun Roy's TRANSLATION OF SEVERAL PRINCIPAL BOOKS, PASSAGES, AND TEXTS OF THE VEDS and William Ward's VIEW OF THE HISTORY, LITERATURE AND MYTHOLOGY OF THE HINDOOS, Pt. III, Sec. XIII, with an introduction on their influence.

--"WALDEN and the SAMHITA of the SAMA VEDA," TSB #96, p. 6.

--"WALDEN: The Wisdom of the Centaur," ELH, XXV (September, 1958), 194-215.
    Thoreau tries to strike a balance between the animal and human traits in mankind.

Stephens, C. A. "The Stranger Guest," HAPS AND MISHAPS ON THE OLD FARM. Boston: Perry, Mason, 1925. pp. 219-227.
    A story of a visit by Thoreau to a Maine farm.

Stern, Madeleine B. "Approaches to Biography," SOUTH ATLANTIC QUARTERLY, XLV (July, 1946), 362-371.
    A study of the types of biography with Thoreau used as the example throughout.

Stevens, Agnes F. "On Walden's Condition," BOSTON HERALD, July ?, 1949.

One of numerous letters to the editor on the
neglect of Walden Pond.

Stevens, Lauren R. THE DOUBLE AXE. New York: Scribners,
1961.
The prize-winning Maxwell E. Perkins Commemorative
Novel about a young couple who use WALDEN in place
of a Bible for their wedding ceremony and then go
out into the Maine Woods in the early years of the
depression to live the simple life. It is a beautifully constructed first novel that is filled with
echoes of WALDEN. Here decidedly is a novel worth
reading and a novelist worth watching. TSB #74.

Stevens, O. A. "Trees: the Original Inhabitants," AMERICAN
FORESTS, LXXIII (February, 1967).
A survey of Thoreau's comments on trees.

Stevens, Peter. "Magpies and Thoreau," COTTONWOOD REVIEW
[University of Kansas, Lawrence, Kansas], ? (1968).
A poem.

Stevenson, Lionel. "A Forgotten English Poem on Thoreau,"
TSB #66.
Included is a poem by Edward Lamplough from HULL AND
YORKSHIRE FRESCOES: A POETICAL YEAR BOOK OF "SPECIMEN
DAYS." The poem is entitled "Thoreau's Walden."

Stevenson, Robert Louis. "Henry David Thoreau: His Character
and Opinions," LIBRARY MAGAZINE, VIII (1881), 41-60.

Stewart, Randall. "The Growth of Thoreau's Reputation,"
AMERICAN LITERATURE: A CRITICAL SURVEY, edited by T.
D. Young and R. E. Fine. New York: American Book Co.,
1968. pp. 164-174.

also in: COLLEGE ENGLISH, VII (January, 1946), 208-
214. A lecture delivered before the Friends of
Brown University Library.

--"The Hawthornes at Wayside, 1860-1864," MORE BOOKS [Bul-
letin of the Boston Public Library], XIX (September, 1944),
263-279.
Contains an estimate of Thoreau written by Mrs.
Hawthorne at the time of his death. Also an excellent picture of Concord life at the time.

--NATHANIEL HAWTHORNE: A BIOGRAPHY. New Haven, Conn.:
Yale University Press, 1948.

Stibbs, John H. "Mountain Fantasy," LIVING WILDERNESS (December, 1946).
A Thoreau devotee climbs Katahdin only to discover
it despoiled by tourists. A plea for conservation.

Stibitz, E. Earle. "Thoreau's Humanism and Ideas on Literature," EMERSON SOCIETY QUARTERLY, LV (1969), 110-116.

Stockton, Edwin L., Jr. "The Figurative and Descriptive Use
of the Sea in the Creative Writings of Henry David Thoreau." University of North Carolina, 1957. Unpublished
master's thesis.

--"Henry David Thoreau: Terrener or Mariner?" RADFORD RE-
VIEW, XX (October, 1966), 143-154.

Stoddard, Donald R. "The Relevance of WALDEN," SKIDMORE
ALUMNI QUARTERLY, XLVII (Spring, 1969), 1-6.

--"Sounding the Depths of WALDEN," EXERCISE EXCHANGE [New
York: Holt], XV (Spring, 1968), 19-20.
Suggests teaching WALDEN by asking students to
write a letter for Emerson to Thoreau's mother
explaining that her son is not a hippie.

Stokes, Thomas L. "Gandhi's Doctrine Out of Thoreau's,"
AUSTIN [Tex.] STATESMAN, November 16, 1956.
A syndicated column on influence of Thoreau on
Gandhi and on current Hungarian resistance. Also
appeared in NEWARK [N. J.] EVENING NEWS, November
14, 1956, as "Hungarian Passive Resistance Has
Thoreau Touch."

Stoller, Leo. AFTER WALDEN: THOREAU'S CHANGING VIEWS ON
ECONOMIC MAN. Stanford University Press, 1957.
It is Mr. Stoller's thesis that when Thoreau at-
tempted to solve his economic problems by going
to Walden Pond and his relation to government by
going to jail, he found these solutions ineffectual
and so moved on to new philosophical positions.
Through his activities as a surveyor he was able to
discover the principle of the succession of forest
trees and so develop a method for managing wood
lots for commercial purposes while also preserving
the forests for spiritual communion. Mr. Stoller
also feels that Thoreau was "compelled" to "recognize that the sucess of the single man in his
private life was dependent on the success of the
community of men in their social life" both in
politics and economics. While we feel that Mr.
Stoller's emphasis on the development of Thoreau's
ideas is significant and valid, we also feel that
he has overstated the negative characteristics of
Thoreau's earlier views and the positive characteristics of his later ones. We doubt that Thoreau
ever considered his Walden experiment a failure.
A valuable by-product of his book is his discovery of a number of forgotten contemporary newspaper comments on Thoreau, which he has listed in
his footnotes. TSB #62.

reviews: AMERICAN HERITAGE, IX (April, 1958), 82-
84, by Bruce Catton.
AMERICAN LITERATURE, XXX (May, 1958), 249-
250.
EMERSON SOCIETY QUARTERLY, XIV (1959), 36.

--"American Radicals and Literary Works of the Mid-nine-
teenth Century: an Analogy," NEW VOICES IN AMERICAN STUD-
IES, edited by Ray B. Browne. Lafayette, Ind.: Purdue
University Press, 1966. pp. 13-20.

--"Civil Disobedience: Principle and Politics," MASSACHU-
SETTS REVIEW, IV (Autumn, 1962), 85-88.

--"A Note on Thoreau's Place in the History of Phenology,"
ISIS, XLVII (June, 1956), 172-181.
Contrary to popular opinion, Thoreau was only one
of many of his contemporaries who was conducting
phenological research in the mid-nineteenth century.

translation: SHI TO SAMBUN, XIV (October, 1966),
14-22, translated into Japanese by Koh Kasegawa.

--"Thoreau and the Economic Order." Columbia University,
1956. Unpublished doctoral dissertation.

--"Thoreau's Doctrine of Simplicity," NEW ENGLAND QUARTERLY,
XXIX (December, 1956), 443-461.
Thoreau "kept returning to the activities of a
more primitive economy because only there could he
find that wholeness of relationship between a man
and his work whose highest realization is in the
life of the artist.

Stone, Edward. VOICES OF DESPAIR. Athens: Ohio University
Press, 1966.
Thoreau, passim.

Stovall, Floyd. AMERICAN IDEALISM. Norman: University of
Oklahoma Press, 1943.
A study of Thoreau's idealism on pp. 73-78.

Stowell, Robert. "Modern Civil Disobedience and Thoreau,"
TSB #69.

--A THOREAU GAZETTEER. Calais, Vermont: Poor Farm Press,
1948.
A set of maps of Thoreau's journeys to the Maine
Woods, Canada, Cape Cod, Concord and Merrimack
Rivers, and Minnesota, and a detailed set of maps
of Concord, all with ample notes. Some of the maps
are Thoreau's own drawings reproduced. This is
both essential and fascinating material for any
student of Thoreau. TSB #23.

--"Thoreau's Influence on an English Socialist," TSB #98,
pp. 1-3.

A discussion of MERRIE ENGLAND by Robert Blatchford.

--"Toward Simple Living: A Theory and Practice of Voluntary
Poverty," FREE SOUL, XI (April, 1953), 3-27.
With many references to Thoreau.

Straker, Robert L. "Thoreau's Journey to Minnesota," NEW ENG-
LAND QUARTERLY (September, 1941).
New information on the Western journey from the
letters of Horace Mann, Jr. who accompanied Thoreau.

Strauch, Carl F. "Emerson Rejects Reed and Hails Thoreau,"
HARVARD LIBRARY BULLETIN, XVI (July, 1968), 257-273.

--"The Essential Romanticism of Thoreau's WALDEN," EMERSON
SOCIETY QUARTERLY, XVIII (1960), 21-23.

Stromberg, R. N. "Thoreau and Marx: A Century After," SO-
CIAL STUDIES, XL (February, 1949), 53-56.
Contrasting "Life without principle" and the "Communist Manifesto." Concludes that the reader of
Thoreau, unlike the reader of Marx, "Will emerge
spiritually refreshed and with, perchance, a philosophy of life."

Stronks, James. "'The Rivals' as a Possible Source for WALDEN,"
TSB #95, p. 5.

Strout, Richard L. "Mr. Thoreau Meet Mr. Zip," CHRISTIAN
SCIENCE MONITOR, November 29, 1962.
A satire on the post office.

Struik, Dirk J. THE ORIGINS OF AMERICAN SCIENCE, NEW ENG-
LAND. New York: Cameron Associates, 1957.
Material on Thoreau's interest in science, pp. 217-
219, et passim.

[Strunsky, Simon]. "Topics of the Times," NEW YORK TIMES,
June 4, 1945.
An editorial on the applicability of Thoreau's
philosophy in these days of rationing.

Strunz, Franz. "Das Fortschrittliche und Neue im Naturge-
fuhl bei Henry David Thoreau," DOKUMENTE DES FORTSCHRITTS
(March, 1910), pp. 203-208.
Eugene F. Timpe's comments (TSB #93) suggest that
Strunz emphasizes Thoreau's Transcendentalism and
his relation to Kant.

--"Naturgefuhl und Naturerkenntnis bei Henry David Thoreau,"
BEITRAGE UND SKIZZEN ZUR GESCHICHTE DER NATURWISSEN-
SCHAFTEN. Hamburg: ? , 1909. pp. 173-185.
Characterizes Thoreau's transcendental approach
to natural science, yet admires his ability to
record precise observations. Though prone to

howlers and plagiarism himself, Strunz notes that
Thoreau was not a competent researcher.

Strutz, William. "Ellery Channing's Copy of A WEEK," TSB #94,
p. 2.

Stuckey, Norman. "Thoreau's Pond," BOSTON POST, January 10,
1945.
A letter claiming Walden Pond for Thoreau's fame
only.

also in: BOSTON HERALD, January 12, 1945, and
SATURDAY REVIEW OF LITERATURE, January 20, 1945.

Stylites, Simeon. "The Inside Story," CHRISTIAN CENTURY,
LXXI (December 29, 1954), 1577.
Letter commemorating centennial of WALDEN.

Sugimura, K. "A Walden Pond Bivouac," INITIATIVE [Tokyo],
XII (March, 1967), 10-14.

"Supreme Individualist," CHRISTIAN SCIENCE MONITOR, July
12, 1967.
Editorial on Thoreau.

"Survey Proves Thoreau Correct; Walden Pond Has Depth of 102
Feet," CONCORD JOURNAL, October 3, 1968.
Report of N. E. Marine Technology Soc. survey.

Swan, Michael. "Living in Concord," A SMALL PART OF TIME.
London: Jonathan Cape, 1957. pp. 95-108.

[Swann, Arthur]. IMPORTANT AUTOGRAPH LETTERS MANUSCRIPTS
DOCUMENTS THE COLLECTION FORMED BY JAMES LORIMER
GRAHAM TOGETHER WITH PROPERTY FROM...A NEW ENGLAND
PRIVATE COLLECTOR. New York: Parke-Bernet, April 29-
30, 1958.
Catalog of sale.

Swann, H. K. "H. D. Thoreau," NATURE IN ACADIE. London:
Bale, 1895.
A long prefatory poem.

Swanson, Donald R. "Far and Fair Within: "A Walk to Wachusett,"
EMERSON SOCIETY QUARTERLY, LVI (1969), 52-53.

Sweeney, James Ross. "The Cosmic Drama in Thoreau's 'Spring',"
EMERSON SOCIETY QUARTERLY, XXIV (1961), 3-6.
Analysis of the WALDEN chapter.

Sweetland, Harriet M. HENRY DAVID THOREAU: 1817-1862: BOOKS,
MANUSCRIPTS, AND ASSOCIATION ITEMS IN DETROIT AND ANN
ARBOR: A CENTENNIAL EXHIBITION. Detroit: Wayne State
University Libraries, 1962.
An annotated catalog. Also distributed as Thoreau
Society Booklet 18.

--"The Significance of Thoreau's Trip to the Upper Mississippi in 1861," TRANSACTIONS OF THE WISCONSIN ACADEMY OF SCIENCE, ARTS AND LETTERS, LI (1962), 267-286.

Swift, Ernest. "They Lived for Conservation," CONSERVATION VOLUNTEER [St. Paul, Minn.], XXVI (November, 1963), 31-34.
        On Thoreau and John Muir.

--"Thoreau and Muir Lived Their Conservation Convictions," CONSERVATION NEWS, XXVIII (February 1, 1963), 1-4.

Swift, Ernie. "Straight Talk," NATIONAL WILDLIFE, VI (June, 1968), 19.
        Comments on Thoreau's "Walking" and "Life without Principle."

Swift, Lindsay. BROOK FARM. New York: Corinth Books, 1961.
        After being out of print for nearly half a century, this best of all studies of the most famous of the Transcendentalist Utopias is now available in a well-printed paperback edition. It contains a wealth of material about many of Thoreau's close friends and associates as well as frequent mention of Thoreau himself. TSB #75.

Stoinoff, Nicolas. "Un Centenaire Bulgara parle," NOTRE ROUTE [Paris], 1964.
        Comments on Thoreau, p. 98.

Talbert, Jay Kennedy. "John Brown in American Literature." University of Kansas, 1941. Unpublished doctoral dissertation.

Talbot, Charles Remington. ROMULUS AND REMUS: A DOG STORY. Boston: Lothrop, 1888.
    A children's novel with much about Thoreau in it.

Tanner, Tony. "Thoreau and the Sauntering Eye," THE REIGN OF WONDER: NAIVETY AND REALITY IN AMERICAN LITERATURE. Cambridge University Press, 1965. pp. 46-63.
    A delightful and perceptive essay. TSB #96.

Targan, Barry. "August 1, 1854," SALAMAGUNDI [Flushing, N. Y.], IX (Spring, 1969), 29.
    A poem based on a Thoreau journal entry.

Taylor, Henry J. "A Deflation of Thoreau," SAN FRANCISCO EXAMINER, July 10, 1968.

Taylor, Horace. "Thoreau's Scientific Interests as Seen in His JOURNAL," MCNEESE REVIEW, XIV (1963), 45-59.

Taylor, J. Golden. NEIGHBOR THOREAU'S CRITICAL HUMOR. Logan, Utah: Utah State University Press, 1958. (Utah State University Monograph Series, VI, January, 1958).
    Although there have been a number of studies of Thoreau's humor published, this is by far the best and the most thorough. Wisely, the emphasis is placed upon Thoreau's use of humor as a technique of criticism, for he rarely used humor for its own sake. And as such, the book makes an excellent survey of Thoreau's criticism of church, state, education, business, etc., as well as a sort of anthology of Thoreau's humorous remarks. It is well that at last we are beginning to get some worthwhile studies of Thoreau's techniques as a writer. And this, in its particular field, is the best one yet. TSB #64.

    reviews: AMERICAN LITERATURE (November, 1959). VOLUNTAD [Montevideo, Uruguary] (January, 1960).

--"Thoreau's Sour Grapes," PROCEEDINGS OF UTAH ACADEMY OF ARTS AND SCIENCES, XLII (1965), 38-49.

translation: SHI TO SAMBUN [Tokyo], XV (March, 1967),
64-73, translated into Japanese by Koh Kasegawa.

Taylor, Lynn. "Thoreau School Named for Author, Naturalist,"
CHICAGO TRIBUNE, April 7, 1966.

Teale, Edwin Way. ADVENTURES IN NATURE. New York: Dodd, Mead,
1959.
Essays reprinted from earlier volumes with many
references to Thoreau.

--CIRCLE OF THE SEASONS. New York: Dodd, Mead, 1953.
An account of a Thoreau Society meeting and many
quotations from Thoreau are included in this delightful series of extracts from Mr. Teale's journals. TSB #46.

--"The Great Companions of Nature Literature," AUDUBON
MAGAZINE, XLVI (December, 1944), 363-366.
A checklist of great nature books with Thoreau
leading the list in frequency.

--"Henry Thoreau and the Realms of Time," TSB #64.
Presidential Address by Edwin Way Teale at the
Annual Meeting of the Thoreau Society, Concord,
Massachusetts, Saturday, July 12, 1958.

translations: "Thoreau y el Reinado del Tiempo,"
translated into Spanish by V. Munoz. EL PLATA
[Montevideo, Uruguay], June 28, 1959.

"Thoreau y el Tiempo," translated into Spanish by
V. Munoz. CENIT (April, 1961?).

--THE LOST WOODS: ADVENTURES OF A NATURALIST. New York:
Dodd, Mead, 1945.
Chapters entitled "On the Trail of Thoreau" and
"Wildlife at Walden" on pp. 81-91 and pp. 273-283.

review: THOREAU SOCIETY BULLETIN #14.

--"Nature in Action: Henry Thoreau's Pond Essentially the
Same," NEWARK [N. J.] STAR-LEDGER, July 15, 1946.

--NORTH WITH THE SPRING. New York: Dodd, Mead, 1951.
This fine study of the advance of spring northward
contains many references to Thoreau and the chapter
"The Crane Fields" tells of a visit to Thoreau's
Concord scenes. TSB #38.

--"Photographs of Walden," OUTDOORS ILLUSTRATED (September-
October, 1950).

--"Report on Walden Pond," LIVING WILDERNESS (Summer, 1951),
pp. 28-29.

Conditions are much improved in the care of the
reservation.

--"Thoreau's Walden," LIFE MAGAZINE (September 22, 1947),
70-73.
A beautiful photographic essay on the pond in
autumn.

--"Walden Pond," CANADIAN NATURE, XII (January, 1950),
16-17.
A superb kodachrome view of Walden Pond.

--WANDERING THROUGH WINTER. New York: Dodd, Mead, 1965.
The final volume in the American Seasons series.
Like the earlier volumes, it frequently quotes
from Thoreau and everywhere shows the impact of
his philosophy. TSB #93.

Teehan, Jack. "Mt. Monadnock Murals Installed in Keene
National Bank Building," NEW HAMPSHIRE SENTINEL, June 28,
1950, p. 1 passim.
A reproduction of the new Thoreau mural and an
article about it.

Teller, Walter. "The World and We That Dwell Therein,"
NEW YORK TIMES BOOK REVIEW, December 22, 1963, p. 1 pas-
sim.
Thoreau and other journal-keepers.

Temmer, M. J. "Rousseau and Thoreau," YALE FRENCH STUDIES,
XXVIII (1961-1962), 112-121.

Temple, F. J. "Thoreau, poete et philosophe," INFORMATIONS
ET DOCUMENTS, CXCL (December 15, 1963), 21-29.
Lengthy and well-illustrated article in French in
a "revue publiee par le Centre Culturel Americain"
[Paris].

Tenenbaum Shea. "Diogenes of Concord," POETS AND GENERATIONS.
New York: Noble, 1955. pp. 55-65.
An essay in Yiddish on Thoreau

--"Henry David Thoreau," LA LIBRE TRIBUNE [Paris], September, 1951, p. 40.
A brief essay in Yiddish.

--"An Oasis," CHICAGO JEWISH COURIER, February 7, 1937.
An essay in Yiddish.

--"Reflections on the Hundred Year Anniversary of WALDEN,"
JEWISH VOICE [Mexico City], March 16, 1946.+
An essay in Yiddish.

"Theosophist Unaware," THEOSOPHY, XXXII (May-June, 1944),
290-295 passim.

A study of Thoreau's philosophy in the light of
Theosophist doctrines.

Thide, Olivia. "Thoreau's Occupations," BROOKLYN EAGLE,
March 7, 1897.
Essay reprinted from BACHELOR OF ARTS.

"This Curious World," SAN FRANCISCO NEWS, August 30, 1945.
This widely syndicated cartoon features a drawing
of the Walden hut and states, "Mohandas Gandhi
derived the idea of non-violent resistance from
reading Henry Thoreau's ON THE DUTY OF CIVIL DIS-
OBEDIENCE, written when the latter was jailed for
non-payment of taxes on his cabin at Walden Pond."

Thomas, John Wesley. JAMES FREEMAN CLARKE: APOSTLE OF GER-
MAN CULTURE IN AMERICA. Boston: Luce, 1949.
This is the first modern book on Thoreau's Unitarian friend. Although biographical detail is
not emphasized, it gives a good background for the
interest of all of the Transcendentalists in German philosophy and literature. It shows surprising
insight into both the men and the times. Unfortunately its use is limited through the lack of any
index. TSB #33.

Thomas, W. Stephen. EMERSON AND THOREAU: A RELATIONSHIP.
Rochester, N. Y.: Philosopher's Club, February 15,
1954.
Mimeographed booklet.

--"His Words Live and Inspire," ROCHESTER [N. Y.] DEM-
OCRAT AND CHRONICLE, May 12, 1953.
A column on Thoreau.

--"Marti and Thoreau: Pioneers of Personal Freedom,"
DOS PUEBLOS [Havana, Cuba] August, 1949, pp. 1-3.
Comparison of Thoreau and the Cuban revolutionary.
Influence of Thoreau on Marti.

--100TH ANNIVERSARY OF THOREAU'S WALDEN: THE SPIRITUAL
MESSAGE OF WALDEN. Rochester, N. Y.: First Unitarian
Church, October 3, 1954 (mimeographed).
A centennial sermon on Walden.

Thomas, William S. "Thoreau as His Own Editor," NEW ENGLAND
QUARTERLY, XV (March, 1942), 101-103.
A 16 stanza poem owned in ms. by the late Doctor
Thomas compared with the 10 stanza version of
"To My Brother."

Thompson, Evan. "Thoreau: A Centenary View," AMONG FRIENDS
[Detroit Public Library], XXVI (Spring, 1962), 7-12.

Thompson, Lawrence. ROBERT FROST: THE EARLY YEARS 1874-1915.

New York: Holt, Rinehart and Winston, 1966.
    Frequent comment on Thoreau's influence on Frost.

Thompson, Ruth. "Minnesota Memories: Jonathan T. Grimes,
    Early Settler," MINNEAPOLIS MORNING TRIBUNE, November
    3, 1947.
        On Thoreau's Minnesota visit.

Thompson, Wade C. "The Aesthetic Theory of Henry David Tho-
    reau." Columbia University, 1959. Unpublished doctoral
    dissertation.

  --"The Impractical Thoreau," COLLEGE ENGLISH (November,
    1957).
        A reply to the Salomon article on Thoreau in the
        January, 1956, COLLEGE ENGLISH.

"Thoreau," BOSTON EVENING TRANSCRIPT, July 19, 1882.

"Thoreau," BOSTON TRANSCRIPT, July 2, 1905.
        This and other bibliographical items of half a
        century ago are taken from a letter by Walter
        Faxon in the Francis H. Allen papers.

"Thoreau," SAN FRANCISCO CHRONICLE, July 4, 1945.
        A centennial editorial.

"Thoreau Among the Ph.D's," TSB #8.
        A listing of completed doctoral dessertations on
        Thoreau from 1934 to 1941. Also listed are dis-
        sertations in progress.

"Thoreau and Chekhov," TSB #98, p. 6.
        "Quotation from a letter from Anton Chekhov to
        V. G. Korolenko of October 17, 1887" as it appears
        in LIFE AND LETTERS OF ANTON CHEKHOV, edited by
        S. S. Koteliansky and Philip Tomlinson. London:
        Cassell, 1925. This may be the "earliest known
        reference to Thoreau in Russia."

"Thoreau and Greeley," NEW YORK TRIBUNE, June 11, 1882.

THOREAU AND INDIA. New Delhi: United States Information
    Service, 1962. [AMERICAN REVIEW].

"Thoreau and Music," TSB #18.
        Musical portrait of Thoreau by Charles Ives, re-
        printed from 114 SONGS, a privately printed volume
        of compositions.

THOREAU AND THE NEW YORK TRIBUNE: A CHECKLIST, by Helen B.
    Morrison. TSB #77+82.
        (Unquestionably Thoreau's most effective publicity
        agent during his lifetime was Horace Greeley, the editor

of the NEW YORK TRIBUNE. The two men met in 1843 when
Thoreau was living on Staten Island and continued their
friendship throughout Thoreau's life. Greeley regularly
acted as Thoreau's literary agent, placing his essays
in various periodicals of the day. But equally important,
he continually kept Thoreau's name before the readers of
the TRIBUNE.

Mrs. Helen B. Morrison, editor of THOREAU TODAY (New
York: Comet, 1957), has made the first intensive search
of the files of the NEW YORK TRIBUNE for mentions of Thoreau and has thus uncovered many, many hitherto unnoticed
items. They are listed here in simple chronological order).

1. January 10, 1843
    An article entitled "The Children of the Mist" is
an answer to a review of a lecture by Mr. Bancroft entitled "Spirit of the Age." It is signed H. Could this
be Thoreau? Sounds like his writing, but no further
identification of H.

2. April 11, 1843
    Issue gives contents of 'The Dial', no. XII, April 1,
1843. Then, "we rather like these lines by Thoreau:"
Then the poem "Haze' which is definitely signed Thoreau.
Then, a comment by the editor on Thoreau's contributions
of some translations from Anacreon. About a half column.

3. October 19, 1843
    In issue under notice of 'The Dial' for October; "We
have not room to speak of 'A Winter's Walk' by H. D.
Thoreau.

4. October 27, 1843
    Almost 2 columns from "A Winter's Walk signed by H. D. T.

5. January 25, 1844
    'The Dial' for January notices: A comment on the lecture
on Poetry by H. D. T. (2 columns).

6. April, 1844
    'The Dial', no. XVI, for April 1844: "The Dial was
filled with admirable papers by R. W. E., C. Lane, W. E.
Channing, H. D. Thoreau, and others of the noblest intel-
lects and the most genial spirits in New England...The
Dial has now closed its fourth annual volume, and we
have heard that it may not be continued. We hope otherwise" etc. etc.

7. May 18, 1844
    "The Dial, the most original and thoughtful periodical
ever published in this country, has suspended its issues
for the present....It has been sustained for three years
by the free-will contributions of R. W. Emerson, Margaret
Fuller, W. E. Channing, Theodore Parker, C. Lane, J. S.
Dwight, C. A. Dana, Henry D. Thoreau, E. Peabody, and

others of the deepest thinkers and most advanced minds
in our country."

8.   November 17, 1848
    Under the title of "Ktaadn and the Maine Woods,"
Mr. H. D. Thoreau of Concord, Mass., has been publishing
a series of sketches in the Union Magazine which are
quite superior to any description of wild-woods life that
we have seen for several years. (Over 4 columns of extracts).

9.   November 18, 1848
    "We give several additional extracts from Mr. Thoreau's
narrative of his journeyings in the Maine Wilderness."
(A full column, followed by:) "We take leave of Mr. Thoreau's narrative by quoting its splendid conclusion--as
fine a peice of unrhymed poetry as we have ever read."
(Begins: "The new world" and goes half a column).

10.   June 13, 1849
    On 1st page under "Reviews of New Books," "H. D. Tho-
reau;s book 'A Week On The Concord and Merrimack Rivers',
(pp. 413. 12 mo.) Boston, Munroe Co. N.Y.G.P. Putnam."
Together with the review, there are 4 extracts from the
text, almost 2 columns. The review criticizes Thoreau's
"misplaced Pantheistic attack on the Christian Faith."
But calls it, "a really new book--a fresh, original,
thoughtful work." Closing: Albeit we love not theological controversary, we proffer our columns to Mr. Thoreau, should he see fit to answer these questions. We
would have preferred to pass the theme in silence, but
our admiration of his book and our reprehension of its
Pantheism forbade that course. May we not hope he will
reconsider his too rashly expressed notions on this head?"

11.   July 25, 1850
    Under the title "The Wreck of the Elizabeth" "....Rev.
Mr. Fuller and Mr. Henry D. Thoreau of Concord, Mass.,
left yesterday for Fire Island."

12.   June 19, 1852
    Under title of NEW PUBLICATIONS: "Sartain for July.
Among other notable articles....a quaint essay on 'The
Iron Horse' by Henry D. Thoreau....Thoreau's musings on
the locomotive are characteristic, Emersonian many will
say. They are that and something more. They draw a
sweet moral from the sourest features of New England."

13.   July 22, 1852
    "Sartain's Magazine for August notes articles by"
....C. P. Cranch, Alice Carey and Thoreau....and others
of which any magazine may well be proud."

14.   August 2, 1854
    Under title: SLAVERY IN MASSACHUSETTS: "An address,

delivered at the Anti-Slavery celebration at Framingham, Mass., July 4, 1854, by Henry D. Thoreau of Concord, Mass." (Almost 3 columns).

15. August 8, 1854
    Under title: NEW PUBLICATIONS: "Life in the Woods, on Wednesday, August 9, Ticknor and Fields will publish Walden, or Life in the Woods by Henry D. Thoreau."
"When I wrote the following pages, or rather the bulk of them, I lived alone in the woods, a mile from any neighbor, in a house which I built myself on the shore of Walden Pond, in Concord, Mass., and earned my living by the labor of my hands only."
At the end of this ad: "This striking and original book will be published in 1 vol. 16 mo. in cloth, at $1."
All 18 chapters are named under table of contents.
The ad is repeated in the Tribune for August 9, 1854, and a smaller ad in the issue for August 10, 1854.

16. October 19, 1855
    Under title: "The Lecture Season", Henry D. Thoreau's name is mentioned among others including, Emerson, Thackery, H. W. Beecher, Bayard Taylor, George W. Curtis, Lucy Stone Blackwell, etc.

16a. July 29, 1854
    Under title NEW PUBLICATIONS, a section headed A MASSACHUSETTS HERMIT: "Ticknor and Fields have in press a work by Henry D. Thoreau, entitled 'Life in the Woods', describing the experience of the author during a solitary residence of two years in a hut on the shore of Walden Pond, in Concord, Massachusetts. The volume promises to be one of curious interest, and by the courtesy of the publishers we are permitted to take some extracts in advance of the regular issue." There are 6 sections with the following headings:

    1. The Hermit Builds His Hut
    2. The Hermit Plants Beans
    3. The Hermit Commences Housekeeping
    4. The Hermit's First Summer
    5. The Hermit Finds a Friend
    6. The Hermit Has Visitors, Many of them Bores

(All in all, almost four columns).

17. November 10, 1856
    Under title THE LECTURING SEASON, Thoreau's name occurs in alphabetical list of lecturers.

18. November 20, 1856
    Under title THE LECTURE SEASON, an extended list of possible lecturers, includes Thoreau's name.

19. September 18, 1857
Under title THE LECTURE SEASON, a list of 56 names of
those "Who lectured with acceptance last winter and are
ready to do so this season." The list contains names
of O. W. Holmes, Herman Melville, and Thoreau.

20. May 21, 1858
In an article by a Boston correspondent, the last para-
graph of which reads:
The Atlantic Monthly for June commences with an
account of a trip to Lake Chesuncook, in Maine.
This is easily seen to be by Thoreau."

21. July 17, 1858
Under title: A WHITE MOUNTAIN EXCURSION. Almost two
columns of description of which one paragraph says,
"....that night of fog and rain Mr. Thoreau, the Concord
Pan, spent in Tuckerman's Ravine with Judge Hoar, his
companion on the Chesunook Tour, two other gentlemen
and a guide. I have been assured by one of the party
that they woke up in the morning perfectly dry, although
they had only a cotton tent for a shelter....Mr. Thoreau
doubtless understands as well as any mountaineer how to
make himself comfortable under such circumstances."

22. October 12, 1858
Under title THE LECTURE SEASON. "The following list
of persons desireous of giving lectures this season is
as complete as we are able to make it." The list contains
over 100 names, including Thoreau of Concord.

23. September 9, 1859
Under title LYCEUM LECTURERS. A list of 194 names,
among which are Alcott, Emerson and Thoreau of Concord.

24. October 12, 1859 [NEW YORK DAILY TRIBUNE]
Under column titled PERSONAL: second paragraph.
"Henry D. Thoreau, who is sometimes called 'The Hermit
of Concord', supplied the desk at Music Hall, Boston,
on Sunday. Mr. Thoreau is an eccentric individual, having
lived until within a short time ago in a hut in the woods
between Concord and Lincoln. He is at present a resident
of the Village of Concord, follows surveying as a business,
and is an intimate friend of Ralph Waldo Emerson. His
subject was 'The Way in Which We Spend Our Lives." It
was an original, racy, and erratic production, and was
listened to the close with interest."

25. November 9, 1859
Under column entitled FROM BOSTON: one paragraph reads:
"Henry D. Thoreau delivered a lecture on John Brown
at the Tremont Temple on Tuesday evening. It was one of
the 'Fraternity' of course. There were some just and
striking remarks in it, and many foolish and ill-natured
ones. Sneers at the Republicans were quite frequent.

Men like General Wilson, and editors like those of The
Tribune and The Liberator, who, while the lecturer was
cultivating beans and killing woodchucks on the margin
of Walden Pond, made a public opinion strong enough on
Anti-Slavery grounds to tolerate a speech from him in
defense of insurrection, deserve better treatment than
they receive from some of the upstart Abolitionists of
the day."

26. May 9, 1860
   Under title NEW PUBLICATIONS is mentioned "Echoes of
Harper's Ferry, comprising the best speeches, sermons,
letters, poems, and other utterances of the leading
minds of America and Europe, called forth by John Brown's
Invasion of Virginia." Thoreau's name included with many
others. "The services at Concord, or Liturgy for a
Martyr, composed by Emerson, Thoreau, Alcott, Sanborn,"
etc. collated and arranged by James Redpath.

27. November 9, 1860
   Under title: NEW PUBLICATIONS. One half column de-
voted to the description of James Redpath's "Echoes of
Harper's Ferry," mentions all the great speeches, sermons,
letters, etc. called forth by John Brown's Invasion.
The closing paragraph: "The Services at Concord, or
'Liturgy for a Martyr! composed by Emerson, Thoreau,
Alcott and Sanborn, etc. unsurpassed in beauty even by
the Book of Common Prayer."

28. July 30, 1861
   Under title: FROM CONCORD, a letter dated Concord,
Massachusetts, July 26, 1861, signed Argos. Describes
a visit to the Concord Battlefield and mentions "The
current reversals at Bull Run and Manuesses in the war
for the union." One sentence toward the end of the
article reads: "I am sorry to say that the excellent
naturalist and poet, Henry D. Thoreau, is in poor health."

29. May 10, 1862, Saturday
   Under title: PERSONAL. "Henry D. Thoreau, the genial
writer on the natural scenery of New England, died at
Concord, Massachusetts on Tuesday, May 6th, after a
protracted illness of more than eighteen months. He
was a native of Boston, but moved with his family at the
age of five years to Concord, where he has since resided.
He graduated at Harvard College in 1837, and was nearly
forty-five years old at the time of his death. His
writings include A WEEK ON THE CONCORD AND MERRIMACK
RIVERS; WALDEN, OR LIFE IN THE WOODS; and various contributions to the periodical literature of the day. They
are remarkable for their freedom and originality of thought,
their quaint humor, and their warm sympathy with all the
manifold aspects of nature. His disease was consumption,
and, as we are informed, 'his humor and cheerful courage
did not forsake him during his sickness, and he met death
as gayly as Theramenes in Xenophon's story.' Mr. Thoreau,

in spite of the racy individuality of his character, was much beloved and respected by his townsmen, and his writings have numerous admirers. He was honored with a public funeral from the Town Hall of Concord, On Friday, the 9th, inst."

30. May 28, 1862
Under title: NEW PUBLICATIONS: "The ATLANTIC opens with a quaint characteristic essay on 'Walking', by the late Henry Thoreau, whose recent decease imports an additional interest to every production of his unique pen."

31. October 21, 1862
Under title: NEW PUBLICATIONS: "The Atlantic Monthly for November, 1862, is now ready. The contents and contributors are enumerated below....WILD APPLES by Henry D. Thoreau," etc., etc.

"Thoreau & Solitude," HOME JOURNAL (August 25, 1880).

"Thoreau and Willa Cather," TSB #20.
Included are echoes of Thoreau in the writings of Willa Cather.

"Thoreau as a Poet," LONDON DAILY CHRONICLE, November 9, 1895.

"Thoreau Borrows a Box of Papers," TSB #106, pp. 7-8.
Included is a letter from Hannah Hunstable to Nathan Brooks in which Thoreau is mentioned in an excerpt.

"Thoreau Cabin Hearth Found," CHRISTIAN SCIENCE MONITOR, June 13, 1946.
The most detailed account of Robbins' discovery yet in print.

also in: THOREAU SOCIETY BULLETIN #16.

"Thoreau Centenary," GRACE, 1 (Spring, 1962), 239.

"Thoreau Collection to be Shown," BOSTON TRAVELLER, September 11, 1945.
A notice of the Museum of Natural History exhibition.

"The Thoreau Collection of The Pierpont Morgan Library of New York City," TSB #19.
A checklist taken directly from the card catalog of the Morgan Library.

"A Thoreau Evening at Cooper Union," TSB #11.
A brief digest of speeches given by Raymond Adams, Roger Baldwin, Henry S. Canby and Roger Payne at a discussion on Thoreau.

"The Thoreau Family," TSB #19.
    A note on the Thoreau geneology by Cephas Guillet of
    New York City.

"A Thoreau Family Tree," TSB #17.
    This family tree was prepared by Raymond Adams.

"Thoreau--Fuel Expert," CHRISTIAN SCIENCE MONITOR, October
    29, 1942.
        An editorial.

Thoreau, Henri [sic] David. "The Citizen's Conscience,"
    THE GIST. Cambridge, Mass.:   ? ,   ? . pp. 77-79.
    A digest of "Civil Disobedience."

Thoreau, Henry David. "Anacreon," SELECTED WRITINGS OF THE
    AMERICAN TRANSCENDENTALISTS, edited by George Hochfield.
    New York: Signet, 1966. pp. 351-356.

    --ANTI-SLAVERY AND REFORM PAPERS. Intro. by Walter Harding.
    Montreal: Harvest House, 1963.
        A new revised collection of Thoreau's political
        essays with commentary.

        reviews: CANADIAN AUTHOR AND BOOKMAN, XXXIX
                  (Summer, 1964), 18.
                  CATHOLIC WORKER (September, 1964).
                  CHATHAM [Ont.] DAILY NEWS, December 31,
                  1963.

    --ANTI-SLAVERY AND REFORM PAPERS, edited and introduced
    by Walter Harding. Montreal: Harvest House, 1966.
        A revised edition.

    --"Aphorisms," EMERSON SOCIETY QUARTERLY, VII (1957),
    37-39.
        Reprinted from the Bibliophile Society FIFTH YEAR
        BOOK.

    --"Autumnal Tints," NEW DOMINION MONTHLY, I (October, 1867),
    14-16.

    --"The Backwoods of Maine," THE STUDENT: A FAMILY MAGA-
    ZINE AND MONTHLY READER, V (January, 1849), 68.
        It is included in the present text of the Ktaadn
        chapter of the MAINE WOODS (Walden edition, p.88ff.)
        TSB #36.

    --CAPE COD, editions of. [Listed chronologically. Included
    are all entries from "Preliminary check-list of the edi-
    tions of CAPE COD by Kenneth Harber TSB #67].

    1865 Boston: Ticknor & Fields. First Edition. Edited
          by Sophia Thoreau and W. E. Channing.

1865 London: Samson Low, Son and Marston. First British Edition and first Thoreau book to be printed abroad.

1866 Boston: Fields, Osgood & Company.

1871? Boston: James R. Osgood & Company.

1877 Boston: Houghton, Osgood & Company.

1881 Boston: Houghton Mifflin. Gilt autograph on cover, uniform with other works.

1894 Boston: Houghton. Riverside Edition-Writings, Vol. IV. Unsigned intro. by Scudder.

1894 The Same. Large paper edition.

1894? London: Constable? British Riverside Edition?

1896 Boston: Houghton Mifflin. Holiday Edition in 2 volumes with Scudder introduction expanded and Watson watercolors.

1906 Boston: Houghton Mifflin. Walden Edition-Writings, Vol. IV. Includes MISCELLANIES. Scudder expanded unsigned introduction and H. W. Gleason photos.

1906 Boston: Houghton Mifflin. Walden Edition-Writings, Vol. IV.

1906 Boston: Houghton Mifflin. Concord Edition-Writings.

1907 New York: Crowell. Intro. by Annie Russell Marble.

1908 New York: Crowell "Second Edition". Intro. and photos by Clifton Johnson.

1912 London: Harrap. Intro. and photos by Clifton Johnson. Visitors edition.

1914 Boston: Houghton Mifflin. Intro. and photos by Charles S. Olcott.

1914 New York: Crowell. Vol. ? of V of thin paper set of works.

1915 Boston: Houghton Mifflin. Vol. IV of XI of Riverside Pocket Edition.

1929 Boston: Houghton Mifflin. Edited by G. O. Blake. Includes MAINE WOODS and MISCELLANIES. Vol. II of V of Concord Edition-Works.

1932 Boston: Houghton Mifflin. Riverside Cambridge Edition-Writings.

1939   Boston: Houghton Mifflin.   Riverside Edition-Writ-
        ings in 8 volumes?

1940   New York: Crowell.   WORKS include Emerson's Bio-
        graphical sketch, WALDEN, MAINE WOODS, WEEK.

1951   New York: Norton; Toronto: George J. McLeod Ltd.
        This is the second in Norton's new Thoreau
        set.   And like the first, it is both delight-
        full and provocative.   Only the highest
        praise can be given to Henry Bugbee Kane's
        line drawings which add so much to the flavor
        of the book and the map endpapers which add
        so much to the understanding.   Henry Beston's
        introduction is brief and to the point.   And
        Dudley Lunt has tried his hand again at ar-
        ranging the text--to our mind far more suc-
        cessfully than he did with the MAINE WOODS.
        He has added to the text the Journal account
        of the 1857 excursion to the Cape.   And he has
        subtracted from the text (placing them in
        the appendix where they are easily consulted)
        a few of the lengthier historical quotations
        which Thoreau himself thought slowed down the
        narrative.   It certainly does not result in
        the definitive text for the scholar, but the
        lay reader will, I think, find it more in-
        teresting reading.   In closing, a word of
        praise for the clear, readable type used in
        this series.   TSB #36.

        reviews: BULLETIN OF THE MASSACHUSETTS AUDU-
                   BON SOCIETY, XXXV (November, 1951),
                   357-358, by Francis H. Allen.
                   CHICAGO TRIBUNE BOOKS, July 1, 1951,
                   by Alfred C. Ames.

1961   New York: Crowell.
        A beautiful new edition, with large, clear
        print, and with decorations by Clare Leighton.
        TSB #77.

1965   New Haven: College and University Press.   Arranged
        with notes by Dudley C. Lunt, an introduction by
        Henry Beston, and illustrated by Henry Bugbee Kane.
        Masterworks of Literature Series.
        A paperback reprint with good clear type and
        lovely illustrations.   TSB #95.

1966   New York: Crowell.   Apollo Edition.
        A good clear paperback reprint.   TSB #95.

1969   New York: Limited Editions Club.   Illustrated with
        38 pencil drawings by Raymond J. Holden.   Limited
        to 1500 copies.

--CAPE COD, translations of
    1962? Stockholm: Tidero. Translated into Swedish by
        Gustav Sandgren.

--CAPE COD, selections from
    "Cape Cod Anecdote," YANKEE (June, 1942), A quotation
    from CAPE COD.

    "What Thoreau Saw at Cohasset," SCITUATE [Mass.] HERALD,
    July 25, 1941. Reprint of part of CAPE COD with notes.

--CIVIL DISOBEDIENCE, editions of
    1942   Harrison Park, N. J.: 5x8 Press.

    1945? London: Peace Pledge Union. Pamphlet #1, "Clas-
          sics of Non-Violence."

    1946   Boonton, N. J.: Liberty Library Published for
          the New York Thoreau Fellowship.

    1948   Chicago: Great Books Foundation [Henry Regnery
          Company, Hinsdale, Ill., Pub.]. Entitled CIVIL
          DISOBEDIENCE AND A PLEA FOR CAPTAIN JOHN BROWN.
          Another inexpensive pamphlet edition of
          Thoreau.

    1950   Saugatuch, Conn.: 5x8 Press.
          A new edition with frontispiece by Roger
          Lyford.

    1963   London: Peace News Pamphlets. With an Intro. by
          Gene Sharp. Entitled ON THE DUTY OF CIVIL DIS-
          OBEDIENCE.

    1964   Westwood, N. J.: Fleming H. Revell Co.
          A handy, well-printed little cloth-bound
          edition with a brief appreciative intro-
          duction in the "Revell Inspirational Clas-
          sic" series. So far as known, the only
          cloth-bound separate edition of the essay
          currently available. TSB #90.

    1965   Santa Ana, Calif.: Freedom Newspapers. Pamph-
          let reprint.

    1966   Kyoto, Japan: Yamaguchi Shoten. Intro. and notes
          by Toshihiko Ogata.
              Text in English, intro. and notes in Jap-
          anese.

    1966   Kyoto, Japan: Apollon-sha. Intro. by M. Higash-
          iyama. Entitled RESISTANCE TO CIVIL GOVERNMENT.
          Privately printed for Leonard Kleinfeld.
          Edition limited to 300 copies.

1967   Tokyo: Bunshido. Edited and annotated by M.
Sakurai. Entitled CIVIL DISOBEDIENCE and WALKING.

1967   New York: Twayne, Annotated and with an intro-
duction by Walter Harding. Entitled THE VARIORUM
CIVIL DISOBEDIENCE.
Companion volume to THE VARIORUM WALDEN.

review: CONCORD JOURNAL, February 29, 1968.

1967   Tarrytown: Horseless Headsman Press. Entitled
WHAT TO DO ABOUT VIET-NAM?
A leaflet reprinting of a condensed "Civil
Disobedience."

1968   New York: Pyramid Books. Entitled ESSAY ON CIVIL
DISOBEDIENCE.
A Little Paperback Classic.

1969   Boston: David R. Godine.
A beautifully printed and bound edition,
limited to 650 copies, with fifty specially
numbered copies bound by hand. Each slip-
cased. TSB #109.

n.d.   London: Fifield.

--CIVIL DISOBEDIENCE, recordings of
1968   Caedmon Records TC1263, read by Archibald Mac-
Leish.
MacLeish reads in a quiet, unpretentious,
clearly enunciated voice which glosses
over some of the stridency of Thoreau's
volatile essay. TSB #105.

--CIVIL DISOBEDIENCE, in collections or journals.
"Civil Disobedience," AMERICAN LITERATURE: AN ANTHOLOGY
AND CRITICAL SURVEY, edited by David, Frederick, and
Mott. New York: Scribners, 1948. I, 782-876.
With excerpts from other works of Thoreau.

"Civil Disobedience," THE ANARCHISTS, edited by Irving
L. Horowitz. New York: Dell, 1964. pp. 311-321.
A condensed version of Thoreau's essay in
an anthology of "the great non-conformists
and dissenters." Karl Schapiro, in "On
the Revival of Anarchism," pp. 572-581
comments on his personal indebtedness to
Thoreau.

"Civil Disobedience," THE DEMOCRATIC TRADITION IN AMER-
ICA, edited by Wheat. Boston: Ginn, 1943. pp. 193-195.
A condensed version for the use of West
Point students!

"Civil Disobedience," FREE SPEECH. Essix: Rolleigh, 1898. pp. 18-52.

"Civil Disobedience," THE LITERATURE OF THE UNITED STATES, edited by Blair, Hornberger, and Stewart. Chicago: Scott, Foresman, 1946. I, pp. 938-979.
> An excellent anthology which also includes "Walking," excerpts from WALDEN and the JOURNALS, and various poems. TSB #22.

"Civil Disobedience," NONVIOLENCE IN AMERICA: A DOCUMENTARY HISTORY, edited by Staughton Lynd. Indianapolis: Bobbs-Merrill, 1966. pp. 57-82.
> Volume also contains many other references to Thoreau's essay and influence.

"Civil Disobedience," PEOPLE SHALL JUDGE. Chicago: University of Chicago Press, 1949.

"Civil Disobedience," TOWARD LIBERAL EDUCATION, edited by Locke et al. New York: Rinehart, 1948.

"Civil Disobedience," THE WORLD'S GREAT THINKERS: MAN AND THE STATE: THE POLITICAL PHILOSOPHERS, edited by Commins, Saxe, and Robert N. Linscott. New York: Random House, 1947. pp. 295-320.
> Thoreau's essay (with a brief introduction) along with an excellent collection of the world's most important political documents. TSB #21.

"On Civil Disobedience," WEEKLY LAW DIGEST [San Francisco, Calif.], XXVI (August 20, 1962), 2-4. Condensed.

"Resistance to Civil Government," AESTHETIC PAPERS. Gainesville, Fla.: Scholars' Facsimiles and Reprints, 1957.
> The first publication of Thoreau's essay on "Civil Disobedience" was so limited that it is the rare person who can locate a copy for his library. Now Scholars' Facsimiles and Reprints have reprinted it in facsimile, with an introduction by Joseph Jones, to make it more readily available. TSB #60.

"Resistance to Civil Government," AMERICAN ESSAYS, edited by Charles B. Shaw. New York: Pelican Mentor Books, 1948. pp. 42-64.
> A reprint with notes.

"Resistance to Civil Government," FREEDOM [London, Eng.], X (October, 1949), 2.
> A condensation of "Civil Disobedience".

--CIVIL DISOBEDIENCE, translations of

1897   "Civil Disobedience," MIDCAREA SOCIALA [Social
        Movement], June 22, 1897.+ Translated into
        Rumanian and published in this small Bucharest
        weekly.

1907   New York: Maisel. Introduced and translated into
        Yiddish by Max Maisel.

1949   Iwanami: ? Translated into Japanese by Akira
        Tomita. Entitled SHIMIN TOSHITE NO HANKO.

1949   Santiago, Chili: Babel. Translated into Spanish
        by Ernesto Montenegro in the Edicion de lujo
        numerada. Entitled DESOBEDIENCIA CIVIL.

1950   Los Angeles: Rocker Publications Committee.
        Translated into Yiddish by Joseph J. Cohen.
        Entitled ON THE DUTY OF CIVIL DISOBEDIENCE.
             The only in-print translation of Thoreau
             into Yiddish.

1953   Rosario, Argentina: Publicaciones de la Union
        Socialista Libertaria de Rosario. Translated
        into Spanish by Ernesto Montenegro. With a pre-
        face by Rudlof Rocker. Entitled DESOBEDIENCIA
        CIVIL.

1959   Hamburg: Aktionkreis fur Gewaltlosigkeit. En-
        titled WIDERSTAND GEGEN DIE REGIERUNG.

1963   Istanbul: Gun Basimevi. Translated into Turkish
        by Vedat Gunyol. Entitled MAKSIG YONETIME KARSI.

1966   Frankfort: Galerie Patio. Translated into German
        by W. E. Richartz. Entitled UBER DIE PFLICHT ZUM
        UNGEHORSAM GEGEN DEN STAAT.
             A hand-printed edition of 150 copies.

1967   Zurich: Diogenes. Translated into German by W.
        E. Richartz. Entitled UBER DIE PFLICHT ZUM
        UNGEHORSAM GEGEN DEN STAAT.

1967   [Paris]: Pauvert [Libertes Nouvelles]. Translated
        into French by M. Flak, C. Demorel, and L. Vernet.
        Entitled LE DESOBEISSANCE CIVILE SUIVIE DE PLAIDOYER
        POUR JOHN BROWN.

1968   Sao Paulo, Brazil: Editora Cultrix. Entitled
        A DESOBEDIENCIA CIVIL E OUTROS ENSAIOS. Tr-
        ducao, prefacio e notas de Jose Paulo Paes.

1968   Copenhagen: Steen Hasselbalchs. Translated into
        Danish by Ingeborg Buhl. Entitled CIVIL LYDIGH-
        EDSNAEGTELSE OG UDVALGTE BREVE.
             Includes also some of Thoreau's letters to
             Blake.

n.d. Buenos Aires: Reconstruir. A Spanish trans-
      lation. Entitled DESOBEDIENCIA CIVIL.

--CIVIL DISOBEDIENCE, selections from
    "Civil Disobedience," CHICAGO TRIBUNE, August 3, 1952.
    Extracts.

    CIVIL DISOBEDIENCE AND WALDEN: SELECTIONS. Chicago:
    Great Books Foundation, 1954.

    "I heartily accept..." South Norwalk, Conn.: Antonio
    Frasconi, [1966?]. A broadside reprinting of the
    opening lines of "Civil Disobedience," Edition limited
    to 50 copies.

--COLLECTED POEMS OF HENRY THOREAU, edited by Carl Bode.
    Chicago: Packard and Company, 1943. Regular and
    Critical editions.

--COLLECTED POEMS, edited by Carl Bode. New enlarged
    edition. Baltimore: Johns Hopkins Press, 1964.
    (paper 1965).
            In 1943 Bode edited the first collected edition
            of Thoreau's poems--and incidentally the first
            variorum edition of any American poet. For
            years now it has been out of print and command-
            ing a real premium on the rare book market. Now
            it has been reprinted from the same plates with
            thirteen additional poems that have since come
            to light appended. It is good to have Thoreau's
            poetry thus readily available once more in an
            edition that is both thoroughly annotated and
            includes all the variants. But it is unfortunate
            that the exigencies of publishing necessitated
            using the old plates thus perpetuating in the
            Thoreau canon two poems he did not write (tho
            a note in the back points out this error) and
            the misreading of several lines in other poems.
            TSB #87.
            reviews: NEW ENGLAND QUARTERLY, XXXVII (Septem-
                      ber, 1964), 393-397.
                      [London] TIMES LITERARY SUPPLEMENT,
                      June 18, 1964.

--"David Henry Thoreau." Hartford: Emerson Society, 1957.
    Facsimile of Thoreau's entry in his Harvard
    classbook.

--"Ding Dong," LIPPINCOTT'S MAGAZINE (May, 1888). First
    publication of this poem.

--EXCURSIONS. Intro. by Leo Marx. New York: Corinth
    Books, 1962.
            The only inexpensive paperback reprint of Tho-

reau's collected travel essays.

--EXCURSIONS, contemporary reviews of
          CONTINENTAL MONTHLY, IV (December, 1863), 708-
          709. A favorable contemporary review.
          INDEPENDENT, December 3, 1863. Reprinted in
          AMERICAN TRANSCENDENTAL QUARTERLY, 11 (1969),
          31.
          NEW YORK TIMES, November 23, 1863. Reprinted
          in the TIMES' centennial A CENTURY OF BOOKS
          1851-1951. p. 5.

--"The House at Walden Pond." Concord: Thoreau Lyceum,
   1967. Brochure.

--"Huckleberries," FLYING QUILL [Goodspeed's Bookstore,
   Boston] (October, 1959).
          Facsimile and description of a Thoreau MS.

--"Humo" and "Inspiration," POESIA ESTADO UNIDENSE. Buenos
   Aires: Ediciones Continental, 1944. pp. 58-60.
          Translated into Spanish by Alfredo Weiss.

--"Independence," FREE VISTAS, edited by Joseph Ishill.
   Berkeley Heights, N. J.: Oriole Press, 1933. p. 177.

--"Independence," ISHILL'S VARIORUM, edited by Joseph
   Ishill. Berkeley Heights, N. J.: Oriole Press, 1963.
   pp. 115-116.

--"Inspiration," CHRISTIAN SCIENCE MONITOR, July 29, 1954.
   A reprinting of Thoreau's poem in part.

--JOURNALS OF THOREAU, THE, editions of
   1949 Boston: Houghton Mifflin. 14 Vols. Forward by
         Henry S. Canby. Re-issue of 1906 Walden edition
         of WORKS.
         reviews: CHICAGO TRIBUNE, April 8, 1951.
                   NEW REPUBLIC, CXXIV (May 7, 1951), 24-
                   26, by Maxwell Geisman.
                   NEW YORK HERALD TRIBUNE, May 20, 1951,
                   by Alfred Kazin.
                   NEW YORK TIMES, May 20, 1951, by Joseph
                   Wood Krutch.
                   NEW YORK WORLD TELEGRAM, June 5, 1951,
                   by Sterling North.
                   NEW YORKER (December 29, 1951).
                   SATURDAY REVIEW OF LITERATURE, Septem-
                   ber 22, 1951, pp. 20-21 passim, by
                   Townsend Scudder.
                   THOREAU SOCIETY BULLETIN #30, January,
                   1950.
                   [London] TIMES LITERARY SUPPLEMENT,
                   April 18, 1952, pp. 257-258.
                   WASHINGTON POST, June 17, 1951, by
                   Sterling North.

1963   New York: Dover. 2 Vols., boxed. Edited by
        Bradford Torrey and Francis H. Allen. Forward
        by Walter Harding.
            The complete 1906 edition reprinted in
            two volumes.

        reviews: EMERSON SOCIETY QUARTERLY, XXXVII
                  (1964), 92.
                  [London] TIMES LITERARY SUPPLEMENT,
                  December 19, 1963, p. 1048.
                  UNIVERSITY [Princeton Alumni Magazine]
                  (Summer, 1964).

--JOURNALS OF THOREAU, THE, in collections
    "Journal," A TREASURY OF THE WORLD'S GREAT DIARIES,
    edited by Philip Dunaway and Mel Evans. New York:
    Doubleday, 1957.

--JOURNALS OF THOREAU, THE, translation of
    1963   Vicenza: G. Stocchiero. Translated into Italian
           by Biancamaria Tedeschini Lalli. Entitled VITA
           DI UNO SCRITTORE. Neri Pozza Editore edition.

--JOURNALS OF THOREAU, THE, selections from
    "Autumn," a contemporary review of. BOSTON ADVERTISER,
    September 14, 1892.

    "Extracts from Thoreau's Journal," LITERARY WORLD, XIV
    (September 8, 1883), 287.

    EARLY SPRING. Cambridge: Riverside Press, 1968.
    Privately printed. Edition limited to 500 copies.

    THE FIRST DAYS OF WINTER. Cambridge: Riverside
    Press, 1962. Privately printed. Edition limited to
    500 copies.

    THE HEART OF THOREAU'S JOURNALS, edited by Odell
    Shepard. New York: Dover, 1961.
                    Although there has been many collections
                    of selections from Thoreau's JOURNALS over
                    the years, none has ever succeeded so well
                    in reflecting the general tenor of the
                    whole fourteen volumes as Odell Shepard's
                    HEART OF THOREAU'S JOURNALS, first pub-
                    lished in 1927, and now reissued in a paper-
                    back edition with a new preface, new foot-
                    notes, and new introductory comments, all
                    presented in a well-printed, handy-size
                    edition. (Dover has also issued at the same
                    time a superb two-volume edition of Audubon'
                    Journals). TSB #75.

    "Immortal American Words," P.M., January 13, 1942,
    p. 22.
                    The newspaper quotes Thoreau's December 4,

1860, journal entry on slavery.

IN THE MIDST OF WINTER. Cambridge: Riverside Press, 1965. Privately printed. Edition limited to 400 copies.

A PIG TALE. New Fairfield, Conn.: Bruce Rogers, 1947.
A pamphlet printing of an excerpt from the Journals, illustrated by C. R. Capon.

SELECTED JOURNALS OF, edited, with a foreword by Carl Bode. New York: Signet Books, 1967.
Excellent selection that gives the flavor of the whole journal. TSB #99.

SELECTIONS FROM THOREAU'S JOURNALS, intro. and notes by R. H. Blyth. Tokyo: Daigakusyorin, 1949. In English.

"So I Go to Walden A-Skating," NEW YORK TIMES MAGAZINE, December 29, 1963, p. 11.
Excerpts from the JOURNAL.

TWO FRAGMENTS FROM THE JOURNALS, edited, with a preface, by Alexander C. Kern. Wood engraving by John Roy. Iowa City: Windhover Press, 1968. Edition limited to 220 copies.
Two unpublished fragments from Thoreau's journal which shed light on his compositorial techniques. And a real typographical gem. TSB #107.

"Winter," a contemporary review of. UNITARIAN REVIEW, XXX (1888), 73.

WINTER AT WALDEN. Cambridge: Riverside Press, 1964. Privately printed. Edition limited to 400 copies.

WINTER: THE FIRST TEN DAYS OF JANUARY. Cambridge: Riverside Press, 1963. Privately printed. Edition limited to 400 copies.

WINTER: PRELUDE TO SPRING. Cambridge: Riverside Press, 1967. Privately printed. Edition limited to 400 copies.

WINTER'S DOMINION. Cambridge: Riverside Press, 1966. Privately printed. Edition limited to 400 copies.

A WRITER'S JOURNAL, selected and edited with an introduction by Laurence Stalpleton. New York: Dover, 1960.
An anthology of selections from Thoreau's JOURNAL with particular emphasis upon his comments on writing as an art and with several long sequences not hitherto available in anything but the full JOURNAL. A perceptive introduction concentrating on Thoreau's interest in "relatedness"--the

tieing together of the phenomena of the
universe. TSB #73.

reviews: JOHN O'LONDON'S WEEKLY, June 15,
          1961.
          LONDON TIMES, June 4, 1961.
          THE SPHERE [London], June 17, 1961.

--JOURNALS OF THOREAU, THE, translations of selections from
   AUTUMN. Zurich: Buchergilde Gutenberg, 1944. Translated into German by Bertha Engler.

   "Parales vielles d'un siecle...et pourtant," L'UNIQUE
   [Orleans, France], April, 1954.
          A French translation of Thoreau's Journal
          entry for July 21, 1851.

   UN PHILOSOPHE DANS LES BOIS. Translated by R. Michaud
   and S. David, with a preface by Roger Asselineau.
   [Paris]: Vent d'Ocust, 1967.
          Selections from the JOURNAL.

   "Un Philosophe dans les Bois," INFORMATIONS AND DOC-
   UMENTS [Paris: American Embassy], CCLIV (December 15,
   1967), 26-32.
          Excerpts from Journals translated into French.

   WINTER, GEDANKEN UND STIMMUNGSBILDER. DEN NACHGELAS-
   SENEN WERKEN THOREAUS ENTNOMMEN. Translated by Emma
   Emmerich. Munich: Concord Verlag, 1900.
          Emmerich's selections from Thoreau's jour-
          nals include entries from winter months on
          a day-by-day basis. Oddly, she does not
          mention H. G. O. Blake's WINTER (1897),
          upon which her translation is modeled. The
          fact that this book went through two further
          printings, Darmstadt: Peters, 1901, and Pader-
          born: Lucus, 1921, indicates that it gained
          a reading public. TSB #105.

--"Let Us Live Deliberately," CLEVELAND UNITARIAN, May 20,
   1944, p. 1.

--LETTERS
   FAMILIAR LETTERS, a contemporary review of. NATION,
   LIX (October 18, 1894), 291-292; TRUTH SEEKER, June
   24, 1893.

   Letter to Stearns Wheeler of November 28, 1838, FLYING
   QUILL [Goodspeed's], August, 1967, p. 1. Facsimile.

   "Letters to Greeley, Blake, and Benton. CIVIL DISOBE-
   DIENCE, and excerpts from WALDEN," AMERICAN LIFE IN
   LITERATURE, edited by Jay B. Hubbell. New York:
   Harper's, 1951.

"Thoreau Writes Emerson on Friendship," WOLF MAGAZINE OF LETTERS, XXI (June, 1955), 9-10.
> Reprints Thoreau's letter of February, 1843.

TWO THOREAU LETTERS. Ysleta, Texas: Edwin B. Hill, 1942.
> Two unpublished letters, the first to a college classmate, the second to a Maine cousin about his Maine excursions.

["Walt Whitman"], THE CENTENARY OF WALT WHITMAN'S LEAVES OF GRASS, edited by Joseph Ishill. Berkeley Heights, N.J.: Oriole Press, 1955. pp. 26-28.
> Reprints Thoreau's letter to Blake on Whitman.

--LIFE WITHOUT PRINCIPLE, editions of
> 1946 Stanford University, California: James L. Delkin Preface by Henry Miller. Entitled LIFE WITHOUT PRINCIPLE: THREE ESSAYS BY HENRY DAVID THOREAU.

> reviews: SAN FRANCISCO CHRONICLE, ? , 1946, by Joseph Henry Jackson.
> TSB #16, July, 1946.

> 1965 Santa Ana, California: Freedom Newspapers. Pamphlet reprint.

--LIFE WITHOUT PRINCIPLE, in collections and journals
> "Life Without Principle," GREAT ENGLISH AND AMERICAN ESSAYS, edited by D. S. Mead. New York: Rinehart, 1950. pp. 95-111.

> "Life Without Principle," OF TIME AND TRUTH, edited by Lorch et al. New York: Dryden, 1946. pp. 557-561.
> > Also includes "Modern Improvements," and "Plea for Captain John Brown."

--LIFE WITHOUT PRINCIPLE, translations of
> "Vida sin Principios," translated into Spanish by V. Munoz. CENIT, May, 1959, pp. 2725-2726 passim.+ Also in VOLUNTAD, IV (May, 1960).

> "Liv uten Prinsipp," FRIHUG [Norway], XI (December, 1962), 6-8. In Norse.

--THE MAINE WOODS, editions of
> 1950 New York: Norton. Edited by Dudley C. Lunt. Illustrated by H. B. Kane.
> > This is the first of a new 4 volume edition of Thoreau. The binding, typography, and the illustrations are beautiful. When one starts to read the text, one finds something very different from the standard MAINE WOODS. Mr. Lunt has completely rearranged the text,

combining Thoreau's three journeys into
one. Since Thoreau himself combined several trips into one in CAPE COD, 2 years
into 1 in WALDEN, etc., Mr. Lunt has some
justification for his scheme. In order to
do it, he has had to relegate parts of the
text to an appendix and to insert explanatory notes to link passages together. Three
chapters have been chopped into sixteen.
Since the trips were taken in different
months in different years, with different
guides and companions, combining them is
confusing. I prefer the original. TSB #31.
reviews: BULLETIN OF THE MASSACHUSETTS AUDUBON
SOCIETY, XXXIV (May, 1950), by Allen.
CHRISTIAN SCIENCE MONITOR, April 29,
1950, by T. Morris Longstreth.
NEW YORK HERALD TRIBUNE, April 14,
1950, by Lewis Gannett.
NEW YORK TIMES, April 8, 1950, by
Charles Poore.
PUNCH, July 11, 1951, by R. C. S.
[London] TIMES LITERARY SUPPLEMENT,
August 10, 1951, p. 498.
WILMINGTON JOURNAL, March 24m 1950.
YANKEE, XIV (June, 1950), 77.

1961   New York: Crowell.

1965   New Haven: College and University Press. Masterworks of Literature Series. Illustrated
paperback reprint of 1950 Norton edition.

1966   New York: Crowell. Decorations by Clare Leighton. Apollo Edition. Paperback.

--THE MAINE WOODS, selections from
"Ktaadn Trout," A TREASURY OF FISHING STORIES, edited
by Charles E. Goodspeed. New York: A. S. Barnes, 1946,
pp. 71-74.

"Outfit for an Excursion," CAPE CODDER [Orleans, Mass.],
August 21, 1947.
Supposedly an unpublished piece of Thoreau's
writing discovered in an old notebook in
Eastham, Mass. It is actually but a copy
of part of the appendix to THE MAINE WOODS.

--THE MAINE WOODS, contemporary review
CONTINENTAL MONTHLY, VI (August, 1864), 235-236.
A favorable contemporary review.

--"Mist," "Smoke," and "Independence," THE POCKET BOOK OF
AMERICAN POEMS. New York: Pocket Books, 1948. pp. 135-136.

--"My Prayer," "Poems for Your Scrapbook," BOSTON POST, August 3, 1942.

     also in: BOSTON POST, July 12, 1943; and BOSTON POST, July 12, 1948.

--"Of Books and Their Titles," edited by R. Baird Shuman. EMERSON SOCIETY QUARTERLY, XVIII (1960), 26-34.
     First accurate transcription of one of Thoreau's college essays with a facsimile of the MS.

--OF FRIENDSHIP, translated into German by Paul Pattlock. Aschaffenburg: Pattlock, 1947.

--PLAN OF NATHANIEL HAWTHORNE'S ESTATE IN CONCORD MASS: SURVEYED BY HENRY D. THOREAU. AUGUST 20, 1860. New York: Grolier Club, 1964. Facsimile reproduction.

--"Plan of Nathaniel Hawthorne's Estate," EMERSON SOCIETY QUARTERLY, XLVIII (1967), 86. Facsimile.

--A PLEA FOR CAPTAIN JOHN BROWN, in collections and journals
     "A Plea for Captain John Brown," MASSES AND MAINSTREAM, VI (October, 1953), 46-50. An abridged version.

     "A Plea for Capt. John Brown," CONSCIENCE IN AMERICA, edited by Lillian Schlissel. New York: Dutton, 1968. pp. 80-87.
          Thoreau is quoted constantly throughout this fascinating collection of documents pertaining to conscientious objection in America from colonial times to today, and he emerges rather as the hero of the book. TSB #106.

--A PLEA FOR CAPTAIN JOHN BROWN, translation of
     Translated into Japanese by Tsutomu Shigematsu. BULL. OF MINAMI KYUSHU JUNIOR COLLEGE, II (November, 1965).

--A PLEA FOR CAPTAIN JOHN BROWN, selection from
     "Beauty Stands Veiled," AND WHY NOT EVERY MAN?, edited by Herbert Aptheker. Berlin: Seven Seas, 1961. pp. 212-217.
          In a anthology of anti-slavery selections.

--"Poems," POETRY OF THE NEW ENGLAND RENAISSANCE. New York: Rinehart Editions, 1950.
     Includes 31 poems by Thoreau (pp. 327-352)--I think the largest selection of his poems in any anthology. TSB #34.

--POEMS OF NATURE, a contemporary review of. ATHENAEUM, October 17, 1896.

--Receipt for payment for estimating the area of the town
  of Lincoln, Mass. August 31, 1860, BICENTENNIAL CELE-
  BRATION OF THE TOWN OF LINCOLN MASSACHUSETTS 1754-1954.
  Lincoln: ?   , 1954?. p. 12. Facsimile reproduction.

--"Rumors from an Aeolian Harp," "To Nature," "Smoke,"
  "The Fisher Boy," A HEBREW ANTHOLOGY OF AMERICAN VERSE,
  translated into Hebrew by Reuben Avinoam. Tel-Aviv:
  Am Oved, 1953. pp. 169-176.

--"The Seasons," EMERSON SOCIETY QUARTERLY, IX (1957), 4.
  Reprint of Thoreau's first essay.

--"The Seven Against Theves," edited by Leo Max Kaiser.
  EMERSON SOCIETY QUARTERLY, XVII (1959), 1-30.
      The first publication of Thoreau's translation of
      the Greek play, with an introduction and many textual
      notes. Based on the MS of Thoreau's rough draft now
      in the Huntington Library.

--SIC VITA! New York: Silverado Press, 1962.
      The first printing of the newly discovered Thoreau
      poem. 30 copies were made on Whatman hand-made
      paper made in 1824; 25 copies, on hand-made Japan
      vellum; and 325 copies on Tuscany hand-made paper.
      A shortened version entitled "Summer Song" appeared
      in THIS WEEK MAGAZINE, June 17, 1962, p. 2.

--SLAVERY IN MASSACHUSETTS, translation of
  1960 Montevideo, Uruguay: Ediciones Voluntad. Trans-
        lated into Spanish by Vladimir Munoz. With
        an introduction by Walter Harding. Entitled
        ESCLAVITUD EN MASSACHUSETTS.

--THE SUCCESSION OF FOREST TREES, illustrated by Thoreau
  MacDonald. Toronto, Canada: Privately printed, 1956.
      A beautifully printed and illustrated brochure.
      TSB #58.

--THE SUCCESSION OF FOREST TREES, selection from
  "Planters of Trees," CHRISTIAN SCIENCE MONITOR, December 14, 1954.

--"The Summer Rail," "Maze," "Conscience," 100 AMERICAN
  POEMS, edited by Selden Rodman. New York: Penquin Signet
  Books, 1948.
      With a long note by Rodman on Thoreau's poetry.
      pp. 8-10. The poems, pp. 52-54.

--SURVEY OF WALDEN POND. Boston: Goodspeed, 1954.
      A beautiful collotype facsimile reproduction of
      Thoreau's hitherto unpublished manuscript survey of
      Walden Pond, showing the location of the cabin, and
      with many comments by Thoreau. It is issued in a

limited edition and would grace any room if framed.

--"To Edith," edited by Kenneth W. Cameron. EMERSON SOCIETY
QUARTERLY, XVIII (1960), 40-41.
First publication of a hitherto unknown poem by
Thoreau.

--"Transportation and Planting of Seeds," MCGUFFEY FIFTH
ECLECTIC READER, 1879 edition.
Reprinted New York: Signet, 1962. p. 290.

--WALDEN, editions of. [Listed chronologically. Included are
all entries of "A Preliminary Checklist of the Editions
of Walden," by Walter Harding. TSB #39.]

1854   Boston: Ticknor and Fields.

1884   Edinburgh: David Douglas; London: Hamilton, Adams.

1886   London: Walter Scott.   Intro. by Dircks.

1888   London: Walter Scott; Toronto: Gage.   Intro. by
Dircks.

1889   Boston: Houghton Mifflin. Riverside Aldine Series.

1893   Boston: Houghton Mifflin.   Riverside Edition,
Vol. II.   Sometimes labeled New Riverside Edition.

1893   The Same.   A large-paper edition.

1895   London: Scott.   Intro. by Dircks.

1897   Boston: Houghton Mifflin.   Holiday Edition.
Intro. by Torrey.

1897   The Same.   London: Gay and Bird.

1897   Boston: Houghton Mifflin.   Popular Edition.
Life by Emerson.

1898   Boston: Houghton Mifflin.   Cambridge Classics
Edition.   Life by Emerson.

1899   New York: Crowell.   Intro. by Roberts.

1902   Boston: Houghton Mifflin.   New Holiday Edition.
Intro. by Torrey.

1902   The Same.   London: Gay and Bird.

1904   London: Simple Life Press.   An abridged edition.

1906   Boston: Houghton Mifflin.   Manuscript Edition
of WORKS.   Intro. unsigned.   Vol. II.

1906 Boston: Houghton Mifflin. Walden Edition of
      WORKS. Intro. unsigned. Vol. II.

1906 London: Oxford University. Intro. by Watts.
      Dutton. World's Classics Edition.

1906 London: Blackie. Intro. by Whiteing.

1908 London: Dent; New York: Dutton. Intro. by
      Raymond. Everyman's Library Edition.

1909 Boston: Bibliophile Society.

1910 New York: Longmans Green. Intro. by Alden.
      Longmans' English Classics Edition.

1910 New York: Merrill. Intro. by Dorey. Merrill's
      English Texts Edition.

1910 Boston: Houghton Mifflin. Intro. by Allen.
      Riverside Literature Series Edition.

1910 New York: Macmillan. Intro. by Rees. Macmillan
      Pocket Classics Edition.

1910 New York: Crowell.

1910 New York: Kelmscott Society.

1911 London: Harrup.

1917 New York: Scott Foresman. Lake English Classics
      Edition.

1919 Boston: Houghton Mifflin. Visitor's Edition.

1920 London: Mudie's Select Library Ltd. Intro. by
      Will H. Dirks. New Camelot Series.

1922 Chicago: Scott Foresman. Lake English Classics
      Edition Revised.

1926 London and Glasgow: Blackie. Intro. by Whiteing.
      Wallet Library Edition.

1927 London: Chapman and Hall.

1927 The Same. Limited Edition.

1929 Boston: Houghton Mifflin. Riverside Library
      Edition.

1929 Boston: Houghton Mifflin. Concord Edition. Vol. ?

1929 New York: Macmillan. Intro. by King. Modern
      Reader's Series Edition.

1930   Chicago: Lakeside Press.   Intro. by Adams.

1931   London: Chapman and Hall.

1932   Boston: Houghton Mifflin.   Riverside Pocket
       Edition of WORKS.   Vol. II.

1936   New York: Grosset and Dunlap.   Universal Library
       Edition.

1936   Boston: Merrymount Press.   Intro. by Canby.
       Limited Editions Club Edition.

1937   New York: Modern Library.   Intro. by Atkinson.
       Includes other Thoreau writings.

1937   Boston: Houghton Mifflin.   Entitled WORKS.
       Includes other Thoreau writings.

1938   Harmonsworth, Middlesex, England: Penquin.

1938   Chicago: American Technical Society.   Intro. by
       Cooper.

1939   New York: Heritage Club.

1940   New York: Crowell.   Entitled WORKS.   Includes
       other Thoreau writings.

1942   New York: Black.   Intro. by Haight.   Classics
       Club Edition.

1942   New York: World.

1942   New York: Penquin.

1944   Mount Vernon: Peter Pauper.   Illus. by Aldren
       Watson.   DeLuxe Artist's Edition.
          "whose brilliant full-page pictures and
          chapter headings in two colors would have
          been loved by Thoreau himself."   Printed
          on specially-made, deckle-edged paper, bound
          with decorated sides and cloth spine, and
          boxed.   TSB #7.

1944   Girard, Kansas: Haldeman-Julius.   A condensed
       version.

1946   New York: Dodd, Mead.   Intro. by Teale.   Illus.
       with 142 photographs.
          With fifty or more editions of WALDEN having
          poured forth from the presses of the world
          since the first edition of 1854, it would
          seem pointless to devote any space in our
          bulletin to another edition.   But Mr. Teale

has done an exceptional piece of work here
and it is worthy of all the notice it can
receive. In his Foreword, the editor announces that he has tried to produce the
WALDEN that "I have often looked for for
my own library." Evidently his tastes co-
incide with those of your reviewer, for he
has produced just the edition that I have
long been looking for. I have twenty-five
or thirty editions on my own bookshelves,
but I know that in the future when I want
to read WALDEN for pure enjoyment, this is
the volume I shall turn to. It is also the
edition that I shall recommend every begin-
ner at Thoreau to turn to.

Mr. Teale's WALDEN is a beautiful edition
and it is a beautiful edition without being
precious. It is as sturdy as the character
of Thoreau himself. It is printed in a type
that is eminently readable. It is bound in
a good, sturdy binding that will stand wear
and tear. It is annotated with the most
lucid and stimulating comments that we have
yet seen. And best of all, Mr. Teale has
succeeded in illustrating it with photographs
that add to rather than detract from the
text. I have just two exceedingly minor
criticisms. On Page 6, the first edition of
WALDEN is given incorrectly as 1845. And
the plates for one or two of the photographs
are slightly muddy. But aside from this,
this is the best edition of WALDEN as yet to
appear on the bookstalls. It is the edition
we have dreamed of and never dared hope to
see. No matter how many other editions he
may already own, I hope that every Thoreau
lover will add this one to his shelves and
that he, like a Gideonite, will distribute
it far and wide among his friends. I do
not very often go all out in praise of a
new edition of an old classic, but from now
on, so far as I am concerned, this is the
edition of WALDEN.   TSB #18.

reviews: ANALYSIS (November, 1946).
            BOSTON POST, December 8, 1946, by
            Henry B. Kane.
            CHICAGO TRIBUNE, November 24, 1946,
            by Frederick Babcock.
            CONCORD JOURNAL, November 28, 1946,
            by W[heeler] R[uth] W.
            NATURAL HISTORY (January, 1947).
            NEW YORK HERALD TRIBUNE, December
            23, 1946, by Lewis Gannet.
            NEW YORK HERALD TRIBUNE BOOKS,

December 8, 1946, by George F.
Whicher.
NEW YORK SUN, December 3, 1946,
by Clayton Hoagland.
NEW YORK TIMES, January 5, 1947,
by Brooks Atkinson.
NEW YORK WORLD TELEGRAM, November
26, 1946, by Harry Hansen.
NEW YORKER (December 28, 1946),
by E. B. White.

1946 New York: Modern Library. Intro. by Atkinson.
Illus. by Charles Locke. Illustrated Modern
Library Edition.

Add to the many new editions of Thoreau's
Masterpiece this new volume in the Illustrated Modern Library. In binding, in typo-
graphy, and in handy size, this volume is
a beauty. Charles Locke's illustrations,
particularly the twelve full-page color reproductions of his oil paintings, are beautiful beyond question. But would we seem
too much of a stickler for detail if we sug-
gested that apparently Mr. Locke never saw
Concord or Walden Pond? He represents some
beautiful landscapes, but they are such as
I've never seen in Concord. More accurate
are the nineteen little black-and-white line
drawings which head the chapters. From them,
one might get a good picture of the Concord
landscape. The introduction by Brooks Atkinson is reprinted from the earlier Modern
Library edition of Thoreau's writings, and as
we have said before, it is one of the best
introductions to the Sage of Walden Pond.
Despite the inaccuracy of the illustrations,
this is a beautiful edition and will make
an excellent gift edition for those of your
friends who have not yet acquired WALDEN for
their library shelves. TSB #18.

1947 Chicago: Packard. Intro. by Whicher. Entitled
WALDEN AND SELECTED ESSAYS.

This inexpensive reprint contains the entire
WALDEN, plus six essays, a long introduction
by Dr. Whicher, and an especially good bibliography. If you are looking for a good edition
of WALDEN to use in your classes, teachers,
here is certainly the best for the money. Dr.
Whicher, as usual succeeds in saying just the
right things about Thoreau. TSB #22.

review: AMERICAN LITERATURE, XX (May, 1948),
256.

1947 Boston: Houghton Mifflin. Edited by Canby.
Entitled WORKS. Includes other Thoreau writings.
Cambridge Edition.

1947 New York: Viking. Intro. by Bode. Entitled
Viking Portable. Includes other Thoreau writings.

1948 New York: Rinehart. Intro. by Pearson. Rinehart
Edition #8. Entitled WALDEN AND ON THE DUTY OF
CIVIL DISOBEDIENCE.

1949 New York: New American Library. Signet Book 747.
A 25 cent reprint, handy for use in liter-
ature courses. Good but brief Introduction.
TSB #30.

1950 New York: Modern Library. Intro. by Atkinson.
Modern Library College Edition. Entitled WALDEN
AND OTHER WRITINGS OF HENRY DAVID THOREAU.
A re-issue in a cheap edition with paper
binding of the well-known Modern Library
edition with its excellent introduction by
Brooks Atkinson and a new foreword by Town-
send Scudder. TSB #32.

1950 New York: Harpers. Intro. by Krutch. Harpers'
Modern Classics Edition.
Excellent type. Sane Introduction. Good
as an inexpensive school text, but lacks
map and annotations. TSB #31.

1950 New York: Doric. Illus. by Anthony Saris.
Type small but clear. No annotations nor
introduction. Drawings show little acquaintance with either Thoreau or Concord. TSB #31

1951 New York: Norton. Intro. by Willey. Illus. by
Kane.
The last in Norton's 3 vol. edition of Thoreau's writings. The introduction, unfortunately, has little of any significance to
say. But Kane's illustrations are on an
equal with the high standard set in his two
previous volumes. It is indeed a pleasure
to have an edition of WALDEN in good, readable type and beautifully illustrated.
TSB #38.

review: CHRISTIAN SCIENCE MONITOR, November 29, 1951, by T. Morris Longstreth.

1955 New York: Dodd, Mead. Edited by Teale. Great
Illustrated Classics Edition.
When Dodd, Mead brought out Teale's edition

258

of WALDEN nine years ago, I was happy
to be able to review it as "the best edition
yet to appear." Unfortunately it has been
out of print now for some time. But at last
they have reprinted it (from the same plates)
in a less expensive format, minus some of the
less important photographic illustrations.
It is still the best edition of WALDEN to own.
Mr. Teale's introductory comments--even
though written nine years ago they are as
pertinent as ever--and photographs add much
to the meaning of the text. And the type is
large and clear. It is unfortunate however
that the publishers derived their text from
a more recent edition than the first and so
have helped to perpetuate some of the print-
ers' errors that have crept in over the years.
TSB #53.

1956   New York: New American Library. Mentor Book MD176.
Entitled WALDEN...AND...CIVIL DISOBEDIENCE.
The cheapest edition of WALDEN now in print,
with CIVIL DISOBEDIENCE thrown in for good
measure. TSB #56.

1957   Boston: Houghton Mifflin. Edited, annotated,
and with an introduction by Sherman Paul. Riverside Editions A14.
A new paperbound edition for college use.
The introduction is by far the best yet to
appear in an edition of WALDEN. It is particularly good on the organic structure of
the book. It may, however, be a little too
complex for the average undergraduate. The
annotations, though few, are decidedly pertinent. Appended is Charles Lane's DIAL
essay on "Life in the Woods," which, while
interesting, adds little to the value of the
book. TSB #59.

1960   New York: Libra Collection. Preface by Krutch.
One of the most beautiful editions of WALDEN
ever published. Large pages; large, clear
print; illustrated with 24 woodcuts from the
ancient Chinese drawing manuals of the Mustard Seeds Garden studio--woodcuts that
mirror exactly the strength and simplicity
and beauty of the text itself; bound in a
beautiful, rough-finish green cloth, and
doubly boxed. It is hard to imagine a more
beautifully conceived edition. The preface
by Mr. Krutch is brief, but very much to
the point. Scholars however will be dis-
turbed by the fact that the "complemental
verses" at the end of the first chapter have

been omitted and that the text itself
perpetuates some of the errors that have
crept into printings since the first edition.
TSB #73.

1960   New York: New American Library. "Afterword" by
Perry Miller. Signet Classics Edition.

1960   Boston: Houghton Mifflin. Intro. by Sherman Paul.
Entitled WALDEN AND CIVIL DISOBEDIENCE. A re-
vision of the Riverside paperback Edition with
CIVIL DISOBEDIENCE added.

1960   Garden City: Doubleday. Dolphin paperback edition
Good, clear type. TSB #72.

1961   New York: Crowell. Intro. by Atkinson.
The introduction is short, but very much to
the point. Unfortunately the text of WALDEN
itself is corrupt at points. For readability
of type and beautiful simplicity of typog-
raphy and decorations, this is unquestionably
the best collected edition of Thoreau's major
works available today. TSB #77.

1961   New York: Holt, Rinehart and Winston. Commentaries by Larzer Ziff.
It is hard to imagine that with 150 or more
editions of WALDEN already in existence,
someone could make an altogether new and useful approach. But Mr. Ziff has done it.
Accompanying the text of WALDEN is a series
of analyses of the chapters demonstrating
how rhetorically and grammatically Thoreau
adapted his style to his subject matter.
While the edition is aimed at college writing
courses, any serious student of Thoreau will
find Mr. Ziff's analyses thought-provoking
and enlightening. TSB #78.

1962   New York: Bantam Books. Intro. by Krutch. En-
titled WALDEN AND OTHER WRITINGS.
Paperback edition with fine introduction.
Includes WALDEN, "Life without Principle,"
"Civil Disobedience," and excerpts from
WEEK, CAPE COD, MAINE WOODS, and JOURNAL.
TSB #83.

1962   New York: Collier Books. Intro. by Charles R.
Anderson.
Text: small print, tiny margins, not particularly accurate. Introduction: "WALDEN
is an experience recreated in words for the
purpose of getting rid of the World altogether
and discovering the Self. Its real theme is

is the search for perfection." TSB #81.

1963 New York: Twayne. Edited and Annotated by
Walter Harding. Entitled THE VARIORUM WALDEN.
The annotations in this edition are far
superior to those in any other, as those
acquainted with Mr. Harding's research would
expect them to be. They are rich indeed,
running to some 50 pages of small print. In
addition to hundreds of identifications of
allusions and people there are useful cross-
references to the JOURNAL and summaries of
scholarship on various points. There is a
brief and interesting introduction. The
format is good. Some annotations are unfortunately out-of-date and there are some unfortunate typographical errors in the text,
but these minor flaws can be corrected in
future printings or editions which will certainly be called for. J. Lyndon Shanley.
TSB #83.

> reviews: CAPITAL TIMES [Madison, Wis.],
> December 20, 1962.
> CHICAGO TRIBUNE, December 9, 1962.
> CONCORD JOURNAL, November 15, 1962.
> NEW ENGLAND QUARTERLY, XXXVII
> (September, 1964), 393-397, by
> Raymond Gozzi.
> ROCHESTER TIMES UNION, December
> 1, 1962.
> WESTERN HUMANITIES REVIEW, XVIII
> (Spring, 1964), 178-180.

1963 The same. New York: Washington Square Press.
Corrects the misprints of the hardcover
edition and adds a number of new annotations.
TSB #85.

1963 Cleveland: Micro Photo. Duopage facsimile of
first edition.

1963 New York: Harper and Row. Intro. by David Aloian.
Harper's Modern Classic Edition for use in secondary schools.

1964 Boston: Student Outline Company. A student's
"trot."

1964 Cleveland: Bell and Howell. Duopage photographic
facsimile of the 1854 first edition.

1964 Boston: Houghton Mifflin. Intro. by E. B. White.
Suggestions for Reading and Discussion by Frank
H. Townsend. For use in secondary schools.

1965   New York: Airmont Pub. Intro. by Frederick
        Langmack. Entitled WALDEN AND CIVIL DISOBEDIENCE.
            Type small but readable. Perceptive intro-
            duction but careless with facts. TSB #95.

1965   New Haven: College and University Press. Intro.
        by Willey. Illus. by Kane. Masterworks of
        Literature Series.
            A well-printed paperback reprint. TSB #95.

1965   New York: Harper and Row. Entitled WALDEN...AND
        ...CIVIL DISOBEDIENCE.
            Handy little edition with clear though small
            type, a fairly accurate text, and a brief
            but lively introduction. TSB #94.

1966   Mount Vernon: Peter Pauper Press. Abridged and
        edited by C. Merton Bancock. Illus. by Aldren
        Watson.
            Beautifully printed and illustrated edition,
            but highly condensed. TSB #96.

1966   New York: Crowell. Intro. by Krutch. Decorations
        by Clare Leighton. Paperback reprint with a new
        introduction.

1966   New York: Franklin Watts. The first "large-type"
        edition available for the use of those with weak
        eyes.

1966   New York: Norton. Edited by Owen Thomas. En-
        titled WALDEN AND CIVIL DISOBEDIENCE: AUTHORI-
        TATIVE TEXTS, BACKGROUND REVIEWS, AND ESSAYS IN
        CRITICISM. Norton Critical Edition.
            Includes an annotated text with background
            excerpts from the JOURNAL and 19 reviews
            and critical essays by authors as varied
            as Daniel Ricketson and Sherman Paul. TSB #

1968   New York: Lancer Books. Magnum Easy Eye Book.
        Entitled WALDEN AND THE ESSAY ON CIVIL DIS-
        OBEDIENCE.
            Printed in exceptionally large type for a
            paperback and on light green "easy to read"
            paper. The only such large type paperback
            edition available. TSB #105.

1968   New York: Washington Square Press. Edited by
        Walter Harding. Entitled THE VARIORUM WALDEN
        AND THE VARIORUM CIVIL DISOBEDIENCE. Paperback
        edition.

1969   New York: Macfadden-Bartell Corp. Adapted by
        Ralph K. Andrist. Ladder Classic.
            "This special edition is for readers for

whom English is a second language. It can
be read by anyone who has learned 2,000
words of English." Adapted to help popu-
larize WALDEN abroad. An example of how it
has been modified: "Most men live all their
lives in quiet despair. A kind of dispair
is hidden even under men's games and pleasures. There is no play in them, because
play is something that follows work." TSB
#108.

[1969] New York: Franklin Watts. Intro. by John Ash-
worth.
For those who want a clear large-type edition, this "Watts Ultratype" edition is the
one. It manages to include a highly readable type in a volume about half the size
of the earlier Watt Large Type edition. It
also has an extra-sturdy binding and particularly durable paper. TSB #108.

n.d.   New York: Burt. Cornell Series.

n.d.   New York: Burt. New Pocket Edition.

n.d.   New York: Burt. The Home Library.

n.d.   Philadelphia: Henry Altemus.

n.d.   London: Frowde. Intro. by Watts-Dunton.

n.d.   Armed Services Edition.

n.d.   London: Fifield. Heretical Booklets Series.

--WALDEN, in collections or journals
"Walden,"AMERICAN LITERARY MASTERS, edited by Charles
Anderson. New York: Holt. 1965. I, 625-830.
With extended prefatory essay analyzing
image and structure of WALDEN.

"Walden,"THE AMERICAN TRADITION IN LITERATURE, edited
by Bradley, Beatty, and Long. New York: Norton, 1967.
I, 1236-1490. Complete text.

"Walden,"CONCORD IDEALISM, edited by R. Stewart and D.
Bethurum. Chicago: Scott, Foresman, 1954. pp. 78-
242.
Complete text of the book in a college textbook.

"Walden," THE GREAT IDEAS TODAY 1965. Chicago: En-
cyclopaedia Britannica, 1965. pp. 437-519. An
abridged edition.

"Walden," THE INDIVIDUAL AMERICAN, edited by Gordon
and Feidelson. Boston: Ginn, 1966. pp. 376-629.
     A complete well-annotated text for use in
     high schools.

"Walden," THE POPULAR EDUCATOR, I (August 2, 1939),
40-46. An abridged edition.

"Walden," READERS DIGEST, XXXVII (September, 1940),
129-136. An abridged edition.

--WALDEN, recordings of
    1958   St. Joseph, Michigan: Audio Book Co. 6 records.
          A recording of the complete text of the firs
          six chapters of WALDEN, read by John Carra-
          dine. Carradine's clipped, polished accent
          may at first seem a little at odds with Tho-
          reau's homely style. But that is more than
          made up for by the clarity and distinctness
          of diction. Except for an occasional under-
          standable verbal substitution (such as a <u>the</u>
          for a <u>their</u>), the text is accurately render-
          ed. On the whole it is a thoughtful and
          enlightening rendition that should be a god-
          send to the blind and a stimulation to any
          student of Thoreau. It is recorded at the
          new 16 rpm speed and all six records pack
          into a beautiful album only 8"x7"x3/4".
          What is more amazing, the album is only $6.9
          We understand the remaining half of WALDEN
          will be recorded later if there is sufficien
          demand for this first half. TSB #65.

          review: AMERICAN RECORD QUIZ, December, 195

    1962   New Rochelle, N. Y.: Spoken Arts. Read by Howard
        Mumford Jones. One long-playing recording.
          A good series of selections from 6 chapters,
          read clearly and distinctly but a little
          pompously. TSB #83.

    1968   Boston: Houghton Mifflin. Caedmon Record TC 1261
        Read by Archibald MacLeish.
          A 12-inch 33 rpm recording of selections
          read very poetically. Perhaps the most
          satisfying recording yet of selections from
          WALDEN. TSB #106.

--WALDEN, translations and foreign editions of
    1897   Munich: Johann Palm's Verlag. Translated by Emma
        Emmerich.
          The earliest translation of WALDEN into a
          foreign language, and in its second edition
          (Munich: Verlag Concord, n.d.) the most ac-
          curate of the German translations. Prefacec

by a well-balanced and intelligent essay,
Emmerich's translation attempts to render
the difficulties of Thoreau's text, his wit,
and his characteristic style. Third editions
of this translation were apparently published
by two separate firms, Loschwitz of Dresden
and Menzel of Baden-Baden. TSB #105.

1900 Moscow: ? . Translated into Russian. Entitled
WALDEN: AN EXPERIMENT IN SIMPLIFYING LIFE. An
abridged edition.

1902 Bussum, Holland: Grentzebach. Translated into
Dutch by von Dawwoude.

1903 Baden-Baden: Menzel. Translated into German by
Loschwitz.

1905 Jena and Leipzig: Eugen Diederichs. Translated
into German by Wielhelm Nobbe.
Tends to simplify and at times interpret
Thoreau's text, particularly in relatively
difficult passages. Nobbe's substantial
introduction refers to a variety of secondary sources including Salt, Lowell, Ellery
Channing, Burroughs, and Bradford Torrey.
TSB #105.

1910 Moscow: ? . Translated into Russian by
Bulanizke. Entitled AN ATTEMPT TO SIMPLIFY LIFE.
An abridged edition.

1911 Tokyo: Bunseisha. Translated into Japanese by
Koichiro Mizushima. Illustrated by Bernard Leach.
Entitled SHINRIN SEIKATSU.

1922 Tokyo: ? . Introduction and notes in Japanese
by Knisaky Shinoda.

1922 Paris: Editions de la Novelle Revue Francaise.
Translated into French by Louis Fabulet.

1922 Berlin: Hendel. Translated into German by Franz
Meyer.
Tends to simplify and qualify Thoreau's
text for the sake of clarity. Reissued
(Weimar: Gustav Kiepenheuer Verlag, 1964)
without mention of the earlier edition.

1922 Jena: Diederichs. Translated into German by
Nobbe.

1924 Prague: Nekovarik. Translated into Czech .

1925 Tokyo: Shinchosha. Translated into Japanese by

Yoshio Imai. Entitled MORI NO SEIKATSU.

1928 Venice, La Nouva Italia: Editrice, 1928. Translated into Italian by Guido Ferrando.

1929 Tokyo: Kenkyusha. Translated into Japanese.

1933 Tokyo: Nantendo Press. Translated into Japanese by Koichiro Mizushima. Entitled TETSUJIN NO SHINRIN SEIKATSU.

1933 ? : ? . Translated into Japanese by Seitaro Furudate. Entitled MORI NO SEIKATSU.

1945 Zurich: Artemis Verlag. Edited and introduced by Fritz Guttinger. Translated into German by Siegfried Lang. Vol. II of the American Series of the Artemis Library.
The most accurate and the most satisfactory of the post-war translations of WALDEN.

reviews: BASLER NACHRICHTEN, March 9, 1946. NEUE ZURCHER ZEITUNG, September 29, 1945 and December 19, 1945. DIE TAT [Zurich], October 20, 1945 DIE WELTWOCHE [Zurich], February 8 1946, by Hans Naf.

1947 Stockholm: Wahlstrom and Widstrand. Translated into Swedish by Frans. G. Bengtsson. Illustrated by Stig Asberg. Entitled SKOGSLIV VID WALDEN.

1948 Tokyo: Chikushi Shobo. Annotated and translated into Japanese by Toru Okamoto.
Pages 1-67 contain "Where I Lived," "Sounds," "Visitors," and "The Ponds." Pages 68-131 are in Japanese, as is the introduction, pp. i-viii.

1948 Tokyo: Dai-sen. Translated into Japanese by Emai Kisei.

1949 Buenos Aires: Espasa Calpe. Translated into Spanish by Justo Garate.
The translation is much closer to the spirit of the original than other Spanish translations. The text is thoroughly annotated, has a good introduction, and also the Gleason map of Concord. He has, however, used more chapter divisions than in the original text. TSB #31.

review: CRITICA, February 11, 1950.

1949 Kobenhavn: Kunst og Kultur. Translated into

Danish by Ole Jacobsen. Illustrated by Mads
Stage. Entitled WALDEN: LIVET IN SKOVENE.
   Knowing no Danish, I cannot evaluate the
   translation. But I can vouch for the fact
   that this is one of the most beautifully
   illustrated editions of WALDEN that I have
   ever seen. It puts our American editions
   to shame. TSB #30.

   reviews: INFORMATION ONSDAG, November 23.
            1949, p. 4.
            KRISTELIGT DAGBLAD, November 23,
            1949.

1949   Leipzig: Dieterich'schen Verlagsbuchhandlung.
       Translated into German by Anneliese Dengel.
          A free translation which, despite fortunate
          and precise phrases, does not suggest Tho-
          reau's sentence sense or the texture of his
          style. Includes an introduction by Walther
          Fischer and selections from "Civil Disobe-
          dience" and "Life without Principle." TSB
          #105.

195?   Athinae: Atlantis. Translated into Greek by
       J. Zaharakis.

1950   Cairo: Societe Orientale Publicite. An Arabic
       translation with the Heritage Club plates.

1950   Tokyo: Mikasa Shobo. Translated into Japanese
       by Miyanishi Hoitsu.

1950   Prague: ?   . Translated into Czech by   ?   .

1951   ? : Iwanami. Translated into Japanese by
       Saburo Kamiyoshi. Entitled MORI NO SEIKATSU.

1951   ? : Yotokusha. Translated into Japanese by
       Katashi Sakai. Entitled WALDEN KOHAN NITE.

1953   Tokyo: Kadikawa Shoten. Translated into Japanese
       by Akira Tomita. Entitled MORI NO SEIKATSU.

1953   Oslo: Dreyers Forlag. Translated into Norwegian
       by Andreas Eriksen. Illustrated by Mads Stage.
       Entitled LIVIT I SKOGENE.

1953   Rio de Janiero: Revista Branca. Translated into
       Portugeuse by E. C. Caldas. Entitled WALDEN E
       OUTROS ESCRITOS.
          A translation of the Modern Library edition,
          including Brooks Atkinson's introduction.

1954   Helsinki: Werner Soderstrom Osakeyhtio. Trans-

267

lated into Finnish by Mikko Kilpi. Entitled
ELAMAA METSASSA.

1955   Kerala: Sree Ram Vilas Press. Translated into
Malayalam.

1957   ? : Kenkyusha. Edited with notes by Kinsaku
Shinoda.

1957   ? : Yamaguchi-shoten. Edited with notes by
Masru Shiga.

1960   New Delhi: Sahitya Akademi. Translated into
Malayalam by Sree Krishna Sarma.

1960   New Delhi: Maktaba Jamia. Translated by Ali
Abbas Husaini. Entitled VALDEN.

1961   Vienna and Munich: Manutiuspresse. Translated
into German with an afterword by Erika Ziha.
Entitled WALDEN: LEBEN EIN UNVERSUCHTES EXPERIMENT
A re-write of Thoreau's text according to
modern journalistic standards. Ziha reproduces expressions characteristic of Lang's
translation. The sixth translation of WALDEN
is the most "readable" and the least accurate

1962   New Delhi: S. Chand and Company. Preface by S.
Schindler.

1962   Moscow: ? .
The first translation of WALDEN into Russian
since the Revolution.

1963   Jerusalem: Bialik Institute. Translated into
Hebrew by Hanoch Kal'ai. Introduction by Simon
Halkin. Illustrated by Louise Shatz. Entitled
VOLDEN (CHAYIM BAYABAR) AND MERIEZRACHI.

review: JERUSALEM POST, January 25, 1963.

1964   New Delhi: Sahitya Akademi. Translated into
Bengali by Kirankumar Ray.

1964   New Delhi: Sahitya Akademi. Translated into
Kannada by Devudu Narasimha Sastri.

1964   New Delhi: Sahitya Akademi. Translated into
Hindi by Banarasidas Chaturvedi.

1964   Meimar: Kiepenheuer. Translated into German by
Franz Meyer.

1964   Milano: Rizzoli. Translated into Italian by
Pietro Sanavio. Entitled WALDEN OVVERO LA VITA
NEI BOSCHI.

1965   New Delhi: Sahitya Akademi. Translated into
        Gujarati by S. G. Betai.

1965   New Delhi: Sahitya Akademi. Translated into
        Punjabi by Dr. Gopal Singh.

[1965] Taipei: Cheng Wen Pub. Service. Translated into
        Chinese by Huang Chien P'ing.

1967   Paris: Aubier Editions. Introduction and trans-
        lation by G. Landre-Augier. Entitled WALDEN OU
        LA VIE SANS LES BOIS.
            A bilingual edition with French and English
            texts on opposite pages.

1967   Paris: Gallimard. Translated into French by L.
        Fabulet. Entitled WALDEN OU LA VIE DANS LES
        BOIS.
            A new edition without the preface.

n.d.   Guntur, India: Maruthi Book Depot. With notes
        by P. Ramachandra Rao.
            Abridged edition with 244 pages of notes
            and comments.

n.d.   New Delhi: Jamia. Translated into Urdu by Ali'
        Abbas Husaini.

n.d.   New Delhi: Sahitya Akademi. Translated into
        Malayalam by Srikrishnasaima. Entitled WALDEN
        ATHAVA ARAMJAJIVITAM.

n.d.   Buenos Aires: Emecé Editores. Translated into
        Spanish by Vedia. Entitled WALDEN o LA VIDA EN
        LOS BOSQUES.

n.d.   London: Blackie. Translated into Braille.

--WALDEN, selections from
    "The Battle of the Ants," ENCORE (July, 1945), pp. 70-76.
            A reprinting of a portion of WALDEN with
            an excerpt from an essay by Kirby and Spence
            on ants which Thoreau used as a source.

    "Building a House at Walden," THE PRACTICE OF EXPOSITION,
    edited by Bachelor and Haley. New York: Appleton-
    Century, 1947. pp. 111-121.
            Excerpt from WALDEN.

    CHAPTERS FROM WALDEN. London: Macmillan, 1921. English
    Literature Series for Schools Edition.

    [Excerpts from WALDEN], HYMNS FOR THE CELEBRATION OF
    LIFE, edited by Arthur Foote II, et al. Boston: Beacon,
    1964. Responsive Reading #395.

"Higher Laws," THE COLLEGE ANTHOLOGY. Chicago: Scott Foresman, 1949. I, 261-269.

"Higher Laws," TREASURY OF PHILOSOPHY, edited by Dagobert D. Runes. New York: Philosophical Library, 1955. pp. 1169-1173. With commentary.

"Higher Laws," BETTER READING, edited by Blair and Gerber. Chicago: Scott, Foresman, 1945. pp. 282-293. Chapter from WALDEN.

HOUSE-WARMING AND WINTER VISITORS. Camden: Haddon Craftsmen, 1936.

"The Loon," THE BIRD WATCHER'S ANTHOLOGY, edited by Roger Tory Peterson. New York: Harcourt, Brace, 1957. pp. 184-186.

"The Pond," THE BOOK OF NATURALISTS, edited by William Beebe. New York: Knopf, 1944. pp. 73-84. Reprinting a chapter from WALDEN.

THE PONDS. New York: Comet Press, 1949. Designed and illustrated by Edwin B. Koleby. Edition limited to 1500 copies. A perfectly delightful reprint of a chapter from WALDEN, issued as a Christmas greeting. TSB #31.

"Reading," ENCORE, Vol. I (February, 1942), 102-110. A reprint of the third chapter of WALDEN.

"Reading" and "Where I Lived," THOUGHT AND EXPERIENCE IN PROSE. New York: Oxford, 1951.

SELECTIONS FROM THOREAU'S WALDEN, with introduction and illustrations by Raymond Barrio. Sunnyvale, Calif.: Ventura Press, [1968]. A series of mimeographed selections illustrated with brush drawings.

SELECTION FROM THOREAU'S WALDEN. Tokyo: ? , 1933.

"Solitude," SELECT ESSAYS, edited by J. Matsumoto and K. Iwata. [Tokyo]: Kobunsha, [1967?], 36-51.

"Sounds," READING FOR IDEAS, edited by Harrison and Christian. New York: Farrar and Rinehart, 1943. Book contains also Dallas Lore Sharp's "Turtle Eggs for Agassiz."

"Thoreau's Thoughts," CANADIAN NATURE, XII (January, 1950), 10.

"Truth Alone Wears Well," U.S.A., Vol. I, No. 11, pp. 58-63.

A reprinting of part of the final chapter
of WALDEN in this OWI magazine for distribution abroad only. Copies are not available
in this country. This is also published in
French, Spanish, Portuguese, Italian, Greek,
Russian and Norwegian. A long introduction
is a fine brief study of Thoreau's significance.

TWO EXTRACTS FROM THE CONCLUDING CHAPTERS OF WALDEN.
Chappaqua: Bibliophile Press, 1930.

WALDEN, OR LIFE IN THE WOODS, edited with notes by H.
Demizu. Tokyo: Kairyudo, 19?.

WALDEN OR LIFE IN THE WOODS. Tokyo(?): Sanseido, 1948.
Selections from WALDEN in English with intro-
duction and notes in Japanese by T. Hijikata.
In the Universal English Series.

WALDEN, with introduction and notes by Kinsaku Shinoda.
"Kenkyusha Pocket English Series." Tokyo: Kenkyusha,
1929.
Prints four chapters with an introduction
and notes.

WHAT I LIVED FOR. New York: Archway Press, 1946.
This little volume is a gem for those who
collect the really unusual in Thoreauviana.
It is a selection of what is probably the
most famous section of WALDEN, the "I went
to the woods..." paragraphs from the second
chapter of the book. They are reproduced
in facsimile of the handwriting of the noted
artist George Salter and illustrated with
tiny line-drawings by Mr. Salter. The whole
is beautifully bound and boxed. Probably
nothing like this has been done since the
days of medieval manuscript production. So
if you want a really unusual book for your
library or if you wish to call a friend's
attention to what are probably the most
significant passages in the whole of Thoreau's
masterpiece, this is the book to purchase.

WHERE I LIVED AND WHAT I LIVED FOR. Waltham Saint
Lawrence: Golden Cockerel Press, 1924.

WHERE I LIVED AND WHAT I LIVED FOR. New York:
Chaucer Head, 1924.

"Where I Lived, and What I Lived For," INTELLIGENT READ-
ING, edited by Tenney. New York: Crofts, 1938. pp. 349-
358.

"Where I Lived, and What I Lived For," EFFECTIVE READING.

Boston: Houghton Mifflin, 1944. pp. 421-429.

"Where I Lived, and What I Lived For," "Brute Neighbors," DOMINANT TYPES IN BRITISH AND AMERICAN LITERATURE, edited by Wimberly and Shaw. New York: Harper, 1949.
    Reprinting two chapters from WALDEN.

"Why I Went to the Woods," A TREASURY OF THE FAMILIAR, edited by Ralph L. Woods. New York: Macmillan, 1942. pp. 361-367.
    An excerpt from WALDEN.

"Winter Animals," WYOMING WILDLIFE (December, 1958).
    Reprinted from WALDEN.

THE WISDOM OF THOREAU. New York: Philosophical Library, 1967.
    A reprint of the central chapters of WALDEN.

--WALDEN, translations of selections from
EINFACHHEIT UND HOHERE GESETZE, translated by Augusta B. Brenner.
    A translation into German of the "Where I Lived and What I Lived For" and "Higher Laws" chapters of WALDEN, with an epilogue by Augusta B. Brenner.

JOURNAL D'UN HOMME LIBRE, translated into French by Genevieve Brallion-Zeude. Paris: Nouveaux Horizons [Editions Seghers], 1965. pp. 214.
    Extracts from WALDEN and "Civil Disobedience."

"Nei Boschi di Walden," VOLONTA [Pistoia, Italy], XXI (January, 1968), 21-24.
    Text in Italian from WALDEN.

"El Pensamiento vivo de Thoreau," CENIT [France] (May, 1958), 2461-2462.
    Excerpts from WALDEN, translated into Spanish by V. Munoz.

THOREAU-CHE SHRAMAJIVAN [Marathi], translated into Hindu by Vaman J. Junte. Pavnar [Wardha]: Paramdham Vidjapith 1957 (2nd edition).
    Translation of the "Economy" chapter of WALDEN

"De Walden o la vida en los bosques," CENIT, VIII (March, 1958), 2375-2376.
    Translation of excerpts from WALDEN into Spanish by V. Munoz.

WOFUR ICH LEBTE, translated by Fritz Krohel. (Munich, 1950).
    Brief selection from WALDEN.

--WALDEN, contemporary reviews of
GRAHAM'S MAGAZINE, XLV (September, 1854),
298-300.
NATIONAL ANTI-SLAVERY STANDARD, December 16,
1854, p. 3.
NATIONAL MAGAZINE, V (September, 1854), 284-
285.
PROVIDENCE [R.I.] JOURNAL, August 11, 1854.
SOUTHERN LITERARY MESSENGER, XX (September,
1854), 575.
EMERSON SOCIETY QUARTERLY, VII (1957), 43.
Reprinted from the MONITOR of June 7, 1862.

--WALDEN, quotations from
"The Good Old Days or Housing a Hundred Years Ago,"
SMITHSONIAN INSTITUTION EMPLOYEES FEDERAL CREDIT UNION.
Letter No. 138. August 1, 1947.
A quotation from WALDEN on the cost of build-
ing the hut.

--A WALDEN CALENDAR. Waterville, Maine: Carl and Clara
Weber, 1953.
A calendar for 1954 with quotations from WALDEN
for each month.

--THE WALK TO LAND'S END. New York: New American Library,
1965.
A condensed, paperback edition with vocabulary
reduced to 2,000 words "for readers for whom
English is a second language."

--"Walking," IN PRAISE OF WALKING. Westport, Conn.:
Redcoat Press, 1943.

--"Walking," THE PLEASURES OF WALKING, edited by E. V.
Mitchell. New York: Vanguard Press, 1948. pp. 129-172.
A new edition of a delightful little anthology
for inveterate hikers, which for the first time
includes Thoreau's memorable essay on the subject.

--"Walking," The Pocket Reader. New York: Pocket Books,
Inc., 1941.

translation: OM AT VANDRE, translated into Danish
by Ole Jacobson. Copenhagen: Kunst og Kultur,
"Walking" and "A Winter Walk."

--A WEEK ON THE CONCORD AND MERRIMACK RIVERS, editions of
1950   Tokyo(?): Hokuseido Press. Entitled A SHORTENED
VERSION OF A WEEK ON THE CONCORD AND MERRIMACK
RIVERS.
With an excellent introduction and notes
by R. H. Blyth.

1954   Boston: Little, Brown. Arranged with notes by
Dudley C. Lunt. Illustrated by Henry Bugbee
Kane. Entitled THE CONCORD AND MERRIMACK RIVERS.
Messrs. Lunt and Kane continue the editing
and illustrating of Thoreau's works which
they started several years ago for the W.
W. Norton Co. in a volume to match that in
format, design, and concept. Here they have
reduced both the contents and the title of
Thoreau's first book approximately one third.
They have removed all the extraneous essays
which Thoreau so gratuitously inserted into
the original text. Ordinarily we are in
haste to disavow such violation of old classics, but we readily admit here that they
have made an improvement. "The Concord and
Merrimack Rivers" is a much more readable
volume than the original book. It flows
smoothly, with no snags or sandbars in the
way. It reveals itself as one of the finest
of all travel books-as H. M. Tomlinson once
called it. It is not, however, as its editor
claims, the first edition to so unclutter
the text. In 1937, when H. S. Canby edited
the omnibus volume THE WORKS OF THOREAU for
Houghton Mifflin, he made a similar reduction
of the text. However, Mr. Lunt's edition
does have helpful explanatory notes and the
superb illustrations by Mr. Kane. TSB #49.

reviews: APPALACHIA, XXX (June, 1955), 451-
452, by Christopher McKee.
BOSTON POST, December 26, 1954.
BOSTON SUNDAY POST, December 26,
1954.
CLEVELAND PLAIN DEALER, February
11, 1955.
CONCORD [Mass.] JOURNAL, October
?, 1954.
NEW YORK WORLD TELEGRAM, November
10, 1954.

1961   New York: New American Library.
After years of having no inexpensive edition
of A WEEK available, here is the second paperback edition out in a few months. This is
less than half the price of the other, but
has a less sturdy binding and smaller margins.
The type readability is about the same in
the two. The brief foreword by Denham Sut-
cliffe manages to make a fairly large number
of misstatements of fact, but it does show
a sympathetic understanding of Thoreau's ideas.

review: NATIONAL FISHERMAN (June, 1962), by
John Gardner.

1961   Boston: Houghton Mifflin. Sentry Edition.
        At last an inexpensive paperback edition
        of Thoreau's first book. A good clear type
        and a sturdy binding as well. TSB #76.

        review: THE SKIPPER (February, 1963), 35.

1961   New York: Crowell.

1963   New York: Rinehart. Edited and introduction by
        Walter Harding.
        Based on 1868 edition, with revisions and
        an enlarged table of quotation identifications.

1963   Cleveland: Micro Photo. Duopage facsimile of
        the first edition.

1964   Cleveland: Bell and Howell. Duopage photographic
        facsimile of the 1849 first edition.

1965   New Haven: College and University Press. Master-
        works of Literature Series. Notes by Dudley C.
        Lunt. Illustrated by H. B. Kane. Under the title:
        THE CONCORD AND MERRIMACK. (paper).
        Reprint of a shortened version of A WEEK.

1966   New York: Crowell. Decorations by Clare Leighton.
        "Apollo Edition."
        Paperback reprint with large, clear type.

1966   [New York]: West Virginia Pulp and Paper Co.
        Foreword by Jean A. Bradnick.
        A boxed limited, beautifully illustrated
        edition, distributed privately as a
        Christmas present by the company.

1967   New Delhi, India: Eurasia Publishing House.
        Introduction by K. R. Chandrasekharan. Classics
        in American Literature Series.

--A WEEK ON THE CONCORD AND MERRIMACK RIVERS, selections from
    "The Call of the River," ENCORE (February, 1947), 97.

    "Hannah Dustin," MURDER: PLAIN AND FANCIFUL WITH SOME
    MILDER MALEFACTIONS, edited by Sandoe. New York:
    Sheridan House, 1948. pp. 300-302.
                We didn't believe it until we saw it our-
                selves, but here is Thoreau as the writer
                of a murder mystery. It is an excerpt from
                A WEEK. A unique piece for your Thoreau
                collection--and good reading if you are a
                whodunit fan.

--A WEEK ON THE CONCORD AND MERRIMACK RIVERS, translations
    of selections from

"El Camino de Sudbury," EL AUTO URUGUAYO [Montevideo, Uruguay] (September, 1958). Translated into Spanish by V. Munoz.

"El Pescador," EL AUTO URUGUAYO, (August, 1958). Translated by V. Munoz.

UBER DIE FREUNDSCHAFT. Aschaffenburg: ? , 1946.
      From the "Wednesday" chapter of Thoreau's
      A WEEK ON THE CONCORD AND MERRIMACK RIVERS.

--A WEEK ON THE CONCORD AND MERRIMACK RIVERS, contemporary
   reviews of
          GODEY'S LADY'S BOOK, XXXIX (September, 1849), 223.
          LONDON SPECTATOR, XXII (October 13, 1849), 975.
          WESTMINSTER REVIEW, LII (January, 1850), 309-310. A favorable review printed in England.
          THE ATHENAEUM (October 27, 1849), 27.
          PICTORIAL NATIONAL LIBRARY, III (1849), 60-61.

--WILD APPLES. Worcester [Mass.]: Achille J. St. Onge, 1956. A beautifully printed, miniature book (measuring only 3"x 1 3/4"), designed by the great Bruce Rogers (his only miniature book), printed by the Marchbanks Press, bound in full pigskin, and stamped in gold. A real treasure for collectors of fine books and a unique addition to any Thoreau library. TSB #58.

--WORKS, editions of
1947 London: Allen and Unwin. Selected and edited by
      H. S. Canby. Entitled THE WORKS OF THOREAU.
      An English reprint.

1963 Cleveland: Micro Photo. 20 Vol. Duopage facsimile
      of the Walden Edition. Entitled THE WRITINGS OF
      HENRY DAVID THOREAU.

1964 Cleveland: Bell and Howell. Duopage photographic
      facsimile of the 1906 Walden Edition. Entitled
      THE WRITINGS.
      Volumes available separately.

1969 New York: AMS Press. 20 Vols. Entitled WRITINGS.
      A facsimile reproduction of the 1906 edition.

--WORKS, selections from
EXCERPTS FROM WORKS OF HENRY DAVID THOREAU, edited by
Arthur G. Volkman. Wilmington, Delaware: The Archaeological Society of Delaware, [1943]. Paper No. 5.
      "The writings of Henry David Thoreau, on
      the amenities of collecting Indian relics."

also in: BULLETIN OF ARCHAEOLOGICAL SOCIETY
OF DELAWARE, 11, 1962, 23-32.

EXCERPTS FROM WRITINGS ON LIBERTY. Chicago: Norman
Press, 1943.
> Produced by a class on typography taught
> by Norman W. Forgue at the American Academy
> of Arts in Chicago.

THE PORTABLE THOREAU, edited by Carl Bode. New York:
Viking, 1947.
> An excellent new anthology of Thoreau's most
> important writings, well edited, with a thor-
> ough introduction, chronology, bibliography,
> and notes on each selection by the editor of
> Thoreau's poems. It is the only inexpensive
> anthology with excerpts from Thoreau's letters,
> poems and journals. It contains selections
> from all of Thoreau's books and the entire
> WALDEN. Our only objection is that it entirely
> omits the important John Brown essays. TSB
> #19.
>
> review: CHICAGO TRIBUNE, March 9, 1947, by
> Frederic Babcock.

THE PORTABLE THOREAU, edited by Carl Bode. New York:
Viking, 1957.
> Revised, paperbound edition of earlier
> anthology.

THE PORTABLE THOREAU: REVISED EDITION, edited by Carl
Bode. New York: Viking, 1964.
> Introduction has been altered, letters
> eliminated, John Brown material added, and
> a new epilogue added, as well as bibliog-
> raphy brought up to date. One of the more
> comprehensive anthologies of Thoreau's writing
> available. TSB #89.

READINGS FROM HENRY D. THOREAU, edited by Yukiji
Tsutani. Tokyo: Taibundo, 1967.
> Selections in English with notes in Japanese.

THE RIVER. New York: Twayne, 1963.
> A selection of Thoreau's comments on his
> hikes, boating trips, and skating trips along
> the Concord rivers, arranged, edited and an-
> noted by Dudley C. Lunt, and illustrated by
> Henry Bugbee Kane. An interesting selection
> that emphasizes just how large a part the
> rivers of Concord played in Thoreau's life.
> The illustrations by Kane, as usual, are out-
> standing. TSB #84.

reviews: CONCORD JOURNAL, July 4, 1963.
NEW YORK TIMES BOOK REVIEW, July
7, 1963.

THE RIVER, edited by Dudley Lunt, illustrated by H.
B. Kane. New Haven: College and University Press,
1965. "Masterworks of Literature Series."
Paperback reprint of selections from Thoreau's writings on rivers.

SELECTED WRITINGS, edited by Lewis Leary. New York:
Appleton-Century-Crofts, 1958.
A volume in the paper-covered Crofts Classics
editions. Contains "Civil Disobedience,"
"Life without Principle," "My Prayer," and
selections from WALDEN and the JOURNAL. It
is good to have the two essays and selections
from the JOURNAL available in a cheap edition,
but it does not seem likely that many will
feel satisfied with a cut version of WALDEN.

SELECTED WRITINGS ON NATURE AND LIBERTY, edited by
Oscar Cargill. New York: Liberal Arts Press, 1952.
A paper-bound selection from Thoreau in
"The American Heritage Series." Contains
a chronology, an introduction (rather care-
lessly written), a brief bibliography, six
poems, "Civil Disobedience," "Walking," an
excerpt from each of WALDEN, CAPE COD, and
A WEEK, seven letters, and annotations.
Thus it does contain a little material not
in other inexpensive editions of Thoreau,
but so much of it is fragmentary that no well-
rounded picture is acheived. TSB #43.

translation: ESCRITOS SELECTOS SOBRE
NATURALELA & LIBERTAD. Buenos Aires: ? ,
1960. A translation into Spanish.

"Selections," AMERICAN MIND, edited by Warfel, Gabriel
and Williams. New York: American Book Co., 1947.

"Selections," ANGLING IN AMERICA: ITS EARLY HISTORY AND
LITERATURE, edited by Charles E. Goodspeed. Boston:
Houghton Mifflin, 1939.
Thoreau on fishing.

"Selection," MASTERS OF AMERICAN LITERATURE, edited by
Pochman and Allen. New York: Macmillan, 1949. pp. 791-
874. For college use.

"Selections," THE TREASURE CHEST, edited by J. Donald
Adams. New York: Dutton, 1946. pp. 153-177.
A group of short selections from Thoreau's
writings admirably chosen in that rather

than reprinting the bits found in every anthology, Mr. Adams has delved into the JOURNALS and come out with some new selections that display perfectly Thoreau's crispness of style. It is a significant sign of Thoreau's growing stature that Mr. Adams, the editor of the NEW YORK TIMES BOOK REVIEW, devotes more space to our Concordian than any other writer in this "anthology of contemplative prose." TSB #16.

SOUNDINGS. Franklin, New Hampshire: Hillside Press, 1964.
"Selections from the Journals, Walden, and The Week." A miniature edition.

THOREAU: PEOPLE, PRINCIPLES, AND POLITICS, edited [with an introduction] by Milton Meltzer. New York: Hill and Wang, 1963.
In both paperback and hard-cover editions. A collection of Thoreau's social and political essays and comments in his journals and letters, edited in chronological order so that one can watch the development of his thoughts.

THOREAU TODAY: SELECTIONS FROM HIS WRITINGS, edited by Helen Barber Morrison. New York: Comet Press, 1957.
Because Mrs. Morrison felt that Thoreau still "had something helpful to say to readers today about the conduct of their lives," she has gathered together several hundred notable quotations from his writings and organized them alphabetically by topic. Her book thus offers a handy cross-index to Thoreau's thoughts that is particularly helpful because the source of each quotation is adequately indicated. Odell Shepard has written a brief introduction. TSB #62.

THE THOUGHTS OF THOREAU, edited by Edwin Way Teale. New York: Dodd, Mead, 1962.
A new anthology of epigrams and aphorisms selected from Thoreau and arranged under such topics as "Freedom," "Birds," "Possessions." Teale not only includes the familiar quotations, but through his long study of Thoreau has found many more worth repeating. A stimulating collection and a handy cross-index to Thoreau's thought. Also available in deluxe edition. TSB #82.

THE THOUGHTS OF THOREAU, edited by Edwin Way Teale. New York: Dodd, Mead, 1963. Paperback Apollo Edition.
Reprint of one of the best anthologies.

"Three essays," THE DEMOCRATIC SPIRIT, edited by
Bernard Smith. New York: Knopf, 1941.
>Edited with an introduction.

"Travel in Concord," GREAT AMERICAN NATURE WRITING,
edited by Joseph Wood Krutch . New York: Sloane, 1950.
pp. 96-125.
>Selections from Thoreau's nature writings in
>what is one of the most beautifully designed
>and edited anthologies I have seen. Also
>includes a long essay by Prof. Krutch on
>American nature writers. TSB #34.

--WORKS, contemporary review of
>DIAL, XLI (October 16, 1906), 232-235 and
>XLII (February 16, 1907), 107-110. [1906-
>Walden edition reviewed].

--WORKS, translations of selections from
CORATGE CIVIC. Barcelona: Edicions D'Aportacio
Catalana, 1967.
>Catalan translations of "Paradise (to be)
>Regained," "Civil Disobedience," and "Life
>without Principle."

DESOBEIR: TRADUIT DE L'ANGLAIS AVEC UN AVANTPROPOS
PAR LEON BAZALGETTE. Paris: Rieder, 1921.
>Includes "Life without Principle," "Civil
>Disobedience," "Slavery in Massachusetts,"
>etc.

ESCRITOS SELECTOS SOBRE NATURALEZA Y LIBERTAD, translated by Mario A. Marino. Buenos Aires: Agora, 1960.
>Selected Writings on Nature and Liberty.

UN FILOSOFO EN LOS BOSQUES. Buenos Aires: Ediciones
Iman, 1937.
>Selections from Thoreau's writings and
>essays on Thoreau by Emerson and Waldo
>Frank, all translated into Spanish by
>Horacio E. Roque.

HENRI DI THORO YAMCE NIVDAK LEKH, translated by Pand-
harinath Balvant Rege. Bombay: G. P. Parchure Prakashan Mandir, 1959.
>Five essays and excerpts from his letters.

MAHATMA THORONI VICARSRSTI, translated by Natvar
Malavi. Bombay: Vora, 1961.
>Selections from the writings of Thoreau.

OPERA SCELTE. Venezia: Neri Pozza Editore, 1958.
>An omnibus of "Natural History of Mas-
>sachusetts," "Wild Apples," A WEEK, WALDEN,
>excerpts from CAPE COD, "Civil Disobedience,"

and "A Plea for Captain John Brown" translated into Italian by Piero Sanavio.

SHIMIN TO SHITE HANKO. Tokyo(?): Iwanami, 1949.
Translation into Japanese of "Civil Diso-
bedience," "Life without Principle," "A
Plea for Captain John Brown," and "Walking."

SHIZEN TO JINSEI. Translated into Japanese by Yosh-
ikatsu Motono. Tokio: Shin-ei-Sha, ? .
A collection of Thoreau's essays.

SHIZENJIN NO MEISO [Meditations of a Recluse]. Translated into Japanese by Sen Yanagida. Tokyo: Shunjusha,
1921.
A miscellaneous collection of Thoreau's
essays.

THOREAU GENKOROKU. Translated into Japanese by Kojiro
Nishikawa. Naigai, 1912.
"Words by Thoreau."

THOREAU NO KOTOBA. Kyoto, ? , 1947.
"Golden Sayings of Thoreau," edited by
Katsushi Shiga.

THOREAU NO KOTOBA. Translated into Japanese by Masaru
Shiga. Nishimurashoten, 1949.
"Words by Thoreau."

THOREAU YANCHE NIVDAK LEKH. Translated into Marathi
by Pandharinah B. Rege. Bombay: G. P. Parchure prakashan mandir, (195?).
Selected writings.

DIE WELT UND ICH. Translated by Fritz Krokel. Guter-
sloh: Bertelsmann Verlag, 1951.
Combines biographical material with selections
from A WEEK, WALDEN, THE MAINE WOODS, a
variety of essays, and Thoreau's letters and
journals. In this fine anthology Krokel
provides the German student with the essence
of Thoreau. TSB #105.

WROTE THOREAUS. Minden [Germany]: J. C. C. Bruns,
circa 1900?.
Translated by Gerhard Guthers. An early
German edition of Thoreau apparently on
the plan of Dreiser's recent LIVING THOUGHTS
OF THOREAU.

--WORKS, quotations from
AMERICA THE BEAUTIFUL IN THE WORDS OF, edited by
Robert L. Polley. New York: William Morrow and Co,
1966.

A large 9" x 12" exhibition format volume
of striking nature photographs, most in color,
with selected quotations from Thoreau as commentary. Some of the photographs are of
areas Thoreau never knew. But other than
that, this is a choice and beautiful volume
that both nature lovers and Thoreau enthusiasts will treasure. TSB #95.

"Be Not Simply Good. Be Good for Something." Rancho
Santa Fe, Calif.: American Educational Publishers, 1965.
A 22" x 5 1/2" poster.

BOOKS AND READING. Ysleta, Texas: Edwin B. Hill, ? .
More quotations from Thoreau's writings.

HENRY DAVID THOREAU: QUOTATIONS FROM HIS WRITINGS.
Selected by Amy W. Smith. Worcester, Mass: Achille
J. St. Onge, 1948.
A deluxe miniature edition limited to 750
copies printed by the Merrymount Press.
Something for the collector of unusual
Thoreauana.

THE LIVING THOUGHTS OF THOREAU PRESENTED BY THEODORE
DREISER. Greenwich, Conn.: Fawcett, 1958.
In 1939 Theodore Dreiser compiled a strange
mosaic of Thoreau's thoughts on religion,
war, evil, friendship, etc. Unfortunately
he did not bother to identify his sources
and he so twisted Thoreau's thoughts that
one reviewer at the time was given the impression that Thoreau was a fascist! Neither
will one get an adequate impression of Thoreau's style from this volume, since Dreiser
eliminated all of Thoreau's specific examples
and thus made him as abstract as Emerson.
The paperback reprint contains all the faults
of the original edition and adds to them a
cover which blares out with "Genius? Prophet?
Madman? A fascinating study of one of America's strangest heroes." TSB #65.

"The Meaning of Life," THINK (March, 1951).
A series of quotations.

PHILOSOPHY OF NATURAL LIFE: COLLECTED THOUGHTS OF
THOREAU. Translated into Russian by Z. G. Nakashdze.
Moscow, 1903.

"Portraits of Winter," EASTERN FAMILY OF FINE PAPERS
[St. Paul, Minn.], I (January, 1967), 9-12.
Quotations illustrated with photographs.

"The Qualities of Nature," COUNTRY BEAUTIFUL, V (1966),
34-49.

Quotations from Thoreau illustrated with
beautiful color photographs.

ONE THOUSAND BEAUTIFUL THINGS, edited by Barrows.
Chicago: People's Book Club, 1947.
Many brief quotations, passim.

THOREAU ON MAN AND NATURE, edited by Arthur Volkman.
Mount Vernon: Peter Pauper Press, 1960.
Volkman, with his sensitivity for gem-like
quotations from Thoreau, and Peter Pauper
Press, with its craft for fine printing,
have joined in producing one of the loveliest
gift-book editions of Thoreau there is. The
quotations are chosen from the full range
of Thoreau's works and cover topics from
nature to man to God to happiness. It is
remarkable how many precisely right quotations
are included. The book is illustrated with
actual leaf prints which are not only fully
appropriate but things of beauty. This is
a volume which Thoreau lovers will be happy
to shower upon their friends. TSB #71.

reviews: VOLUNTAD (August, 1960).
WILMINGTON [Del.] MORNING NEWS,
April 19, 1960.

"Thoreau on Uncommon Schools," NEW YORK HERALD TRIBUNE,
April 30, 1944.
A WALDEN quotation.

THOREAUS WORTE, translated by Gutherz Gerhard. Minden:
Bruns, 1909.
A selection of quotations from Thoreau's
works.

"Thoughts from Thoreau," THE VEGETARIAN MESSENGER AND
HEALTH REVIEW [Manchester, England], XLV (February,
1948), 39.
Quotations with portrait.

THE THOUGHTS OF THOREAU, edited by Edwin Way Teale.
New York: Dodd, Mead, 1962.
A new anthology of epigrams and aphorisms
selected from Thoreau and arranged under
such topics as "Freedom," "Birds," "Possessions." Teale not only includes the familiar
quotations, but through his long study of
Thoreau has found many more worth repeating.
A stimulating collection and a handy cross-
index to Thoreau's thought. Also available
in deluxe edition. TSB #82.

reviews: AUDUBON MAGAZINE (July, 1963).

CAPITAL TIMES [Madison, Wisc.],
December 20, 1962.
CHICAGO TRIBUNE, December 9, 1962.
CONCORD JOURNAL, December 6, 1962.
NATIONAL PARKS MAGAZINE (January,
1963).
NEW YORK TIMES, November 26, 1962.

"Words that Will Live," WORKER [New York], December 14,
1954.
Quotations from Thoreau in the Communist
newspaper.

"Why should we not meet..." [Chicago: Privately printed
for Daniel E. Hager, 1946].
A quotation from Thoreau printed for framing.

THE WISDOM OF THOREAU. New York: Pyramid Books, 1968.
Selected quotations from his writings. A
"Little Paperback Classic."

"A written word is the choicest of relics." Geneseo,
New York: Gaudeamus Press, 1966.
Limited edition of a broadside.

--A YANKEE IN CANADA. Montreal: Harvest House, 1961.
The first separate printing of this "excursion"
with notes and introduction by Maynard Gert-
ler. An Emulation Book.

reviews: CANADIAN LITERATURE, XII (Spring,
1962), 79-80.
WHITEHORSE [Yukon] STAR, January
27, 1964.

--A YANKEE IN CANADA, WITH ANTI-SLAVERY AND REFORM PAPERS.
New York: Haskell House, 1968.
Facsimile reprint of 1892 edition.

translation: UN YANKEE AU CANADA. Translated into French by Adrien Therio. Montreal:
Les Editions de l'Homme, 1962.

--and Ralph Waldo Emerson. CIVIL DISOBEDIENCE AND, SELF-
RELIANCE, edited with notes by Koh Kasegawa. Tokyo:
Hokuseido Press, 1960.
Text in English, notes and introduction in
Japanese.

"The Thoreau House in Boston," TSB #17.
The article includes an excerpt from RAMBLES IN OLD
BOSTON, NEW ENGLAND (Boston, 1887), edited by Edward
G. Porter. pp. 116-117.

"Thoreau House Museum Plans Are in Danger," NEW YORK HERALD
      TRIBUNE, August 8, 1948.
            On unsuccessful drive to buy the Thoreau-Alcott
            House.

"Thoreau Island," DOWN EAST (October, 1967), p. 19.
            On the naming of an island in Grand Lake Matagamon
            in Maine for Thoreau.

"Thoreau in Holland," TSB #14.
            Included is a short history by C. W. Bieling of "the
            little socialistic community named Walden founded
            near Amsterdam by Frederik van Eeden." Also included
            is Bieling's translation of van Eeden's FORWORD TO
            THE DUTCH EDITION OF WALDEN (written in Walden, Nether-
            lands, September 7, 1902).

"Thoreau in Minnesota," TSB #57.
            A photostatic copy of "A Week on the Frontier" from
            the MINNEAPOLIS STATE ATLAS for July 3, 1861.

"Thoreau in Stained Glass," TSB #32.
            Included is a reproduction of the stained glass
            window at Trinity College in Hartford, Connecticut.

"The Thoreau Library of Alfred W. Hosmer," TSB #30.

"Thoreau Lyceum Open House," CONCORD JOURNAL, December 8, 1966.

Thoreau, Mary. "The Thoreau Centenary," JERSEY WEEKLY POST,
      May 12, 1962.
            A centennial tribute to Thoreau in an Isle of Jersey
            newspaper by a distant relative of Thoreau.

"Thoreau Memorial at Site of Cabin Completed Monday," CONCORD
      JOURNAL, April 1, 1948, p. 1.

"Thoreau, a Natural Maverick," SENIOR SCHOLASTIC, XCIV (March
      14, 1969), 11.

"Thoreau on Fighting Injustice," DES MOINES [Iowa] REGISTER,
      August 7, 1967.
            An editorial.

"Thoreau on Housing," TOMORROW'S TOWN (April, 1947).
            An excerpt from Thoreau in the publication of the
            National Committee on Housing, Inc.

"Thoreau on the Price of a House," NEW YORK SUN, May 12, 1947.

"Thoreau on Trial," REVIEW OF RESEARCH AND REFLECTION, I
      (Winter, 1960), 24-27.
            Defends Thoreau from Buranelli's recent attack.

"Thoreau--oppdaget i Norge," NORDISK TIDENDE [Brooklyn, N. Y.],
      August 9, 1962.

On Grimnes' winning trip to U. S. from Norway
for his essay on Thoreau.

"Thoreau Pencils," TSB #24.
Included is a reproduction of an original Thoreau
pencil wrapper.

"Thoreau: Pflicht zum Ungehorsam," DER, SPIEGAL, December 4,
1967.
On the current influence of "Civil Disobedience"
in Germany.

"A Thoreau scenario," "The Talk of the Town," THE NEW YORKER
(February 12, 1944), p. 16.

THOREAU SOCIETY, publications of

---BOOKLETS

#1   Adams, Raymond, et al. THE THOREAU SOCIETY OF AMER-
ICA: BOOKLET #1. Chapel Hill, N. C.: Orange Print
Shop, 1942. 19pp.

#2   [Adams, Raymond]. THE THOREAU SOCIETY: BOOKLET #2.
Chapel Hill, N. C.: Orange Print Shop, 1943. 4pp.

#3   Curtis, George William. REMINISCENCES OF THOREAU.
Northfield, Mass.: Walter Harding, [1945]. [2pp.]

#4   Jones, Samuel Arthur. THOREAU'S INCARCERATION.
Bridgewater, Mass.: Thoreau Society, 1946. [8pp.]

#5   [Harding, Walter]. THOREAU'S DIPLOMA. New Brunswick,
New Jersey: Thoreau Society, 1948. 2pp.

#6   Alcott, May. CONCORD SCENES. New Brunswick, New
Jersey: Thoreau Society, 1949. [8pp.]

#7   Allen, Francis H. THOREAU'S EDITORS HISTORY AND
REMINISCENCE. Monroe, N. C.: Nocalore Press, 1950.
28pp.

#8   Houston, Walter Scott. AN INDEX TO THE FIRST 10
YEARS OF THOREAU SOCIETY PUBLICATIONS. Charlottesville, Va.: Thoreau Society, 1953. 2pp.

#9   West, Herbert Faulkner. MR. EMERSON WRITES A LETTER
ABOUT WALDEN. Lunenburg, Vt.: Stinehour Press, 1954.
[18pp.]

#10   Hosmer, Joseph, et al. THE CONCORD FREEMAN: THOREAU
ANNEX. Charlottesville, Va.: Thoreau Society, 1955.
4pp.

#11   Harding, Walter. THOREAU'S LIBRARY. Charlottesville,
Va.: University of Virginia Press, 1957. 102pp.

#12 Robinson, Kenneth Allen. THOREAU AND THE WILD APPETITE. [Geneseo, N. Y.: Thoreau Society], 1957. 29pp.

#13 Todd, Mabel Loomis. THE THOREAU FAMILY TWO GENERATIONS AGO. Berkeley Heights, N. J.: Oriole Press, 1958. 23pp.

#14 H[arding], W[alter]. TWO FORGOTTEN BITS OF THOREAUVIANA. Geneseo, N. Y.: Thoreau Society, 1959. 4pp.

#15 Shanley, J. Lyndon. PLEASURES OF WALDEN. [Geneseo, N. Y.: Thoreau Society, 1960. 8pp.]

#16 Harding, Walter. THOREAU'S MINNESOTA JOURNEY: TWO DOCUMENTS. Geneseo, N. Y.: Thoreau Society, 1962. 60pp.

#17 [Hicks, John]. A CENTENARY GATHERING FOR HENRY DAVID THOREAU. Amherst, Mass.: University of Massachusetts, 1962. 228pp. [Issued also as THE MASSACHUSETTS REVIEW, Autumn, 1962.]

#18 Stoller, Leo. HENRY DAVID THOREAU: 1817-1862: BOOKS, MANUSCRIPTS, AND ASSOCIATION ITEMS IN DETROIT AND ANN ARBOR. Detroit, Mich.: Wayne State University Library, [1963]. 13pp.

#19 Taylor, J. Golden. THE WESTERN THOREAU CENTENARY. Logan, Utah: Utah State University, 1963. 63pp.

#20 Harding, Walter. SOPHIA THOREAU'S SCRAPBOOK. Geneseo, N. Y.: Thoreau Society, 1964. 66pp.

#21 Harding, Walter. THE THOREAU CENTENNIAL. Albany: State University of New York Press, 1964. 119pp.

#22 Harding Walter. AN INDEX TO THE FIRST 100 THOREAU SOCIETY BULLETINS. Geneseo, N. Y.: Thoreau Society, 1968. 4pp.

#23 Harding, Walter. THEO BROWN AND HENRY THOREAU. Rochester: Gaudeamus Press, 1968. 7pp.

#24 Garate, Justo. THOREAU AND THE SPANISH LANGUAGE: A BIBLIOGRAPHY. Geneseo, N. Y.: Thoreau Society, 1970. 12pp.

#25 Fenn, Mary Gail. THOREAU'S EASTERBROOK COUNTRY. Geneseo, N. Y.: Thoreau Society, 1970. 1p.

THOREAU SOCIETY BULLETINS, dates of publication

No.	
1. October, 1941	3. April, 1942
2. January, 1942	4. July, 1943

THOREAU SOCIETY, transactions of
        1944   "If Thoreau Came Back," BOSTON HERALD, July 9, 1944.
                An editorial on the Concord meeting.

                "Reminder from Concord," NEW YORK SUN, July 13, 1944.
                An editorial on the Concord meeting. It set
                off the following exchange of letters to the
                editors: Willard, Simon. "Thoreau's Deacons."
                July 20, 1944; Kennedy, J. R. "Thoreau Defended."
                July 27, 1944; Willard, Simon. "Thoreau's As-
                sertions." August 16, 1944; Hanna, W. J. "In
                Defense of Walden's Sage." August 30, 1944;
                Willard, Simon. "Unsecluded Walden." Septem-
                ber 16, 1944.

        1945   Guy, Don. "Plan Simple Ceremonies at Walden Pond,"
                TAUNTON [Mass.] DAILY GAZETTE, July 3, 1945.
                On the Concord meeting.

                "Mark Thoreau Centenary," BOSTON POST, July 5, 1945.
                Brief account of Concord meeting.

                "Simple Walden Centenary Rite," BOSTON HERALD, July
                5, 1945.
                Another account of the Concord meeting.

                "Thoreau Addicts Form Chapter of National Society,"
                CHICAGO TRIBUNE, November 25, 1945.
                An account of the Chicago meeting. The TRIBUNE
                gave several notices of the meeting in earlier
                issues.

                "Tribute Paid Thoreau at Walden Ceremony," BOSTON
                GLOBE, July 5, 1945.
                Account of the Concord meeting, with photo-
                graph of speakers.

                "Walden Centenary," CONCORD JOURNAL, June 28, 1945.
                Some miscellaneous notes on the celebration.

                "Walden Centenary Is Observed by Concord Folks,"
                CONCORD ENTERPRISE, July 5, 1945.
                Account of the Concord meeting.

                "Walden Pond Comes of Age, Marks Thoreau Experiment,"
                PAWTUCKET [R.I.] TIMES, July 3, 1945.
                Announcement of the Concord meeting, illus-
                trated.

                "Walden Revisited," CONCORD JOURNAL, July 5, 1945.
                The most detailed account of the meeting at
                Concord.

        1946   "In Commemoration Thoreau Society," BOSTON HERALD,
                July 14, 1946.
                An account of the annual meeting.

"Memorial to Thoreau," CONCORD JOURNAL, July 18,
1946.
   A report of the meeting.

"Propose Memorial to Thoreau at Famous Cabin Site,"
LOWELL [Mass.] SUN, July 15, 1946.
   A detailed account of the annual meeting.

"Thoreau Enthusiasts Visit Writer's Haunts at
Walden," CHRISTIAN SCIENCE MONITOR, July 13, 1946.
   A notice of the meeting.

"Thoreau Memorials Proposed," CONCORD ENTERPRISE,
July 18, 1946.
   A report of the meeting.

"Thoreau Society Meets Saturday," NEW YORK SUN,
July 10, 1946.
   A notice of the meeting.

1947   "Thoreau's Cabin Site Marked with Granite at Walden
Pond," BOSTON HERALD, July 13, 1947.
   Account of the annual meeting, with photograph
   of the dedication ceremonies.

"Thoreau's Home Marked," NEW YORK TIMES, July 13,
1947.
   An account of the Concord meeting.

"Site of Thoreau's Cabin at Walden is Marked by
Granite Shaft July 12," CHRISTIAN SCIENCE MONITOR,
July 7, 1947.
   Announcement of annual meeting.

1948   "Annual Thoreau Meeting Held," CONCORD ENTERPRISE,
July 15, 1948.

1949   "Thoreau Group Meets in Concord," CONCORD ENTER-
PRISE, July 14, 1949.
   Detailed account of annual meeting and election.

"Thoreau Society Inducts at Concord," LOWELL SUN,
July 11, 1949.
   Account of annual meeting with photograph of
   officers of society.

"Thoreau Society Meets in Concord," BOSTON GLOBE,
July 10, 1949.
   Account of annual meeting.

"Thoreau Society to Observe Centennial of Two
Publications," CONCORD JOURNAL, July 7, 1949.
   Announcement of annual meeting.

1950　"National Thoreau Society Holds Meeting in Concord,"
LOWELL SUN, July 17, 1950.
　　　Reports of the annual meeting.

"National Thoreau Society to Meet at Concord July
15," LOWELL SUN, July 9, 1950.
　　　Reports of the annual meeting.

"Society Meeting Honors Thoreau," CONCORD ENTERPRISE,
July 20, 1950.
　　　On the annual meeting of the society.

"Thoreau Group to Meet Here on July 15th," CONCORD
ENTERPRISE, June 22, 1950.
　　　On the annual meeting of the society.

"Thoreau Meeting This Saturday," CONCORD ENTERPRISE,
July 13, 1950.
　　　On the annual meeting of the society.

"Thoreau Society Meets in Concord," LOWELL SUN,
July 18, 1950.
　　　Reports of the annual meeting with photograph
　　　of officers.

1951　"Thoreau Group Again Conducts Meeting Here,"
CONCORD ENTERPRISE, July 12, 1951.
　　　Annual meeting.

"Thoreau Group to Meet Here on Saturday," CONCORD
ENTERPRISE, July 5, 1951, p. 67.
　　　A poem.

1952　"Thoreau Club Meeting Here on Saturday," CONCORD
ENTERPRISE, July 10, 1952.
　　　An annual meeting.

"Thoreau Society Annual Meeting at Concord Shrine,"
BOSTON GLOBE, July 13, 1952.
　　　Annual meeting.

1953　Howe, R. D.　"Society Meets in Concord," [Harris-
burg, Pa.] HOME STAR, July 22, 1953, p. 1.
　　　Annual meeting.

"The Thoreau Society to Meet July 11," CONCORD
JOURNAL, July 9, 1953, p. 1.

1954　"Group Honors Thoreau," NEW YORK TIMES, July 11,
1954.
　　　Account of Thoreau Society annual meeting.

REPORT ON A PRELIMINARY MEETING AT THE ROCHESTER
MUSEUM OF ARTS AND SCIENCES, JULY 8, 1954 TO FORM
THE ROCHESTER CHAPTER OF THE THOREAU SOCIETY.

Rochester, N. Y.: 1954 (mimeographed).
A detailed account of the organizational
meeting of this new chapter.

"Thoreau Society Planning Special 'Walden' Meeting,"
CONCORD JOURNAL, July 8, 1954.
Announcement of annual meeting.

1955   "H. F. West Named President of Thoreau Society,"
BOSTON GLOBE, July 10, 1955.
Account of annual meeting.

"Thoreau Group Meets Here on Saturday," CONCORD
ENTERPRISE, July 7, 1955.
Announcement of annual meeting.

"Thoreau Group Pick New Officers Here; Blodgett
Speaker," CONCORD ENTERPRISE, July 14, 1955.
Account of annual meeting.

"Thoreau Society Annual Meeting," CONCORD JOURNAL,
July 14, 1955, pp. 1 passim.

"Thoreau Society Annual Meeting Here Saturday
July 9," CONCORD JOURNAL, July 7, 1955.
Announcement of annual meeting.

1956   "Annual Meeting of National Thoreau Society in
Concord," LOWELL SUN, July 15, 1956.
With photograph of speakers and officers.

"At Thoreau Society Meeting," LOWELL SUN, July 19,
1956.
Account of annual meeting.

"Maryland Man Heads Thoreau Society," BOSTON HERALD,
July 15, 1956.
Account of annual meeting.

"Thoreau Admirers Meet at Concord," CONCORD ENTER-
PRISE, July 19, 1956.
Account of annual meeting.

"Thoreau Club Meeting Here on Saturday," CONCORD
ENTERPRISE, July 12, 1956.

"Thoreau Group to Meet Here on July 14th," CONCORD
ENTERPRISE, June 23, 1956.

1959   "Thoreau Group Hold Meeting at Concord," CONCORD
ENTERPRISE, July 16, 1959.
Report on annual meeting.

"Thoreau Meeting," CONCORD JOURNAL, July 16, 1959.
Report on annual meeting.

1961   "Uncle Dudley." "Meditation on Concord River,"
        BOSTON GLOBE, July 15, 1961.
                Editorial on the 1961 society annual meeting.

        "Thoreau Society Meeting Here," CONCORD JOURNAL,
        July 20, 1961.

        "Thoreau Society Meeting on Saturday at First
        Parish Church," CONCORD JOURNAL, July 13, 1961.

1962   [Seim, Erling].   "Amerika minnest Thoreau,"
        FRIHUG [Norway], VIII (September, 1962), 4-5.
                Account of centennial meetings.

        "Thoreau Society Meeting Saturday," CONCORD JOURNAL,
        July 12, 1962.
                Announcement of annual meeting.

1963   "Thoreau Society Holds Annual Meeting," CONCORD
        JOURNAL, July 18, 1963.
                Detailed account.

1964   Wheeler, Ruth R.   "Annual Meeting of Thoreau Soci-
        ety," CONCORD JOURNAL, July 16, 1964.

        Sherwood, Mary P.   "The National Thoreau Society
        Soars Toward It's 'Sweet Day'," CONCORD FREE PRESS,
        July ?, 1964.
                On annual meeting.

        Sherwood, Mary P.   "Walter Harding, Thoreau Society
        President," CONCORD TOWN (July, 1964), pp. 16-17.

1965   "Thoreau Society Annual Meeting," CONCORD JOURNAL,
        July 19, 1965.

1966   "Special Programs, Exhibits Planned for Open House
        at Thoreau Lyceum," CONCORD FREE PRESS, December
        8, 1966.

        "Thoreau Society Holds Annual Meeting," CONCORD
        JOURNAL, July 14, 1966.

1967   Report of Thoreau Society annual meeting.   CONCORD
        JOURNAL, July 20, 1967.

        ANNUAL MEETING.   Concord, Mass.: Thoreau Society,
        1967.   Illustrated by Thoreau MacDonald.   Unpaged
        pamphlet.

1968   "Thoreau Society Annual Meeting," CONCORD JOURNAL,
        July 18, 1968.

        "Thoreau Society Hears Well-Known Writer on 'Science
        vs Technology'," CONCORD FREE PRESS, July 18, 1968.

Report on annual meeting.

"Thoreau, Society Meeting," CONCORD JOURNAL, July
17, 1968.

1969   Reyman, Vernon. "Henry David Thoreau," RUTLAND
[Vt.] DAILY HERALD, July 17, 1969.
Account of Thoreau Society annual meeting.

"Thoreau Society Hears Unpublished Essay," CONCORD
FREE PRESS, July 17, 1969.
On annual meeting.

"Thoreau Tablet is Dedicated at Walden Pond," BOSTON GLOBE,
July 13, 1947.
A news account.

"Thoreau Underground," CONCORD JOURNAL, October 18, 1945.
A member of the Danish Underground requests a photograph of Thoreau's grave as his reward for rescuing
an American flyer.

"Thoreau.   Unpublished notes read to the Concord School,"
BOSTON DAILY ADVERTISER, July 25, 1885.
Report of a lecture by H. G. O. Blake.

"Thoreau Visits Japan via the Sierra Club," SIERRA CLUB BUL-
LETIN, L (January, 1965), 15.
Photographic exhibit.

"Thoreauana Show Largest Yet Held," NEW YORK SUN, June 22, 1945.
A description of the museum exhibition.

"Thoreau's Bright World," BOSTON TRANSCRIPT, March 16, 1907.

"Thoreau's Example," SPECTATOR, LVI (February 17, 1883), 239-240

"Thoreau's Hut at Walden Pond." West Concord, Mass.: J. Ritchie
(1954?).
A water-color drawing of the Walden hut.

"Thoreau's Indian Relics," TSB #105, p. 8.
A quote from the THIRD ANNUAL REPORT OF THE TRUSTEES
OF THE PEABODY MUSEUM OF AMERICAN ARCHAEOLOGY AND
ETHNOLOGY is included.

"Thoreau's Lecture on Sir Walter Raleigh," TSB #75, p. 4.
Reprinted from the CONCORD FREEMAN, February 10, 1843,
p. 2.

"Thoreau's Manuscript on Wellfleet Oysterman to be Lodged in
Wellfleet," CAPE CODDER, June 5, 1958.
With facsimile of MS.

"Thoreau's Plan of a Farm," TSB #20.

Included is a "hitherto unpublished survey done by Thoreau on March 23, 1858."

"Thoreau's Unpublished Journals," NEW YORK TRIBUNE, August 15, 1880.

"Thoreau's Verses," SATURDAY REVIEW OF LITERATURE, LXXXI (January 18, 1896), 55.

"Thoreau's WALDEN Is Now 100," DES MOINES [Iowa] SUNDAY REGISTER, July 8, 1945.
 A centennial editorial.

"Thoreau's Walden Reverie Upset by Sunday Visitors," NEW YORK TIMES BOOK REVIEW, April 15, 1923.
 A cartoon.

"Thoreau's Wild Wood Philosophy," NEW YORK TRIBUNE, July 26, 1885.

Thorovian. "Questions Raised," CONCORD JOURNAL, September 12, 1946.
 Questioning the recently discovered hut site.

Thorp, Willard. "Thoreau's Huckleberry Party," TSB #40.
 Contains excerpts from Hawthorne's NOTEBOOKS and Emerson's JOURNAL which pertain to Thoreau.

Thorpe, James. "English and American Literature in the Mc-Cormick Collection: Some Bibliographical Notes," PRINCETON UNIVERSITY LIBRARY CHRONICLE, X (November, 1948), 16-41.
 Includes an account of the Thoreau manuscripts and first editions in this collection.

"Thoughts of Martin Buber on Henry Thoreau based on a conversation in Jerusalem, July 25, 1962 with W. Stephen Thomas," TSB #85, p. 1.

Three Brief Reviews of Thoreau's WEEK. TSB #29.
 Three contemporary reviews.

"Through the Arch," VILLAGER [New York City], August ?, 1945.
 A columnist suggests a style promotion on "Walden Men's Wear" with suggestions from Thoreau's color tastes.

Tilden, Freeman. "Two Concord Men in a Boat," NATIONAL PARKS MAGAZINE, XXXVIII (July, 1964), 8-10.
 Thoreau and Emerson contrasted.

Tillinghast, C. A. "The West of Thoreau's Imagination: The Development of a Symbol," THOTH [Syracuse University], VI (1965), 42-50.

Timms, Cartwright. "The Philosophy of Henry David Thoreau,"
    LONDON QUARTERLY AND HOLBURN REVIEW, CLXXII (April, 1947),
    152-156.
        An essay in the official publication of British
        Methodism.

Timpe, Eugene F. "The Macrocosm of WALDEN," PROCEED. OF IVth
    CONG. OF INTERNAT. COMP. LIT. ASSOC., 1966, 73-79.

    --"Thoreau in Germany," TSB #93, pp. 1-3.

Tinker, Edward Larocque. "New Editions, Fine & Otherwise,"
    NEW YORK TIMES BOOK REVIEW, March 29, p. 21.
        Traces Thoreau's THE DUTY OF CIVIL DISOBEDIENCE
        and his non-cooperation to Etienne La Boetie's
        DISCOURSE SUR LA SERVITUDE VOLUNTAIRE, translated
        by Harry Kurz under the title ANTI-DICTATOR [Colum-
        bia University Press, 1942.]

"Today's Hippies--Are They Carbon Copies of Thoreau?" STUDENT
    REVIEW, II (September, 1967), 3.

Todd, Edgeley W. "Philosophical Ideas at Harvard College,
    1817-1837," NEW ENGLAND QUARTERLY, XVI (March, 1943), 63-90
        A study of the influence of Harvard philosophy
        courses upon Emerson and Thoreau.

Tolman, George. Letter to Editor. BOSTON TRAVELER (October
    17, 1890).
        Says the new family stone in the Thoreau lot at
        Sleepy Hollow was erected from Aunt Maria Thoreau's
        bequest to Mr. Thatcher in Bangor.

T[olman], W. N. Letter to the editor. NEW YORK SUN, April
    6, 1945.
        The cairn controversy.

Tolstoi, Leo. LA GRAN TRAGEDIA. Barcelona, Spain: Maucci,
    1907.
        A full paragraph on Thoreau on p. 84.

Tolstoy, Leo. "Letter to Dr. Eugen Heinrich Schmitt,"
    TOLSTOY'S WRITINGS ON CIVIL DISOBEDIENCE AND NON-VIOLENCE.
    New York: Bergman, 1967. pp. 169-172.

Tomita, Akira. H. D. THOREAU. Tokyo: Kenkvusha, 1934.
        A critical study of Thoreau, in Japanese.

Toperoff, Sam. "Dollars and Sense in Walden," EMERSON SOCIETY
    QUARTERLY, XLIII (1966), 87-88.

"Topics of the Times," NEW YORK TIMES, February 25, 1958.
        On Thoreau's pencils.

Torrey, Brandford. "A Text from Thoreau," BOSTON TRANSCRIPT,
    November 14, 1900.

Later reprinted in THE CLERK OF THE WOODS.

Transtromer, Tomas. "Ode to Thoreau," WESTERN HUMANITIES
REVIEW, VIII (Spring, 1954), 86.
A poem.

Trayser, Donald. "Once Upon A Time on Cape Cod," CAPE CODDER,
October 7, 1948, p. 2.
On Thoreau on Cape Cod.

Treat, Robert and Betty Treat. "Thoreau and Institutional
Christianity," AMERICAN TRANSCENDENTAL QUARTERLY, I (1969),
44-47.

Tripp, Raymond P., Jr. "A Recipe for WALDEN Criticism,"
NEW ENGLAND REVIEW, I (July, 1969), 11-14.

--"Thoreau and Marcus Aurelius: A Possible Borrowing,"
TSB #107, p. 7.

Trottenburg, Arthur D. "Cape Cod Revisited," HARVARD ALUMNI
BULLETIN, LXII (November 7, 1959), 163-173.
Photographs of Cape Cod with quotations from
Thoreau's CAPE COD.

--"Poem about Concord," HARVARD ALUMNI BULLETIN, LXV
(September 29, 1962), 19-28.
Picture essay on Thoreau's haunts.

Troubetzkoy, Ulrich. "Emerson Would be Pleased," CHRISTIAN
SCIENCE MONITOR, February 25, 1946.
Concord as it appears today to the literary pilgrim.

Troy, Jack. "Pot-Hunting at Concord and Walden," TSB #101, p. 6.

Tryon, W. S. PARNASSUS CORNER: A LIFE OF JAMES T. FIELDS,
PUBLISHER TO THE VICTORIANS. Boston: Houghton Mifflin,
1963.
Includes some new information on Thoreau's relations
with his publishers.

--and William Charvat. THE COST BOOKS OF TICKNOR, AND
FIELDS AND THEIR PREDECESSORS 1832-1858. New York:
Bibliographical Society of America, 1949.
The accounts of the publishers of Thoreau's WALDEN.

Tuerk, Richard Carl. "Circle Imagery in the Prose of Emerson
and Thoreau from NATURE (1836) to WALDEN (1854)."
Johns Hopkins University, 1967. Unpublished doctoral
dissertation.
Abstract is reproduced in TSB #107, pp. 5-6.

--"Thoreau and Chaucer's Dream, TSB #103, p. 1.

Turner, Lorenzo Dow. ANTI-SLAVERY SENTIMENT IN AMERICAN

LITERATURE PRIOR TO 1865. Port Washington, N. Y.:
Kennikat, 1966.
    Reprint of a 1929 book. Thoreau, pp. 98-99.

Two photographs of Walden Pond. CHRISTIAN SCIENCE MONITOR,
    September 26, 1955, p. 6.

Tyler, Alice F. FREEDOM'S FERMENT. Minneapolis: University
    of Minnesota Press. 1944.
        An intellectual history of the United States.
        Thoreau, pp. 56-59.

Tynan, Katherine. "Thoreau at Walden," LOUISE DE LA VALLIERE
    AND OTHER POEMS. ? : ? , p. 90.
        A poem by one of W. B. Yeats' friends.

Ueland, Brenda.   IF YOU WANT TO WRITE...   New York: Putnam,
     1938.
          A high school student criticizes Stevenson's
          evaluation of Thoreau, pp. 150-156.

"Uncle Dudley."   "The Sun is But a Morning Star," BOSTON
     GLOBE, July 1, 1945.
          A two-column editorial appreciation of Thoreau.

   --"Thoreau on Maneuver," BOSTON DAILY GLOBE, November
     15, 1941.
          An editorial based on Webb Miller's I FOUND NO PEACE
          and on the Barlow cartoon in the NEW YORKER (October
          18, 1941).

"The Uncommon Man," GARDEN CITY [N. Y.] NEWSDAY, January 11,
     1960.
          Editorial on Thoreau.

Updegraff, Robert R.   "Time for Everything," THE ROTARIAN,
     LX (February, 1942), 29-30 passim.
          On page 28 is a portrait of Thoreau as one who
          was self-appointed "inspector of snowstorms and
          rainstorms."

Uphaus, Willard.   "Conscience and Disobedience," MASSACHUSETTS
     REVIEW, IV (Autumn, 1962), 104-108.

"Upton Sinclair on Thoreau," TSB #71, p. 3.
          A letter from Sinclair to Harding on Thoreau.

Urzidil, Johannes.   "Adalbert Stifter und Henry Thoreau,"
     WELT UND WORT, V (1950), 225.
          Suggests that Thoreau was directly influenced by
          Stifter's HOCHWALD (1842).

   --"Henry David Thoreau oder Natur und Freideit," CASTRUM
     PEREGRINI, XXX (1956), 13-31.
          An appreciation of Thoreau which lyrically describes
          his relation to nature and praises his Walden sojourn,
          his civil disobedience, and his abolitionism.

   --"Weltreise in Concord," NEUE LITERARISCHE WELT, May 10,
     1953, p. 8.
          Again calls attention to the resemblance between
          Thoreau and Stifter.

Valenti, Jack. "He Sat by a Pond, His Words Tilted Planet,"
     HOUSTON POST, August 18, 1956.
          Appreciative essay.

--"Thoreau," TEN HEROES AND TWO HEROINES. Houston, Texas:
     Premier Printing, 1957. pp. 35-37.
          Brief essay by Lyndon Johnson's chief assistant.

Vance, William Silas. "Carlyle and American Transcendentalists.
     Harvard University, 1936. Unpublished doctoral disser-
     tation.

Van Dore, Wade. "The Language and Message of WALDEN," CHRIS-
     TIAN SCIENCE MONITOR, January 12, 1967.

--"New Bust in the Hall of Fame," CHRISTIAN SCIENCE MONITOR,
     October 4, 1962.
          Thoreau's philosophy for today.

--"A Poem Was My Road Map," CHRISTIAN SCIENCE MONITOR,
     August 16, 1969.
          How the author was influenced by Emerson and Thoreau.

--"Thoreau Lyceum Plans an Ambitious Future," CHRISTIAN
     SCIENCE MONITOR, August 10, 1967.

--VERSE WITH A VENGEANCE. Boston: Bruce Humphries, 1961.
          A collection of vitriolic verses with frequent
          reference to Thoreau in the foreword, the dedication,
          and even the copyright statement! On p. 43 it in-
          cludes a poem entitled, "Two Reasons Why the Unique
          and Great Henry Thoreau Will Never Be a Popular
          Author." The poem: "He does not ever pet or dandle
          us. His truth is so true it is scandalous." TSB#77.

Van Doren, Mark. HENRY DAVID THOREAU: A CRITICAL STUDY. New
     York: Russell and Russell, 1961.
          Van Doren's 1916 undergraduate honors thesis at the
          University of Illinois was the first study to make
          extensive use of the complete JOURNAL. As such it
          offered some good insight into Thoreau's ideas on
          friendship, solitude, the well-rounded man, and
          reading (although this last has been superseded by
          the studies of Whaling, Willson and others). Best
          is his discussion of Thoreau's use of the specific
          in his writing. Weakest is his claim that Thoreau

in his later years felt his life to be a failure.
Van Doren's book has been out-of-print and almost
impossible to obtain for many, many years. Thoreau
scholars will welcome this opportunity to add it to
their shelves. TSB #76.

--NATHANIEL HAWTHORNE. New York: William Sloane Associates,
1949.
Another in the new American Men of Letters Series.
Van Doren has much of significance to say on Haw-
thorne, including a little on his relationship with
Thoreau. We are glad to see that the newer volumes
in the series are including critical bibliographies.
TSB #27.

van Kranendonk, A. G. GESCHIEDENIS VAN DE AMERIKAANSE LITER-
ATUUR. Amsterdam, Holland: Oorschot, 1946.
On Thoreau, pp. 55-57.

VanNostrand, A. D. "Thoreau Beside Himself," EVERYMAN HIS
OWN POET. New York: McGraw-Hill, 1968. pp. 92-112.
An enlightening discussion of Thoreau's use of
metaphor in WALDEN and particularly on his ability
to, as Emerson says, draw "universal law from
single fact." TSB #107.

Vazques Amaral, Jose. HENRY DAVID THOREAU. Paris: Umbral,
May, 1968. Text in Spanish.

Verma, Prakash. "Satyagraha: the Non-Violence of Gandhi,"
SOUTH DAKOTA REVIEW, VI (Summer, 1968), 3-9.
Comments on Thoreau's influence on Gandhi.

Vernet, Laurence. "Actualite de Thoreau," FRANCE AMERIQUE
MAGAZINE [Paris], 1968, pp. 94-98.

--"Marcel Proust: Admirateur Imprevu de Thoreau," EUROPE
[Paris], XLVII (Janvier, 1969), 217-224.

Very, Jones. "On Visiting the Graves of Hawthorne and Thoreau," POEMS AND ESSAYS. Boston: Houghton Mifflin,
1886. p. 519.
An apparently hitherto unnoticed poem on Thoreau
by his personal friend and Greek tutor at Harvard.

Very, Lydia L. A. "The Thoreau Field Club," POEMS AND PROSE
WRITINGS. Salem, Mass.: Salem Press, 1890. pp. 362-367.
An amusing account, by Jones Very's sister, of an
early nature club named after Thoreau.

Vivancos. "The Perception of Beauty," TIME MAGAZINE (September 16, 1966).
Painting illustrating a quotation from Thoreau
as an advertisement for the Container Corp. of
America.

Volkman, Arthur G. "The Hound, Bay-Horse, and Turtle Dove," TSB #103, pp. 6-7.

--"A Note on Japp's Life of Thoreau," TSB #107, pp. 6-7. A discussion of "an 'Authors Edition: From Advance Proof Sheets', of THOREAU: HIS LIFE AND AIMS, by H. A. Page, (pseudonym of A. H. Japp), published in Boston by James R. Osgood and Company, 1877."

--"Thoreau on the Brandywine," DELAWARE TODAY, VI (August, 1967), 14 passim.

Von Brandt, Ralph Van Kirk. HENRY D. THOREAU: CORRESPONDENCE. Trenton, N. J.: Published by the author, (1944?). A series of free-verse letters to Thoreau in heaven and his imagined replies.

von Ende, A. "Henry David Thoreau," BEILAGE ZUR ALLGEMEINEN ZEITUNG, No. 197 (August 26, 1896), 1-3. Celebrates the fact that Thoreau, like Whitman, actually practiced individualism, unlike most Americans, who tend to be individualists in theory only. Calls attention to Thoreau's opposition to majority views and considers him the greatest writer among the Transcendentalists and the most original and powerful personality in American literature.

W., C. "The Man Who Knows His Village," FREEDOM [London, England], XV (August 21, 1954), 2.

W., D. E. "Thoreau's Hut," BOSTON TRANSCRIPT, August 6, 1904.

Waggoner, Hyatt H. "'Grace' in the Thought of Emerson, Thoreau, and Hawthorne," EMERSON SOCIETY QUARTERLY, LIV (1969), 68-72.

Wakefield, Dan. "Marked in Mustard and Sauerkraut," NEW YORK HERALD TRIBUNE BOOK WEEK, November 8, 1964.
    A visit to Walden Pond.

"Walden," EMERSON SOCIETY QUARTERLY, VII (1957), 43.
    Facsimile reprint of tribute to Thoreau from the May 17, 1862 Concord MONITOR.

"Walden Ideals," NEW YORK TIMES, June 17, 1945.
    A centennial editorial.

"Walden in Retrospect," NEW YORK SUN, June 18, 1945.
    An editorial on the museum exhibit.

"Walden Pond," FRIENDS (May, 1957), pp. 12-15.
    A series of beautiful color photographs from the Chevrolet house organ.

"Walden Pond--A century after Thoreau Lived There," NEW YORK HERALD TRIBUNE, September 18, 1938.
    A page of rotogravure photographs.

"Walden Pond Inflation," OGDEN [Utah] STANDARD-EXAMINER, June 21, 1969.
    Editorial on cost of Walden cabin replica.

"Walden Pond Park Growing," CLEVELAND [Ohio] PLAIN DEALER, December 13, 1955.
    On the addition to the reservation.

"Walden Pond Preserve," HOBBIES, LII (October, 1947), 143.
    A brief note on the state reservation.

"Walden Pond Still Endangered," LIVING WILDERNESS (Spring, 1959), pp. 32-33.

"Walden Pond Today," TSB #28.

"Walden Will Be Thoreau's Crown," FITCHBURG SENTINEL, May 10, 1922.
>Account of gift of Walden Reservation to state by Emersons.

Waldinger, Ernst. "An Thoreau," DIE KUHLEN BAUERNSTUBEN. Vienna: ? ,   ? . pp. 67-68.
>A poem.

Waldrep, Reef. "Saving Thoreau's Pond," CHICAGO TRIBUNE, July 7, 1969.
>Letter to editor.

Walker, Edyth. "Walden--A Calming Influence," TSB #42.
>"A condensation of a paper read at the 1952 annual meeting of the Thoreau Society."

Walker, James. "The Ancestry of Thoreau," SATURDAY REVIEW OF LITERATURE, September 8, 1945, p. 8.
>A letter to the editor from a New Zealander giving some new light on Thoreau's ancestry, with a note by Henry S. Canby. Important for study of Thoreau's biography. TSB #13.

Walker, Paul. "Fate of Famed Cabin Is Told," HARRISBURG [Pa.] HOME STAR, July 8, 1953, p. 1.
>On the later history of the Walden cabin.

--"Your New York," PATRIOT [Harrisburg, Pa.], June 29, 1945.
>On the museum exhibition and the author's interest in Thoreau.

Walker, Roy. "The Natural Life: An Essay on Thoreau," THE VEGETARIAN NEWS [London, England], XXVI (Spring, 1948), 3-8.
>An excellent general study with new material on the influence of early American vegetarians on Thoreau. TSB #23.

Wall, Mary B. "Verdict of Time," KALEIDOGRAPH (August, 1948).
>A poem on Thoreau.

Wallace, Archer. "Poor Men Who Made Us Rich," TARGET, XCIII (May 27, 1933).
>Thoreau for children.

Wallis, Charles L. "Gandhi's Source Book," CHRISTIAN REGISTER, CXXVIII (September, 1949), 31-32.
>On influence of CIVIL DISOBEDIENCE.

Wang, Li. M. A. "The Orient in Henry David Thoreau," ABSTRACTS OF MASTERS'THESES. Athens, Ohio: Ohio University Press, 1949. p. 43.
>The results of this study reveal that the mystical elements in Thoreau were strongly influenced by

Oriental philosophy, and that Thoreau took, not
only figures and sentences, but ideas as well,
from his Oriental reading. R.A. TSB #30.

Warner, F. L. "Spring Cleaning Time at Concord," CHRISTIAN
SCIENCE MONITOR, May 13, 1941.
Much about the Thoreau exhibit in the Antiquarian
House.

Warren, Austin. "Henry David Thoreau," THE NEW ENGLAND CON-
SCIENCE. Ann Arbor: University of Michigan Press, 1966.
pp. 102-118.

Wasserstrom, William. "Howells' Mansion and Thoreau's Cabin,"
COLLEGE ENGLISH, XXVI (February, 1965), 366-372.

Watson, Bruce. "The Origin of Civil Disobedience," FELLOWSHIP,
XXXI (March, 1965), 14-16.

Watson, Ellen. "Thoreau Visits Plymouth," TSB #21.

--"Thoreau's Escape," JOHN O'LONDON'S WEEKLY [London, Eng-
land], January 9, 1948.
A reprint of a portion of "Thoreau Visits Plymouth"
from TSB #31.

Watt, W. W. "So Long Thoreau!" NEW YORK HERALD TRIBUNE,
March 3, 1943.
A poem.

Weaver, Richard M. "Two Types of American Individualism,"
MODERN AGE, VII (Spring, 1963), 119-134.
A contrast of Thoreau and John Randolph of Roanoke.

"Webb Miller, Famed UP War Correspondent Drew Courage to
Endure Tough Job from Thoreau's WALDEN," NEW BEDFORD
STANDARD TIMES, September 8, 1957.

Weeks, Brigitte. "Homage to Thoreau," BOSTON, LX (May, 1968),
52-57.
On Thoreau Lyceum.

Weeks, Edward. "What Happens to Walden," IN FRIENDLY CANDOR.
Boston: Little Brown, 1959. pp. 244-248.
An essay on the destruction of trees at Walden
Pond.

Weiss, John. POEM READ AT THE ANNUAL DINNER OF THE CLASS OF
EIGHTEEN HUNDRED AND THIRTY SEVEN FEBRUARY 26, 1874.
Boston: Deland, 1874.
Commemorative poem about Thoreau.

also in: EMERSON SOCIETY QUARTERLY, VII (1957),
35-37. Facsimile of poem.

--"Thoreau," EMERSON SOCIETY QUARTERLY, VII (1957), 6-17.
Facsimile reprint of review of Thoreau's books
from CHRISTIAN EXAMINER for July, 1865.

"Weiss on Thoreau," TSB #21.
A portion of "Poem Read at the Annual Dinner of
the Class of Eighteen Hundred and Thirty Seven"
is included.

Welch, Donovan L. "A Chronological Study of the Poetry of
Henry David Thoreau." University of Nebraska, 1966.
Unpublished doctoral dissertation.

Welker, Robert Henry. BIRDS & MEN: AMERICAN BIRDS IN SCIENCE,
ART, LITERATURE, AND CONSERVATION. Cambridge: Harvard
University Press, 1955.
"Literary Birdman: Henry David Thoreau," pp. 91-115.
The first study to place Thoreau's interest in and
knowledge of birds against the background of his
times. Also makes a provocative study of the chronological development of Thoreau's interest in birds.
And, finally, contrasts Thoreau's attitude towards
nature with that of Emerson. A thoughtful, interesting book, particularly for those interested in
19th century American science. TSB #54.

Wellek, Rene. A HISTORY OF MODERN CRITICISM: 1750-1950:
THE AGE OF TRANSITION. New Haven: Yale University Press,
1965.
Contains several pages on Thoreau's criticism.

Wells, Anna Mary. DEAR PRECEPTOR: THE LIFE AND TIMES OF
THOMAS WENTWORTH HIGGINSON. Boston: Houghton Mifflin,
1963.
Higginson has unfortunately been one of the most
neglected minor figures of American Transcendentalism,
but now at last he has received due recognition
in a highly readable biography that has, incidentally,
much to say about his relationship with Thoreau and
his part in the development of Thoreau's posthumous
fame. DEAR PRECEPTOR is one of those rare gems--a
highly readable book that is obviously based on
sound scholarship. TSB #84.

Wells, Henry W. "An Evaluation of Thoreau's Poetry," AMER-
ICAN LITERATURE, XVI (May, 1944), 99-109.
One of the fullest studies of Thoreau's poetry
yet published.

Welti, Albert J. "Ein ameritanischer Einsiedler," DER BUND
[Bern, Switzerland], December 21, 1945.
A brief essay on Thoreau.

Wershba, Joseph. "Of Fame and a Woman," NEW YORK POST, May
6, 1962.
Interview with Malvina Hoffman about her Hall of

Fame bust of Thoreau.

West, Herbert Faulkner. "Strange Interlude--Thoreau Voice
of America," REBEL THOUGHT. Boston: Beacon, 1953. pp.
196-210.
A thoughtful discussion of Thoreau as an unorthodox
thinker. Contains excerpts from 3 unpublished
letters: one from Thoreau to the American Association
for the Advancement of Science; one from Louisa May
Alcott to Sophia Foord on the death of Thoreau, and
one from Emerson to his English publisher urging
publication of WALDEN in England. TSB #43.

--"Thoreau and the Younger Generation," TSB #56.

--"Values in Thoreau," TSB #20.
This is a condendation of the lecture delivered
at the annual meeting in Concord on July 12, 1947.

Westbrook, Perry. "John Burroughs and the Transcendentalists," EMERSON SOCIETY QUARTERLY, LV (1969), 47-55.

--"Thoreau: The Theme of the Quest," ENGLISH RECORD, VIII
(Winter, 1958), 13-17.

Westphal, Paul. "Thoreau als Befrier," DIE TAT, XII (1920),
501-506.
Suggests that Thoreau's social principles could
be of help to the German people in the aftermath
of World War I.

Weygandt, Cornelius. ON THE EDGE OF EVENING: THE AUTOBIOGRAPHY
OF A TEACHER AND WRITER WHO HOLDS TO THE OLD WAYS. New
York: Putnam, 1946.
This quite charming, conversational autobiography
of a University of Pennsylvania English professor
is filled with such tributes to Thoreau as, "The
man and his writing are seldom long out of mind
with me," or, "I conned over A WEEK and WALDEN
and fairly devoured his journals." The quiet,
friendly spirit of the book will delight many; its
dry humor, even more. It is unfortunate that the
captions under the photographs opposite page 132
have become interchanged, labeling Thoreau "Henry
Reed" and vice versa. TSB #17.

W[heeler], J. A. "Reflections on an Early American Anarchist,"
WHY?, II (July-August, 1943), 2-3.
An answer to the Woodcock article.

Wheeler, Jo Ann. "Duty of Civil Disobedience," MONEY, XIV
(June, 1949), 5.
On the centennial of Thoreau's essay.

--"A Thoreauvian Adventure," TSB #13.

--"Thoreau's Duty," MONEY, IV (January, 1950), 8.
        On centennial of "Civil Disobedience."

Wheeler, Mary C.   "Concord Sketches," TSB #46.
        This short article is accompanied by three sketches
        done by Mary C. Wheeler in "1862, the year of Tho-
        reau's death, when Miss Wheeler was 16." The
        sketches are: "(1) the summer-house which Thoreau
        and Alcott built for Emerson; (2) the pencil factory;
        and (3) the Minot house, showing the old woodshed
        where Thoreau loved to sit with old George Minot
        and listen to his stories."

Wheeler, Richard.   "Some of Us Are More Desperate Than Others,"
        SATURDAY EVENING POST, April 11, 1959, p. 34.
        A poem.

Wheeler, Ruth Robinson.   CONCORD: CLIMATE FOR FREEDOM.   Concord,
        Mass.: Concord Antiquarian Society, 1966.   Edition
        limited to 1500 copies.
        A delightfully readable account of life in Thoreau's
        home town from the town's establishment to the Civil
        War, based on years of research by the authority
        on Concord history, and embellished with 100 illus-
        trations.   It is a book that no student of Thoreau
        can afford to be without and the type of history
        that every town should have.   TSB #102.

--THE CONCORD FRIENDLY AID SOCIETY.   Concord: Privately
   printed, 1950.
        A history with much about the charitable activities
        of Thoreau's mother and an excellent background
        picture of Concord in Thoreau's day. TSB #46.

--THE HISTORY OF THE COLONIAL INN.   Concord, Mass.:
   Colonial Inn, (1948?).
        A pamphlet history of a building in which Thoreau
        once lived.

--"Isaac Hecker and Concord," CONCORD JOURNAL, May 5, 1960.
        Including his stay with the Thoreaus.

--"Old Virginia Road," CONCORD JOURNAL, April 30, p. 6.

--OUR AMERICAN MILE.   Concord Antiquarian Society, 1957.
        An illustrated history of Lexington Road, tracing
        the history of each individual house back to its
        origin.   Filled with details of interest to the
        Thoreau scholar.

--"Thoreau Alcott House," TSB #24.

--"Thoreau and Capital Punishment," TSB #86, p. 1.
        Printed is a partial list of those who signed a
        document entitled "Protest of 400 inhabitants of

308

Concord to the hanging of Washington Goode."
Henry Thoreau's name is included. This article is
reprinted from the CONCORD JOURNAL, December 26, 1963.

--"Thoreau Farm," TSB #42.
"This was a paper delivered at the 1952 annual
meeting," and is printed with a picture of Thoreau's birthplace. "All the materials in direct
quotations is from Thoreau's Journals and is in-
dexed there."

--"A Thoreau Herbarium," TSB #29.

--"The Thoreau House," TSB #31.
A revised and corrected version of an article
originally appearing in the CONCORD JOURNAL for
May 14, 1942.

--"Thoreau's Village Background," TSB #100, pp. 1-6.

--"Concord Houses:" How They Grew," CONCORD JOURNAL, December 3, 1959.
Details on the Thoreau birthplace.

--"John Brown in Concord," CONCORD JOURNAL, October 15,
1959, pp. 1 passim.
With much on Thoreau's interest in Brown.

--"Masonic Building Has Long History," CONCORD JOURNAL,
November 30, 1961.
New information on Thoreau's teaching in the public
schools of Concord.

--"Ricketson House to be Restored," CONCORD JOURNAL, Jan-
urary 17, 1963.
Announces campaign to restore and open to public
Brooklawn, the home of Thoreau's New Bedford
friend.

--"A Yankee Trick," CONCORD JOURNAL, December 14, 1961.
Thoreau's JOURNAL solves a Concord surveying
mystery.

--HENRY DAVID THOREAU 1817-1862. Concord: Minute Man Press,
1967.
A guide to the Thoreau sites in Concord for free
distribution to tourists.

--HISTORIC CONCORD MASSACHUSETTS. Concord: Board of Trade,
(1947?).
A leaflet guide to Concord with much on Thoreau.

[Wheeler, Ruth]. "Thoreau Still Lives," CONCORD JOURNAL,
December 18, 1958.
Notes on W. B. Yeats' interest in Thoreau.

--"The Wright Tavern," CONCORD JOURNAL, July 25, 1957.
Includes material on the Thoreau family.

Wheeler, Wilfred. "Thoreau in Concord," TSB #45.
A communication in response to Prof. Adams article
in the previous bulletin.

"When Summer Comes to Boston," BOSTON POST, June 16, 1948.
Brief essay on Walden Pond.

"Where Do We Stand to Put All America Behind Us?" CAPE CODDER,
August 16, 1962.
Cartoon about Thoreau pilgrims.

"Where Thoreau's Writing Was Found," CAPE CODDER [Orleans,
Mass.], September 4, 1947.
More information on the source for "Outfit for an
Excursion," CAPE CODDER, August 21, 1947.

Whicher, George F. "Reflections on an Anniversary," AMHERST
ALUMNI NEWS, VI (April, 1954), 5.
Mr. Whicher's last chapel talk before his untimely
death on March 7, 1954.

--WALDEN REVISITED: A CENTENNIAL TRIBUTE TO HENRY DAVID
THOREAU. Chicago: Packard, 1945.

reviews: CHICAGO SUN TRIBUNE, July 8, 1945, by
Fred Babcock.
CHRISTIAN CENTURY, LXII (August 1, 1945),
885, by W. E. G[arrison].
CHRISTIAN SCIENCE MONITOR, July 11, 1945,
by T. Morris Longstreth.
NATION, August 4, 1945 by Joseph Wood Krutch
NEW ENGLAND QUARTERLY, XVIII (September,
1945), 415-416, by Arvin Newton.
NEW YORK HERALD TRIBUNE, September 11, 1945,
by Gerald W. Johnson.
NEW YORK HERALD TRIBUNE BOOKS, October 28,
1945, pp. 1-2, by Isabel Paterson.
NEW YORK TIMES BOOK REVIEW, August 5, 1945,
by E. B. Garside.
PROBE (Autumn, 1945), pp. 14-15, by Walter
Harding.
THOREAU SOCIETY BULLETIN #12.

--, editor. THE TRANSCENDENTALIST REVOLT AGAINST MATERIALISM.
Boston: Heath, 1949.
A textbook for American civilization courses. Con-
tains Arthur Schlesinger's "Jacksonian Democracy
and Literature;" Emerson's "Transcendentalist" and
"Ode to Channing;" H. S. Commager's "Theodore Parker;"
and Louisa Alcott's "Transcendental Wild Oats."
It is thus probably the most thorough anthology on
Transcendentalism available and an ideal introduction
to the movement. TSB #28.

Whicher, Stephen. "An Appointment in American Literature,"
COLLEGE ENGLISH, XXI (May, 1960), 466-469.
Includes some pleasant spoofs on current Thoreau
scholarship.

--and Robert Spiller, editors. THE EARLY LECTURES OF
RALPH WALDO EMERSON: 1833-1836. Vol. 1. Cambridge:
Harvard University Press, 1959.
The first scholarly edition of Emerson's essays,
with much incidental background material on
Thoreau. TSB #70.

Whitaker, Alex. "Henry David Thoreau Comments on University
Life in WALDEN," CAVALIER DAILY [Charlottesville, Va.],
February 17, 1955, p. 2.
A series of cartoons.

White, E. B. "Retort Transcendental," THE NEW YORKER, XVIII
(April 4, 1942), 12.

--"A Slight Sound at Evening," THE POINTS OF MY COMPASS.
New York: Harper, 1962.
Essay on Thoreau.

--"Visitors to the Pond," NEW YORKER, XXIX (May 23, 1953),
28-31.
Senator McCarthy investigates Thoreau. Delightful
satire.

--"Walden," ONE MAN'S MEAT. New York: Harper and Brothers,
1942. pp. 98-107.
Reprinted from HARPER'S MAGAZINE, June, 1939, and
reprinted with Thoreau's "Civil Disobedience," in
READINGS FOR CITIZENS AT WAR, edited by Theodore
Morrison and others. (New York: Harper and Brothers,
1943.)

--"Walden" and "A Slight Sound of Evening," AN E. B. WHITE
READER. New York: Harper and Row, 1966. pp. 226-244.

--"Walden: A Letter to Henry Thoreau," A COLLECTION OF
TRAVEL IN AMERICA, BY VARIOUS HANDS, edited by George
Bradshaw. New York: Farrar Straus, 1948. pp. 351-358.
Also includes excerpts from Thoreau's CAPE COD,
pp. 359-372.

--"Walden--1954," YALE REVIEW, XLIV (September, 1954),
13-22.
A delightful essay on the significance of Thoreau
today. TSB #49.

White, Elliott Adams. "Distance at Walden," SATURDAY REVIEW
OF LITERATURE, August 4, 1945.
A letter to the editor on the Cairn controversy.

--Letter to the editor. CONCORD JOURNAL, June 28, 1945.
Cairn controversy.

White, Morton and Lucia White. THE INTELLECTUAL VERSUS THE
CITY. New York: New American Library, 1964.
Frequent comment on Thoreau.

WHITE POND IN CONCORD. Concord, Mass.: Brierdale Farm, ? .
Concerns Thoreau's relations to White Pond.

White, Stewart Edward. "Apostolic Mike," ESQUIRE (February,
1946).
A short story with passage after passage para-
phrased from Thoreau.

White, Viola C. "A Teacher's Avocation," TSB #13.
Includes excerpts from correspondence between Dr.
Julian Willis Abernethy and Mr. Edwin B. Hill.

White, William. "Thoreau Among the Nudists," TSB #104, p. 5.
Discusses the following article: Austin, Thomas D.
"Thoreau, the First Hippie," ANKH, Vol. I, No. 4,
Spring Quarter 1968.

--"Three Unpublished Thoreau Letters," NEW ENGLAND QUARTERLY,
XXXIII (September, 1960), 372-374.
Prints fuller texts of the letters of September 25,
1843 from Margaret Fuller; of April 13, 1855 and
August 8, 1855 to George William Curtis.

--"Unpublished MSS in Booksellers' Catalogues: A Thoreau
Letter," SERIF [Kent State University], I (December, 1944),
28-29.
Letter to Watson of October 4, 1954.

--"An Unpublished Thoreau Poem," AMERICAN LITERATURE, XXXIV
(March, 1962), 119-121.
The new "Sic Vita."

--"An Unpublished Thoreau Poem: A Correction," TSB #82, p. 2.

--"A WEEK in The Feinberg Collection," TSB #85, p. 2.

White, William Chapman. "Get Moving, Thoreau!" NEW YORK HERALD
TRIBUNE, July 21, 1953, p. 22.
If Thoreau should return to life today. An essay.

Whitford, Kathryn. "Thoreau and the Woodlots of Concord,"
NEW ENGLAND QUARTERLY, XXIII (September, 1950), 291-306.
A very significant study of Thoreau as an ecologist.
Important for an understanding of Thoreau as a
scientist. TSB #34.

Whitford, Phillip and Kathryn Whitford. "Thoreau: Pioneer
Ecologist and Conservationst," SCIENTIFIC MONTHLY, LXXIII
(November, 1951), 291-296.

312

By far the best study yet of Thoreau's contributions
to science. Evaluates both Thoreau's work and other
attempts to study his work. Particularly good on
his study of tree growth. One minor error: despite
what they say, Thoreau did read Darwin's ORIGIN OF
SPECIES. TSB #38.

translation: SMI TO SAMBUN [Tokyo], XVI (October,
1967), 40-49, translated into Japanese by Koh
Kasegawa.

Whitman, Howard. A REPORTER IN SEARCH OF GOD. New York:
Doubleday, 1953.
Recounts a visit to Walden, pp. 233-234.

Whitman, Walt. THE CORRESPONDENCE OF WALT WHITMAN. Vol. I,
1842-1867; Vol. II, 1868-1875. New York: New York University Press, 1961.
Occasional references to Thoreau.

Whittemore, R. C. "Henry David Thoreau," MAKERS OF THE AMER-
ICAN MIND. New York: Morrow, 1964. pp. 185-196.

Wickenden, Dan. THE WAYFARERS. New York: Morrow, 1945.
A novel with some notes (p. 226) on Thoreau and
Emerson in relation to nature and loneliness.

Widmer, Kingsley. THE LITERARY REBEL. Carbondale: Southern
Illinois, University Press, 1965.
Comments on Thoreau passim.

Wiener, Harvey S. "To a Fairer World: Thoreau's Last Hours,"
JOURNAL OF HISTORICAL STUDIES, I (Autumn, 1968), 361-365.

Wild, Paul H. "Flower Power: a Student's Guide to Pre-Hippie
Transcendentalism," ENGLISH JOURNAL, LVIII (January, 1969),
62-68.
On teaching WALDEN to high school students as a
hippie document.

Wilder, Thornton N. "The American Loneliness," ATLANTIC
MONTHLY, CXC (August, 1952), 65-69.
A most provocative essay on Thoreau as the epitome
of the American sense of loneliness. TSB #40.

--"Wrestling with Henry David Thoreau." Oberlin, Ohio:
Oberlin College, June 9, 1952 (mineographed).
A commencement address.

"The Will of H. G. O. Blake," TSB #68.
A portion of the will is reprinted.

Willard, Simon. Letter to the editor. NEW YORK SUN, June
18, 1945.
Disparaging Thoreau's culture.

--"Thoreau's Revolt," NEW YORK SUN, July 12, 1946.
       A letter to the editor belittling Thoreau's
       civil disobedience.

Williams, Cecil B. "Thoreau of Walden," COLLEGE ENGLISH,
    XXIII (January, 1962), 401.
       A sonnet.

Williams, Donald L. "T. W. Higginson on Thoreau and Maine,"
    COLBY LIBRARY QUARTERLY, VII (March, 1965), 29-32.

Williams, Eric D. "Henry David Thoreau: Enchantment With
    Life," TSB #101, p. 6.

   --"Thoreau: Prophet of World Faith," THOREAU JOURNAL
    QUARTERLY, I (January 15, 1969), 14-16.

Williams, Frances M. "Thoreau's Views on Violence." San
    Diego State College, 1963. Unpublished master's thesis.

Williams, Jonathan. "The Distances to a Friend," AN EAR IN
    BARTRAM'S TREE: SELECTED POEMS. Chapel Hill: University
    of North Carolina Press, 1968. p. 30.
       Poem on Thoreau.

Williams, Paul O. "At Thoreau's Grave," CARDINAL POETRY
    QUARTERLY, II (Fall, 1966), 18.
       A poem.

   --"The Borrowed Axe--A Biblical Echo in WALDEN?" TSB #83,
    p. 2.

   --"The Concept of Inspiration in Thoreau's Poetry," PMLA,
    LXXIX (September, 1964), 466-472.

   --"Emerson Guided: Walks with Thoreau and Channing,"
    EMERSON SOCIETY QUARTERLY, XXXV (1964), 66-68.

   --"Thoreau and Purslane," TSB #91, p. 3.

   --"Thoreau in the BOATSWAINTS WHISTLE," EMERSON SOCIETY
    QUARTERLY, XXVIII (1965), 133.
       Little known early printing of Thoreau.

   --"Thoreau's "It is no dream of mine': A New Proposal,"
    TSB #86, pp. 3-4.

   --"Walden Organized," EMERSON SOCIETY QUARTERLY, XXXIII
    (1963), 49.
       A poem.

Willis, Lonnie L. "Folklore in the Published Writings of
    Henry David Thoreau: A Study and a Compendium-Index."
    University of Colorado, 1968. Unpublished doctoral
    dissertation.

Abstract appears in TSB #109, p. 8.

Wills, Garry. "Why Did Thoreau Start It?" NATIONAL CATHOLIC
REPORTER, November 17, 1965.
    On Civil Disobedience.

Willson, Lawrence. "Another View of the Pilgrims," NEW
ENGLAND QUARTERLY, XXXIV (June, 1961), 160-177.
    A thorough study of Thoreau's comments on the
    Pilgrims, particularly in CAPE COD.

--"Central Theme of Thoreau's Life Seen Relevant to 20th
Century," UNIVERSITY OF CALIFORNIA CLIP SHEET, XXXIX
(July 30, 1963), 5.

--"The Great Reversal," DALHOUSIE REVIEW, XXXIX (Spring,
1959), 5-18.
    Contrasts present moral confusion in America to
    moral clarity of Thoreau and his contemporaries.

--"Thoreau and the French in Canada," REVUE DE L'UNIVERSITE
D'OTTAWA, XXIX (July-September, 1959), 281-297.
    A study of Thoreau's attitude toward the French
    in Canada, based on the unpublished Canadian and
    Indian Notebooks.

--"Thoreau and the Natural Diet," SOUTH ATLANTIC QUARTERLY,
LVII (Winter, 1958), 86-103.
    An important study of Thoreau's dietary principles
    with much unpublished material from Thoreau's
    Indian notebooks. TSB #65.

--"Thoreau and New England's Weather," WEATHERWISE, XII
(June, 1959), 91-94 passim.
    The first authoritative study of Thoreau's interest
    in the weather, with many quotations from his works,
    including many from unpublished notebooks. TSB #68.

--"Thoreau and Roman Catholicism," CATHOLIC HISTORICAL
REVIEW, XLII (July, 1956), 157-172.
    Summarizes Thoreau's comments on Catholicism and
    discusses the many Jesuit accounts of early Amer-
    ican exploration he read.

--"Thoreau--Citizen of Concord," EMERSON SOCIETY QUARTERLY,
XIV (1959), 7-12.
    On Thoreau's interest in the history of Concord.

--"Thoreau: Student of Anthropology," AMERICAN ANTHROPOL-
OGIST, LXI (April, 1959), 279-289.
    A detailed study of the Indian notebooks.

--"Thoreau's Canadian Notebook," HUNTINGTON LIBRARY QUAR-
TERLY, XXII (May, 1959), 179-200.
    A detailed analysis of the "Canadian Notebook."

Among the most important studies to appear in
recent years.

--"Thoreau's Medical Vagaries," JOURNAL OF HISTORY OF
MEDICINE, XV (January, 1960), 64-74.

--"The Transcendentalist View of the West," WESTERN HUMAN-
ITIES REVIEW, XIV (Spring, 1960), 183-191.
   Thoreau's literal and figurative opinions of the
   West.

Wilson, Carroll A. THIRTEEN AUTHOR COLLECTIONS OF THE NINE-
   TEENTH CENTURY AND FIVE CENTURIES OF FAMILIAR QUOTATIONS,
   edited by Jean Wilson and David Randall. New York:
   Scribners, 1950. 2 Vol.
   Contains a detailed account of 13 first editions,
   a MS letter, a Thoreau pencil, and the 1837 Harvard
   graduation program all in Mr. Wilson's collection.

Wilson, Eddie W. "Conclusion," LIVING WILDERNESS, XXI (Fall,
   1956), 8.
   A poem based on Thoreau's journal.

--"Thoreau and Birds," CHAT, IX (November, 1945), 70-72.
   A centennial essay in the Bulletin of the North
   Carolina Bird Club.

--"Thoreau's Wildness," LIVING WILDERNESS, XV (Spring, 1950),
   18.
   A poem.

Wilson, Edmund. "The Extrovert of Walden Pond," NOTE-BOOKS
   OF NIGHT. San Francisco: Colt Press, 1942. pp. 11-12.

Wilson, John Byron. "Darwin and the Transcendentalists,"
   JOURNAL OF HIST. OF IDEAS, XXVI (April-June, 1965),
   286-290.

--"Henry Thoreau's 'Village School'," ADULT EDUCATION, XV
   (Autumn, 1964), 17-22.

--"Transcendental Activity in the Dissemination of Culture
   in America, 1830-1860." University of North Carolina,
   1941. Unpublished doctoral dissertation.

--"The Transcendentalists' 'Idea of a University',"
   EDUCATIONAL FORUM, XXXIII (March, 1969), 343-354.

Wilson, Will Erwin. "Drums," WINGS (Winter, 1953), p. 13.
   A poem on Thoreau.

Winn, O. Howard. "A Sentence for Thoreau," MIDWEST QUARTERLY,
   IX (Summer, 1968), 380.
   A poem.

Winslow, Grace Sewell. "Concord," BOSTON POST, February 27, 1942.
> A poem.

--"The Old Oysterman's House," YANKEE (June, 1940), pp. 17 passim.
> A visit to the home of Thoreau's Cape Cod friend.

Winsten, Stephen. SALT AND HIS CIRCLE. London: Hutchinson, 1951.
> The first biography of Thoreau's English biographer Henry S. Salt. It contains much of interest to the Thoreau student for it gives a good picture of the interest in Thoreau in late 19th century England and of Salt's own longstanding devotion to the man. TSB #39.

Winterich, John T. "Walden," TWENTY-THREE BOOKS AND THE STORIES BEHIND THEM. Philadelphia: Lippincott, 1938. pp. 165-174.

Wisbey, Herbert A., Jr. "Thoreau's Last Trip to Cape Cod," CAPE COD MAGAZINE (1959).
> Brief essay on Thoreau's last excursion to the Cape.

Wood, James Playsted. A HOUND, A BAY HORSE AND A TURTLE-DOVE. New York: Pantheon, 1963.
> A "life of Thoreau for the young reader," Wood's book tells briefly and succinctly the facts of Thoreau's life and then sums up some of his major ideas and their impact on the world since. Wood is obviously well acquainted and sympathetic with Thoreau's life. He makes a number of minor errors of fact, but none of them are particularly important. We are sorry however he devotes but a paragraph to Ellen Sewall and nothing at all to the fire on Fair Haven Bay. On the whole the book is engagingly written, but for a rugged portrayal of Thoreau's life, we still prefer August Derleth's CONCORD REBEL. TSB #86.

> reviews: BOOK WEEK (April 12, 1964).
> NEW YORK TIMES, November 10, 1963.

--"Mr. Thoreau Writes a Book," THE NEW COLOPHON, I (October, 1948), 367-376.
> An account of the 1849 publication of A WEEK.

Wood, Virginia. "Mrs. Collier of Cohasset Is an Avid Reader at 101," SOUTH SHORE NEWS [Scituate, Mass.], June 4, 1961.
> An interview with Ellen Sewall's daughter.

Woodbury, Benjamin C. "The Unco Guid; or Finding What One Is Looking For," JOURNAL OF THE AMERICAN INSTITUTE OF HOMEOPATHY, XI (January, 1947), 23-25.

On the first great disciple of Thoreau, Samuel
Arthur Jones, with a note on the Thoreau Society.

Woodcock, George. CIVIL DISOBEDIENCE. Toronto: Canadian
Broadcasting Co. Publications, 1966.
Text of 6 radio lectures with many comments on
Thoreau.

--"Thoreau," WAR COMMENTARY [London] (January, 1943).
On Thoreau as an anarchist.

--"Thoreau's WALDEN," FREEDOM [London] (January 19, 1952),
p. 2.
A commentary.

Woodford, Hubert G. "Interpretations of Life: VII. Thoreau's
WALDEN," INQUIRER [London, England], November 22, 1947.
A general essay.

Woodlief, Annette M. "The Literary Humor of Thomas Carlyle
and Henry David Thoreau." Wake Forest University, 1963.
Unpublished master's thesis.

Woodring, Paul. "Was Thoreau a Hippie?" SATURDAY REVIEW OF
LITERATURE, December 16, 1967, p. 68.

Woodruff, Stuart. "Thoreau as Water-Gazer: 'The Ponds',"
EMERSON SOCIETY QUARTERLY, XLVII (1967), 16-17.

Woods, Eleanor. "Cost What It May," HUMANIST, XXI (March, 1961),
77-86.
On the application of Thoreau's principles of civil
disobedience today.

Woods, Frederick. "Henry David Thoreau: The Artist as Individualist," STAND [London], X (Summer, 1955), 10-12.
A strong denunciation of Thoreau.

Woods, Ralph L. "New England's Ice Age," COLUMBIA, XL (Decem-
ber, 1960), 20-21 passim.
A survey of commercial ice harvesting in New
England with material on WALDEN.

Woodson, Thomas. "The Two Beginnings of WALDEN: A Distinction
of Styles," ELH, XXXV (September, 1968), 440-473.

Woodward, C. Donald. Letter to Editor. NEW BEDFORD [Mass.]
STANDARD TIMES, January 24, 1968.
On Thoreau's views and the war in Vietnam.

Woodress, James. DISSERTATIONS IN AMERICAN LITERATURE 1891-
1966. Durham: Duke University Press, 1968.
Lists all known doctoral dissertations on Thoreau.

Woodward, Robert H. "Thoreau's Diction," TSB #95, p. 5.

[Woolf, Virginia]. "Thoreau," TIMES LITERARY SUPPLEMENT
     (July 12, 1917), pp. 325-326.
          Kirkpatrick's new bibliography of Woolf reveals
          this annoymous centennial essay to have been
          written by her.

"The Work of Fannie Hardy Eckstorm," TSB #15.
          Discusses OLD JOHN NEPTUNE by Fanny Hardy Eckstorm,
          available in a limited edition only from the author.
          Mentions the PENOBSCOT.

"Work on Thoreau Site Yields New Proofs," CONCORD JOURNAL,
     September 5, 1946.
          Another "After Reading Thoreau" sonnet.

"World Famous Walden Pond at Concord Scene of Thoreau 'Exper-
     iment in Living' Marks Centennial Tomorrow," BOSTON
     TRAVELER (July 3, 1945).
          Features a large composite photograph.

Worthington, John W. "Thoreau's Route to Katahdin," APPALACHIA
     (June, 1946), pp. 3-14.
          With illustrations and map.

Worthington, Marjorie. MISS ALCOTT OF CONCORD. New York:
     Doubleday, 1958.
          A biography of Louisa May Alcott. The author
          describes it as a labor of love. But unfortunately
          love's labor is lost. It adds nothing in either
          fact or interpretation to the already published
          biographies of Stern, Meigs, and several others
          and is filled with parenthetical remarks that are
          irrelevant and inane. Thoreau appears occasionally
          in these pages, but nothing significant is said
          about him except an uncalled-for accusation that
          he deserted Bronson Alcott at Fruitlands. TSB #65.

"Would Have School Named for Thoreau," CONCORD ENTERPRISE,
     July 24, 1947.
          Rella Ritchell presents her plan for a Thoreau
          monument.

Wright, Brooks. "Bradford Torrey," MORE BOOKS, XXIII (Dec-
     ember, 1948), 363-371.
          On the editor of the standard edition of Thoreau's
          WORKS.

Wright, Guy. "Solitary Protestor," SAN FRANCISCO EXAMINER,
     May 17, 1968.
          Thoreau and hippies.

     --"Thoreau the Square," SAN FRANCISCO EXAMINER, May 16, 1968.

Wright, Nathalia. "Emily Dickinson's Boanerges and Thoreau's
     Atropos: Locomotives on the Same Line," MODERN LANGUAGE

NOTES, LXXII (February, 1957), 101-103.
    WALDEN as a source for one of her poems.

Wyeth, N. C. "Walden Revisited," DELAWARE TODAY, VI (August,
    1967), 15.
        Painting reproduced.

  --"Thoreau, His Critics, and the Public," TSB #37.

Wykes, Alan. A CONCISE SURVEY OF AMERICAN LITERATURE. New
    York: Library Publishers, 1955.
        Several pages of commentary on Thoreau.

Wykoff, George S. "Walden Pond 1955," CEA CRITIC (December,
    1955), p. 7.
        Account of a recent visit to Walden Pond.

Wylie, Evan M. "Thoreau Trails," HOLIDAY, IV (September,
    1948), 105ff.
        On Thoreau's 1857 visit to the Maine Woods, illus-
        trated with kodochromes by George Burns. A par-
        ticularly beautiful piece of work. TSB #25.

Wyllie, John Cook. "Delugeous or Detergeous or ?" CEAA NEWS-
    LETTER, II (July, 1969), 3.
        More on the puzzling word in Thoreau's Carlyle
        essay.

Yahagi, Kodo. "On the Position of Henry David Thoreau in Relation to the Formation of Americanism," TAISHO DIAGAKU KENKYUKIYO, XLIV (March, 1959), 1-40. In Japanese.

Yamasaki, Tokihito. "Before WALDEN, H. D. Thoreau's Theory of Civil Disobedience at Its Genesis," JOURNAL OF LAW AND POLITICS [Osaka City University, Japan] (February, 1964).

--"The Meaning of CIVIL in CIVIL DISOBEDIENCE," QUARTERLY JOURNAL OF LAW AND POLITICS [Osaka City University, Japan], LXXVII (March, 1965). Text in Japanese.

--"Resistance and Political Thoughts of H. D. Thoreau, 1845-1854," OSAKA CITY UNIVERSITY LAW ASSOCIATION PUBLICATIONS: LAW REVIEW, VIII (January, 1962).

"Young Pioneer Turns Back Time on Lone, Long Stay in Deep Woods," TRENTON [N. J.] TIMES, September 3, 1958.
      Account of George Gardner, Thoreau follower, who lives alone in the Adirondacks.

Young, T. D. and Ronald Fine, editors. "Henry David Thoreau," AMERICAN LITERATURE: A CRITICAL SURVEY. New York: American Book Company, 1968. pp. 163-212.
      Reprints Randall Stewart, "The Growth of Thoreau's Reputation": Reginald Cook, "Thoreau in Perspective": Lauriat Lane, "On the Organic Structure of WALDEN": Sherman Paul, "Resolution at Walden"; and George Hendrick, "The Influence of Thoreau's 'Civil Disobedience' on Gandhi's SATYAGRAHA."

Young, Vernon. "Mary Austin and the Earth Performance," SOUTHWEST REVIEW, XXXV (Summer, 1950), 153-163.
      Thoreau compared unfavorable with Mary Austin as a writer.

Zabriskie, F. N. "Brown Bread and Baked Beans," LIPPINCOTT'S
MAGAZINE (October, 1888).
On Thoreau.

Zahniser, Howard. THOREAU AND THE PRESERVATION OF WILDNESS.
Washington: The Wilderness Society, 1957.
Mimeographed text of annual meeting address.

also in: CONCORD JOURNAL, July 18, 1957, and
LIVING WILDERNESS, XXIII (Spring, 1958), 20-22.

excerpts: NEW OUTLOOK, X (December, 1957), 68-74,
and THOREAU SOCIETY BULLETIN #60.

--"Thoreau and the Wilderness," CONGRESSIONAL RECORD (November 2, 1962).

also in: THOREAU SOCIETY BULLETIN #80, pp. 3-4.

[Zahniser, Howard]. "Thoreau Honored and Presented," LIVING
WILDERNESS (Winter, 1947-1948), pp. 23-24.
Reviews of WALDEN REVISITED, WALDEN AND SELECTED
ESSAYS, THE PORTABLE THOREAU, and COLLECTED POEMS
OF HENRY THOREAU.

Zalamea, Luis. "Thoreau Today," AMERICAS, XIV (March, 1962),
27-32.
A centennial essay. Published in both English and
Spanish.

Zalowitz, N. "The Celebrated American Writer Who Lived Two
Years Alone in a Wood," DAILY FORWARD [New York City],
July 14, 1945.
A centennial essay on Thoreau, in Yiddish.

--"98 Years After His Death They Admit Thoreau to the Hall
of Fame," DAILY FORWARD, November 8, 1960.
An article in Yiddish.

Zardoya, Concha. HISTORIA DE LA LITERATURE NORTEAMERICANA.
Barcelona, Spain: Editorial Labor, 1956.
Includes section on Thoreau.

Zahner, J. Alex. "About Henry David Thoreau," CARNEGIE
MAGAZINE, XXXVI (May, 1962), 149-152.
A centennial tribute.

Ziemann, Mrs. Glennie T. "Teacher Writes Fan Letter to H.
D. Thoreau," ENGLISH HIGH LIGHTS, XV (November, 1957),
3.
Report of a high school class's reaction to WALDEN.

Ziff, Larzar. "Walden: Considerations and Assignments,"
EXERCISE EXCHANGE, IX (November, 1961), 30-31.
Excerpts from his commentaries in his edition of
WALDEN.

Zimmer, F. "Emerson...Thoreau...Hawthorne," NEW YORK TIMES
BOOK REVIEW, March 13, 1955, p. 2.
A cartoon.

--"Which Way to Walden Pond?" NEW YORK TIMES BOOK REVIEW,
June 6, 1954, p. 2.
A cartoon.

Zumaran, Adriana. "Desobediencia Civil," RECONSTRUIR [Buenos
Aires], January 4, 1952.
On Thoreau's "Civil Disobedience."

Zwanzig, Karl Joachim. "Henry David Thoreau als Kritiker
der Gesellschaft." Freie Universitat. Berlin, 1956.
Unpublished doctoral dissertation.
A rigorous and systematic study of Thoreau's
social thought. Calls attention to the importance
of Thoreau's journals in any consideration of
Thoreau's criticism of society. According to
Zwanzig, Thoreau's social philosophy is a natural
outgrowth of his attempt to lead a satisfactory
life. The key to Thoreau's social thought is his
attitude toward reform. Thoreau was often opposed
to reform movements because they violated individualism even though they were rooted in idealism.
Argues that the mature Thoreau was led to a position
more radical than civil disobedience and that he
became increasingly concerned with the welfare of
society at large. TSB #105.